The Urban Community

The Urban Community

W. Allen Martin
The University of Texas at Tyler

PEARSON

Prentice
Hall

Upper Saddle River, New Jersey 07458

Library of Congress Cataloging-in-Publication Data

The urban community / edited by W. Allen Martin
    p. cm.
     ISBN 0-13-098423-X
   1. Cities and towns–United States. 2. Sociology, Urban–United
States. 3. Sociology, Urban. 4. Community. I. Martin, W. Allen

   HT123 .U7427 2004
   307.76'0973--dc21

                       2003004756

Executive Editor: Chris DeJohn
Publisher: Nancy Roberts
Editorial Assistant: Veronica D'Amico
Director of Marketing: Beth Gillette Meija
Marketing Assistant: Adam Laitman
Production Liaison: Joanne Hakim
Assistant Manufacturing Manager: Mary Ann Gloriande
Cover Design: Bruce Kenselaar
Cover Illustration/Photo: Robert Crawford, "Urban Street"
Image Permission Coordinator: Frances Toepfer
Composition/Full Service Project Management: John Shannon, Pine Tree Composition, Inc.
Printer/Binder: Hamilton Printing Company

Credits and acknowledgments borrowed from other sources and reproduced, with permission, in this textbook appear on pages 335–336.

Pearson Education LTD.
Pearson Education Singapore, Pte. Ltd
Pearson Education Canada, Ltd.
Pearson Education – Japan
Pearson Education Australia PTY, Limited

Pearson Education North Asia Ltd
Pearson Educación de Mexico, S.A. de C.V.
Pearson Education Malaysia, Pte. Ltd
Pearson Education, Upper Saddle River,
  New Jersey

10 9 8 7 6 5 4 3 2 1
ISBN 0-13-098423-X

CONTENTS

IV   THE MODERN HOLISTIC STUDY   299

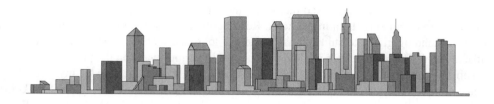

PREFACE

One of the few good reasons to construct a book of readings is getting to talk with the authors of the finest articles recently published in prestigious journals and other outlets. I asked most of them for permission to cut some parts of their articles. Who would want that to happen? Nobody, but quite readily they understood that space in books is at a premium and condensing things is routine, hence they were almost eager to allow this chopping. They also realized that students, and readers generally, prefer material that does not require deep mathematical reading. Thus, they permitted me to ax statistical tables that one must acknowledge represent a great deal of hard work and outstanding scholarship. I encourage students who have already had parametric statistics to read the complete works in the journals: I am sure you will agree that the authors, all of them, used the appropriate statistics in reaching their conclusions.

Putting together this reader required a great deal of reading, but that is no complaint. I enjoy reading urban and community sociology and urban geography and design are favorites of mine. At my campus, The University of Texas at Tyler, which opened only a couple of years before I moved here, I started and directed a master's degree in Public Planning and Administration and still teach in the area. Similarly, I started the geography program here and taught geography until we could hire a tenure-tract geographer. With these experiences my appreciation for sociology's sister disciplines continues to grow. As broad and open a discipline as sociology is, our friends in related disciplines have much to contribute to the understanding of cities and communities.

ACKNOWLEDGEMENTS

This project proceeded surprisingly swiftly. I presented the idea to Christopher M. DeJohn, Executive Editor at Prentice Hall who immediately saw its value, and hence I soon had my hands full. Here at my university, I was helped by two of the finest graduate students. One, Amy S. Glenn, Ed.D., helped locate copies of the articles and prepared them for Chris and his assistant, Veronica. Throughout most of the process, I was fortunate to have Clay Winskie who essentially was my partner. He read the articles, discussed them with me, offered his views of how to edit the articles, and helped with organizing them in the book. Reading the greatest works in one's field and working with outstanding graduate students has made my long hours at the office a pleasure. I would also like to thank Thean Hancke, a student who helped in various ways on the project.

My efforts were made all the more pleasant through the encouragement of my wife, Debbie (who just completed a second master's degree), and our two grown children, Zach (Sgt. USMC), now a full-time college student; and Michelle, at Austin College, off for her junior year in France.

W. Allen Martin
The University of Texas at Tyler

INTRODUCTION

Scholars writing about cities and the nature of community have produced some of the most well-known works in the social sciences. The early works were often about how cities develop and how they differ from rural areas and ways of living. Cities are where modern people live; more than eighty percent of the populations of developed countries live in cities. In fact being urban and being developed or modern correlate closely. Not only is the United States more than eighty percent urban, we are more than eighty percent metropolitan. Our more urban states are the ones that are more productive, more educated, and wealthier. The historic path shows clearly the developmental connection between the rise of cities and the rise of things modern. City people invent things and social organizations, and in turn we live in the environments that we create. How urban life began and how it has changed is fundamental to understanding urban lives today.

Change has been the subject of much of the writing about cities, but also the study of cities has evolved in response to shifts during the twentieth century in cities and the world. Cities grew larger as smaller places shrank. The power went to large places and so did the rural populations. Instead of free-standing cities and towns spread across the land, metropolitan areas became the residences of power and people. Thus, the lives of people were changing. Simple, old arrangements became complex and fast paced, white picket fences and endless discussions in the parlor were replaced by television and computer. People have seen the death of cities as independent places; they have wondered if communities, by any previous definition, are already dead.

Well, urban configurations and lives changed but their essence has not. Understanding these changes is fundamental to social scientific understanding of where we are today. Thus *The Urban Community* traces the earlier approaches to understanding cities as it looks at some of the most important works of decades gone by. For the most part however, the articles included here are works from the past five years that represent the best analyses of the modern city and community. The student will do well to appreciate the finest of the older works, as they appear in the first section of this book, and to consider if the best of the modern works, to be seen in the latter three sections, will some day be viewed as classics of a similar stature.

Urban sociology during the early twentieth century introduced human ecology—urban ecology—and it was all the rage. But then sociologists found short-comings and misdirections in the ecological approach. The idea of the "biotic community" (Park) was quickly seen to be a false step, but it was to be expected for a scholarly direction beginning with an analogy for its inspiration. In just a few decades many social scientists demanded a more global view, arguing that studying local spatial and economic structures misses the larger problems that vex cities and communities. Sociologists in particular saw and continue to see the distortion in focusing only on cities in one developed country, and the problem is a larger one than might first meet the eye. Sociologists and many others have been denouncing the idea that inner-city problems are simply local and the fault of the benighted residents. Social scientists have long recognized blaming the victim as an outrage, thus whether the view is of the dispossessed in big American cities or of poor countries caught in the untenable "dependency" foisted upon them by world-wide capitalism, the emphasis is often upon the actions of distant powers and the consequences for the downtrodden. Are there purely local independent variables that cause urban problems, or is the local community merely the backdrop or a façade for the real problems caused by huge forces that know no bounds?

By reading *The Urban Community*, you will see if such studies have importance and explanatory power even in the face of overwhelming worldwide events and even though writings by Marx and Engles and also of Wallerstein and Hayak may be relevant also. Furthermore, we need to discuss urban communities as the homes of people who live ordinary lives. Certainly cities have their own modes of operating and the feel of one city differs from that of another. Is it not true that big city people live differently from small town people? Don't people in some cities have different rates of joining and participating than people in other cities of similar scale?

The United States may not be totally unique, but we are in some ways. We have so much more money, power, technology, and pop-cultural icons, and the media to broadcast them—the many components of the imperialism that we are charged with—all this undergirds the fury that often works its way into urban sociology. Migrants from different streams and with various motives made new relationships and rules here in a developing country that deliberately threw off some of the old ways as they made new towns that would become cities. These cities composed of immigrant communities form the firmament of our living arrangements. What these arrangements did and continue to do to our institutions, families, and mind sets may or may not have been fundamentally different from life conditions in Old World cities, but it is an interesting issue. Sociologists cite de Tocqueville as a wise observer of America's uniqueness much more than they charge him with blind sentimentality. American cities and communities are fascinating and thus so are our lives.

The Urban Community focuses on the North American metropolis and the constituent cities and communities in which we live. We will investigate macro-level issues, beginning with the first two human ecological articles. Then we will leave the macro-perspective and "bring people back in," i.e., in the second section we will see how individuals build and participate in communities. We will return in the third section to the geographic and demographic perspectives in understanding urban life. *The Urban Community* presents a variety of positions both in terms of theoretical stance and disciplinary category; the only goal is to expose students to the many interesting issues and angles posed by scholars in studying life in the modern American city. The fourth section is one big and beautiful study by Molotch, Freudenburg, and Paulsen, who provide us with an engrossing holistic study that compares Ventura and Santa Barbara, California; this work compares favorably with any comprehensive urban study ever to appear in the *American Sociological Review*.

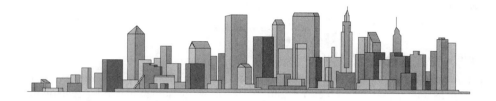

SECTION INTRODUCTIONS

I   URBAN CLASSICS

Some of the most well-known works in sociology, and the social sciences generally, were written by urban and community sociologists. In particular these were writings about how cities develop and how they differ from rural areas and rural ways of living. Cities are where modern people live, more than eighty percent of the populations of developed countries live in cities: in fact, being urban and being developed or modern correlate closely. Not only is the United States more than eighty percent urban, we are more than eighty percent metropolitan. Our states that are more urban are the ones that are more productive and more educated and richer. The historic path shows clearly the developmental connection between urban development and the rise of things modern. City people invent things and social organization.

A. Urban Development: Urban Ecological Perspectives

Our emphasis is not so much on these sweeping generalities but rather on the way that people find themselves organized, the ways and the results that people live from day to day doing what people do. At one end of the casual view, people come to live in metropolitan areas, but moreover they reside in particular communities within the larger urban network. How this happens and how the metropolis becomes organized was the interest of Ernest Burgess and Robert Park, two of the founders of the Chicago School of Human Ecology. Park and Burgess were two of the founders of the Chicago School of Human Ecology, and they laid the foundations for understanding how cities grow and how they work.

Burgess (1925) and Park (1936) focused on cities as human population centers arranged in a "natural" way within a geographic space. Burgess sought in an *a priori* model to show how ecological units organize themselves. He saw that certain ecological processes resulted in "concentric zones," and he boldly stated exactly what was in those rings. Robert E. Park perceived a master mechanism in cities, that he termed "competitive cooperation" (1936, 23). The winners and losers in the struggle for money and space lead to cities being divided up into "natural areas" where people form themselves into communities. Thus Park propounds a definition of community that is one of the most used even today.

B. Human Relations: Sociocultural Perspectives

The *community* is a "unit idea" in Robert A. Nisbet's (1966) *The Sociological Tradition*. He lists five unit ideas and *community* is the first, and ". . .the most fundamental and far-reaching of sociology's unit-ideas. . ." (p. 47). "Community is a fusion of feeling and thought, of tradition and commitment, of membership and volition" (p. 48). In short, community is where we live and what we seek. The large city and metropolis are too big and heterogeneous—at that level of living and analysis we have to rely on formal arrangements—what Tonnies and so many others have called "contractual society." Ferdinand Tonnies makes explicit the inescapable dichotomy between the community and the larger society or city. In *Community and Society*, Tonnies essentially asks the Hobbesian question about human relations, "Why do we live together and why do we stay together?" Thus Tonnies discusses the will, placing the natural will with the community, the Gemeinschaft. The Gesellschaft, the city or urban society, is marked by individualism where natural association is replaced by secondary relationships in which individuals use others for their own gain. Tonnies (1887) discusses how small-town people of earlier eras associated and lived differently from modern-era big-city people. The big city comes to be a fearful place, and the great classic scholar, Georg Simmel, explores the reactions of people to living in the big city. He shows what happens to people as they are constantly assaulted by big city processes and changes, and by the fast pace and precision of the modern "bulk city" (1903). Simmel (1903) found that living in a big city has an unfortunate impact upon our thoughts and feelings. These two early sociologists shaped the classic view of human relations in the cities. Louis Wirth (1938) followed this view, and states that, "Typically, our physical contacts are close but our social contacts are distant" (p. 55). Wirth looked across the city of Chicago and defined what cities were becoming, and, in keeping with other social thinkers of the era, found that burgeoning cities were causing huge problems for their residents.

C. The Case Study: Local Community Perspectives

The focus turns more to community as we leave the urban classics of a century ago, moving to the days when sociologists began recognizing that cities are composed of communities. Roland Warren looked back from his vantage point in the 1960s to trace the previous fifty years, including the pathfinding case studies such as the Lynds' *Middletown in Transition* (1937). Such cities in the United States developed rather autonomously but became more related and similar with "The Great Change" (Warren 1963) in the early and mid-twentieth century. With the expansion of the federal government, giant corporations, and mass media, cities became less independent and more like cogs in the metropolitan machine. The more positive spin is that now layers of governmental overseers challenge local abuses of powers—"Boss Hog;" much-vilified Wal-Mart has driven out inefficient and overpriced retailers, and television is wretched but better than constant gossip and unrelieved boredom. Cities have been flourishing, and even though they have become copies of each other, we can still cheer them for having led us up and away from "the idiocy of rural life" (Marx and Engels 1848, p. 13).

Following Warren and with essentially the same interest, Albert Hunter (1978) reviews mainly more recent studies and changing perspectives of the notable community thinkers. Through his analysis of cities and suburbs, Hunter demonstrates that the perennial features of community have weathered change, and though different in some respects, they continue to prosper. Hunter introduces us to new ways of looking at communities; by using the "emergent view," for example we can see that neighborhoods create and change the ways that people feel and act in regard to their communities or cities. After the vast sweeps and deep thoughts of Warren and Hunter, Robert K Merton weighs in with a pleasant little study, "Types of Influentials: The Local and the Cosmopolitan." Though writing years earlier than Warren and Hunter, Merton's study still holds up as an insightful view of how influence and power is spread among all levels and neighborhoods of each city. Furthermore his research is in the sociology of communications framework and shows the great sociologist's procedures in working on the research project. We see that ideas and influence do not simply drop down from the top (as Marx saw it) but circulate within a stratum wherein the "influentials" are just community members who have some informal claim to expertise or experience.

The sociologists of this section find that people create their cultures as well as come to live in and be shaped by them; there is agency in what people do and decide; thus people transform cities and make them or at least their neighborhoods unique. From these older studies which still have major power in informing us of how we live in cities, let us turn to recent ideas and research.

II   COMMUNITY IN THE MODERN CITY

A. Community Building

William Drayton is a proponent of gardens, "Secret Gardens" (2000), that are placed in the interior of blocks. These communal sites of flora along with private gardens are a delight wherever they are found, but because of the configuration of property laws, they are not found very often. Clare Cooper Marcus (2001) has a similar vision of urban design that advances shared community space as a major theme. She presents notable cases of where residents can walk and play on common greens while still having the feeling of ownership or of being an insider who belongs there. Marcus highlights the principles of such successful outdoor space as the central focus of good community building.

Steuteville is a notable proponent of "The New Urbanism" (2000). This urban movement in neighborhood development is growing fast and is widely respected. It may be seen as a reaction and a solution to a pair of the nation's great problems—the over use of the car/SUV and urban sprawl. By building tightly organized, attractive housing developments close together and close in to the heart of the city, urbanites can combine several goals of how they live their lives and structure the cities. There is much to think about in the "New Urbanism," and there are a growing number of examples sprouting all around the country.

Just as community gardens began with substantial funding by a rich man who wanted to see people of middle incomes remain in the city, planners have had to work at promoting sustainable community development by increasing social capital. Bridger and Luloff (2001) find that social capital is indeed important, but it cannot be given to people and cannot be controlled by officials, it must grow and develop on its own. So there is a circularity: Social capital makes communities work and last, and these sustainable communities are the hosts of social capital. Some Vietnamese in a (Martin 1988) little study saw uncooperativeness as one of their basic traits: "One Vietnamese is better that three Japanese, but three Vietnamese aren't worth one Japanese." But this community in Port Arthur, Texas, of 5,000 Vietnamese refugees bought shrimp boats and established a seafood company, became owners of a dock, one was a marine insurer, others started marine service and hardware companies, their wives ran seafood. restaurants, and their children worked in various parts of the business sector. This was an emergent ethnic enclave, an incipient version of what Wilson and Martin (1982) found amongst the Cubans of Miami. Ethnic enclaves develop all of the types of capital leading to their having "ethnic enclave economies." Much goes into making ethnic enclaves work, and Raijman and Tienda discuss one part, the "Training Functions of Ethnic Economies: Mexican Entrepreneurs in Chicago" (2000). This issue is important because entrepreneurs are accused of having little concern for the community. Is this charge justified in terms of hiring community members—outside of the family? Like the Vietnamese and the Cubans, the Mexican entrepreneurs support each other in their rise through the firms that they start. Does this mean that entrepreneurs are mostly a positive factor in community development and participation?

One way to encourage social capital is through the help of community development corporations. At a meeting in the 1992 Pittsburgh ASA, a small group of sociologists and social workers visited Fairywood, a named community and a CDC wherein the residents were receiving federal assistance. After hearing presentations, touring the residential area, and watching so many children playing in a huge community swimming pool, one of us asked the question: "Where are the men?" The answer was one of amazement, "Well, they can't live here"—but obviously they visit. The federal rules were changing by the late 1990s, and CDCs were changing too. Robert Silverman (2001) investigates how CDCs have changed with a case study in Jackson, Mississippi. He compares the CDCs with the larger population of the city. Silverman finds the usual situation: Poor blacks live in CDCs where the community development industry plays a large role, and the CDC is "less autonomous and grassroots."

B. Community Participation
Social Connections

The last chapter of Robert Wuthnow's book, *Loose Connections: Joining Together in America's Fragmented Communities* (1998), begins our look at community participation. This chapter, "The Larger Picture," wraps up the changes discussed in previous chapters. Wuthnow looks broadly at our poor communities and our prosperous ones, small towns and large metropolises. In the early part of the chapter preceding our selection, Wuthnow says that we are losing our clearly defined institutions and roles, leaving us without a feeling of continuity in the good works that we wish to do. "In short, broad social and cultural patterns interact with specific kinds of communities to produce different repertoires of civic involvement" (p. 204). The role of big companies in community drives and routines is now less constant and dependable but more "porous." Wuthnow sees these business changes as leading to our not joining civic organization as much as previously. The extension includes less civility leading to lower levels of trust. And indeed, the corporations are a major cause of our moving from one place to another. This too, separates people from those whom they have come to know well, but then after we move, it is often the corporate world that provides new friends.

After reading "Loose Connections" the feeling of many forces shaping our sense of self and our place in society is almost overwhelming. Thus you may welcome Lemann's (1996) review, "Kicking in Groups." Lemann takes us on a tour of some influential writing on the topic of how atomized people become. He reviews Banfield's early study of the civics of Italy, which presaged his widely read book, *The Unheavenly City*, and then Lemann turns to Putnam's book *Making Democracy*

Work. Here we see the argument that civic culture leads to trust that leads to community development. Putnam then wrote "Bowling Alone," an article whose ready acceptance amazes Lemann in that he sees quite the opposite, thus the title of Lemann's article reprinted here, "Kicking in Groups."

Social Isolation

A specific question has arisen often: Is race or poverty the more important issue when considering particular problems within such communities? Sucoff and Upchurch (1998) delve into a sensitive issue along these lines: "Neighborhood Context and the Risk of Childbearing Among Metropolitan-Area Black Adolescents." This issue is straightforward but difficult to untangle, thus I have left the one table—in this whole book—that shows parametric statistical results. The authors smoothly address various methodological issues on their way to answering their research question. Note issues of norm differences within a race and the idea of "person-environment fit."

Small and Newman (2001) wrote a fine *Annual Review of Sociology* article, reprinted here, in which they explore "Urban Poverty After *The Truly Disadvantaged*: The Rediscovery of the Family, the Neighborhood, and Culture." Small and Newman jump into their study with William Julius Wilson's work beginning with *The Truly Disadvantaged* (1987). "The New Urban Poverty" began when the economy abandoned the industrial/manufacturing jobs and people in favor of the information/service economy. The significance of this change falls into many categories, but for the matter at hand the big problem was that good, quickly acquired, liveablewage jobs were replaced by positions requiring higher education and spatial mobility. No longer could a man with few skills simply take a job that supported him and his family in a stable position. Thus the next generation after World War II found that the cities and nation had moved on, while they were left with nowhere to turn. The part of Small and Newman's work that is reprinted here is the second of their three sub-titled sections, "The Neighborhood." The issue is, can neighborhoods cause poverty? The authors help us get through the methodological difficulties of the question as they review the recent literature on urban communities as causes of poverty.

One of the best works cited by Small and Newman (our book's next article) is "Neighborhood Poverty and the Social Isolation of Inner-City African American Families" by Rankin and Quane (2000). As is so often necessary, to answer big, complex questions, we need to get down to a case study to see how things really work in a particular place. Rankin and Quane chose Chicago and study it with sophisticated statistical analyses. As usual, I will spare you the advanced parametric statistics, but as always, you can be assured that the authors did a fine job in using the best methods to arrive at their conclusion. The results are not simple and immediately satisfying because the relationships are not always direct and linear. Furthermore, we see that studying social networks and their members requires sensitivity that is difficult to achieve. One issue here is raised again in other articles in the *The Urban Community:* Is the nature of community changing fundamentally thereby changing such notions as social isolation and the idea that members of a household experience the community in the same way: perhaps the members of each household have different communities?

C. Community Action

"The Effectiveness of Neighborhood Collective Action" (Mesch and Schwirian 1996) is crucial for determining if community is a level at which people should work. Neighborhoods that are higher in socioeconomic status are more effective substantially because they have more and better organizational resources and have the greatest ties to extra-community organizations. Community associations have success with social action, except for low income areas, especially when working on environmental threats. A former student of mine, Clarke Hammond, is the president of a neighborhood association in Austin, Texas. The group succeeds in their initiatives such as the opening of a Home Depot store in their neighborhood. The huge chain store desired to move in and the residents set the conditions including, building style, landscaping, signage, and paying for the neighborhood's annual party. Why does community action work for some and not for other locales? Mesch and Schwirian give us a good base from which to answer that question.

Etzioni (1996) argues that our communities are where we should be working. The community is neither the greedy individual nor the oppressive state but in the middle, just right, the third way. That is, not the political right nor the left–but another position in the spectrum of political positions, sort of a non-politics. The community is a level where things can work, where we care, and where we can have some control. Etzioni has produced many works on communitarianism and can be considered the leading proponent. In "The Responsive Community: A Communitarian Perspective," he works with the concepts of "responsive" and "authentic" communities, and he argues the need for the pairing of rights and needs. Etzioni gives us good material for discussing the most important issues in the social sciences.

III   MODERN ECOLOGICAL VIEWS OF THE CITY

A. Socio-Geographic Views

Geography and sociology have moved so close that only remote sensing and geomorphology seem distant from what sociologists do. I began the teaching of geography at my rather new campus and eventually hired a full-time geographer (Darrel McDonald); we began a long-running Geographic Information Systems study of neighborhood clustering, apparently the first full GIS study in sociology (1995). This section's first selection is a GIS study on the topic of locations of hazardous waste. Mitchell, Thomas, and Cutter (1999) begin with the understanding that certain areas of the country and then selected areas in particular seem to be the spots for dangerous refuse. Data are divided for urban, suburban, and rural areas, but this article does not focus on types of places and uses only aggregate data. We see, however, how race, residence and income are related to toxic places with interesting results that were possible only with the fine use of longitudinal analysis. Turning to an entirely different sort of sociogeographical treatment, we see James Kunstler's "Home From Nowhere" (1996). One can imagine his saying, "No matter where you go for the first time, you've seen it all before." Our sprawling suburbs and similar places are bland or worse. But how could this have happened in such a rich country? The answers are complex but neatly presented. Have you spent much time thinking about zoning ordinances? Well here's your chance. What do you think about urban planning; did you ever think that it is part of the problem? Communities matter to us, but some of the basic civic things we tacitly support may be the opposite of what we really want. In my prosperous city of Tyler there are many beautiful neighborhoods, and the ugliest courthouse. Nobody wanted the little run-down eyesore, but as Kunstler notes such monstrosities were built when the United States was at its zenith in the 1950s. In other writings Kunstler argues that principles of the "New Urbanism" can help the poor and abandoned to live decent lives. One of the issues that geographers have helped with is the study of ethnic enclave economics and one of the leaders is David Kaplan. The geography of ethnic enclave economics always includes good detail of location and also mapping that helps in understanding the relation to communities and their resources such as Kaplan's study of "The Creation of an Ethnic Economy: Indochinese Business Expansion in Saint Paul" (1997). The article selected here is a review of "The Spatial Structure of Urban Ethnic Economies" (1998).

B. Socio-Demographic Views

Demography is a field closely attached to sociology, at least in North America. Sociological demographers study populations to learn about many topics such as residential mobility and segregation. Of course, these studies require geographic units and boundaries, and geographers are major users of census data. It is not surprising that population geography is well established as a sub-discipline and that when we think of geographic studies as different from demographic studies, we are usually talking about only a matter of emphasis.

Myers' (2000) study reprinted here uses demographic data to examine how family instability is related to neighborhood instability. He investigates the relation between childhood mobility and later living arrangements, i.e., if parents move frequently from one community to another, their children may grow into unsettled family lives of their own. An obvious extension of the thought is that stable families produce stable neighborhoods and communities.

Another pattern that relates to neighborhood stability and desirability is segregation. Charles (2000) studies intensively the causes of neighborhood preferences as that leads to residential segregation. Recall that the Chicago School of Human Ecology studied the process of "invasion" where different ethnic groups (or other types of ecological units) move into neighborhoods, often inducing the residents to move out. Thus a turnover of the occupants may grow into "succession" in which the new group displaces the former. Why this happens and how this differs among the various majority and minority groups is complex, but Charles clarifies the issue in the case of Los Angeles.

IV   THE MODERN HOLISTIC STUDY

This wrap-up section is small but the article reprinted in this volume is perhaps the largest ever to appear in the *American Sociological Review*. Moloch, Freudenburg, and Paulsen (2000) compare and contrast sister cities. Their research question is, "What makes two places that should be so similar actually so dissimilar?" The answers require a lot of work and deep insight. That the authors accomplish their task is striking and makes for interesting reading and is a triumph of good sociology. The concluding article takes us far away from the focus and style of the previous section or two. The history and geography of place is brought in as essential to understanding cities. Similarly, Moloch, Freudenburg, and Paulsen discuss the role of business as not just an amorphous presence but particularly, rather as they show the importance of architecture. The result is a holistic study of unusual comprehensiveness and explanatory power.

The Urban Community

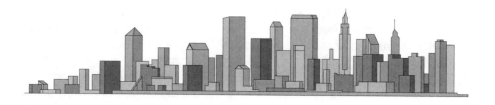

I   URBAN CLASSICS

Here are some great, old works, some of the treasures of sociology, by three authors who contemplate what the urban environment does to people. The view is negative, but were they wrong? Much of modern thought embraces their insights. Tonnies (1887) is the scholar most identified with lamenting the loss of the old community and concern about the bustling new city. His book is still cited anytime a sociologist discusses the dichotomy, indeed the clumsy German words he used still ring out, Gemeinschaft und Gesellschaft. *Simmel was a scholar and lecturer who discussed everything from the nature of two and three to the aesthetic significance of the nose. But his great classic is about the big city, the "bulk city" as translated from the German, a place of 100,000 and more people. His emphasis was on the crush of people, time, and money in the city—not the metropolis, an area with urban, suburban, and rural components and at least 50,000 people in a central place. The hundred-year-old German does not fit well with modern English. Read Simmel's (1903) work for the feel and spirit, don't get bogged down in the syntax. Following Simmel's classic writing is the defining, literally, work by Louis Wirth (1938), in which he condemns not only the big, modern city but also urban society*

The third section of the Urban Classics has three authors of the post-World War II era. Warren is one of the great community sociologists of the period and a scholar of the study of community studies. By reading this part of Warren's book, students can learn about the seminal American community studies. Warren's writings went on in single authorship, including The Community in America *(1963) and two later editions, and then he coauthored* New Perspectives on American Community *(1983) with Larry Lyon. Lyon went on to write* The Community in Urban Society

(1987)—a fine textbook. Following Warren's chapter that focuses on studies of the 1920s through the 1950s, we turn to Hunter's (1978) review of the ethnographies of the 1960s and 1970s. Merton's (1949) writing here is a methodological study stemming from the sociology of communication. "Types of Influentials: The Local and The Cosmopolitan" is a splendid use of ideal types, and it is fun to contemplate as you deal with people in your community.

A.
Urban Development: Urban Ecological Perspectives

THE GROWTH OF THE CITY: AN INTRODUCTION TO A RESEARCH PROJECT

Ernest W. Burgess

The outstanding fact of modern society is the growth of great cities. Nowhere else have the enormous changes which the machine industry has made in our social life registered themselves with such obviousness as in the cities. In the United States the transition from a rural to an urban civilization, though beginning later than in Europe, has taken place, if not more rapidly and completely, at any rate more logically in its most characteristic forms.

All the manifestations of modern life which are peculiarly urban—the skyscraper, the subway, the department store, the daily newspaper, and social work—are characteristically American. The more subtle changes in our social life, which in their cruder manifestations are termed "social problems," problems that alarm and bewilder us, as divorce, delinquency, and social unrest, are to be found in their most acute forms in our largest American cities. The profound and "subversive" forces which have wrought these changes are measured in the physical growth and expansion of cities. That is the significance of the comparative statistics of Weber, Bücher, and other students.

These statistical studies, although dealing mainly with the effects of urban growth, brought out into clear relief certain distinctive characteristics of urban as compared with rural populations. The larger proportion of women to men in the cities than in the open country, the greater percentage of youth and middle-aged, the higher ratio of the foreign-born, the increased heterogeneity of occupation increase with the growth of the city and profoundly alter its social structure. These variations in the composition of population are indicative of all the changes going on in the social organization of the community. In fact, these changes are a part of the growth of the city and suggest the nature of the processes of growth.

The only aspect of growth adequately described by Bücher and Weber was the rather obvious process of the *aggregation* of urban population. Almost as overt a process, that of *expansion,* has been investigated from a differ-

3

ent and very practical point of view by groups interested in city planning, zoning, and regional surveys. Even more significant than the increasing density of urban population is its correlative tendency to overflow, and so to extend over wider areas, and to incorporate these areas into a larger communal life. This paper, therefore, will treat first of the expansion of the city, and then of the less-known processes of urban metabolism and mobility which are closely related to expansion.

EXPANSION AS PHYSICAL GROWTH

The expansion of the city from the standpoint of the city plan, zoning, and regional surveys is thought of almost wholly in terms of its physical growth. Traction studies have dealt with the development of transportation in its relation to the distribution of population throughout the city. The surveys made by the Bell Telephone Company and other public utilities have attempted to forecast the direction and the rate of growth of the city in order to anticipate the future demands for the extension of their services. In the city plan the location of parks and boulevards, the widening of traffic streets, the provision for a civic center, are all in the interest of the future control of the physical development of the city.

This expansion in area of our largest cities is now being brought forcibly to our attention by the Plan for the Study of New York and Its Environs, and by the formation of the Chicago Regional Planning Association, which extends the metropolitan district of the city to a radius of 50 miles, embracing 4,000 square miles of territory. Both are attempting to measure expansion in order to deal with the change, that accompany city growth. In England, where more than one-half of the inhabitants live in cities having a population of 100,000 and over, the lively appreciation of the bearing of urban expansion on social organization is thus expressed by C. B. Fawcett:

One of the most important and striking developments in the growth of the urban populations of the more advanced peoples of the world during the last few decades has been the appearance of a number of vast urban aggregates, or conurbations, far larger and more numerous than the great cities of any preceding age. These have usually been formed by the simultaneous expansion of a number of neighboring towns, which have grown out toward each other until they have reached a practical coalescence in one continuous urban area. Each such conurbation still has within it many nuclei of denser town growth, most of which represent the central areas of the various towns from which it has grown, and these nuclear patches are connected by the less densely urbanized areas which began as suburbs of these towns. The latter are still usually rather less continuously occupied by buildings, and often have many open spaces.

These great aggregates of town dwellers are a new feature in the distribution of man over the earth. At the present day there are from thirty to forty of them, each containing more than a million people, whereas only a hundred years ago there were, outside the great centers of population on the waterways of China, not more than two or three. Such aggregations of people are phenomena of great geographical and social importance; they give rise to new problems in the organization of the life and well-being of their inhabitants and in their varied activities. Few of them have yet developed a social consciousness at all proportionate to their magnitude, or fully realized themselves as definite groupings of people with many common interests, emotions and thoughts.[1]

In Europe and America the tendency of the great city to expand has been recognized in the term "the metropolitan area of the city," which far overruns its political limits, and in the case

[1]"British Conurbations in 1921," *Sociological Review,* XIV (April, 1922), 111–12.

of New York and Chicago, even state lines. The metropolitan area may be taken to include urban territory that is physically contiguous, but it is coming to be defined by that facility of transportation that enables a business man to live in a suburb of Chicago and to work in the loop, and his wife to shop at Marshall Field's and attend grand opera in the Auditorium.

EXPANSION AS A PROCESS

No study of expansion as a process has yet been made, although the materials for such a study and intimations of different aspects of the process are contained in city planning, zoning, and regional surveys. The typical processes of the expansion of the city can best be illustrated, perhaps, by a series of concentric circles, which may be numbered to designate both the successive zones of urban extension and the types of areas differentiated in the process of expansion.

This chart represents an ideal construction of the tendencies of any town or city to expand radially from its central business district—on the map "The Loop" (I). Encircling the downtown area there is normally an area in transition, which is being invaded by business and light manufacture (II). A third area (III) is inhabited by the workers in industries who have escaped from the area of deterioration (II) but who desire to live within easy access of their work. Beyond this zone is the "residential area" (IV) of high-class apartment buildings or of exclusive "restricted" districts of single family dwellings. Still farther, out beyond the city limits, is the commuters' zone—suburban areas, or satellite cities—within a thirty- to sixty-minute ride of the central business district.

This chart brings out clearly the main fact of expansion, namely, the tendency of each inner zone to extend its area by the invasion of the next outer zone. This aspect of expansion may be called *succession,* a process which has

been studied in detail in plant ecology. If this chart is applied to Chicago, all four of these zones were in its early history included in the circumference of the inner zone, the present business district. The present boundaries of the area of deterioration were not many years ago those of the zone now inhabited by independent wage-earners, and within the memories of thousands of Chicagoans contained the residences of the "best families." It hardly needs to be added that neither Chicago nor any other city fits perfectly into this ideal scheme. Complications are introduced by the lake front, the Chicago River, railroad lines, historical factors in the location of industry, the relative degree of the resistance of communities to invasion, etc.

Besides extension and succession, the general process of expansion in urban growth involves the antagonistic and yet complementary processes of concentration and decentralization. In all cities there is the natural tendency for local and outside transportation to converge in the central business district. In the down-town section of every large city we expect to find the department stores, the skyscraper office buildings, the railroad stations, the great hotels, the theaters, the art museum, and the city hall. Quite naturally, almost inevitably, the economic, cultural, and political life centers here. The relation of centralization to the other processes of city life may be roughly gauged by the fact that over half a million people daily enter and leave Chicago's "loop." More recently sub-business centers have grown up in outlying zones. These "satellite loops" do not, it seems, represent the "hoped for" revival of the neighborhood, but rather a telescoping of several local communities into a larger economic unity. The Chicago of yesterday, an agglomeration of country towns and immigrant colonies, is undergoing a process of reorganization into a centralized decentralized system of local communities coalescing into sub-business areas visibly or invisibly dominated by the central business district. The actual processes of what may be called centralized decentralization are now being studied in the development of the chain store, which is only one illustration of the change in the basis of the urban organization.[2]

Expansion, as we have seen, deals with the physical growth of the city, and with the extension of the technical services that have made city life not only livable, but comfortable, even luxurious. Certain of these basic necessities of urban life are possible only through a tremendous development of communal existence. Three millions of people in Chicago are dependent upon one unified water system, one giant gas company, and one huge electric light plant. Yet, like most of the other aspects of our communal urban life, this economic co-operation is an example of co-operation without a shred of what the "spirit of co-operation" is commonly thought to signify. The great public utilities are a part of the mechanization of life in great cities, and have little or no other meaning for social organization.

Yet the processes of expansion, and especially the rate of expansion, may be studied not only in the physical growth and business development, but also in the consequent changes in the social organization and in personality types. How far is the growth of the city, in its physical and technical aspects, matched by a natural but adequate readjustment in the social organization? What, for a city, is a normal rate of expansion, a rate of expansion with which controlled changes in the social organization might successfully keep pace?

SOCIAL ORGANIZATION AND DISORGANIZATION AS PROCESSES OF METABOLISM

These questions may best be answered, perhaps, by thinking of urban growth as a resultant of organization and disorganization analogous to the anabolic and katabolic processes of metabolism in the body. In what way are individuals incorporated into the life of a city? By what process does a person become an organic part of his society? The natural process of acquiring culture is by birth. A person is born into a family already adjusted to a social environment—in this case the modern city. The natural rate of increase of population most favorable for assimilation may then be taken as the excess of the birth-rate over the death-rate, but is this the normal rate of city growth? Certainly, modern cities have increased and are increasing in population at a far higher rate. However, the natural rate of growth may be used to measure the disturbances of metabolism caused by any excessive increase, as those which followed the great influx of southern Negroes into northern cities since the war. In a similar way all cities show deviations in composition by age and sex from a standard population such as that of Sweden, unaffected in recent years by any great emigration or immigration. Here again, marked variations, as any great excess of males over females, or of females over males, or in the proportion of children, or of grown men or women, are symptomatic of abnormalities in social metabolism.

Normally the processes of disorganization and organization may be thought of as in reciprocal relationship to each other, and as co-operating in a moving equilibrium of social order toward an end vaguely or definitely regarded as progressive. So far as disorganization points to reorganization and makes for more efficient adjustment, disorganization must be conceived not as pathological, but as normal. Disorganization as preliminary to reorganization of attitudes and conduct is almost invariably the lot of the newcomer to the city, and the discarding of the habitual, and often of what has been to him the moral, is not infrequently accompanied by sharp mental conflict and sense of personal loss. Oftener, perhaps, the change gives sooner

---

[2]See E. H. Shideler, *The Retail Business Organization as an Index of Community Organization* (in preparation).

or later a feeling of emancipation and an urge toward new goals.

In the expansion of the city a process of distribution takes place which sifts and sorts and relocates individuals and groups by residence and occupation. The resulting differentiation of the cosmopolitan American city into areas is typically all from one pattern, with only interesting minor modifications. Within the central business district or on an adjoining street is the "main stem" of "hobohemia," the teeming Rialto of the homeless migratory man of the Middle West.[3] In the zone of deterioration encircling the central business section are always to be found the so-called "slums" and "bad lands," with their submerged regions of poverty, degradation, and disease, and their underworlds of crime and vice. Within a deteriorating area are rooming-house districts, the purgatory of "lost souls." Near by is the Latin Quarter, where creative and rebellious spirits resort. The slums are also crowded to overflowing with immigrant colonies—the Ghetto, Little Sicily, Greek-town, Chinatown—fascinatingly combining old world heritages and American adaptations. Wedging out from here is the Black Belt, with its free and disorderly life. The area of deterioration, while essentially one of decay, of stationary or declining population, is also one of regeneration, as witness the mission, the settlement, the artists' colony, radical centers—all obsessed with the vision of a new and better world.

The next zone is also inhabited predominatingly by factory and shop workers, but skilled and thrifty. This is an area of second immigrant settlement, generally of the second generation. It is the region of escape from the slum, the *Deutschland* of the aspiring Ghetto family. For *Deutschland* (literally "Germany") is the name given, half in envy, half in derision, to that region beyond the Ghetto where successful neighbors appear to be imitating German Jewish standards of living. But the inhabitant of this area in turn looks to the "Promised Land" beyond, to its residential hotels, its apartment-house region, its "satellite loops," and its "bright light" areas.

This differentiation into natural economic and cultural groupings gives form and character to the city. For segregation offers the group, and thereby the individuals who compose the group, a place and a role in the total organization of city life. Segregation limits development in certain directions, but releases it in others. These areas tend to accentuate certain traits, to attract and develop their kind of individuals, and so to become further differentiated.

The division of labor in the city likewise illustrates disorganization, reorganization, and increasing differentiation. The immigrant from rural communities in Europe and America seldom brings with him economic skill of any great value in our industrial, commercial, or professional life. Yet interesting occupational selection has taken place by nationality, explainable more by racial temperament or circumstance than by old-world economic background, as Irish policemen, Greek ice-cream parlors, Chinese laundries, Negro porters, Belgian janitors, etc.

The facts that in Chicago one million (996,589) individuals gainfully employed reported 509 occupations, and that over 1,000 men and women in *Who's Who* gave 116 different vocations, give some notion of how in the city the minute differentiation of occupation "analyzes and sifts the population, separating and classifying the diverse elements.[4] These figures also afford some intimation of the complexity and complication of the modern industrial mechanism and the intricate segregation and isolation of divergent economic

---

[3]For a study of this cultural area of city life see Nels Anderson, *The Hobo*, Chicago, 1923.

[4]Weber, *The Growth of Cities*, p. 442.

groups. Interrelated with this economic division of labor is a corresponding division into social classes and into cultural and recreational groups. From this multiplicity of groups, with their different patterns of life, the person finds his congenial social world and—what is not feasible in the narrow confines of a village—may move and live in widely separated, and perchance conflicting, worlds. Personal disorganization may be but the failure to harmonize the canons of conduct of two divergent groups.

If the phenomena of expansion and metabolism indicate that a moderate degree of disorganization may and does facilitate social organization, they indicate as well that rapid urban expansion is accompanied by excessive increases in disease, crime, disorder, vice, insanity, and suicide, rough indexes of social disorganization. But what are the indexes of the causes, rather than of the effects, of the disordered social metabolism of the city? The excess of the actual over the natural increase of population has already been suggested as a criterion. The significance of this increase consists in the immigration into a metropolitan city like New York and Chicago of tens of thousands of persons annually. Their invasion of the city has the effect of a tidal wave inundating first the immigrant colonies, the ports of first entry, dislodging thousands of inhabitants who overflow into the next zone, and so on and on until the momentum of the wave has spent its force on the last urban zone. The whole effect is to speed up expansion, to speed up industry, to speed up the "junking" process in the area of deterioration (II). These internal movements of the population become the more significant for study. What movement is going on in the city, and how may this movement be measured? It is easier, of course, to classify movement within the city than to measure it. There is the movement from residence to residence, change of occupation, labor turnover, movement to and from work, movement for recreation and adventure. This leads to the question: What is the significant aspect of movement for the study of the changes in city life? The answer to this question leads directly to the important distinction between movement and mobility.

MOBILITY AS THE PULSE OF THE COMMUNITY

Movement, per se, is not an evidence of change or of growth. In fact, movement may be a fixed and unchanging order of motion, designed to control a constant situation, as in routine movement. Movement that is significant for growth implies a change of movement in response to a new stimulus or situation. Change of movement of this type is called *mobility.* Movement of the nature of routine finds its typical expression in work. Change of movement, or mobility, is characteristically expressed in adventure. The great city, with its "bright lights," its emporiums of novelties and bargains, its palaces of amusement, its underworld of vice and crime, its risks of life and property from accident, robbery, and homicide, has become the region of the most intense degree of adventure and danger, excitement and thrill.

Mobility, it is evident, involves change, new experience, stimulation. Stimulation induces a response of the person to those objects in his environment which afford expression for his wishes. For the person, as for the physical organism, stimulation is essential to growth. Response to stimulation is wholesome so long as it is a correlated *integral* reaction of the entire personality. When the reaction is *segmental,* that is, detached from, and uncontrolled by, the organization of personality, it tends to become disorganizing or pathological. That is why stimulation for the sake of stimulation, as in the restless pursuit of pleasure, partakes of the nature of vice.

The mobility of city life, with its increase in the number and intensity of stimulations, tends inevitably to confuse and to demoralize the person. For an essential element in the mores and in personal morality is consistency, consistency of the type that is natural in the social control of the primary group. Where mobility is the greatest, and where in consequence primary controls break down completely, as in the zone of deterioration in the modern city, there develop areas of demoralization, of promiscuity, and of vice.

In our studies of the city it is found that areas of mobility are also the regions in which are found juvenile delinquency, boys' gangs, crime, poverty, wife desertion, divorce, abandoned infants, vice.

These concrete situations show why mobility is perhaps the best index of the state of metabolism of the city. Mobility may be thought of in more than a fanciful sense, as the "pulse of the community." Like the pulse of the human body, it is a process which reflects and is indicative of all the changes that are taking place in the community, and which is susceptible of analysis into elements which may be stated numerically.

The elements entering into mobility may be classified under two main heads: (1) the state of mutability of the person, and (2) the number and kind of contacts or stimulations in his environment. The mutability of city populations varies with sex and age composition, the degree of detachment of the person from the family and from other groups. All these factors may be expressed numerically. The new stimulations to which a population responds can be measured in terms of change of movement or of increasing contacts. Statistics on the movement of urban population may only measure routine, but an increase at a higher ratio than the increase of population measures mobility. In 1860 the horse-car lines of New York City carried about 50,000,000 passengers; in 1890 the trolley-cars (and a few surviving horse-cars) transported about 500,000,000; in 1921, the elevated, subway, surface, and electric and steam suburban lines carried a total of more than 2,500,000,000 passengers.[5] In Chicago the total annual rides per capita on the surface and elevated lines were 164 in 1890; 215 in 1900; 320 in 1910; and 338 in 1921. In addition, the rides per capita on steam and electric suburban lines almost doubled between 1916 (23) and 1921 (41), and the increasing use of the automobile must not be overlooked.[6] For example, the number of automobiles in Illinois increased from 131,140 in 1915 to 833,920 in 1923.[7]

Mobility may be measured not only by these changes of movement, but also by increase of contacts. While the increase of population of Chicago in 1912–22 was less than 25 per cent (23.6 per cent), the increase of letters delivered to Chicagoans was double that (49.6 per cent)—(from 693,084,196 to 1,038,007,854).[8] In 1912 New York had 8.8 telephones; in 1922, 16.9 per 100 inhabitants. Boston had, in 1912, 10.1 telephones; ten years later, 19.5 telephones per 100 inhabitants. In the same decade the figures for Chicago increased from 12.3 to 21.6 per 100 population.[9] But increase of the use of the telephone is probably more significant than increase in the number of telephones. The number of telephone calls in Chicago increased from 606,131,928 in 1914 to 944,010,586 in 1922,[10] an increase of 55.7 per cent, while the population increased only 13.4 per cent.

Land values, since they reflect movement, afford one of the most sensitive indexes of mo-

[5]Adapted from W. B. Munro, *Municipal Government and Administration,* II, 377.

[6]*Report of the Chicago Subway and Traction Commission,* p. 81, and the *Report on a Physical Plan for a Unified Transportation System,* p. 391.

[7]Data compiled by automobile industries.

[8]Statistics of mailing division, Chicago Post-office.

[9]Determined from *Census Estimates for Intercensual Years.*

[10]From statistics furnished by Mr. R. Johnson, traffic supervisor, Illinois Bell Telephone Company.

bility. The highest land values in Chicago are at the point of greatest mobility in the city, at the corner of State and Madison streets, in the Loop. A traffic count showed that at the rush period 31,000 people an hour, or 210,000 men and women in sixteen and one-half hours, passed the southwest corner. For over ten years land values in the Loop have been stationary, but in the same time they have doubled, quadrupled, and even sextupled in the strategic corners of the "satellite loops,"[11] an accurate index of the changes which have occurred. Our investigations so far seem to indicate that variations in land values, especially where correlated with differences in rents, offer perhaps the best single measure of mobility, and so of all the changes taking place in the expansion and growth of the city.

In general outline, I have attempted to present the point of view and methods of investigation which the department of sociology is employing in its studies in the growth of the city, namely, to describe urban expansion in terms of extension, succession, and concentration; to determine how expansion disturbs metabolism when disorganization is in excess of organization; and, finally, to define mobility

[11]From 1912–23, land values per front foot increased in Bridgeport from $600 to $1,250; in Division-Ashland-Milwaukee district, from $2,000 to $4,500; in "Back of the Yards," from $1,000 to $3,000; in Englewood, from $2,500 to $8,000; in Wilson Avenue, from $1,000 to $6,000; but decreased in the Loop from $20,000 to $16,500.

and to propose it as a measure both of expansion and metabolism, susceptible to precise quantitative formulation, so that it may be regarded almost literally as the pulse of the community. In a way, this statement might serve as an introduction to any one of five or six research projects under way in the department. The project, however, in which I am directly engaged is an attempt to apply these methods of investigation to a cross-section of the city—to put this area, as it were, under the microscope, and so to study in more detail and with greater control and precision the processes which have been described here in the large. For this purpose the West Side Jewish community has been selected. This community includes the so-called "Ghetto," or area of first settlement, and Lawndale, the so-called "Deutschland," or area of second settlement. This area has certain obvious advantages for this study, from the standpoint of expansion, metabolism, and mobility. It exemplifies the tendency to expansion radially from the business center of the city. It is now relatively a homogeneous cultural group. Lawndale is itself an area in flux, with the tide of migrants still flowing in from the Ghetto and a constant egress to more desirable regions of the residential zone. In this area, too, it is also possible to study how the expected outcome of this high rate of mobility in social and personal disorganization is counteracted in large measure by the efficient communal organization of the Jewish community.

HUMAN ECOLOGY

Robert Ezra Park

I. THE WEB OF LIFE

Naturalists of the last century were greatly intrigued by their observation of the interrelations and co-ordinations, within the realm of animate nature, of the numerous, divergent, and widely scattered species. Their successors, the botanists, and zoölogists of the present day, have turned their attention to more specific inquiries, and the "realm of nature," like the concept of evolution, has come to be for them a notion remote and speculative.

The "web of life," in which all living organisms, plants and animals alike, are bound together in a vast system of interlinked and interdependent lives, is nevertheless, as J. Arthur Thompson puts it, "one of the fundamental biological concepts" and is "as characteristically Darwinian as the struggle for existence."[1]

Darwin's famous instance of the cats and the clover is the classic illustration of this interdependence. He found, he explains, that humblebees were almost indispensable to the fertilization of the heartsease, since other bees do not visit this flower. The same thing is true with some kinds of clover. Humblebees alone visit red clover, as other bees cannot reach the nectar. The inference is that if the humblebees became extinct or very rare in England, the heartsease and red clover would become very rare, or wholly disappear. However, the number of humblebees in any district depends in a great measure on the number of field mice,

which destroy their combs and nests. It is estimated that more than two-thirds of them are thus destroyed all over England. Near villages and small towns the nests of humblebees are more numerous than elsewhere and this is attributed to the number of cats that destroy the mice.[2] Thus next year's crop of purple clover in certain parts of England depends on the number of humblebees in the district; the number of humblebees depends upon the number of field mice, the number of field mice upon the number and the enterprise of the cats, and the number of cats—as someone has added—depends on the number of old maids and others in neighboring villages who keep cats.

These large food chains, as they are called, each link of which eats the other, have as their logical prototype the familiar nursery rhyme, "The House that Jack Built." You recall:

The cow with the crumpled horn,
That tossed the dog,
That worried the cat,
That killed the rat,
That ate the malt
That lay in the house that Jack built.

Darwin and the naturalists of his day were particularly interested in observing and recording these curious illustrations of the mutual adaptation and correlation of plants and animals because they seemed to throw light on the origin of the species. Both the species and their

---

[1] *The System of Animate Nature* (Gifford Lectures, 1915–16), II (New York, 1920), 58.

[2] J. Arthur Thompson, *Darwinism and Human Life* (New York, 1911), pp. 52–53.

mutual interdependence, within a common habitat, seem to be a product of the same Darwinian struggle for existence.

It is interesting to note that it was the application to organic life of a sociological principle—the principle, namely, of "competitive co-operation"—that gave Darwin the first clue to the formulation of his theory of evolution.

"He projected on organic life," says Thompson, "a sociological idea," and "thus vindicated the relevancy and utility of a sociological idea within the biological realm."[3]

The active principle in the ordering and regulating of life within the realm of animate nature is, as Darwin described it, "the struggle for existence." By this means the numbers of living organisms are regulated, their distribution controlled, and the balance of nature maintained. Finally, it is by means of this elementary form of competition that the existing species, the survivors in the struggle, find their niches in the physical environment and in the existing correlation or division of labor between the different species. J. Arthur Thompson makes an impressive statement of the matter in his *System of Animate Nature*. He says:

The hosts of living organisms are not.... isolated creatures, for every thread of life is intertwined with others in a complex web.... . Flowers and insects are fitted to one another as hand to glove. Cats have to do with the plague in India as well as with the clover crop at home. . . . . Just as there is a correlation of organs in the body, so there is a correlation of organisms in the world of life. When we learn something of the intricate give and take, supply and demand, action and reaction between plants and animals, between flowers and insects, between herbivores and carnivores, and between other conflicting yet correlated interests, we begin to get a glimpse of a vast self-regulating organization.

These manifestations of a living, changing, but persistent order among competing organisms—organisms embodying "conflicting yet correlated interests"—seem to be the basis for the conception of a social order transcending the individual species, and of a society based on a biotic rather than a cultural basis, a conception later developed by the plant and animal ecologists.

In recent years the plant geographers have been the first to revive something of the earlier field naturalists' interest in the interrelations of species. Haeckel, in 1878, was the first to give to these studies a name, "ecology," and by so doing gave them the character of a distinct and separate science, a science which Thompson describes as "the new natural history."[4]

The interrelation and interdependence of the species are naturally more obvious and more intimate within the common habitat than elsewhere. Furthermore, as correlations have multiplied and competition has decreased, in consequence of mutual adaptations of the competing species, the habitat and habitants have tended to assume the character of a more or less completely closed system.

Within the limits of this system the individual units of the population are involved in a process of competitive co-operation, which has given to their interrelations the character of a natural economy. To such a habitat and its inhabitants—whether plant, animal, or human—the ecologists have applied the term "community."

The essential characteristics of a community, so conceived, are those of: (1) a population, territorially organized, (2) more or less completely rooted in the soil it occupies, (3) its individual units living in a relationship of mutual interdependence that is symbiotic rather

---

[3]*Ibid.,* p. 72.

[4]"Ecology," says Elton, "corresponds to the older terms Natural History and Bionomics, but is methods are now accurate and precise." See article, "Ecology," *Encyclopedia Britannica* (14th ed.).

than societal, in the sense in which that term applies to human beings.

These symbiotic societies are not merely unorganized assemblages of plants and animals which happen to live together in the same habitat. On the contrary, they are interrelated in the most complex manner. Every community has something of the character of an organic unit. It has a more or less definite structure and it has "a life history in which juvenile, adult and senile phases can be observed."[5] If it is an organism, it is one of the organs which are other organisms. It is, to use Spencer's phrase, a superorganism.

What more than anything else gives the symbiotic community the character of an organism is the fact that it possesses a mechanism (competition) for (1) regulating the numbers, and (2) preserving the balance between the competing species of which it is composed. It is by maintaining this biotic balance that the community preserves its identity and integrity as an individual unit through the changes and the vicissitudes to which it is subject in the course of its progress from the earlier to the later phases of its existence.

II. THE BALANCE OF NATURE

The balance of nature, as plant and animal ecologists have conceived it, seems to be largely a question of numbers. When the pressure of population upon the natural resources of the habitat reaches a certain degree of intensity, something invariably happens. In the one case the population may swarm and relieve the pressure of population by migration. In another, where the disequilibrium between population and natural resources is the result of some change, sudden or gradual, in the conditions of life, the pre-existing correlation of the species may be totally destroyed.

[5]Edward J. Salisbury, "Plants," *Encyclopaedia Britannica* (14th ed.).

Change may be brought about by a famine, an epidemic, or an invasion of the habitat by some alien species. Such an invasion may result in a rapid increase of the invading population and a sudden decline in the numbers if not the destruction of the original population. Change of some sort is continuous, although the rate and pace of change sometimes vary greatly. Charles Elton says:

> *The impression of anyone who has studied animal numbers in the field is that the "balance of nature" hardly exists, except in the minds of scientists. It seems that animal numbers are always tending to settle down into a smooth and harmonious working mechanism, but something always happens before this happy state is reached.*[6]

Under ordinary circumstances, such minor fluctuations in the biotic balance as occur are mediated and absorbed without profoundly disturbing the existing equilibrium and routine of life. When, on the other hand, some sudden and catastrophic change occurs—it may be a war, a famine, or pestilence—it upsets the biotic balance, breaks "the cake of custom," and releases energies up to that time held in check. A series of rapid and even violent changes may ensue which profoundly alter the existing organization of communal life and give a new direction to the future course of events.

The advent of the boll weevil in the southern cotton fields is a minor instance but illustrates the principle. The boll weevil crossed the Rio Grande at Brownsville in the summer of 1892. By 1894 the pest had spread to a dozen counties in Texas, bringing destruction to the cotton and great losses to the planters. From that point it advanced, with every recurring season, until by 1928 it had covered practically all the cotton producing area in the United States. Its progress took the form of a territorial succession. The consequences to agriculture

[6]"Animal Ecology," *ibid.*

were catastrophic but not wholly for the worse, since they served to give an impulse to changes in the organization of the industry long overdue. It also hastened the northward migration of the Negro tenant farmer.

The case of the boll weevil is typical. In this mobile modern world, where space and time have been measurably abolished, not men only but all the minor organisms (including the microbes) seem to be, as never before, in motion. Commerce, in progressively destroying the isolation upon which the ancient order of nature rested, has intensified the struggle for existence over an ever widening area of the habitable world. Out of this struggle a new equilibrium and a new system of animate nature, the new biotic basis of the new world-society, is emerging.

It is, as Elton remarks, the "fluctuation of numbers" and "the failure" from time to time "of the regulatory mechanism of animal increase" which ordinarily interrupts the established routine, and in so doing releases a new cycle of change. In regard to these fluctuations in numbers Elton says:

These failures of the regulating mechanism of animal increase—are they caused by (1) internal changes, after the manner of an alarm clock which suddenly goes off, or the boilers of an engine blowing up, or are they caused by some factors in the outer environment— weather, vegetation, or something like that?[7]

and he adds:

It appears that they are due to both but that the latter (external factor) is the more important of the two, and usually plays the leading rôle.

The conditions which affect and control the movements and numbers of populations are more complex in human societies than in plant and animal communities, but they exhibit extraordinary similarities.

[7]*Ibid.*

The boll weevil, moving out of its ancient habitat in the central Mexican plateau and into the virgin territory of the southern cotton plantations, incidentally multiplying its population to the limit of the territories and resources, is not unlike the Boers of Cape Colony, South Africa, trekking out into the high veldt of the central South African plateau and filling it, within a period of one hundred years, with a population of their own descendants.

Competition operates in the human (as it does in the plant and animal) community to bring about and restore the communal equilibrium, when, either by the advent of some intrusive factor from without or in the normal course of its life-history, that equilibrium is disturbed.

Thus every crisis that initiates a period of rapid change, during which competition is intensified, moves over finally into a period of more or less stable equilibrium and a new division of labor. In this manner competition brings about a condition in which competition is superseded by co-operation.

It is when, and to the extent that, competition declines that the kind of order which we call society may be said to exist. In short, society, from the ecological point of view, and in so far as it is a territorial unit, is just the area within which biotic competition has declined and the struggle for existence has assumed higher and more sublimated forms.

III. COMPETITION, DOMINANCE AND SUCCESSION

There are other and less obvious ways in which competition exercises control over the relations of individuals and species within the communal habitat. The two ecological principles, dominance and succession, which operate to establish and maintain such communal order as here described are functions of, and dependent upon, competition.

In every life-community there is always one or more dominant species. In a plant community this dominance is ordinarily the result of struggle among the different species for light. In a climate which supports a forest the dominant species will invariably be trees. On the prairie and steppes they will be grasses.

Light being the main necessity of plants, the dominant plant of a community is the tallest member, which can spread its green energy-trap above the heads of the others. What marginal exploitation there is to be done is an exploitation of the dimmer light below this canopy. So it comes about in every life-community on land, in the cornfield just as in the forest, that there are layers of vegetation, each adapted to exist in a lesser intensity of light than the one above. Usually there are but two or three such layers; in an oak-wood for example there will be a layer of moss, above this herbs or low bushes, and then nothing more to the leafy roof; in the wheatfield the dominating form is the wheat, with lower weeds among its stalks. But in tropical forests the whole space from floor to roof may be zoned and populated.[8]

But the principle of dominance operates in the human as well as in the plant and animal communities. The so-called natural or functional areas of a metropolitan community—for example, the slum, the rooming-house area, the central shopping section and the banking center—each and all owe their existence directly to the factor of dominance, and indirectly to competition.

The struggle of industries and commercial institutions for a strategic location determines in the long run the main outlines of the urban community. The distribution of population, as well as the location and limits of the residential areas which they occupy, are determined by another similar but subordinate system of forces.

[8]H. G. Wells, Julian S. Huxley, and G. P. Wells, *The Science of Life* (New York, 1934), pp. 968–69.

The area of dominance in any community is usually the area of highest land values. Ordinarily there are in every large city two such positions of highest land value—one in the central shopping district, the other in the central banking area. From these points land values decline at first precipitantly and then more gradually toward the periphery of the urban community. It is these land values that determine the location of social institutions and business enterprises. Both the one and the other are bound up in a kind of territorial complex within which they are at once competing and interdependent units.

As the metropolitan community expands into the suburbs the pressure of professions, business enterprises, and social institutions of various sorts destined to serve the whole metropolitan region steadily increases the demand for space at the center. Thus not merely the growth of the suburban area, but any change in the method of transportation which makes the central business area of the city more accessible, tends to increase the pressure at the center. From thence this pressure is transmitted and diffused, as the profile of land values discloses, to every other part of the city.

Thus the principle of dominance, operating within the limits imposed by the terrain and other natural features of the location, tends to determine the general ecological pattern of the city and the functional relation of each of the different areas of the city to all others.

Dominance is, furthermore, in so far as it tends to stabilize either the biotic or the cultural community, indirectly responsible for the phenomenon of succession.

The term "succession" is used by ecologists to describe and designate that orderly sequence of changes through which a biotic community passes in the course of its development from a primary and relatively unstable to a relatively permanent or climax stage. The main point is that not merely do the individual plants and animals within the communal habitat grow but the community itself, i.e., the system of relations between the species, is likewise involved in an orderly process of change and development.

The fact that, in the course of this development, the community moves through a series of more or less clearly defined stages is the fact that gives this development the serial character which the term "succession" suggests.

The explanation of the serial character of the changes involved in succession is the fact that at every stage in the process a more or less stable equilibrium is achieved, which in due course, and as a result of progressive changes in life-conditions, possibly due to growth and decay, the equilibrium achieved in the earlier stages is eventually undermined. In such case the energies previously held in balance will be released, competition will be intensified, and change will continue at a relatively rapid rate until a new equilibrium is achieved.

The climax phase of community development corresponds with the adult phase of an individual's life.

> In the developing single organism, each phase is its own executioner, and itself brings a new phase into existence, as when the tadpole grows the thyroid gland which is destined to make the tadpole state pass away in favour of the miniature frog. And in the developing community of organisms, the same thing happens—each stage alters its own environment, for it changes and almost invariably enriches the soil in which it lives; and thus it eventually brings itself to an end, by making it possible for new kinds of plants with greater demands in the way of mineral salts or other riches of the soil to flourish there. Accordingly bigger and more exigent plants gradually supplant the early pioneers, until a final balance is reached, the ultimate possibility for that climate.[9]

The cultural community develops in comparable ways to that of the biotic, but the process is more complicated. Inventions, as well as sudden or catastrophic changes, seem to play a more important part in bringing about serial changes in the cultural than in the biotic community. But the principle involved seems to be substantially the same. In any case, all or most of the fundamental processes seem to be functionally related and dependent upon competition.

Competition, which on the biotic level functions to control and regulate the interrelations of organisms, tends to assume on the social level the form of conflict. The intimate relation between competition and conflict is indicated by the fact that wars frequently, if not always, have, or seem to have, their source and origin in economic competition which, in that case, assumes the more sublimated form of a struggle for power and prestige. The social function of war, on the other hand, seems to be to extend the area over which it is possible to maintain peace.

IV. BIOLOGICAL ECONOMICS

If population pressure, on the one hand, co-operates with changes in local and environmental conditions to disturb at once the biotic balance and social equilibrium, it tends at the same time to intensify competition. In so doing it functions, indirectly, to bring about a new, more minute and, at the same time, territorially extensive division of labor.

Under the influence of an intensified competition, and the increased activity which competition involves, every individual and every species, each for itself, tends to discover the particular niche in the physical and living environment where it can survive and flourish with the greatest possible expansiveness consistent with its necessary dependence upon its neighbors.

It is in this way that a territorial organization and a biological division of labor, within

[9]*Ibid.*, pp. 977–78.

the communal habitat, is established and maintained. This explains, in part at least, the fact that the biotic community has been conceived at one time as a kind of super-organism and at another as a kind of economic organization for the exploitation of the natural resources of its habitat.

In their interesting survey, *The Science of Life,* H. G. Wells and his collaborators, Julian Huxley and G. P. Wells, have described ecology as "biological economics," and as such very largely concerned with "the balances and mutual pressures of species living in the same habitat.[10]

"Ecology," as they put it, is "an extension of Economics to the whole of life." On the other hand the science of economics as traditionally conceived, though it is a whole century older, is merely a branch of a more general science of ecology which includes man with all other living creatures. Under the circumstances what has been traditionally described as economics and conceived as restricted to human affairs, might very properly be described as Barrows some years ago described geography, namely as human ecology. It is in this sense that Wells and his collaborators would use the term.

The science of economic—at first it was called Political Economy—is a whole century older than ecology. It was and is the science of social subsistence, of needs and their satisfactions, of work and wealth. It tries to elucidate the relations of producer, dealer, and consumer in the human community and show how the whole system carries on. Ecology broadens out this inquiry into a general study of the give and take, the effort, accumulation and consumption in every province of life. Economics, therefore, is merely Human Ecology, it is the narrow and special study of the ecology of the very extraordinary community in which we live. It might have been a better and brighter science if it had begun biologically.[11]

Since human ecology cannot be at the same time both geography and economics, one may adopt, as a working hypothesis, the notion that it is neither one nor the other but something independent of both. Even so the motives for identifying ecology with geography on the one hand, and economics on the other, are fairly obvious.

From the point of view of geography, the plant, animal, and human population, including their habitations and other evidence of man's occupation of the soil, are merely part of the landscape, of which the geographer is seeking a detailed description and picture.

On the other hand ecology (biologic economics), even when it involves some sort of unconscious co-operation and a natural, spontaneous, and non-rational division of labor, is something different from the economics of commerce; something quite apart from the bargaining of the market place. Commerce, as Simmel somewhere remarks, is one of the latest and most complicated of all the social relationships into which human beings have entered. Man is the only animal that trades and traffics.

Ecology, and human ecology, if it is not identical with economics on the distinctively human and cultural level is, nevertheless, something more than and different from the static order which the human geographer discovers when he surveys the cultural landscape.

The community of the geographer is not, for one thing, like that of the ecologist, a closed system, and the web of communication which man has spread over the earth is something different from the "web of life" which binds living creatures all over the world in a vital nexus.

[10]*Ibid.*

[11]H. H. Barrows, "Geography as Human Ecology," *Annals Association American Geographers,* XIII (1923), 1–14. See H. G. Wells, *et al., op. cit.,* pp. 961–62.

V. SYMBIOSIS AND SOCIETY

Human ecology, if it is neither economics on one hand nor geography on the other, but just ecology, differs, nevertheless, in important respects from plant and animal ecology. The interrelations of human beings and interactions of man and his habitat are comparable but not identical with interrelations of other forms of life that live together and carry on a kind of "biological economy" within the limits of a common habitat.

For one thing man is not so immediately dependent upon his physical environment as other animals. As a result of the existing worldwide division of labor, man's relation to his physical environment has been mediated through the intervention of other men. The exchange of goods and services have co-operated to emancipate him from dependence upon his local habitat.

Furthermore man has, by means of inventions and technical devices of the most diverse sorts, enormously increased his capacity for reacting upon and remaking, not only his habitat but his world. Finally, man has erected upon the basis of the biotic community an institutional structure rooted in custom and tradition.

Structure, where it exists, tends to resist change, at least change coming from without; while it possibly facilitates the cumulation of change within.[12] In plant and animal communities structure is biologically determined, and so far as any division of labor exists at all it has a physiological and instinctive basis. The social insects afford a conspicuous example of this fact, and one interest in studying their habits, as Wheeler points out, is that they show the extent to which social organization can be developed on a purely physiological and instinctive basis, as is the case among human beings in the natural as distinguished from the institutional family.[13]

In a society of human beings, however, this communal structure is reinforced by custom and assumes an institutional character. In human as contrasted with animal societies, competition and the freedom of the individual is limited on every level above the biotic by custom and consensus.

The incidence of this more or less arbitrary control which custom and consensus imposes upon the natural social order complicates the social process but does not fundamentally alter it—or, if it does, the effects of biotic competition will still be manifest in the succeeding social order and the subsequent course of events.

The fact seems to be, then, that human society, as distinguished from plant and animal society, is organized on two levels, the biotic and the cultural. There is a symbiotic society based on competition and a cultural society based on communication and consensus. As a matter of fact the two societies are merely different aspects of one society, which, in the vicissitudes and changes to which they are subject remain, nevertheless, in some sort of mutual dependence each upon the other. The cultural superstructure rests on the basis of the symbiotic substructure, and the emergent energies that manifest themselves on the biotic level in movements and actions reveal themselves on the higher social level in more subtle and sublimated forms.

---

[12]Here is, obviously, another evidence of that organic character of the interrelations of organisms in the biosphere to which J. Arthur Thompson and others have referred. It is an indication of the way in which competition mediates the influences from without by the adjustment and readjustment of relations within the community. In this case "within" coincides with the orbit of the competitive process, at least so far as the effects of that process are substantive and obvious. See Simmel's definition of society and the social group in time and space quoted in Park and Burgess, *Introduction to the Science of Sociology* (2d ed.), pp. 348–56.

---

[13]William Morton Wheeler, *Social Life among the Insects* (Lowell Institute Lectures, March, 1922), pp. 3–18.

However, the interrelations of human beings are more diverse and complicated than this dichotomy, symbiotic and cultural, indicates. This fact is attested by the divergent systems of human interrelations which have been the subject of the special social sciences. Thus human society, certainly in its mature and more rational expression, exhibits not merely an ecological, but an economic, a political, and a moral order. The social sciences include not merely human geography and ecology, but economics, political science, and cultural anthropology.

It is interesting also that these divergent social orders seem to arrange themselves in a kind of hierarchy. In fact they may be said to form a pyramid of which the ecological order constitutes the base and the moral order the apex. Upon each succeeding one of these levels, the ecological, economic, political, and moral, the individual finds himself more completely incorporated into and subordinated to the social order of which he is a part than upon the preceding.

Society is everywhere a control organization. Its function is to organize, integrate, and direct the energies resident in the individuals of which it is composed. One might, perhaps, say that the function of society was everywhere to restrict competition and by so doing bring about a more effective co-operation of the organic units of which society is composed.

Competition, on the biotic level, as we observe it in the plant and animal communities, seems to be relatively unrestricted. Society, so far as it exists, is anarchic and free. On the cultural level, this freedom of the individual to compete is restricted by conventions, understandings, and law. The individual is more free upon the economic level than upon the political, more free on the political than the moral.

As society matures control is extended and intensified and free commerce of individuals restricted, if not by law then by what Gilbert Murray refers to as "the normal expectation of mankind." The mores are merely what men, in a situation that is defined, have come to expect.

Human ecology, in so far as it is concerned with a social order that is based on competition rather than consensus, is identical, in principle at least, with plant and animal ecology. The problems with which plant and animal ecology have been traditionally concerned are fundamentally population problems. Society, as ecologists have conceived it, is a population settled and limited to its habitat. The ties that unite its individual units are those of a free and natural economy, based on a natural division of labor. Such a society is territorially organized and the ties which hold it together are physical and vital rather than customary and moral.

Human ecology has, however, to reckon with the fact that in human society competition is limited by custom and culture. The cultural superstructure imposes itself as an instrument of direction and control upon the biotic substructure.

Reduced to its elements the human community, so conceived, may be said to consist of a population and a culture, including in the term culture (1) a body of customs and beliefs and (2) a corresponding body of artifacts and technological devices.

To these three elements or factors—(1) population, (2) artifacts (technicological culture), (3) custom and beliefs (non-material culture)—into which the social complex resolves itself, one should, perhaps, add a fourth, namely, the natural resources of the habitat.

It is the interaction of these four factors—(1) population, (2) artifacts (technicological culture), (3) custom and beliefs (non-material culture), and (4) the natural resources that maintain at once the biotic balance and the social equilibrium, when and where they exist.

The changes in which ecology is interested are the movements of population and of artifacts (commodities) and changes in location and occupation—any sort of change, in fact, which affects an existing division of labor or the relation of the population to the soil.

Human ecology is, fundamentally, an attempt to investigate the processes by which the biotic balance and the social equilibrium (1) are maintained once they are achieved and (2) the processes by which, when the biotic balance and the social equilibrium are disturbed, the transition is made from one relatively stable order to another.

B.
Human Relations: Sociocultural Perspectives

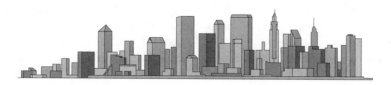

COMMUNITY AND SOCIETY (GEMEINSCHAFT UND GESELLSCHAFT)

Ferdinand Tönnies

Translated and Edited by Charles P. Loomis

BASES OF SOCIAL RELATIONS

1. *Social Entities (soziale Wesenheiten).* Sociology as a special science has as its subject the "things" which result from social life, and only from social life. They are products of human thinking and exist only for such thinking; that is, primarily for individuals themselves who are bound together and who think of their collective existence as dominating them and as a something which is represented as a person capable of volition and action, to which they give a name. The existence of such a something, a social person, can be recognized and acknowledged by outsiders, who may themselves be single or associated individuals, or by a social entity formed by such persons. Such recognition, if mutual, may create a new, essentially similar entity, in the most perfect case, a new social person, which again is existent immediately for its founders but can also be observed, recognized, and acknowledged by outsiders. The manner of existence of this social thing or person is not unlike that of the gods, which, being imagined and thought of by men who are bound together, are also created in order to be glorified, whether the form be that of an animal, a human being, or mixed being. There is, however, an obvious difference in that the gods disappear for the people to whom they belong when their existence is no longer believed in, even though they remain as subjects of the theoretical, historical, and sociological thinking. In contradistinction, social "entities," as we call them, do not require such belief or delusion. They can be thought of as subjects of common volition and operation in clear perception of their imaginary nature. Of course, it is also possible, indeed not an infrequent occurrence, that to the social entities, just as in the case of the gods, a supernatural, or, better stated, a metaphysical nature will be ascribed. The fanciful mythological thinking to which man has always been inclined constantly prevails in this sense and will, therefore, often confuse the inventions and fantasies of one or

the other type; the social entities, especially the collective persons, are superior, powerful, and exalted, and so are the gods. Thus, in the social entity there exists at least some of the godlike characteristics. They stand under the special protection of the gods, especially when to such an entity a supernatural origin is ascribed, as in the case of the church.

When the god is himself represented as a powerful and feared or as a benevolent and kind ruler, he is ruler over the earthly ruler, giving the latter his consecration, confirming and befriending him, establishing his right, especially the right of hereditary succession, as a god-given right. By the grace of God the earthly ruler reigns, enjoying a godlike veneration. All kinds of veneration, as they spring from natural feeling as childish adoration or as awe of the weak for the strong, who may be hated and detested, are interwoven one with another and with the gods in whom they find their consummation and shine forth as religion. As obedient servants of the gods, powerful men are agents and interpreters of the will of God and thereby increase their own power.

Even though this mere creature of thought does not live in the clouds or on Olympus but has ascribed to it an existence such as that which is perhaps embodied in the assembly of an armed force or other meeting of the people, it will not easily avoid that condition in which its existence is brought into relationship with that of the gods. The belief in the gods can support the belief in the republic just as the belief in the church and the veneration of the priesthood are directly related. The scientific critical attitude destroys all of these illusions. It recognizes that only human thought and human will are contained in all these imaginary realms, that they are based upon human hopes and fears, requirements and needs, and that in their exalted forms they are comparable to poetical works of art on which the spirit of the ages has worked.

Thus, we return to the simple problem and thought: what, why, and how do thinking human beings will and want? The simple and most general answer is: they want to attain an end and seek the most appropriate means of attaining it. They strive toward a goal and seek the correct way leading thereto. This is the action, the behavior, which in the affairs of practical life, of daily work, of struggle, of trade, has through the ages been directed and made easier by pleasure and devotion, by hope and fear, by practice and habit, by model and precept.

2. *Human Volition.* The general human volition, which we may conceive as natural and original, is fulfilled through knowledge and ability and is also fundamentally conditioned through reciprocal interaction with them. The whole intellect, even in the plainest man, expresses itself in his knowledge and correspondingly in his volition. Not only what he has learned but also the inherited mode of thought and perception of the forefathers influences his sentiment, his mind and heart, his conscience. Consequently I name the will thought of in this latter sense natural will *(Wesenwille),* contrasting it with the type of rational will *(Kürwille),* in which the thinking has gained predominance and come to be the directing agent. The rational will is to be differentiated from intellectual will. Intellectual will gets along well with subconscious motives which lie deep in man's nature and at the base of his natural will, whereas rational will eliminates such disturbing elements and is as clearly conscious as possible.

Deliberation, the thought form of ends and means, can separate the two, one from the other. From this results the inference that the means are not fundamentally connected to the end; that is to say, the means and end are not allied, interwoven, or identical. The means may rather be completely isolated and therefore possibly even stand in strong opposition to the ends. In this case the end under consideration requires that the means be as suitable to it as possible, that no means or segment thereof be used which is not conditioned by the end, but that the means most suitable for the attainment of a given end be chosen and used. This implies a definite divorce and differentiation of end and means which, therefore, permits no consideration of means other than that of their perfect suitability for the attaining of the end. The principle of the rationalization of the means develops everywhere as a necessary consequence the more thought, in accordance with the desire and intention, is intensively focused on the end or the goal. This signifies, therefore, an attitude of indifference to the means with respect to every consideration other than their greatest effectiveness in attaining the end. This indifference is frequently attained only by overcoming resistance resulting from motives other than the consideration of the end, which motives may hinder, dissuade, or frighten one from the application of this means. Thus, action which adjusts the means to the end desired may be viewed with definite reluctance, also with fear and anxiety, or, more characteristically, with aversion and, what is akin thereto, with feelings of opposition such as come with remorse. With some exaggeration, Goethe says the acting man is always "without conscience." In reality, the acting person often finds it necessary, if he "unscrupulously" follows his goal, to repress or overcome his conscientiousness. On account of this necessity, many consider themselves justified in despising or disowning such feelings, and sometimes they even find their satisfaction in bravado and arrogance, making themselves free from all such considerations.

This means, therefore, that on the one hand there is the simple emotional (impulsive) and, therefore, irrational volition and action, whereas on the other there is the simple rational volition and action in which the means are arranged, a condition which often stands in conflict with the feelings. Between these two extremes all real volition and action takes place. The consideration that most volition and action resembles or is inclined toward either one or the other makes it possible to establish the concepts of natural will and rational will, which concepts are rightly applied only in this sense. I call them normal concepts. What they represent are ideal types, and they should serve as standards by which reality may be recognized and described.

3. *Gemeinschaft and Gesellschaft.* It is not a question of contrasting the rational will with the nonrational will, because intellect and reason belong to natural will as well as to rational will. Indeed, intellect in natural will attains its fruition in the creative, formative, and artistic ability and works and in the spirit of the genius. This is true even though in its elementary forms natural will means nothing more than a direct, naïve, and therefore emotional volition and action, whereas, on the other hand, rational will is most frequently characterized by consciousness. To the latter belongs manufacturing as contrasted with creation; therefore, we speak of mechanical work (as expressed in the German and other languages) referring to forging plans, machinations, weaving intrigues, or fabrications which are directed to the objective of bringing forth the means, the exclusive determination of which is that of producing the outward effects necessary to attain our desired ends.

When these concepts are applied to associations, it should not be understood that we are thinking only of the regular motives leading to the entrance into an association, creating of a confederation, or organizing of a union or special interest group, or even the founding of a commonwealth. It is, however, of importance to recognize what motives lie at the basis of and explain the existence of all kinds of association or cause their persistence, and while we are here interested only in positive bases, this holds also for negative motives upon which persistence may be based. In this connection it is not to be understood that the bases belong fundamentally and persistently either to the one or the other category, that is, of natural will or rational will. On the contrary a dynamic condition or process is assumed which corresponds to the changeable elements of human feeling and thinking. The motives fluctuate so that they are now of one category, then of the other. However, wherever such development takes place a certain regularity or even "law," in the sense of a tendency toward abstract rational forms, may be observed.

I call all kinds of association in which natural will predominates Gemeinschaft, all those which are formed and fundamentally conditioned by rational will, Gesellschaft. Thus, these concepts signify the model qualities of the essence and the tendencies of being bound together. Thus, both names are in the present context stripped of their connotation as designating social entities or groups, or even collective or artificial persons; the essence of both Gemeinschaft and Gesellschaft is found interwoven in all kinds of associations, as will be shown.

SOCIAL SYSTEMS

1. *Relationships, Collectives, Social Organizations.* As social entities or forms, I differentiate: (1) Social relationships (*Verhältnisse*), (2) Collectives (*Samtschaften*), (3) Social organizations or corporate bodies (*Körperschaften*) (leagues, fellowships, associations, or special-interest groups).

The third form is always thought of as a kind of human person capable of creating a definite unified will which, as the will of the natural or artificial persons belonging to it, binds and constrains them to act in conformity with such will, which may be directed inwardly or outwardly. In the social relationship it is not the relationship itself which is so considered, even though it be designated by a special name. However, it is essential that its subjects or bearers, who may be considered as "members" of the relationship, are conscious of it as a relationship which they will affirmatively and thus establish as an existing reality. This manner of establishing a social relationship represents in embryonic or emergent form what is evolved to perfection in the establishment of a social organization or corporation capable of willing and acting.

The collective lies between the social relationship and the social organization. It is thought of as a plurality which, like the social organization, includes a multitude of persons so held together that there result common intentions, desires, inclinations, disinclinations—in short, common feelings and ways of thinking. However, the collective is not capable of real volition. It can reach no decision as long as it does not "organize" itself into a committee, special-interest group, or council.

2. *The Social Relationship.* The social relationship is the most general and simplest social entity or form. It also has the deepest foundation, because it rests partly upon the original, natural, and actual conditions as the causes of connections, of mutual dependence, and of attachment among men, and because it rests partly on the most fundamental, most universal, and most necessary requirements of human beings. The one basis, like the other, is raised to consciousness with different effects. If a natural relationship exists, as for example between my brother and me, on one hand, or between my brother-in-law, my stepbrother, adopted or foster brother and me, on the other, I have the feeling that we are intimate, that we affirm each other's existence, that ties exist between us, that we know each other and to a certain extent are sympathetic toward each other, trusting and wishing each other well. This is true although in the latter case, involving persons who are not blood brothers, the relation-

ship is not so natural as in the first where I know the same mother gave birth to both my brother and me. From this it follows that we have certain values in common, whether it be that we are obliged to manage an estate together, or that we divide possessions as inheritances between us, or that the matter of intellectual goods or ideals is involved. At any rate, out of each such relationship, even between two, there results the recognition and acknowledgment of the social relationship as such on the part of each and therefore the knowledge of each that definite mutual action must regularly result therefrom. This action is expected and demanded of each by the other, and each expects and demands of himself that it be carried out in relation to the other. In this lies the embryo of "rights" which each claims for himself but also concedes to the other, as well as "duties" to which one feels obligated but which one puts upon oneself knowing that the other party wills that he be and considers that he is so obligated.

However, when I become conscious of my most urgent needs and find that I can neither satisfy them out of my own volition nor out of a natural relation, this means that I must do something to satisfy my need; that is, engage in free activity which is bound only by the requirement or possibly conditioned by the need but not by consideration for other people. Soon I perceive that I must work on other people in order to influence them to deliver or give something to me which I need. Possibly in restricted individual cases my mere requests will be granted, as, for example, in the case of a piece of bread or a glass of water. However, as a rule when one is not receiving something in a Gemeinschaft-like relationship, such as from within the family, one must earn or buy it by labor, service, or money which has been earned previously as payment for labor or service.

I now enter or have already entered into a social relationship, but it is of a different kind. Its prototype is barter or exchange, including the more highly developed form of exchange, the sale and purchase of things or services, which are the same as things and are therefore thought of as capable of being exchanged for things or for other services. All action which is of an intellectual nature, and consequently oriented by reason, is of this type because comparison and thinking are necessary to it and furnish a basis for it. Social relationships which result from such barter or exchange are primarily momentary in that they involve a momentary common volition. However, they come to have duration partly through repetition resulting in regularity of the exchange act and partly through the lengthening of the individual act by the postponement of fulfillment on the part of one or both sides. In this latter case there results a relationship, the distinguishing characteristic of which is a one-sided or mutual "promise." It is a real social relationship of obligation or mutual dependence resulting first of all from mutual promises, even though they may be expressly stated by one side and only tacitly understood by the other as such an eventual promise.

Also, the relationships which come to us from nature are in their essence mutual, are fulfilled in mutual performance. The relations produce this mutuality and demand, require, or make it necessary. Having these characteristics, they resemble the exchange relationship. However, the natural relationship is, by its very essence, of earlier origin than its subjects or members. In such natural relationships it is self-evident that action will take place and be willed in accordance with the relationship, whether it be what is contained on the one hand in the simplest relationships resulting from desire and inclination, from love or habit, or on the other hand from reason or intellect contained in the feeling of duty. These latter types of natural will change into one another, and each can be the basis of Gemeinschaft.

On the other hand, in the purest and most abstract contract relationship the contracting parties are thought of as separate, hitherto and otherwise independent, as strangers to each other, and perhaps even as hitherto and in other respects inimical persons. *Do, ut des* (I give, so that you will give) is the only principle of such a relationship. What I do for you, I do only as a means to effect your simultaneous, previous, or later service for me. Actually and really I want and desire only this. To get something from you is my end; my service is the means thereto, which I naturally contribute unwillingly. Only the aforesaid and anticipated result is the cause which determines my volition. This is the simplest form of rational will.

Relationships of the first type are to be classified under the concept Gemeinschaft, those of the other type under the concept of Gesellschaft, thus differentiating Gemeinschaft-like and Gesellschaft-like relationships. Gemeinschaft-like relationships differ to the extent that there is assumed, on the one hand, a real, even if not complete, equality in knowledge or volition, in power and in authority on the part of the participants, and on the other hand, an essential inequality in these respects. This also holds for the relations of Gesellschaft. In accordance with this distinction we shall differentiate between the fellowship type and the authoritative type of social relationship. Let us now consider this difference.

A. In Gemeinschaft-like Relationships. (a) The Fellowship Type. The simplest fellowship type is represented by a pair who live together in a brotherly, comradely, and friendly manner, and it is most likely to exist when those involved are of the same age, sex, and sentiment, are engaged in the same activity or have the same intentions, or when they are united by one idea.

In legend and history such pairs occur frequently. The Greeks used to honor such friendships as those of Achilles and Patroclus, Orestes and Pylades, Epaminondas and Pelopidas, to the extent that to Aristotle is ascribed

the paradox: He who has friends has no friend. In the German language and literature it is customary to designate such sentiments, the nature of which the Greeks glorified as mutual happiness and sorrow, as a brotherly relationship. This characterization is based more on the thought of the ideal than on actual observation, but it is correct in so far as brothers actually make the most natural as well as the most probable pairs of friends, more because of their origin than because of a motive.

(b) Authoritative Type. The relationship of father to child, as observations in everyday life will prove, is to be found in all the strata of society in all stages of culture. The weaker the child and the more it is in need of help, the greater the extent to which the relationship is represented by protection. Protection of necessity always carries with it authority as a condition, because protection regularly can be carried out only when the protected party follows the directions and even the commands of the protector. Although all authority has a tendency to change into the use of force, in the case of the father as well as the mother relationship such a tendency is arrested by love and tenderness. These sentiments, being of animal and vegetative origin, are more likely to be regularly accorded to a child born to a parent than to any other possessed and protected person. The general character of the father relationship can be easily extended to include similar relationships involving protection, examples of which are the step-father, foster father, the general house father, and the guardian, even though these, as representatives of the father, do not necessarily legally stand in Gemeinschaft-like relation to the ward. The authority of the father is the prototype of all Gemeinschaft-like authority. It is especially true in the case of the priesthood, even though the basis may be different. This rests primarily upon mythological conceptions which place the father in Olympus or in heaven and perhaps ascribe numberless children to the father of the gods and men. Or in a less sensual, more re- fined form, the father may be represented by an only son whom the struggle against polytheism tends almost to identify with the father. Little wonder that the title Pope (*Papa,* literally "fa- ther") in the original church of all bishops was raised to the pinnacle of spiritual dignity in the Roman Church and that in the Oriental Church the especially high priests are called fathers *(Popen)* in the language of the common people. Also, world and political authority, which is often mixed with and may not be less sancti- fied than the spiritual, easily takes on the char- acter of the well-wishing father, as is most plainly expressed in the term "father" of a country. The fatherly authority, however, is the special case of authority of age, and the pres- tige-giving quality of age expresses itself most perfectly in the authority of the father. This easily explains the eminence which is attrib- uted to the senator in the worldly and the pres- byter in the spiritual commonwealth.

(c) Mixed Relationships. In many Gemein- schaft-like relationships the essence of author- ity and that of fellowship are mixed. This is the case in the most important of the relationships of Gemeinschaft, the lasting relation between man and woman which is conditioned through sexual needs and reproduction, whether or not the relationship is called marriage.

B. In Gesellschaft-like Relationships. The difference between the fellowship and authori- tative types is also to be found in the Gesellschaft-like relationships. It can, how- ever, be derived only from the fact that the au- thority is based upon a free contract whether between individuals, as service contracts, or by agreement of many to recognize and place a master or head over them and to obey him con- ditionally or unconditionally. This may be a natural person or a collective person which re- sults directly from individuals uniting in a so- ciety, social organization, or corporate body which is capable of volition and action and can be represented through its own totality. The Gesellschaft-like authority attains its consum- mation in the modern state, a consummation which many predecessors strove to attain until the democratic republic came into existence and allowed for development beyond the Gesellschaft-like foundation. The actual au- thority results, however, in the simple Gesellschaft-like relationship, from the differ- ence in the power of two parties, as in the labor contract. Such authority results from contracts made between the individual "employer" and individual "employee," and also from the con- dition out of which come "peace treaties" be- tween victor and conquered. Apparently it is a contract, but in actuality it is coercion and abuse.

3. *The Collective.* The second concept of social entity or form is that of the collective. I make distinctions between natural, psychical, and social collectives. Our concept concerns only social collectives, but these rest partly on natural and partly on psychical collectives, partly on both. This is because the essence of a social collective is to be found in the natural and psychological relationships forming the basis of the collective and are consciously af- firmed and willed. This phenomenon appears everywhere in the life of a people and in many forms of mutualities, as, for example, in forms of life and customs, superstitions and religion. It is especially in evidence in the distinguishing characteristic through which a segment of a people, that is, certain classes, are given promi- nence, nobility, and authority. A distinguishing characteristic which has this function is partly an objective phenomenon and partly something positive in the people's consciousness. The con- sciousness of belonging to a controlling estate makes its appearance in a distinct manner as pride and haughtiness—feelings which in turn are coupled with the submission and modesty of those "lower" classes over which authority is exercised so long as the controlling estates, as such, are honored, and so long as their excel- lence, or even their divinity, is believed in.

In the case of the collective the concepts of Gemeinschaft and Gesellschaft should also be applied. The social collective has the characteristics of Gemeinschaft in so far as the members think of such a grouping as a gift of nature or created by a supernatural will, as is expressed in the simplest and most naïve manner in the Indian caste system. Here, to be fixed to a given calling is just as necessary and natural as being born, and the professional estate or group has the same significance as a large family for which the pursuit and means of making a livelihood, even if this should be accomplished by thievery, is represented as something inherited which it is a duty to retain and nurture. In all systems of ranks or estates, traces of this condition are to be found because (and to the extent that) a complete emancipation from the social relationships established at birth seldom occurred and was often impossible. Thus, man as a rule submits to the social status in which parents and forebears, or, as it is wont to be expressed, "God," has placed him as if it were his lot to bear, even though it be felt as a burden, which, however, is habit and is lightened by the recognition that it cannot be changed. Indeed, within these limits there can exist an intellectual self-consciousness which affirms this estate (rank) even though it be recognized as one of the less significant. This intellectual basis manifests itself partly as the group extols itself for certain superiorities or virtues, the lack of which in the dominating estate is noticed and complained about. Also, the intellectual basis is to be found partly in the consciousness of special knowledge and skill of the group, as, for example, its art, craftsmanship, and skill, which are thought of as being at least the equivalent of the other honored or ruling estates.

Consciousness of a social collective has different results when directed toward the attainment of definite and important ends which it knows to be and claims are its own characteristics. This happens in a pronounced way in the political and intellectual struggle in which the social strata of a people stand against each other as classes. The more the consciousness of authority as a feeling of superiority results in putting one class in such a position of power as to force the lower class to stay in its place, the more this latter will strive toward the attainment of equality and therefore the more indignant it becomes concerning oppression and arrogance on the part of the controlling class, which it attempts to restrict and displace.

Whether this process is called class struggle (*Klassenkampf*) or struggle of estates (*Ständekampf*) is not important. The struggle among the estates usually takes place earlier, is less radical, and can be allayed. The lower estates strive only for the opportunity to participate in the satisfactions of life and fundamentals of authority, allowing the controlling estate to remain in power. This latter remains in power by proclaiming its own fitness and disparaging that of the lower estates and by exerting effort to reduce these lower strata to submission.

The class struggle is more unconditional. It recognizes no estates, no natural masters. In the foreground of the consciousness of the whole class which feels that it is propertyless and therefore oppressed, stands the ideal of the Gemeinschaft of property in field and soil and all the implements of labor. These latter have been acquired through the art of trade or as inherited property belonging by "law" to the small minority which, as the propertied class, is set off against the propertyless class. Therefore, the class struggle becomes more conscious and general than the struggle among the estates. However, even though there be no definite form of struggle there is a corresponding consciousness which makes itself felt in many ways. The great propertyless masses prefer to think of themselves as the people (*Volk*), and the narrow class which is in control of property and its use thinks of itself as society, even though each expression is all inclusive. "The" people *(Volk),* as in the case of the estate, resembles the Gemeinschaft; "the" society, like the class, has, in the sense in which it is here used, the basic characteristic of Gesellschaft.

4. *The Social Organization.* The third and most important category of pure or theoretical sociology is the social organization or corporate body, a social body or union known by many other names. It is never anything natural, neither can it be understood as a mere psychical phenomenon. It is completely and essentially a social phenomenon and must be considered as composed of several individuals. Capacity for unified volition and action, a capacity which is demonstrated most clearly as competency to pass resolutions, characterizes it. Just as the thinking individual is capable of making decisions, so is a group of several individuals when they continuously agree or agree to the extent that there prevails and is recognized a definite will as the will of all or sufficient consensus to be the will of the social organization or corporate body. Thus, the volition of such a group can be represented by the will of a natural person behind whom the will of the whole social organization or corporate body stands. Continuing our discussion of social organizations or corporate bodies, we may make the following observations:

(1) A social organization or corporate body can originate from natural relationships provided these are social relationships. In this connection, kinship, the most universal and natural bond which embraces human beings, comes to our attention. The most important social organization or corporate body which originates therefrom and which among all known peoples occurs as the original form of a common life is the kinship group, the gens, clan, or whatever name is applied to designate this ancient union or unity.

Whether or not the totality of adult persons includes the women, whether their council ends in agreement which is sanctioned by a supposed will of God, or whether they rejoice in and willingly accept the decisions of a leader and head, it is under these conditions that there is formed the embryo of a consciousness which matures into something beyond a mere feeling of belonging together, and there is established and affirmed an enduring self or ego in the totality.

(2) A common relation to the soil tends to associate people who may be kinsfolk or believe themselves to be such. Neighborhood, the fact that they live together, is the basis of their union; it leads to counseling and through deliberations to resolutions. Here again the two principles of fellowship and authority will be involved. The outstanding example of an association of this type is the rural village community, which attains its consummation in the cultivation of the soil practiced in common and the possession of common property in village fields or land held in common by the village, and in the Mark-community which comes to represent the unity of several neighboring village communities which originally may have formed one unit.

The rural village community is frequently identical with a great family or clan but the more alien elements are taken in the more it loses its kinship characteristics. The bond of field and soil and living together first takes its place along with and later more and more supplants the bond of common ancestry. Especially when an alien tribe and its leaders become the conquerors of a territory and establish themselves in the seats of control without extirpating or driving out all the former residents and owners does this tendency manifest itself, molding a new people *(Volk)* from the two groups, even though the one was subjected to new masters. The existence of the village community as a social organization or corporate body ordinarily continues in the form of a fellowship. Such a village community, however, may be modified by the power and rights of feudal lords.

(3) In the more intimate and close living together in the town, the fellowship and co-operative quality attains a new level. Living together tends to depend less on common nature. People not related by blood tend to assemble in the towns since these originally were walled-in villages or strongholds whose inhabitants were forced to co-operate for defense and for the maintenance of peace and order among themselves and thereby to form a political community, either under the rule of a lord or as citizens of equal rights. This was the great mission and service of the town *(Stadt)* community, the *"Polis"* which grew to be that commonwealth which later in Europe and elsewhere up to our time has bequeathed its character and name to the state *(Staat),* the mightiest of all corporate bodies. That assembly of the sovereign people, the religious association *(Ekklesia),* the other great commonwealth of the Roman and post-Roman period, loaned its name to the Church and spread its glory throughout the world in a similar manner.

These social bodies and communities retain their common root in that original state of belonging together, which according to our concept is the Gemeinschaft. Indeed, although the original state of common being, living, and working is changed, it retains and is able to renew its mental and political form and its co-operative functions. Thus, a people *(Volk)* which feels itself bound together by a common language, when held together within a national association or even when only striving to become a nation, will desire to be represented in a unity or *Volksgemeinschaft,* which may become intensified by national consciousness and pride, but may also thereby lose its original genuineness.

5. *Capitalistic, Middle-Class, or Bourgeois Society (bürgerliche Gesellschaft).* During this development, the original qualities of Gemeinschaft may be lost because there takes place a continued change in the original basis upon which living together rests. This change reaches its consummation in what is frequently

designated as individualism. Through this development social life in and of itself is not diminished, but social life of the Gemeinschaft is impaired and a new phenomenon develops out of the needs, interests, desires and decisions of persons who previously worked co-operatively together and are acting and dealing one with another. This new phenomenon, the "capitalistic society," increases in power and gradually attains the ascendancy. Tending as it does to be cosmopolitan and unlimited in size, it is the most distinct form of the many phenomena represented by the sociological concept of the Gesellschaft.

A great transformation takes place. Whereas previously the whole of life was nurtured and arose from the profoundness of the people *(Volk),* the capitalistic society through a long process spreads itself over the totality of this people, indeed over the whole of mankind. As a totality of individuals and families it is essentially a collective of economic character composed primarily of those who partake in that wealth which, as land and capital, represents the necessary means to the production of goods of all kinds. Within narrow or far-flung borders which are determined by actual or supposed kinship bonds, of the existence of which the language group is the most valuable sign, it constructs its state, that is to say, a kind of unity resembling a town community which is capable of willing and acting. It develops as the capitalistic middle-class republic and apparently finally attains its perfection in the social republic. It considers the state a means of attaining its ends, of which not the least important is protecting its person and property as well as the intellectual attitude which gives status and honor to its supporters.

However, since this capitalistic middle-class society cannot, without betraying itself, admit its uniqueness as a collective of Gesellschaft in contradistinction to the people *(Volk)* or, so to speak, herald this difference by raising its own flag, it can only assert its existence through claiming to be identical with, as well as representative and advocate of, the whole people to which it furnishes guidance. This process, which does not stop with conferring equal political rights on all citizens, to a certain extent closes the always widening hiatus between the wealth monopoly of the narrow and real Gesellschaft and the poverty of the people, but it cannot change the essential character of the hiatus. Indeed, it deepens it, spreading and strengthening the consciousness of the "social question."

By means of political and other intellectual organization promoted by town and, to a greater extent, by city life, the consciousness of the Gesellschaft gradually becomes the consciousness of an increasing mass of the people. The people come more and more to think of the state as a means and tool to be used in bettering their condition, destroying the monopoly of wealth of the few, winning a share in the products. Thus, the laborer would be allowed a share in proper proportion to his reasonable needs and the leaders in production their share of certain goods which are to be divided for consumption, and those things suitable for continued common utilization would be retained as common property of the Gesellschaft, which is to say of the people or their organized association, the state

THE BULK CITIES
AND THE MENTAL LIFE

Georg Simmel

The deepest problems of modern life originate out of the individual's claim to protect the independence and peculiarity of his existence against the historically inherited and dominant society. The external superficial culture and techniques of life are the last transformation of the battle achieved with nature in order that the primitive human being may lead about his existence.

May the 18th century's call for liberation of all historically developed relationships among countries and religion, in morals and economy, allow the originally good nature of all human beings to freely develop. May the 19th century not only demand more freedom but also the peculiarity of the human being and his performance which makes the individual incomparable and as indispensable as possible while also making him depend all the more narrowly on the complementary effects of other individuals. May Nietzsche see the condition for the full development of individuals in the most ruthless fight of individuals or in socialism holding down and suppressing their own competition; all from the same basic motive—the resistance of the subject in the social/technical mechanism against being leveled and used by others.

Where the products of the specialized modern life [urbanites] are asked about their inner feelings, so to speak, the body of the culture in their own souls, the answer will have to be found in an equation between the individual and the forces shaping that individual, through the adaptations of the personality, and the manner in which the individual deals with the external powers.

The psychological basis, upon which the personalities of bulk city* individuals arise, merges the increase of stress, which is a result of the fast and non-stop change of outer and inner impressions.

The human being is a "difference" system. This means that his consciousness is stimulated by the difference between the current impression as opposed to the preceding one; and immediate impressions and most insignificant differences, . . . , all use less consciousness than the swift compression of shifting pictures, sheer disance, what one gathers at a glance, and unexpected impressions, all of which impose themselves.

Because the bulk city creates these psychological conditions—with every walk down the street, with the speed and variety of the economic, the vocational, and one's social life—it creates a distinct contrast to the already sensual foundations of one's inner consciousness, in the degree/quantity of consciousness, it demands this from us because of our constituted difference systems in distinction to the town and country life, which has a slower, more accustomed, more even-flowing rhythm of the inner-consciousness' image.

The intellectual character of the bulk city inner life becomes comprehensible in contrast to the rural, small-town arrangement that rather

---

*The German *grosstadt* translates as "bulk city" meaning a city with 100,000 or more people.

concentrates on nature and instinctive relationships. These are rooted in the more unconscious layers of the soul and grow best in calm evenness and uninterrupted habituations.

In the transparent, conscious, uppermost layers of our soul resides our intellect; which is the most adaptable of our inner strengths; it can make the change and contrast of appearances without the disruptions and inner turnovers.

Because of that the bulk city person, who of course is surrounded by thousands of individual modifications, has a protective "organ" [consciousness] against getting uprooted by the currents and discrepancies of the milieu that threaten him. Instead of using nature, he essentially responds with his intellect, which is obtained by increased consciousness, so that every reaction to appearances is transferred from the depth of the personality into the least sensitive, outer consciousness.

This intellectuality shields the subjective life against the rapes of the bulk city, ramifies and connects with multiple separate appearances.

The bulk cities have always been the central organs of the economy because the diversity and the accumulation of the economic exchange give a certain importance to the means of exchange—that would not have occurred with the dearth of the sparse rural exchange traffic.

However, money economy and intellectual power stand in close context. The pure objectivity in the treatment of people is combined with unkind harshness.

The purely rational human being is indifferent to everything involving purely human relations, because such relationships and reactions that are created cannot be understood by the logical mind. Whereas this condition results exactly from individuality, the money principle is the opposite: It asks only about what is common, the exchange value, which levels all the quality and peculiarity to the one question, "how much?"

All natural relationships between people are based on their individuality, while intellectuals calculate human beings just like numbers and indifferent elements—just like the bulk city dweller with his suppliers and buyers, his servant, and, often enough, with the people of his social compulsory reckonings, is in contrast to the character of the smaller town, in which the inevitable knowledge of the individualities generates a more sentimental mode of behavior that stands opposite to the assessment of performance and return.

The essential thing in the economic field is that in more primitive circumstances, products are produced for the customer, who orders them, so that producers and buyers know each other.

However, the modern city feeds almost completely from the production for the market, for someone completely unknown, whom the producer has never seen before. Because of this, the interest of both parties is a merciless objectivity, its rational, calculating, economic egoism does not have to fear any distraction from the inevitability of personal relationships found in small towns.

The market economy is devoid of this fear of the personal, and it dominates the cities where it drives away the last remains of the people's ownership of production and reduces them to customers who work more and more every day—in such close interaction that no one can really say, whether the intellectual state of mind was first pushed toward the money economy or whether this was the decisive factor for the condition.

Certainly the bulk city life is the most fertile ground for this interaction; this I wish to cover with the most significant English historian of the state of minds: in the course of the whole of English history, London has never dwelled in the heart of England—but often as its mind and always its purse!

. . . . The modern spirit became more and more a calculating one; as the bulk city caused once insignificant mental streams to unite themselves. The ideal of science, to change the world into a mathematical example, to fix each part with mathematical formulas, corresponding with the mathematical accuracy of the practical life which was created by the money economy; by weighing mathematically and reducing qualitative values to quantitative ones, the money economy filled up the day of so many people.

Through the arithmetical nature of money, the relationships of the elements of life are precise and secure in the regulation of equalities, dissimilarities, and clarity of those appointments-just like the clarity prompted by the spread of pocket watches.

However, it is the conditions of the city that are cause as well as effect for this characteristic trend.

The relationships and issues of the typical city-dweller are habitually so manifold and complicated, above all: through the conglomeration of so many people with such varied interests, their relationships and activities interlock as a single organism with numerous appendages that without punctuation in promises and performances everything would collapse to an inextricable chaos.

If in Berlin, all clocks would suddenly go wrong in different directions even if only in the span of an hour, its whole economic and other traffic life would be destroyed. In addition, if this occurs, one may find himself making trips in vain due to unfulfilled expectations and appointments.

So, the technology of bulk city life is not at all possible without all activities and interrelations being organized on a most punctual, fixed, and more than subjective time scheme.

Now the task of making a whole from these contemplations steps forward; from each point at the surface of existence, only from this does it seem to arise, an anchor gets sent into the depths of a soul so that all banal formalities through directional lines are formally connected by the ultimate decisions on life's purpose and style.

The punctuality, calculability, and accuracy that the complications and extension of the bulk city life force upon it, stands not only in closest context to its money-economic and intellectual character but must also color the contents of life and the exclusion of those irrational, instinctive, sovereign character traits and impulses that want to determine the form of life instead of accepting it as a general schematically specified one from the outside.

Even if through such characterized and autocratic existences they are impossible, so they are opposite for its figure and from it, the ardent hate of natures like Ruskin and Nietzsche against the city, they find alone in the unsystematically odd and not for everyone, all equally specified the value of life, and therefore their hate of the city streams from the same source as the hate against the money economy and against intellectual existence.

The same factors, because of the minute precision of life, make the structure very impersonal, but because its functioning pieces are coagulated, it is simultaneously very personal.

Perhaps there is no mental appearance that is as typical for the city as that of blasé/indifference.*

Blasé/indifference is the consequence of things changing quickly and people finding contrasts with their narrowly crowded nerve irritations from which also the increase of bulk city intellectualism seems to emerge; why also stupid and the mentally incapable are then not in the habit of being blasé.

An extremely leisurely life makes one arrogant and blasé, because it excites for a very long time the nerves to their strongest reactions until they get no more reaction from the nerves—also they force the nerves to react with violent answers through contrast and swiftness of its changes so their last reserves of

*Editor is aware of this redundancy.

strength are drained and if this continues in this manner, they will not have time to gather new strength for additional reactions.

With the psychological source of blasé/indifference in the city and emerging inability to garner new strength, they are unable to react with the proper energy to new irritations. This incompetence is blasé and is exhibited by every child in a city compared to rural children.

With this physiological source of the bulk city blasé/indifference, flows the money economy.

The nature of blasé/indifference is the conditioning against the changes in things, not in the sense that they would not be perceived, but the difference of things is nullified and causes less of a reaction.

These things appear to the blasé person in an equally weak and gray tinge, no one is dear, or to be preferred by others.

This mindset is the trusted subjective reflex of the completely permeated market economy; in that the money offsets all varieties of things evenly, expresses all qualitative differences between them in terms of how much, in that the money, with its lack of color and indifference, tosses itself up to the general denominator of all values, the most terrifying equalizer, its incomparability hollows out the core of the things, their peculiarity and their specific value.

They all swim in the continuously moving money stream with the same specific weight, lie at the same level, and differ only in the size of the pieces that each discovers on this level.

This coloring or rather bleaching of things may be unrecognizably small in the individual cases through their equivalence with money, in the relationship that the rich have with commodities, however in the total character, the public spirit now gives these objects everywhere, it is accumulated to a very noticeable size. The cities are therefore, the headquarters of the money traffic . . . and the blasé attitude.

That success of the congregation of people provokes in the individual his highest nerve performance, a peak in the success of the congregation of humans and things that irritate; through the merely quantitative increase of the same conditions, this success changes into its opposite, into this particular adaptation of this blasé feeling, in which the nerves accept the last possibility to come with the contents of the bulk city life, they fail themselves in the reaction toward adaptation—self preservation of certain natures, about the price, to debase the whole objective world, then in the end what pulls down the personality inevitably into feeling of same debasement.

While the subject has to arrange this form of existence, completely with himself, his preservation demands of the bulk city no less than the negative side of social nature. One will be allowed to call the mental attitude of the city dwellers toward each other, reservation or reserve in the formal sense.

If so many inner reactions are supposed to answer the continuous outer confrontations with the unending number of humans, like in the little town in which you know most everybody you meet and where you have a positive relationship with all, then one would atomize himself and fall into an unimaginable state.

Partly this psychological circumstance, partly the right to mistrust, that we have toward the elements of big city life, that are roving and fleeting in touch, is the reason we do not know year-long neighbors even by appearance, which is viewed by the small town dwellers as cold and heartless.

Yes, if I am not mistaken, the inside of this outer reserve is not only indifference, but more frequently than we realize, it is a quiet aversion and brings a mutual foreignness and repulsion, that would immediately sprout, in a moment of a somehow induced introduction, hates and fights.

The whole inner organization of a so extended and busy life is based on an extremely manifold step construction of sympathies, indifferences, and aversions of the shortest as well as in the longest type.

This sphere of the indifference is not as big as it seems to be; however, the activity of our soul responds to almost every impression with an almost certain sensation of volatility and change. . . .

Actually this latter would be just as unnatural for us, as the intolerable fog of indiscriminate mutual suggestion. . . . Two typical dangers of the city remain: antipathy—the latent one and practical antagonism, the blatant one, indifference causes the distances and preventions, without which this type of life could not exist at all: its dimensions and its mixtures, the rhythm of its emergence and disappearance, the forms, in which it is sufficed this form's inseparable total of the bulk city life formation with the motives, standardizing in the narrower sense: what appears directly in this as dissolution is only one of its elementary socialization forms in reality.

However, this reservation with the overtone of hidden aversion now reappears as "form or garment" of a much more general intellectual nature of the city. It grants the individual a type and measure of personal freedom—to which there is not any analogy in other circumstances: it goes back to one of the big developmental tendencies of social life. . . .

The earliest stage of social formations that finds itself in history as well as at present time is this: a relatively small circle, with strong opposition against neighboring, foreign, or somehow antagonistic circles, forms as one all the closer union in itself, this circle allows the individual member little room for the development of special and diverse qualities.

So political and informal groups, according to party formations, cooperatively begin religion; the self-preservation of very young unions demands strict boundaries and a centralized unit and can therefore, not grant the individual any freedom and peculiarity of inner and outer development. From this stage, the social evolution goes after two different, and nevertheless, corresponding sides simultaneously.

To the extent, in which the group grows, numerically, spatially, in meaning and life contents—even loosens its immediate inner unit for itself, the sharpness of the original demarcation against others is moderated by interrelations and context; and at the same time, an individual wins freedom of movement, far over the first limitation of jealousy, and a peculiarity and specialty to which the work division [division of labor] gives opportunity and constraint to the group that became larger.

After this formula, the state and religion, guilds and political parties and innumerable other groups developed and naturally modified the particular conditions and strength of the individual in the general scheme.

However, it clearly also seems to me recognizable that individuality developed within the urban life.

The town life in antiquity, like in the middle ages, prevented individuals' relationships from having independence and differentiation—this would suffocate the modern human being, whether he is a small town dweller or a city dweller.

The smaller that a circle is, that forms our surroundings, the more narrowly related are the relationships, the more fearfully it watches the individual's fundamental attitudes and lifestyles, and the sooner a quantitative and qualitative special type of urban person would explode the framework of the totality. The antique Polis seems to have had the character of the town completely in this way.

The continuing threat of the existence of enemies near and far causes that taut cohesion in political and military relationships, that supervision of the citizen by the citizen, the jealousy of the totality against the individual, whose special life could hold down and could take advantage of most citizens through despotism.

The immense agitation and emotionality and the unique variety of colors, of the Athenian life, might be explained as people of incomparable individuality aim their personalities against the constant inner and outer pressures of the de-individualized town.

This created an atmosphere of tension in which the weaker were oppressed, and the strong ones were encouraged to the most ardent self-affirmations. Through this Athens got famous for being the most "generally human" in the intellectual development of our type.

Because this is the connection . . . the farthest and most general contents and forms of life are dearly interconnected with the most individualized ones. . . .

As in feudal times, the "free" man was the one who stood in the country . . . under the right of the biggest social structure, the un-free were those in the narrow circle of the feudal association, under exclusion of that—in one ethereal and refined sense the city dweller is "free" in contrast to the pettiness and prejudices today that constrict the small town dweller.

Because of reserve and indifference, the mental life conditions in big circles that are never felt stronger in the individual's independence as in the densest milling crowd of the bulk city, because the mental distance makes the physical proximity and narrowness really clear; it apparently is only this freedom, if nowhere conceivably so secluded one feels himself at ease, even in the bulk city crowd; because here like otherwise it is not at all necessary that the freedom of the human being is mirrored in his emotional life as well-being.

. . .The field of vision, the economic, the personal, mental relationships of the city, increase its ideal soft picture, as in geometrical progression, as soon as a certain border first is crossed; every achieved dynamic expansion within like by itself always . . . a bigger next expansion that profits by growing within the city just as the unearned increment of the retirement pension from the owner, through the mere increase in traffic.

At this point, the quantity of the life converts directly into quality and character.

The sphere of town life is decided mainly in and of itself.

For the city, this is crucial that its interior life stretches over one wide national or international district in a sequence of waves.

. . .The most significant nature of the city is in this functional size beyond its physical border: and this effectiveness reacts again and gives its life weight consideration and responsibility.

Like a human being, the borders of his body or the district that he fills up directly with his activity, but only with the sum of the effects that stretches temporally and spatially from him: so, also the city consists only of the totality of the effects stretching over its immediacy.

This is its real scope in which its being is pronounced. This already points out the original freedom, the logical and historic supplement limb of such wideness, not to understand, only in the negative sense, as mere freedom of movement and discontinuation of prejudices and debilitating conservatism; however, it is essential that the peculiarity and incomparability of every nature has somewhere been expressed through the formation of life.

That we follow the loss of our own nature—this is freedom—then becomes for us and others quite clear and convincing, if the remarks of this nature differ also from those others, first our uniqueness from others proves that our existence type is not forced upon us by others.

The cities are the seats of the most highly economic work division . . . the city offers more and more of the crucial conditions of its expansion to the work division: a circle, that is receptive for an extremely manifold multiplicity of performances through its size, while the compression of the individuals, their fight for the buyer at the same time are forcing the individual to a specialization of the performance from which he cannot be easily ousted by another.

The crucial one is that the city life changed the fight for food acquisition against nature into a fight against human beings: the profit is not granted from nature, but rather from the human being. . . .

The necessity to specialize the performance to find a not yet discovered acquirement source, to find a not easily replaceable function enrichment of the public needs that must lead, obviously, to grow personality differences within this public, pushes on differentiation and refinement.

And this leads over to the individualization of mental qualities, mental in the narrower sense, to which the city gives cause in the relationship of its size.

A series of causes is at hand.

At first the difficulty is to bring the personality to the validity and the dimensions of the bulk city life.

Where the quantitative increase from meaning and energy comes to its border, one reaches for qualitative specialization in order to somehow win through arousal of the difference sensitivity, win the consciousness of the social circle for itself: what then leads to the most tendentious oddities, to the specific bulk city extravagances of the distinctive being, the atmosphere whose sense not anymore in the contents of such conduct but lies only in the form of being different from the nonconformists and through it becoming noticeable—for many natures remaining only the single means, on the detour of the consciousness of others, a self estimation and the consciousness to fill a place saved for itself.

In the same sense, an inconspicuous one takes effect, but those effects, however, add up to only moments: the brevity and the rarity of the meetings, that each individual has with the other, compared with the traffic of a small city. . . .

Because the temptation is strongest to behave oneself when crowded together, characteristically as possible, as where frequent and long meeting provides an already unambiguous picture of the personality in the other.

This seems to me the deepest reason, from which the bulk city suggests, the instinct straight to the most individual personal existence, meanwhile just as much where always rightly and always with success.

The development of the modern culture characterizes through the force of what one can call the objective spirit, winning over that which is subjective, in the production technology like in the art, in the science like in the objects of the domestic surroundings is the sum of spirit and body, whose mental growth is always incomplete and much slower than the daily physical growth.

Do we really overlook the immense culture nearby in institutions and in bodily comfort, do we compare the cultural advances of the individuals in the same time—at least in the higher classes—with such an alarming difference in growth? Yes, in some aspects of the decline of the culture for individuals in reference to spirituality, tenderness, and idealism.

This discrepancy essentially is the success of growing work division; because such a division requires the individual to be ever more one sided and with every increase in this performance, his personality wastes away.

Less and less is the individual able to handle the overgrowing of the objective culture.

Maybe less consciously, as in the practice and in the dark total feelings that originate it is quite depressed to a negligible quantity, to a grain of dust compared to an immense organization of things and powers, that all advances and spiritualities play values from the hand gradually, and it transfers from the form of the subjective one into those of a purely objective life.

The bulk city is the arena where the culture is growing over all things personal.

Buildings and educational establishments along with miracles and progressing technology provide for the forms of living together in institutions that are so strong that our personalities become weak and cannot stay fully crystallized against all of their influences. Our personalities change or fade and become all virtually the same impersonalized spirit.

For it is making life infinitely easy on the one hand because of stimulation, interests are offered from all sides and they carry on as if in a stream, in which it hardly even needs its own swimming movements.

On the other hand, however, life is composed more and more of these impersonal contents and performances, that displace the actually personal colorings and distinctions; now in order for this most personal aspect to save itself one must be extreme in exerting peculiarity and specialty; and one must exaggerate these in order to make a statement.

The atrophy of the individual through the hypertrophy of the bulk city's objective culture is a reason for hate, as philosophers like Nietzsche might say of the most outer individualism, but this is a reason why they are so loved in the bulk cities—to the city dweller they appear to be the preachers and redeemers of unsatisfied longings.

In asking two forms of individualism, which are nurtured by the quantitative circumstances of the city for the historical position, the individual independence and the education of a personal, special type, the city wins a quite new value in the world history of the spirit.

The 18th century found the individual in political and agrarian relationships, competent and religious type, that became raping and pointless-cramming and compressing that forced unnatural and unfair differences between human beings.

In this situation, the call of freedom and equality was created—the belief in an individual's full freedom of movement, in all social and mental circumstances, that would let all the common noble core immediately step forward, like nature placed in everyone and only society and history would deform it.

Beside this idea of liberalism in the 19th century, grew, through Goethe and the romanticism on the one hand, the economic work division on the other hand, the following: the individuals freed from the historic relationships now wanted to differ also from each other.

No more does the "general human being" reside in each individual but qualitative singularity and uniqueness are now the bearers of his values. In the fight and the devouring of these two types, to find that subject's role within the totality, the outer as well as the inner history of our time proceeds.

It is the function of the bulk cities, the place for the dispute and the attempt to unite, in that their particular conditions reveal themselves as opportunities and attractions to the development of both.

. . . .

Just as the powers grew into the roots as well as into the crown of the whole historical life, we, in a fleeting existence, belong as only a part of a cell—our task is not to accuse or to forgive but only to understand.

. . . .

URBANISM AS A WAY OF LIFE

Louis Wirth

I. THE CITY AND CONTEMPORARY CIVILIZATION

Just as the beginning of Western civilization is marked by the permanent settlement of formerly nomadic peoples in the Mediterranean basin, so the beginning of what is distinctively modern in our civilization is best signalized by the growth of great cities. Nowhere has mankind been farther removed from organic nature than under the conditions of life characteristic of great cities. The contemporary would no longer present a picture of small isolated groups of human beings scattered over a vast territory, as Sumner described primitive society.[1] The distinctive feature of the mode of living of man in the modern age is his concentration into gigantic aggregations around which cluster lesser centers and from which radiate the ideas and practices that we call civilization.

The degree to which the contemporary world may be said to be "urban" is not fully or accurately measured by the proportion of the total population living in cities. The influences which cities exert upon the social life of man are greater than the ratio of the urban population would indicate, for the city is not only in ever larger degrees the dwelling-place and the workshop of modern man, but it is the initiating and controlling center of economic, political, and cultural life that has drawn the most remote parts of the world into its orbit and woven diverse areas, peoples, and activities into a cosmos.

The growth of cities and the urbanization of the world is one of the most impressive facts of modern times. Although it is impossible to state precisely what proportion of the estimated total world-population of approximately 1,800,000,000 is urban, 69.2 percent of the total population of those countries that do distinguish between urban and rural areas is urban.[2] Considering the fact, moreover, that the world's population is very unevenly distributed and that the growth of cities is not very far advanced in some of the countries that have only recently been touched by industrialism, this average understates the extent to which urban concentration has proceeded in those countries where the impact of the industrial revolution has been more forceful and of less recent date. This shift from a rural to a predominantly urban society, which has taken place within the span of a single generation in such industrialized areas as the United States and Japan, has been accompanied by profound changes in virtually every phase of social life. It is these changes and their ramifications that invite the attention of the sociologist to the study of the differences between the rural and the urban mode of living. The pursuit of this interest is an indispensable prerequisite for the comprehen-

[1]William Graham Sumner, *Folkways* (Boston, 1906), p. 12.

[2]S. V. Pearson, *The Growth and Distribution of Population* (New York, 1935), p. 211.

sion and possible mastery of some of the most crucial contemporary problems of social life since it is likely to furnish one of the most revealing perspectives for the understanding of the ongoing changes in human nature and the social order.[3]

Since the city is the product of growth rather than of instantaneous creation, it is to be expected that the influences which it exerts upon the modes of life should not be able to wipe out completely the previously dominant modes of human association. To a greater or lesser degree, therefore, our social life bears the imprint of an earlier folk society, the characteristic modes of settlement of which were the farm, the manor, and the village. This historic influence is reinforced by the circumstance that the population of the city itself is in large measure recruited from the countryside, where a mode of life reminiscent of this earlier form of existence persists. Hence we should not expect to find abrupt and discontinuous variation between urban and rural types of personality. The city and the country may be regarded as two poles in reference to one or the other of which all human settlements tend to arrange themselves. In viewing urban-industrial and rural-folk society as ideal types of communities, we may obtain a perspective for the analysis of the basic models of human association as they appear in contemporary civilization.

---

[3]Whereas rural life in the United States has for a long time been a subject of considerable interest on the part of governmental bureaus, the most notable case of a comprehensive report being that submitted by the Country Life Commission to President Theodore Roosevelt in 1909, it is worthy of note that no equally comprehensive official inquiry into urban life was undertaken until the establishment of a Research Committee on Urbanism of the National Resources Committee. (Cf. *Our Cities: Their Role in the National Economy* [Washington: Government Printing Office, 1937].)

II. A SOCIOLOGICAL DEFINITION OF THE CITY

Despite the preponderant significance of the city in our civilization, however, our knowledge of the nature of urbanism and the process of urbanization is meager. Many attempts have indeed been made to isolate the distinguishing characteristics of urban life. Geographers, historians, economists, and political scientists have incorporated the points of view of their respective disciplines into diverse definitions of the city. While in no sense intended to supersede these, the formulation of a sociological approach to the city may incidentally serve to call attention to the interrelations between them by emphasizing the peculiar characteristics of the city as a particular form of human association. A sociologically significant definition of the city seeks to select those elements of urbanism which mark it as a distinctive mode of human group life.

The characterization of a community as urban on the basis of size alone is obviously arbitrary. It is difficult to defend the present census definition which designates a community of 2,500 and above as urban and all others as rural. The situation would be the same if the criterion were 4,000, 8,000, 10,000, 25,000, or 100,000 population, for although in the latter case we might feel that we were more nearly dealing with an urban aggregate than would be the case in communities of lesser size, no definition of urbanism can hope to be completely satisfying as long as numbers are regarded as the sole criterion. Moreover, it is not difficult to demonstrate that communities of less than the arbitrarily set number of inhabitants lying within the range of influence of metropolitan centers have greater claim to recognition as urban communities than do larger ones leading a more isolated existence in a predominantly rural area. Finally, it should be recognized that census definitions are unduly influenced by the fact that the city, statistically speaking, is always an administrative concept in that the corporate limits play a decisive role in delineating the urban area. Nowhere is this more clearly apparent than in the concentrations of population on the peripheries of great metropolitan centers which cross arbitrary administrative boundaries of city, county, state, and nation.

As long as we identify urbanism with the physical entity of the city, viewing it merely as rigidly delimited in space, and proceed as if urban attributes abruptly ceased to be manifested beyond an arbitrary boundary line, we are not likely to arrive at any adequate conception of urbanism as a mode of life. The technological developments in transportation and communication which virtually mark a new epoch in human history have accentuated the role of cities as dominant elements in our civilization and have enormously extended the urban mode of living beyond the confines of the city itself. The dominance of the city, especially of the great city, may be regarded as a consequence of the concentration in cities of industrial and commercial, financial and administrative facilities and activities, transportation and communication lines, and cultural and recreational equipment such as the press, radio stations, theaters, libraries, museums, concert halls, operas, hospitals, higher educational institutions, research and publishing centers, professional organizations, and religious and welfare institutions. Were it not for the attraction and suggestions that the city exerts through these instrumentalities upon the rural population, the differences between the rural and the urban modes of life would be even greater than they are. Urbanization no longer denotes merely the process by which persons are attracted to a place called the city and incorporated into its system of life. It refers also to that cumulative accentuation of the characteristics distinctive of the mode of life which is associated with the growth of cities, and finally to the changes in the direction of modes of life recognized as urban which are apparent among peo-

ple, wherever they may be, who have come under the spell of the influences which the city exerts by virtue of the power of its institutions and personalities operating through the means of communication and transportation.

The shortcomings which attach to number of inhabitants as a criterion of urbanism apply for the most part to density of population as well. Whether we accept the density of 10,000 persons per square mile as Mark Jefferson[4] proposed, or 1,000, which Willcox[5] preferred to regard as the criterion of urban settlements, it is clear that unless density is correlated with significant social characteristics it can furnish only an arbitrary basis for differentiating urban from rural communities. Since our census enumerates the night rather than the day population of an area, the locale of the most intensive urban life—the city center—generally has low population density, and the industrial and commercial areas of the city, which contain the most characteristic economic activities underlying urban society, would scarcely anywhere be truly urban if density were literally interpreted as a mark of urbanism. Nevertheless, the fact that the urban community is distinguished by a large aggregation and relatively dense concentration of population can scarcely be left out of account in a definition of the city. But these criteria must be seen as relative to the general cultural context in which cities arise and exist and are sociologically relevant only in so far as they operate as conditioning factors in social life.

The same criticisms apply to such criteria as the occupation of the inhabitants, the existence of certain physical facilities, institutions, and forms of political organization. The question is not whether cities in our civilization or in oth-

---

[4]"The Anthropogeography of Some Great Cities," *Bull. American Geographical Society,* XLI (1909), 537–66.

[5]Walter F. Willcox, "A Definition of 'City' in Terms of Density," in E. W. Burgess, *The Urban Community* (Chicago, 1926), p. 119.

ers do exhibit these distinctive traits, but how potent they are in molding the character of social life into its specifically urban form. Nor in formulating a fertile definition can we afford to overlook the great variations between cities. By means of a typology of cities based upon size, location, age, and function, such as we have undertaken to establish in our recent report to the National Resources Committee,[6] we have found it feasible to array and classify urban communities ranging from struggling small towns to thriving world-metropolitan centers; from isolated trading-centers in the midst of agricultural regions to thriving world-ports and commercial and industrial conurbations. Such differences as these appear crucial because the social characteristics and influences of these different "cities" vary widely.

A serviceable definition of urbanism should not only denote the essential characteristics which all cities—at least those in our culture—have in common, but should lend itself to the discovery of their variations. An industrial city will differ significantly in social respects from a commercial, mining, fishing, resort, university, and capital city. A one-industry city will present different sets of social characteristics from a multi-industry city, as will an industrially balanced from an imbalanced city, a suburb from a satellite, a residential suburb from an industrial suburb, a city within a metropolitan region from one lying outside, an old city from a new one, a southern city from a New England, a middle-western from a Pacific Coast city, a growing from a stable and from a dying city.

A sociological definition must obviously be inclusive enough to comprise whatever essential characteristics these different types of cities have in common as social entities, but it obviously cannot be so detailed as to take account of all the variations implicit in the manifold classes sketched above. Presumably some

[6]*Op. cit.*, p. 8.

of the characteristics of cities are more significant in conditioning the nature of urban life than others, and we may expect the outstanding features of the urban-social scene to vary in accordance with size, density, and differences in the functional type of cities. Moreover, we may infer that rural life will bear the imprint of urbanism in the measure that through contact and communication it comes under the influence of cities. It may contribute to the clarity of the statements that follow to repeat that while the locus of urbanism as a mode of life is, of course, to be found characteristically in places which fulfil the requirements we shall set up as a definition of the city, urbanism is not confined to such localities but is manifest in varying degrees wherever the influences of the city reach.

While urbanism, or that complex of traits which makes up the characteristic mode of life in cities, and urbanization, which denotes the development and extensions of these factors, are thus not exclusively found in settlements which are cities in the physical and demographic sense, they do, nevertheless, find their most pronounced expression in such areas, especially in metropolitan cities. In formulating a definition of the city it is necessary to exercise caution in order to avoid identifying urbanism as a way of life with any specific locally or historically conditioned cultural influences which, while they may significantly affect the specific character of the community, are not the essential determinants of its character as a city.

It is particularly important to call attention to the danger of confusing urbanism with industrialism and modern capitalism. The rise of cities in the modern world is undoubtedly not independent of the emergence of modern power-driven machine technology, mass production, and capitalistic enterprise. But different as the cities of earlier epochs may have been by virtue of their development in a preindustrial and precapitalistic order from the great cities of today, they were, nevertheless, cities.

For sociological purposes a city may be defined as a relatively large, dense, and permanent settlement of socially heterogeneous individuals. On the basis of the postulates which this minimal definition suggests, a theory of urbanism may be formulated in the light of existing knowledge concerning social groups.

III. A THEORY OF URBANISM

In the rich literature on the city we look in vain for a theory of urbanism presenting in a systematic fashion the available knowledge concerning the city as a social entity. We do indeed have excellent formulations of theories on such special problems as the growth of the city viewed as a historical trend and as a recurrent process,[7] and we have a wealth of literature presenting insights of sociological relevance and empirical studies offering detailed information on a variety of particular aspects of urban life. But despite the multiplication of research and textbooks on the city, we do not as yet have a comprehensive body of compendent hypotheses which may be derived from a set of postulates implicitly contained in a sociological definition of the city, and from our general sociological knowledge which may be substantiated through empirical research. The closest approximations to a systematic theory of urbanism that we have are to be found in a penetrating essay, "Die Stadt," by Max Weber,[8] and a memorable paper by Robert E. Park on "The City: Suggestions for the Investigation of Human Behavior in the Urban Environment."[9] But even these excellent contributions are far from constituting an ordered and coherent framework of theory upon which research might profitably proceed.

In the pages that follow we shall seek to set forth a limited number of identifying characteristics of the city. Given these characteristics we shall then indicate what consequences or further characteristics follow from them in the light of general sociological theory and empirical research. We hope in this manner to arrive at the essential propositions comprising a theory of urbanism. Some of these propositions can be supported by a considerable body of already available research materials; others may be accepted as hypotheses for which a certain amount of presumptive evidence exists, but for which more ample and exact verification would be required. At least such a procedure will, it is hoped, show what in the way of systematic knowledge of the city we now have and what are the crucial and fruitful hypotheses for future research.

The central problem of the sociologist of the city is to discover the forms of social action and organization that typically emerge in relatively permanent, compact settlements of large numbers of heterogeneous individuals. We must also infer that urbanism will assume its most characteristic and extreme form in the measure in which the conditions with which it is congruent are present. Thus the larger, the more densely populated, and the more heterogeneous a community, the more accentuated the characteristics associated with urbanism will be. It should be recognized, however, that in the social world institutions and practices may be accepted and continued for reasons other than those that originally brought them into existence, and that accordingly the urban mode of life may be perpetuated under conditions quite foreign to those necessary for its origin.

Some justification may be in order for the choice of the principal terms comprising our definition of the city. The attempt has been

---

[7]See Robert E. Park, Ernest W. Burgess, *et al., The City* (Chicago, 1925), esp. chaps. ii and iii; Werner Sombart, "Städtische Siedlung, Stadt," *Handwörterbuch der Soziologie*, ed. Alfred Vierkandt (Stuttgart, 1931); see also bibliography.

[8]*Wirtschaft und Gesellschaft* (Tübingen, 1925), Part II, chap. viii, pp. 514–601.

[9]Park, Burgess, *et al., op. cit.,* chap. i.

made to make it as inclusive and at the same time as denotative as possible without loading it with unnecessary assumptions. To say that large numbers are necessary to constitute a city means, of course, large numbers in relation to a restricted area or high density of settlement. There are, nevertheless, good reasons for treating large numbers and density as separate factors, since each may be connected with significantly different social consequences. Similarly the need for adding heterogeneity to numbers of population as a necessary and distinct criterion of urbanism might be questioned, since we should expect the range of differences to increase with numbers. In defense, it may be said that the city shows a kind and degree of heterogeneity of population which cannot be wholly accounted for by the law of large numbers or adequately represented by means of a normal distribution curve. Since the population of the city does not reproduce itself, it must recruit its migrants from other cities, the countryside, and—in this country until recently—from other countries. The city has thus historically been the melting-pot of races, peoples, and cultures, and a most favorable breeding-ground of new biological and cultural hybrids. It has not only tolerated but rewarded individual differences. It has brought together people from the ends of the earth *because* they are different and thus useful to one another, rather than because they are homogeneous and like-minded.[10]

There are a number of sociological propositions concerning the relationship between (*a*) numbers of population, (*b*) density of settlement, (*c*) heterogeneity of inhabitants and

[10]The justification for including the term "permanent" in the definition may appear necessary. Our failure to give an extensive justification for this qualifying mark of the urban rests on the obvious fact that unless human settlements take a fairly permanent root in a locality the characteristics of urban life cannot arise, and conversely the living together of large numbers of heterogeneous individuals under dense conditions is not possible without the development of a more or less technological structure.

group life, which can be formulated on the basis of observation and research.

Size of the Population Aggregate

Ever since Aristotle's *Politics*,[11] it has been recognized that increasing the number of inhabitants in a settlement beyond a certain limit will affect the relationships between them and the character of the city. Large numbers involve, as has been pointed out, a greater range of individual variation. Furthermore, the greater the number of individuals participating in a process of interaction, the greater is the *potential* differentiation between them. The personal traits, the occupations, the cultural life, and the ideas of the members of an urban community

[11]See esp. vii. 4. 4–14. Translated by B. Jowett, from which the following may be quoted:

"To the size of states there is a limit, as there is to other things, plants, animals, implements; for none of these retain their natural power when they are too large or too small, but they either wholly lose their nature, or are spoiled. . . . . [A] state when composed of too few is not as a state ought to be, self-sufficing; when of too many, though self-sufficing in all mere necessaries, it is a nation and not a state, being almost incapable of constitutional government. For who can be the general of such a vast multitude, or who the herald, unless he have the voice of a Stentor?

"A state then only begins to exist when it has attained a population sufficient for a good life in the political community: it may indeed somewhat exceed this number. But, as I was saying, there must be a limit. What should be the limit will be easily ascertained by experience. For both governors and governed have duties to perform; the special functions of a governor are to command and to judge. But if the citizens of a state are to judge and to distribute offices according to merit, then they must know each other's characters; where they do not possess this knowledge, both the election to offices and the decision of lawsuits will go wrong. When the population is very large they are manifestly settled at haphazard, which clearly ought not to be. Besides, in an overpopulous state foreigners and metics will readily acquire the rights of citizens, for who will find them out? Clearly, then, the best limit of the population of a state is the largest number which suffices for the purposes of life, and can be taken in at a single view. Enough concerning the size of a city."

may, therefore, be expected to range between more widely separated poles than those of rural inhabitants.

That such variations should give rise to the spatial segregation of individuals according to color, ethnic heritage, economic and social status, tastes and preferences, may readily be inferred. The bonds of kinship, of neighborliness, and the sentiments arising out of living together for generations under a common folk tradition are likely to be absent or, at best, relatively weak in an aggregate the members of which have such diverse origins and backgrounds. Under such circumstances competition and formal control mechanisms furnish the substitutes for the bonds of solidarity that are relied upon to hold a folk society together.

Increase in the number of inhabitants of a community beyond a few hundred is bound to limit the possibility of each member of the community knowing all the others personally. Max Weber, in recognizing the social significance of this fact, pointed out that from a sociological point of view large numbers of inhabitants and density of settlement mean that the personal mutual acquaintanceship between the inhabitants which ordinarily inheres in a neighborhood is lacking.[12] The increase in numbers thus involves a changed character of the social relationships. As Simmel points out:

> [If] the unceasing external contact of numbers of persons in the city should be met by the same number of inner reactions as in the small town, in which one knows almost every person he meets and to each of whom he has a positive relationship, one would be completely atomized internally and would fall into an unthinkable mental condition.[13]

The multiplication of persons in a state of interaction under conditions which make their

contact as full personalities impossible produces that segmentalization of human relationships which has sometimes been seized upon by students of the mental life of the cities as an explanation for the "schizoid" character of urban personality. This is not to say that the urban inhabitants have fewer acquaintances than rural inhabitants, for the reverse may actually be true; it means rather that in relation to the number of people whom they see and with whom they rub elbows in the course of daily life, they know a smaller proportion, and of these they have less intensive knowledge.

Characteristically, urbanites meet one another in highly segmental roles. They are, to be sure, dependent upon more people for the satisfactions of their life-needs than are rural people and thus are associated with a greater number of organized groups, but they are less dependent upon particular persons, and their dependence upon others is confined to a highly fractionalized aspect of the other's round of activity. This is essentially what is meant by saying that the city is characterized by secondary rather than primary contacts. The contacts of the city may indeed be face to face, but they are nevertheless impersonal, superficial, transitory, and segmental. The reserve, the indifference, and the blasé outlook which urbanites manifest in their relationships may thus be regarded as devices for immunizing themselves against the personal claims and expectations of others.

The superficiality, the anonymity, and the transitory character of urban-social relations make intelligible, also, the sophistication and the rationality generally ascribed to city-dwellers. Our acquaintances tend to stand in a relationship of utility to us in the sense that the role which each one plays in our life is overwhelmingly regarded as a means for the achievement of our own ends. Whereas, therefore, the individual gains, on the one hand, a certain degree of emancipation or freedom from the personal and emotional controls of in-

---

[12]*Op. cit.,* p. 514.

[13]Georg Simmel, "Dia Grossstädte, und das Geistesleben," *Dia Grossziadt,* ed. Theodor Petermann (Dresden, 1903), pp. 187–206.

timate groups, he loses, on the other hand, the spontaneous self-expression, the morale, and the sense of participation that comes with living in an integrated society. This constitutes essentially the state of *anomie* or the social void to which Durkheim alludes in attempting to account for the various forms of social disorganization in technological society.

The segmental character and utilitarian accent of interpersonal relations in the city find their institutional expression in the proliferation of specialized tasks which we see in their most developed form in the professions. The operations of the pecuniary nexus leads to predatory relationships, which tend to obstruct the efficient functioning of the social order unless checked by professional codes and occupational etiquette. The premium put upon utility and efficiency suggests the adaptability of the corporate device for the organization of enterprises in which individuals can engage only in groups. The advantage that the corporation has over the individual entrepreneur and the partnership in the urban-industrial world derives not only from the possibility it affords of centralizing the resources of thousands of individuals or from the legal privilege of limited liability and perpetual succession, but from the fact that the corporation has no soul.

The specialization of individuals, particularly in their occupations, can proceed only, as Adam Smith pointed out, upon the basis of an enlarged market, which in turn accentuates the division of labor. This enlarged market is only in part supplied by the city's hinterland; in large measure it is found among the large numbers that the city itself contains. The dominance of the city over the surrounding hinterland becomes explicable in terms of the division of labor which urban life occasions and promotes. The extreme degree of interdependence and the unstable equilibrium of urban life are closely associated with the division of labor and the specialization of occupations. This interdependence and instability is

increased by the tendency of each city to specialize in those functions in which it has the greatest advantage.

In a community composed of a larger number of individuals than can know one another intimately and can be assembled in one spot, it becomes necessary to communicate through indirect mediums and to articulate individual interests by a process of delegation. Typically in the city, interests are made effective through representation. The individual counts for little, but the voice of the representative is heard with a deference roughly proportional to the numbers for whom he speaks.

While this characterization of urbanism, in so far as it derives from large numbers, does not by any means exhaust the sociological inferences that might be drawn from our knowledge of the relationship of the size of a group to the characteristic behavior of the members, for the sake of brevity the assertions made may serve to exemplify the sort of propositions that might be developed.

Density

As in the case of numbers, so in the case of concentration in limited space, certain consequences of relevance in sociological analysis of the city emerge. Of these only a few can be indicated.

As Darwin pointed out for flora and fauna and as Durkheim[14] noted in the case of human societies, an increase in numbers when area is held constant (i.e., an increase in density) tends to produce differentiation and specialization, since only in this way can the area support increased numbers. Density thus reinforces the effect of numbers in diversifying men and their activities and in increasing the complexity of the social structure.

On the subjective side, as Simmel has suggested, the close physical contact of numerous

[14]E. Durkheim, *De la division du travail social* (Paris, 1932), p. 248.

individuals necessarily produces a shift in the mediums through which we orient ourselves to the urban milieu, especially to our fellow-men. Typically, our physical contacts are close but our social contacts are distant. The urban world puts a premium on visual recognition. We see the uniform which denotes the role of the functionaries and are oblivious to the personal eccentricities that are hidden behind the uniform. We tend to acquire and develop a sensitivity to a world of artefacts and become progressively farther removed from the world of nature.

We are exposed to glaring contrasts between splendor and squalor, between riches and poverty, intelligence and ignorance, order and chaos. The competition for space is great, so that each area generally tends to be put to the use which yields the greatest economic return. Place of work tends to become dissociated from place of residence, for the proximity of industrial and commercial establishments makes an area both economically and socially undesirable for residential purposes.

Density, land values, rentals, accessibility, healthfulness, prestige, aesthetic consideration, absence of nuisances such as noise, smoke, and dirt determine the desirability of various areas of the city as places of settlement for different sections of the population. Place and nature of work, income, racial and ethnic characteristics, social status, custom, habit, taste, preference, and prejudice are among the significant factors in accordance with which the urban population is selected and distributed into more or less distinct settlements. Diverse population elements inhabiting a compact settlement thus tend to become segregated from one another in the degree in which their requirements and modes of life are incompatible with one another and in the measure in which they are antagonistic to one another. Similarly, persons of homogeneous status and needs unwittingly drift into, consciously select, or are forced by circumstances into, the same area. The different parts of the city thus acquire specialized

functions. The city consequently tends to resemble a mosaic of social worlds in which the transition from one to the other is abrupt. The juxtaposition of divergent personalities and modes of life tends to produce a relativistic perspective and a sense of toleration of differences which may be regarded as pre-requisites for rationality and which lead toward the secularization of life.[15]

The close living together and working together of individuals who have no sentimental and emotional ties foster a spirit of competition, aggrandizement, and mutual exploitation. To counteract irresponsibility and potential disorder, formal controls tend to be resorted to. Without rigid adherence to predictable routines a large compact society would scarcely be able to maintain itself. The clock and the traffic signal are symbolic of the basis of our social order in the urban world. Frequent close physical contact, coupled with great social distance, accentuates the reserve of unattached individuals toward one another and, unless compensated for by other opportunities for response, gives rise to loneliness. The necessary frequent movement of great numbers of individuals in a congested habitat gives occasion to friction and irritation. Nervous tensions which derive from such personal frustrations are accentuated by the rapid tempo and the complicated technology under which life in dense areas must be lived.

Heterogeneity

The social interaction among such a variety of personality types in the urban milieu tends to break down the rigidity of caste lines and to

---

[15]The extent to which the segregation of the population into distinct ecological and cultural areas and the resulting social attitude of tolerance, rationality, and secular mentality are functions of density as distinguished from heterogeneity is difficult to determine. Most likely we are dealing here with phenomena which are consequences of the simultaneous operation of both factors.

complicate the class structure, and thus induces a more ramified and differentiated framework of social stratification than is found in more integrated societies. The heightened mobility of the individual, which brings him within the range of stimulation by a great number of diverse individuals and subjects him to fluctuating status in the differentiated social groups that compose the social structure of the city, tends toward the acceptance of instability and insecurity in the world at large as a norm. This fact helps to account, too, for the sophistication and cosmopolitanism of the urbanite. No single group has the undivided allegiance of the individual. The groups with which he is affiliated do not lend themselves readily to a simple hierarchical arrangement. By virtue of his different interests arising out of different aspects of social life, the individual acquires membership in widely divergent groups, each of which functions only with reference to a single segment of his personality. Nor do these groups easily permit of a concentric arrangement so that the narrower ones fall within the circumference of the more inclusive ones, as is more likely to be the case in the rural community or in primitive societies. Rather the groups with which the person typically is affiliated are tangential to each other or intersect in highly variable fashion.

Partly as a result of the physical footlooseness of the population and partly as a result of their social mobility, the turnover in group membership generally is rapid. Place of residence, place and character of employment, income and interests fluctuate, and the task of holding organizations together and maintaining and promoting intimate and lasting acquaintanceship between the members is difficult. This applies strikingly to the local areas within the city into which persons become segregated more by virtue of differences in race, language, income, and social status, than through choice or positive attraction to people like themselves. Overwhelmingly the city-dweller is not a home-owner, and since a transitory habitat does not generate binding traditions and sentiments, only rarely is he truly a neighbor. There is little opportunity for the individual to obtain a conception of the city as a whole or to survey his place in the total scheme. Consequently he finds it difficult to determine what is to his own "best interests" and to decide between the issues and leaders presented to him by the agencies of mass suggestion. Individuals who are thus detached from the organized bodies which integrate society comprise the fluid masses that make collective behavior in the urban community so unpredictable and hence so problematical.

Although the city, through the recruitment of variant types to perform its diverse tasks and the accentuation of their uniqueness through competition and the premium upon eccentricity, novelty, efficient performance, and inventiveness, produces a highly differentiated population, it also exercises a leveling influence. Wherever large numbers of differently constituted individuals congregate, the process of depersonalization also enters. This leveling tendency inheres in part in the economic basis of the city. The development of large cities, at least in the modern age, was largely dependent upon the concentrative force of steam. The rise of the factory made possible mass production for an impersonal market. The fullest exploitation of the possibilities of the division of labor and mass production, however, is possible only with standardization of processes and products. A money economy goes hand in hand with such a system of production. Progressively as cities have developed upon a background of this system of production, the pecuniary nexus which implies the purchasability of services and things has displaced personal relations as the basis of association. Individuality under these circumstances must be replaced by categories. When large numbers have to make common use of facilities and institutions, an arrangement must be made to adjust the facilities and institutions to the needs of the average person rather than to those of particular individuals. The services of the public utilities, of the recreational, educational, and cultural institutions must be adjusted to mass requirements. Similarly, the cultural institutions, such as the schools, the movies, the radio, and the newspapers, by virtue of their mass clientele, must necessarily operate as leveling influences. The political process as it appears in urban life could not be understood without taking account of the mass appeals made through modern propaganda techniques. If the individual would participate at all in the social, political, and economic life of the city, he must subordinate some of his individuality to the demands of the larger community and in that measure immerse himself in mass movements.

IV. THE RELATION BETWEEN A THEORY OF URBANISM AND SOCIOLOGICAL RESEARCH

By means of a body of theory such as that illustratively sketched above, the complicated and many-sided phenomena of urbanism may be analyzed in terms of a limited number of basic categories. The sociological approach to the city thus acquires an essential unity and coherence enabling the empirical investigator not merely to focus more distinctly upon the problems and processes that properly fall in his province but also to treat his subject matter in a more integrated and systematic fashion. A few typical findings of empirical research in the field of urbanism, with special reference to the United States, may be indicated to substantiate the theoretical propositions set forth in the preceding pages, and some of the crucial problems for further study may be outlined.

On the basis of the three variables, number, density of settlement, and degree of heterogeneity, of the urban population, it appears possible to explain the characteristics of urban life and to account for the differences between cities of various sizes and types.

Urbanism as a characteristic mode of life may be approached empirically from three interrelated perspectives: (1) as a physical structure comprising a population base, a technology, and an ecological order; (2) as a system of social organization involving a characteristic social structure, a series of social institutions, and a typical pattern of social relationships; and (3) as a set of attitudes and ideas, and a constellation of personalities engaging in typical forms of collective behavior and subject to characteristic mechanisms of social control.

Urbanism in Ecological Perspective

Since in the case of physical structure and ecological processes we are able to operate with fairly objective indices, it becomes possible to arrive at quite precise and generally quantitative results. The dominance of the city over its hinterland becomes explicable through the functional characteristics of the city which derive in large measure from the effect of numbers and density. Many of the technical facilities and the skills and organizations to which urban life gives rise can grow and prosper only in cities where the demand is sufficiently great. The nature and scope of the services rendered by these organizations and institutions and the advantage which they enjoy over the less developed facilities of smaller towns enhances the dominance of the city and the dependence of ever wider regions upon the central metropolis.

The urban-population composition shows the operation of selective and differentiating factors. Cities contain a larger proportion of persons in the prime of life than rural areas which contain more old and very young people. In this, as in so many other respects, the larger the city the more this specific characteristic of urbanism is apparent. With the exception of the largest cities, which have attracted the bulk of the foreign-born males, and a few other special types of cities, women predominate numerically over men. The heterogeneity of the urban population is further indicated along racial and ethnic lines. The foreign born and their children constitute nearly two-thirds of all the inhabitants of cities of one million and over. Their proportion in the urban population declines as the size of the city decreases, until in the rural areas they comprise only about one-sixth of the total population. The larger cities similarly have attracted more Negroes and other racial groups than have the smaller communities. Considering that age, sex, race, and ethnic origin are associated with other factors such as occupation and interest, it becomes clear that one major characteristic of the urban-dweller is his dissimilarity from his fellows. Never before have such large masses of people of diverse traits as we find in our cities been thrown together into such close physical contact as in the great cities of America. Cities generally, and American cities in particular, comprise a motley of peoples and cultures, of highly differentiated modes of life between which there often is only the faintest communication, the greatest indifference and the broadest tolerance, occasionally bitter strife, but always the sharpest contrast.

The failure of the urban population to reproduce itself appears to be a biological consequence of a combination of factors in the complex of urban life, and the decline in the birth-rate generally may be regarded as one of the most significant signs of the urbanization of the Western world. While the proportion of deaths in cities is slightly greater than in the country, the outstanding difference between the failure of present-day cities to maintain their population and that of cities of the past is that in former times it was due to the exceedingly high death-rates in cities, whereas today, since cities have become more livable from a health standpoint, it is due to low birth-rates. These biological characteristics of the urban population are significant sociologically, not merely because they reflect the urban mode of existence but also because they condition the growth and future dominance of cities and their basic social organization. Since cities are the consumers rather than the producers of men, the value of human life and the social estimation of the personality will not be unaffected by the balance between births and deaths. The pattern of land use, of land values, rentals, and ownership, the nature and functioning of the physical structures, of housing, of transportation and communication facilities, of public utilities—these and many other phases of the physical mechanism of the city are not isolated phenomena unrelated to the city as a social entity, but are affected by and affect the urban mode of life.

Urbanism as a Form of Social Organization

The distinctive features of the urban mode of life have often been described sociologically as consisting of the substitution of secondary for primary contacts, the weakening of bonds of kinship, and the declining social significance of the family, the disappearance of the neighborhood, and the undermining of the traditional basis of social solidarity. All these phenomena can be substantially verified through objective indices. Thus, for instance, the low and declining urban-reproduction rates suggest that the city is not conducive to the traditional type of family life, including the rearing of children and the maintenance of the home as the locus of a whole round of vital activities. The transfer of industrial, educational, and recreational activities to specialized institutions outside the home has deprived the family of some of its most characteristic historical functions. In cities mothers are more likely to be employed, lodgers are more frequently part of the household, marriage tends to be postponed, and the proportion of single and unattached people is greater. Families are smaller and more frequently without children than in the country. The family as a unit of social life is emancipated from the larger kinship group characteristic of the country, and the individual members pursue their own diverging interests in their vocational, educational, religious, recreational, and political life.

Such functions as the maintenance of health, the methods of alleviating the hardships associated with personal and social insecurity, the provisions for education, recreation, and cultural advancement have given rise to highly specialized institutions on a community-wide, statewide, or even national basis. The same factors which have brought about greater personal insecurity also underlie the wider contrasts between individuals to be found in the urban world. While the city has broken down the rigid caste lines of pre-industrial society, it has sharpened and differentiated income and status groups. Generally, a larger proportion of the adult-urban population is gainfully employed than is the case with the adult-rural population. The white-collar class, comprising those employed in trade, in clerical, and in professional work, are proportionately more numerous in large cities and in metropolitan centers and in smaller towns than in the country.

On the whole, the city discourages an economic life in which the individual in time of crisis has a basis of subsistence to fall back upon, and it discourages self-employment. While incomes of city people are on the average higher than those of country people, the cost of living seems to be higher in the larger cities. Home ownership involves greater burdens and is rarer. Rents are higher and absorb a larger proportion of the income. Although the urban-dweller has the benefit of many communal services, he spends a large proportion of his income for such items as recreation and advancement and a smaller proportion for food. What the communal services do not furnish the urbanite must purchase, and there is virtually no human need which has remained unexploited by commercialism. Catering to thrills and furnishing means of escape from drudgery, monotony, and routine thus become one of the major functions of urban recreation, which at its best furnishes means for creative self-expression and spontaneous group association, but which more typically in the urban world results in passive spectatorism on the one hand, or sensational record-smashing feats on the other.

Being reduced to a stage of virtual impotence as an individual, the urbanite is bound to exert himself by joining with others of similar interest into organized groups to obtain his ends. This results in the enormous multiplication of voluntary organizations directed toward as great a variety of objectives as there are human needs and interests. While on the one hand the traditional ties of human association are weakened, urban existence involves a much greater degree of interdependence between man and man and a more complicated, fragile, and volatile form of mutual interrelations over many phases of which the individual as such can exert scarcely any control. Frequently there is only the most tenuous relationship between the economic position or other basic factors that determine the individual's existence in the urban world and the voluntary groups with which he is affiliated. While in a primitive and in a rural society it is generally possible to predict on the basis of a few known factors who will belong to what and who will associate with whom in almost every relationship of life, in the city we can only project the general pattern of group formation and affiliation, and this pattern will display many incongruities and contradictions.

Urban Personality and Collective Behavior

It is largely through the activities of the voluntary groups, be their objectives economic, political, educational, religious, recreational, or cultural, that the urbanite expresses and develops his personality, acquires status, and is able to carry on the round of activities that constitute his life-career. It may easily be inferred, however, that the organizational framework which these highly differentiated functions call into being does not of itself insure the consistency and integrity of the personalities whose interests it enlists. Personal disorganization, mental breakdown, suicide, delinquency, crime, corruption, and disorder might be expected under these circumstances to be more prevalent in the urban than in the rural community. This has been confirmed in so far as comparable indices are available; but the mechanisms underlying these phenomena require further analysis.

Since for most group purposes it is impossible in the city to appeal individually to the large number of discrete and differentiated individuals, and since it is only through the organizations to which men belong that their interests and resources can be enlisted for a collective cause, it may be inferred that social control in the city should typically proceed through formally organized groups. It follows, too, that the masses of men in the city are subject to manipulation by symbols and stereotypes managed by individuals working from afar or operating invisibly behind the scenes through their control of the instruments of communication. Self-government either in the economic, the political, or the cultural realm is under these circumstances reduced to a mere figure of speech or, at best, is subject to the unstable equilibrium of pressure groups. In view of the ineffectiveness of actual kinship ties we create fictional kinship groups. In the face of the disappearance of the territorial unit as a basis of social solidarity we create interest units. Meanwhile the city as a community resolves itself into a series of tenuous segmental relationships superimposed upon a territorial base with a definite center but without a definite periphery and upon a division of labor which far transcends the immediate locality and is worldwide in scope. The larger the number of persons in a state of interaction with one another the lower is the level of communication and the greater is the tendency for communication to proceed on an elementary level, i.e., on the basis of those things which are assumed to be common or to be of interest to all.

It is obviously, therefore, to the emerging trends in the communication system and to the production and distribution technology that has come into existence with modern civilization that we must look for the symptoms which will indicate the probable future development of urbanism as a mode of social life. The direction of the ongoing changes in urbanism will for good or ill transform not only the city but the world. Some of the more basic of these factors and processes and the possibilities of their direction and control invite further detailed study.

It is only in so far as the sociologist has a clear conception of the city as a social entity and a workable theory of urbanism that he can hope to develop a unified body of reliable knowledge, which what passes as "urban sociology" is certainly not at the present time. By taking his point of departure from a theory of urbanism such as that sketched in the foregoing pages to be elaborated, tested, and revised in the light of further analysis and empirical research, it is to be hoped that the criteria of relevance and validity of factual data can be determined. The miscellaneous assortment of disconnected information which has hitherto found its way into sociological treatises on the city may thus be sifted and incorporated into a coherent body of knowledge. Incidentally, only by means of some such theory will the sociologist escape the futile practice of voicing in the name of sociological science a variety of often unsupportable judgments concerning such problems as poverty, housing, city-planning, sanitation, municipal administration, policing, marketing, transportation, and other technical issues. While the sociologist cannot solve any of these practical problems—at least not by himself—he may, if he discovers his proper function, have an important contribution to make to their comprehension and solution. The prospects for doing this are brightest through a general, theoretical, rather than through an *ad hoc* approach

C.
The Case Study:
Local Community Perspectives

OLDER AND NEWER APPROACHES
TO THE COMMUNITY

Roland L. Warren

The systematic study of the community has developed around the general focus of shared living based on common locality. In a sense, the community is the meeting place of the individual and the larger society and culture. It is in his or her own locality, characteristically, that, throughout most of human history and to a very great extent today, the individual confronts society's institutions, its manner of religious expression, its ways of regulating behavior, its ways of family living, its ways of socializing the young, its ways of providing sustenance, its ways of esthetic expression. Fresh eggs in the local store, services at the local church, places to amuse oneself, a source of employment, streets and roads to get to these facilities, a school for one's children, organizations to which to belong, friends and relatives with whom to visit—all these and many other basic ingredients of everyday life remain largely a function of the local arena, and the way people organize themselves to procure them in locality groups is the special subject matter of the study of the community.

The fact that many of these locality-based ways of doing things are patterns provided in a larger regional, national, or international culture and that much of the structure and function of local institutions is influenced from outside the locality is an important topic that this book will treat. But to recognize explicitly the outside influence, the stamp of the mass culture on the individual community, is not to deny the fact that individuals typically have their principal encounters with mass culture through institutions that are deployed on a locality basis so as to be readily accessible to them. The fact that they are so distributed makes these localities, with their clusters of people and institutions, important units of society and significant units for study.

This chapter reviews some of the different ways of approaching communities as objects of study and some of the chief contributions to knowledge about communities that these different approaches have yielded in the past. It also considers some new approaches to supplement the findings that the older ones continue to contribute.

THE COMMUNITY AS SPACE

One question to be raised about the local clustering of people and institutions has to do with their *spatial relationships*. Obviously, people are not found to be distributed evenly throughout geographical space but are sparsely distributed in some areas, thickly clustered in others. The thickly clustered areas tend in the United States also to be centers of institutional services. Generally speaking, the larger the cluster of people, the more numerous and varied the institutional services in the area.

Urban community studies

The spatial relationships of the urban community likewise received extensive early attention, but they were studied with a somewhat different approach, by an almost entirely different group of sociologists. While rural sociologists were attached to the large state agricultural colleges and thus tied in with the Extension Service of the United States Department of Agriculture, urban sociologists were based in the large public or private universities located in large cities. The markedly separate paths of urban and rural community studies have led to a consequent isolation, disadvantageous to both groups of students. Working independently becomes progressively untenable as the process of urbanization spreads urban cultural patterns to the rural areas and as suburbs arise, which show marked characteristics differentiating them from the rural communities and from the larger urban centers.

If one is to look, however, for a counterpart to the great spurt in rural community studies, which resulted from the discovery of the rural community as a significant sociological unit, one must go to Chicago, where during the 1920s and 1930s, largely under the leadership of Robert E. Park but nurtured by a whole generation of outstanding sociologists, a creative surge forward was made in the study of the urban community. The city containing the University of Chicago became the best-researched city in the world.

Urban studies have been much more deliberately related to human ecology than have rural community studies. In McKenzie's words,

> The spatial and sustenance relations in which human beings are organized are ever in process of change in response to the operation of a complex of environmental and cultural forces. It is the task of the human ecologist to study these processes of change in order to ascertain their principles of operation and the nature of the forces producing them.[1]

McKenzie went on to define the community in ecological terms: "A community, then, is an ecological distribution of people and services in which the spatial location of each unit is determined by its relation to all other units." He added: "A network of interrelated communities is likewise an ecological distribution."[2]

Park and his associates at the University of Chicago became absorbed with the idea of studying the spatial distribution of people and functions in the urban context. What gave their studies special impetus was their belief that what they were learning in Chicago would apply, with appropriate modifications, to other cities as well. "There is implicit in all these studies the notion that the city is a thing with a characteristic organization and a typical

---

[1]R. D. McKenzie, "The Scope of Human Ecology," in Ernest W. Burgess, ed., *The Urban Community: Selected Papers from the Proceedings of the American Sociological Society, 1925,* p. 167. Copyright 1926 by The University of Chicago Press, Chicago, Ill.

[2]"Human Ecology," p. 169.

life-history, and that individual cities are enough alike so that what one learns about one city may, within limits, be assumed to be true of others."[3]

It is a common observation that certain parts of various cities are very much alike, even though they are thousands of miles apart. Indeed, they are often more like each other than other parts of the city, which may be just a few blocks away. Alert travelers have noticed the remarkable similarity between such characteristic urban areas as the better-class hotel districts, tenement slum districts, skidrow amusement centers, shopping centers, and so on. Since such similar areas grow up in similar sized cities, regardless of their geographic separation, they must be the product of cultural and ecological forces that operate similarly in all such cities. The Chicago sociologists determined to study the operation of these forces in Chicago, so that their findings could then be applied to other cities and modified if necessary. Basically, they emerged with two important spatial concepts, the urban zone and the natural area. They found Chicago to be describable in terms of five concentric zones, of which the central business district, or Loop, constituted the center. Proceeding outward, one passed through a Zone in Transition, a Zone of Independent Workingmen's Homes, a Zone of Better Residences, and a Commuter's Zone.[4] The zones were found to differ from each other in a number of major ways, some of which became the basis of special studies, such as Reckless's study of the distribution of commercialized vice in Chicago, the study by Faris and Dunham of the ecology of mental disorders, Mowrer's study of types of family disorganization, and his later summary of types of personal and social disorganization as found in Chicago.[5] A host of other studies were made, and numerous other aspects of community living were found to vary characteristically according to the zonal pattern.

Natural areas, on the other hand, were smaller than zones, products of the natural growth of the city, each showing its own customary type of land use, social activity, people, and so on. Natural areas were produced by the natural interplay of social forces, and these were studied in relation to one another. They formed important focuses for investigation in such works as Shaw's study of delinquency areas, Wirth's study of the ghetto, Zorbaugh's study of the Gold Coast and the slum, and many others.[6] Such natural areas constituted important sociological units, standing to each other in an intricate network of spatial and functional relationships as the significant units whose interrelated aggregate constituted the vast city community.

Concentric zones and natural areas were seen not as static areas whose characteristics were fixed but as the arenas and the resultants of important social and ecological processes. The more specific ecological processes included concentration and dispersion of people, centralization and decentralization of functions, segregation, invasion, and succession.

[3]Robert E. Park, "The City as a Social Laboratory," in T. V. Smith and Leonard D. White, eds., *Chicago: An Experiment in Social Science Research* (Chicago: University of Chicago Press, 1929), p. 8.

[4]Ernest W. Burgess, "Urban Areas," in *The Urban Community.*

[5]See Walter C. Reckless, *Vice in Chicago* (Chicago: University of Chicago Press, 1933); Robert E. L. Faris and H. Warren Dunham, *Mental Disorders in Urban Areas: An Ecological Study of Schizophrenia and Other Psychoses* (Chicago: University of Chicago Press, 1939); Ernest R. Mowrer, *The Family: Its Organization and Disorganization* (Chicago: University of Chicago Press, 1932); and Ernest R. Mowrer, *Disorganization, Personal and Social* (New York: Lippincott, 1942).

[6]See Clifford R. Shaw, *Delinquency Areas* (Chicago: University of Chicago Press, 1929); and Clifford R. Shaw and H. D. McKay, *Juvenile Delinquency and Urban Areas* (Chicago: University of Chicago Press. 1942; Louis Wirth, *The Ghetto* (Chicago: University of Chicago Press, 1928); and Harvey W. Zorbaugh, *The Gold Coast and the Slum* (Chicago: University of Chicago Press, 1929).

Competition was seen as a basic, if not *the* basic, process underlying the others.

Thus, the Chicago sociologists evolved a dynamic conception of the urban community as the resultant of an ecological process in which there was an interdependence of spatial and social functions through time and according to which a sort of comparative morphology for the study of urban communities could be developed. They provided a basis for subsequent developments in urban sociology, developments that, incidentally, had the effect of disappointing some of the more optimistic hopes of the students of the Chicago community.

For as studies were made in other cities, it was found that these cities did not all follow a concentric zone pattern. Many of the other findings in Chicago seem to have been related more to the peculiar exigencies of time and place, the Chicago of the twenties and thirties, than to American cities in general. In his 1960 book Maurice Stein has made an excellent critique of the Chicago group, pointing out its undeniable contribution but also indicating the extent to which the phenomena that it reported so well were peculiarly influenced by the city's rapid growth and the heavy influx of various ethnic groups during the period of the studies and in the decades immediately preceding them.[7] He points out that one of the difficulties of arriving at scientific generalizations from community studies is the fact that community phenomena vary so much in time and place. In developing an approach that will help community studies to "add up" rather than constitute discrete, noncumulative entities, he calls for a dynamic theory of community change and suggests one based on the interrelated processes of urbanization, bureaucratization, and industrialization. In effect, he maintains that generalization from individual community studies will be facilitated if investigators will first locate their communities within these three dimensions of moving change. In this respect, Stein represents a more recent tendency to come to grips with the two related problems of the difficulty of generalizing from individual community studies and the need for an adequate theoretical framework within which to locate the community studied within a change sequence.[8]

THE COMMUNITY AS PEOPLE

Early recognition that a community was more than a mere municipal jurisdiction, but involved an interdependent complex of living patterns on the local level, made appropriate a consideration of the people themselves who made up *the community's population.* The federal Census supplied data on the numbers and characteristics of people according to geographic locality, and the recording of vital statistics for purposes of keeping track of what was happening to people in terms of births, deaths, and marital status provided a constant source of statistical material about the constitution of the population and what was happening to it. The usefulness of such demographic material in community studies became apparent in several ways.

Perhaps most obviously, the individual character of a community is determined to a great extent by the kinds of people who live there. Thus, the high proportion of children and people sixty-five and over in many small villages has its influence on village social life.

[7]*The Eclipse of Community: An Interpretation of American Studies* (Princeton: Princeton University Press, 1960).

[8]A broad selection of studies in human ecology, many related to local communities, is given in George A. Theodorson, ed., *Studies in Human Ecology* (Evanston, Ill.: Row, Peterson & Co., 1961). Subsequent work continuing the Chicago School inquiry has emphasized more of the cultural aspects of ecology. See Gerald D. Suttles, *The Social Construction of Communities* (Chicago: University of Chicago Press, 1972) and Albert Hunter, *Symbolic Communities: The Persistence and Change of Chicago's Local Communities* (Chicago: The University of Chicago Press, 1974).

New mining and lumber communities reflect in their robust vigor the predominance of males in the prime of life and the relative absence of mothers, sisters, and wives. "Cultural islands" of racial and nationality groups stamp their special imprint on a city, as the Irish in Boston and the Mormons in Salt Lake City. Thus, it is customary for studies of individual communities to make a careful analysis of the kinds of people who reside there: the number and percentage in various age groups, the ratio of the sexes to each other by age groups, the numbers and percentage of people of different racial or nationality groups. In communities of any but the smallest size such analysis for different geographical segments of the community is particularly enlightening. Several studies describing the peculiar constitution of the population in various types of natural areas have been made. The differences in age and sex alone between, say, a skid-row section, a middle-class residential area, and an apartment and rooming-house area may be tremendous.[9] An additional aspect of the population often studied is that of the mobility of people, both within the community and between communities.

For the study of the individual community, an additional dimension is that of time. Thus, changes and rates of change through a period of time may be established and a picture acquired of what has been happening with respect to the kinds of people who make up the community. Of greater practical importance, projections of population estimates of various groups or of various sections of the community can be made for the future, affording a basis for future planning of community policies, services, and facilities.

Such demographic material has been found useful on a more general level as well. Beyond the task of understanding the precise situation in any particular community lies the larger task of making general statements about communities, with size, functional specialization, spatial organization, growth in population, and so on held constant. Thus, it is possible to make general statements about communities of a particular type. As an example, one might ask, How does the population of the suburbs differ, generally, from that of central cities, or from cities that are independent of metropolitan areas? Here is an earlier answer based on careful demographic research executed in 1950:

> *Whether the comparison is with their own central cities or with independent cities, suburbs are distinctive in a series of interrelated traits. The suburban population is relatively homogeneous, ethnically; that is, a high proportion is native white. It enjoys a relatively high socio-economic status, as indicated by occupational composition, average educational attainment, or income. The suburban population shows evidences of a stronger familistic bent than the other urban population, in its comparatively high proportions married and levels of fertility, and its low rate of female labor force participation.[10]*

Similar statements can be made about cities with rapid growth rates in contrast to those with slow growth or declining rates; about cities in one region as compared with those in another; about large cities as compared with medium-sized or smaller ones; about manufacturing cities as compared with trade-center cities, and so on.

Demographic analysis thus provides an approach to community studies that enables the student to proceed beyond the limited task of describing a specific community to the scientifically more important task of making general statements about a whole class of phenomena, in this case, a whole category of cities. Such analysis, as already indicated above, need not confine itself to the more conventional demo-

---

[9]Calvin F. Schmid, *Social Trends in Seattle* (Seattle: University of Washington Press, 1944), p. 92.

[10]Reprinted with permission from Otis Dudley Duncan and Albert J. Reiss, Jr., *Social Characteristics of Urban and Rural Communities, 1950* (New York: John Wiley & Sons, copyright 1956), p.6.

graphic data, but may take into consideration any statistically ascertainable and socially significant variable, such as per capita income, percentage of people on public welfare rolls, percentage of married females working, crime rates, and so on. Thus, Seeley and his associates made interesting analyses seeking to ascertain statistically what variables were positively associated with successful community chest and united fund campaigns.[11] Thorndike made a series of studies of "goodness" of American communities, attempting to establish the existence of significant statistical relationships between such "goodness" and a number of different variables that he thought might be related to it. His method of measuring "goodness" and "badness" was courageous, ingenious, and naive, but his efforts represented a significant attempt to translate such vague but important terms into operational definitions and then to test hypotheses with a number of cities in order to arrive at general, scientifically verifiable statements.[12]

Later, Robert Cooley Angell conducted a series of intercommunity studies using various measures that could be constructed from available statistical material. His purpose was to investigate what factors were associated with high moral integration in American cities, whether positively or negatively. He found that a combined crime index and welfare-effort index constituted the most efficient indicator of moral integration. On this basis, he assigned 43 cities with 100,000 or more population in 1940 an "integration index." He then tested the relationship between nine variables and moral integration in these cities. Four variables proved to show no significant relationship: size, income level, church membership, and percentage of people in small businesses among all business

people. The remaining five showed a significant relationship to moral integration, in each case inverse. These were heterogeneity, mobility, rate of city growth, percentage of married women working, and rental spread. Of these, heterogeneity and mobility were crucial in the sense that they alone accounted for about as much variation as all five indicators combined.[13]

There have been no notable recent studies paralleling in scope and objective those of Thorndike and Angell; however a few writers have considered which characteristics would go into a "good" community.[14]

A somewhat different type of approach permits classification of social areas within the city according to economic, family, and ethnic status. This type of "social area analysis" has been developed particularly by Shevky and Bell.[15]

---

[13]See Robert C. Angell, "The Social Integration Of American Cities of More than 100,000 Population," *American Sociological Review,* vol. 12, no. 3 (June 1947), and *The Moral Integration of American Cities* (Chicago: University of Chicago Press, 1951). Parts of both of these reports are incorporated into "The Moral Integration of American Cities," in Paul K. Hatt and Albert J. Reiss, Jr., *Cities and Society: The Revised Reader in Urban Sociology* (Clencoe, Ill.: The Free Press, 1957).

[14]Lawrence Haworth, *The Good City* (Bloomington: Indiana University Press, 1963); Roland L. Warren, "The Good Community—What Would It Be?," *Journal of the Community Development Society,* vol. 1, no. 1 (Spring 1970); and "Toward A Non-Utopian Normative Model of the Community," *American Sociological Review,* vol. 35, no. 4 (April 1970); Leonard S. Cottrell, Jr., "The Competent Community," chapter 11 in Berton H. Kaplan, Robert N. Wilson, and Alexander H. Leighton, eds., *Further Explorations in Social Psychiatry* (New York: Basic Books, 1976).

[15]See Eshref Shevky and Wendell Bell, *Social Area Analysis* (Stanford, Calif.: Stanford University Press, 1955); Eshref Shevky and Marilyn Williams, *The Social Areas of Los Angeles: Analysis and Typology* (Berkeley: University of California Press, 1949); and Wendell Bell, "Social Areas: Typology of Urban Neighborhoods," in Marvin B. Sussman, ed., *Community Structure and Analysis* (New York: Thomas Y. Crowell, 1959). For a collection of ecological and demographic studies of urban communities, see Leo F. Schnore, *The Urban Scene: Studies in Human Ecology and Demography* (New York: Free Press, 1965).

---

[11]John R. Seeley et al., *Community Chest: A Case Study in Philanthropy* (Toronto: University of Toronto Press, 1957).

[12]See E. L. Thorndike, *Your City* (New York: Harcourt, Brace, 1939), and *144 Smaller Cities* (New York: Harcourt, Brace, 1940).

THE COMMUNITY AS SHARED INSTITUTIONS AND VALUES

The community concept, in addition to factors of space and population, includes the notion of *shared institutions and values*. Putting this another way, geographic area and people do not in themselves constitute a community. One must also look for institutions commonly shared and values commonly held by the local population. As we have seen, the area of shared institutional services, far from being secondary, is actually one of the most important ways of delineating communities. But more than this, the shared institutional services are thought to constitute a shared way of life, a level of participation on which people come together in significant relationships for the provision of certain necessary living functions. As indicated earlier, the function of making accessible locally the various institutional facilities for daily living needs is, from the ecological standpoint, the chief reason for existence of the community. If these institutional provisions are conceived broadly, they go far beyond the provision of employment opportunities, stores, and personal or professional services. In aggregate, they constitute a total pattern of living, involving the comprehensive organization of behavior on the locality basis.

The study of communities as a total pattern of living was for a long time largely the interest of anthropologists, whose investigations were directed almost exclusively at the relatively "primitive" communities of cultures remote from western civilization. Such communities were relatively small, simple, and self-sufficient, although their relation to the surrounding tribe, society, or culture area was seldom overlooked by ethnographers.

The study of an American community with such a comprehensive frame of reference was embodied in the Lynds' investigations of "Middletown." Consciously eyeing the work of the cultural anthropologists, the Lynds sought to apply their broad framework of analysis to a small American city. In their words:

> *This study, accordingly, proceeds on the assumption that all the things people do in this American city may be viewed as falling under one or another of the following six main-trunk activities: Getting a living, Making a home, Training the young, Using leisure in various forms of play, art, and so on, Engaging in religious practices, Engaging in community activities. . . . By viewing the institutional life of this city as simply the form which human behavior under this particular set of conditions has come to assume, it is hoped that the study has been lifted on to an impersonal plane that will save it from the otherwise inevitable charge at certain points of seeming to deal in personalities or to criticize the local life. . . . Even though such a venture in contemporary anthropology may be somewhat hazy and distorted, the very trial may yield a degree of detachment indispensable for clearer vision.*[16]

The fieldwork for the first study was completed in 1925. A restudy of the community was made in 1935, after a decade marked by the violent swing from unprecedented national prosperity to severe depression.[17] This second study likewise used a broad institutional approach to the total community. In addition, it extended the time dimension, which was already included in the first study, by incorporating as much pertinent baseline data from the year 1890 as was available. The Middletown studies marked a milestone in the development of knowledge about American communities,

[16]Robert S. Lynd and Helen Merrell Lynd, *Middletown: A Study in Contemporary American Culture* (New York: Harcourt, Brace, 1929), pp.4–5.

[17]Robert S. Lynd and Helen Merrell Lynd, *Middletown in Transition: A Study in Cultural Conflicts* (New York: Harcourt, Brace, 1937).

and we shall return to them in greater detail later.

A few years after the second Middletown study, another study was made, even more deliberately anthropological, of a small community in the central part of the United States. For purposes of anonymity, the community was called Plainville, and the author, an anthropologist, did not reveal his own name but used the pseudonym James West. The fieldwork was done during the summers of 1939, 1940, and 1941. West attempted "to learn specifically and in detail how one relatively isolated and still 'backward' American farming community reacts to the constant stream of traits and influences pouring into it from cities and from more 'modern' farming communities."[18] In the course of the study West came to recognize three aspects of Plainville's development to be of crucial importance, and he gave them special attention. The first was the local system of social stratification, according to which people behaved differently and were differentially treated. Another was the process of socialization, according to which the young were inculcated with the values and behavior patterns of the somewhat distinctive local culture. The third was the "agony of social and economic reorientation" in which Plainville and the surrounding region found themselves as a result of the impact of the recently established federal agencies of the New Deal.

Like the Middletown studies, this study of Plainville represented an attempt to describe the major institutions of everyday living—the ways people get their living, their religious activities, their clubs and organizations, and so on—not only in terms of the structure of their organizations but in terms of the behavior patterns and belief systems that went along with them. Numerous other studies have employed what might be considered an institutional approach to the study of the community. An additional focus of interest and investigation has been the major values that the people in a community hold. Both West and the Lynds had acknowledged the important role of values, the underlying, often unverbalized principles according to which things were judged to be "good" or "bad." The chapter on "The Middletown Spirit" in the second Middletown volume is widely known not only for its deliberate and extensive attempt to articulate some of these principal values held by the people of Middletown, but also because it pointed out many of the self-contradictions in the values themselves.

Shared values are thought of not only as a basic component of what is meant by the community, but also as an important item on which communities often differ greatly from each other.

A study was made of two communities less than fifty miles apart in the southwestern section of the United States. Though alike in many circumstances, they showed marked differences in behavior, differences that could be summarized by the statement that "the stress upon *community cooperation* in Rimrock contrasts markedly with the stress upon *individual independence* found in Homestead."[19] The investigators attributed this great difference in values underlying community behavior to the fact that Rimrock settlers started early in their habits of cooperation, perhaps because of their common adherence to the Mormon Church, while in Homestead the earlier settlers had come as individual families from various parts of the country farther east and had settled on individual farmsteads, a pattern that tended to reinforce the stress on individualism.

---

[18]James West, *Plainville, U.S.A.* (New York: Columbia University Press, 1945), p. vii. A restudy two decades later was made by Art Gallaher, Jr., *Plainville Fifteen Years Later* (New York: Columbia University Press, 1961).

[19]Evon Z. Vogt and Thomas F. O'Dea, "A Comparative Study of the Role of Values in Social Action in Two Southwestern Communities," *American Sociological Review* 18, no. 6 (December 1953): 648.

Du Wors stated in his study: "The 'community' originates in the common acceptance of like definitions of recurring life situations. This acceptance of like definitions gives a certain uniqueness, a separateness a 'personality,' that marks a community as one and not another."[20] Shared values are expressed through such like definitions of life situations and the behavior that results from such like definitions.

THE COMMUNITY AS INTERACTION

A fourth general area of interest in community studies has been the *interaction* of local people, their association with one another and their behavior with regard to one another. The usual procedure has been to investigate the behavior associated with such major institutional areas as the family, the church, government, education, economic endeavor, and so on, thus considering the processual aspects of the community's institutions as well as their merely structural aspects. Another approach has been to use as a point of departure certain basic social processes such as conflict, competition, disorganization, and dissociation and explore their operation on the community level.[21]

A few decades ago it did not appear particularly difficult to describe the major areas of community behavior and the behavior patterns discernible therein. With the rapid increase in complexity of American communities and the attendant increasing orientation of units within the community toward extracommunity systems, however, the delineation and description of community behavior becomes more difficult. A current resolution of this difficulty being developed by a number of stu-

dents of the community is called the *community action* approach. These investigators point out that a clear distinction must be made between local behavior that actually is a community phenomenon and local behavior that nevertheless is only remotely related to the community. Let us consider this distinction briefly.

Not all behavior occurring in the local community is a product of the interaction of people at the community level. Behavior within the family, for example, is largely determined by role patterns within the family group that tend to follow patterns in the larger culture rather than patterning themselves community by community. On the other hand, certain organizations operating in the community follow a patterned structure and patterned procedures that are prescribed by a national organization and show little variation by communities. If some local behavior is more relevant to the community as a social entity than other behavior, it becomes important to establish criteria with which one can recognize community-oriented behavior. Behavior meeting these criteria may then be appropriately studied as community behavior, while other behavior may best be studied in terms of the extracommunity systems (for example, the United States Post Office) or intracommunity systems (for example, individual families) to which it is most closely related.

Investigators who have followed this community action approach generally agree that there should be no rigid dichotomy between community behavior and other behavior that takes place locally, but that community-relatedness should be considered a variable. Any particular local action should be identifiable somewhere along a continuum from the least community-related to the most community-related. A local referendum on floating a school bond issue would be replete with community relevance and far over toward that ex-

---

[20]"Persistence," p. 211.

[21]This was the specific approach of Jessie Bernard's *American Community Behavior* (New York: Dryden Press, 1949).

treme of the scale, while the institution of a change in postal rates at the local post office branch would be far over toward the opposite extreme.

Thus, community behavior as such is much narrower than the whole range of behavior that takes place at the local level, and the community should not be considered as embracing all social life in a geographic area, the entire "locality agglomerate," as one writer has called it, but rather as the "interactional community."[22]

Various sets of criteria have been offered as a basis for identifying local actions with community relevance. One student has proposed the following set of dimensions for differentiating community actions: "(1) the degree of comprehensiveness of interests pursued and needs met, (2) the degree to which the action is identified with the locality, (3) relative number, status, and degree of involvement of local residents, (4) relative number and significance of local associations involved, (5) degree to which the action maintains or changes the local society, and (6) extent of organization of the action."[23]

Kaufman has gone further and suggested that community behavior be studied not so much from the standpoint of a circumscribed locality in space as from the standpoint of an "interactional field," somewhat related to Kurt Lewin's "field theory" analysis.[24] "The interactional field," writes Kaufman, "probably has several dimensions, the limits and interrelation of which need to be determined. The community field is not a Mother Hubbard which contains a number of other fields, but rather is to be seen as only one of the several interactional units in a local society."[25]

Community action sociologists, then, circumscribe the concept of community, making it much narrower than the local society as a whole. Their other special emphasis is on the study of individual actions of the community, rather than on general processes or structure. This represents a radical departure from the usual theoretical approach, one whose possibilities will no doubt be explored more fully in the next few years. In addition, as Green and Mayo assert,

> *Even in those studies of communities in which the functions performed by structural elements have been featured, the group or organization itself is the major focus or unit of analysis. . . . Would not a more direct approach be desirable, i.e., to focus attention on action per se rather than on the structure which gave it birth? This, it is believed, can be accomplished by making an action itself the unit of analysis. If this is done, however, it is necessary to revise rather radically the customary method of carrying on community research; a revision of the usual sociological framework is required.[26]*

[22]Harold F. Kaufman, "Toward an Interactional Conception of Community," *Social Forces* 38, no. 1 (October 1959): 13. Copyright © 1959, University of North Carolina Press (by assignment from Williams and Wilkins Company). A similar distinction has been made between "community" and "local society." See Willis A. Sutton, Jr., and Jiri Kolaja, "Elements of Community Action," *Social Forces* 38, no. 4 (May 1960): 325.

[23]Kaufman, "Interactional Conception of Community," p. 13. A somewhat similar set of criteria is offered by Sutton and Kolaja in "The Concept of Community," *Rural Sociology,* vol. 25, no. 2 (June 1960). See also their "Elements of Community Action." Green and Mayo use five criteria for the classification of community actions: "These are: (1) locale, (2) temporal limits, (3) action orientation, (4) action objects, and (5) the actor," Cf. James W. Green and Selz C. Mayo, "A Framework for Research in the Actions of Community Groups," *Social Forces* 31, no. 4 (May 1953): 321ff. Copyright © 1953, University of North Carolina Press (by assignment from Williams and Wilkins Company).

[24]See Kurt Lewin, *Field Theory in Social Science,* ed. Dorwin Cartwright (New York: Harper & Brothers, 1951).

[25]Interactional Conception of Community," p. 10.

[26]Community Groups," pp. 320–21.

Such an approach leads to the consideration of the community not primarily as a locality group but rather as a series of interrelated actions. The full implications of this theoretical orientation have not yet been fully explored.[27]

It has been possible for community-action sociologists not only to develop a set of criteria for identifying community actions, but also a set of criteria for the study of actions through time. Green and Mayo suggest that community actions be analyzed in terms of four stages: "(1) the initiation of action or 'idea'; (2) goal definition and planning for achievement; (3) the implementation of plans; and (4) goal achievement and consequences." They give guidelines for the analysis of action at each of these stages.[28]

Kaufman proposes a five-phase model, pointing out that two or more phases may be carried on concurrently. These phases are: (1) rise of interest, (2) organization and maintenance of sponsorship, (3) goal setting and the determination of specific means for their realization, (4) gaining and maintaining participation, and (5) carrying out the activities that represent goal achievement.[29]

The development of a field of interest around the process of community development has led to an interest in action models that arise in the process of planned social change. The field of community action and community development comprises the subject matter of chapter 10 of this book.

---

[27]Recently Kaufman has explored further the community interaction approach, and Wilkinson has dealt with the subject using the concept of "field." See, for example, Harold F. Kaufman and Kenneth P. Wilkinson, *Community Structure and Leadership* (Mississippi State University, Social Science Research Center Bulletin 13, June 1967), and Kenneth P. Wilkinson, "The Community as a Social Field," *Social Forces,* vol. 48, no. 3 (March 1970).

[28]"Community Groups," pp. 323ff.

[29]"Interactional Conception of Community," p. 13.

THE COMMUNITY AS A DISTRIBUTION OF POWER

Few developments in the field of community studies in recent years have made such a vast impact on community theory, research, and practice as the growth of *community power-structure* analysis. This has been a means of coming to grips with the observable fact that certain individuals in the community exercise much more influence on what goes on than do others. Recent study has been concerned with ascertaining the extent to which this is true, just how much influence is wielded, by whom, how, on what issues, and with what results.

The concept of differential ability to influence social behavior is not itself a new one. Thrasymachus, in Plato's *Republic,* gives a vivid description of how members of a ruling group are able to utilize the state and political institutions for their purposes, and a "ruling class" theory has developed through such classic works as those of Machiavelli, Marx, Mosca, and Pareto. The concept of social power is related to this special degree in which some people influence the actions of others. A classical definition of such power was given by Max Weber, who wrote, "In general, we understand by 'power' the chance of a man or of a number of men to realize their own will in a communal action even against the resistance of others who are participating in the action."[30] For centuries it has been realized that such influence over collective action is not confined to the prerogatives of a formal office, such as king, president, general, and so on, but that it can be of other types, as well.

In the second Middletown study the Lynds devoted an entire chapter to "The X Family: A

---

[30]*From Max Weber: Essays in Sociology,* trans. and ed. H. H. Gerth and C. Wright Mills (New York: Oxford University Press, 1946), p. 180.

Pattern of Business-Class Control" and pointed out the inordinate influence that members of this leading industrial family exerted in various aspects of the institutional life of that city and the channels through which this influence was exercised.[31] Likewise, in the Yankee City study Warner and his associates described the manner in which concentrated power was wielded by the upper classes in that community, and Hollingshead, in his social class analysis of the youth of a small midwestern city, showed specifically how the school system was controlled by a small number of upper-class people and made to function for their own interests.[32]

The more recent interest and activity in the field of the exercise of social power at the community level was largely set in motion by a study of community power structure by Floyd Hunter. Defining power as "a word that will be used to describe the acts of men going about the business of moving other men to act in relation to themselves or in relation to organic or inorganic things," he studied community power in a southeastern city that is a regional center of finance, commerce, and industry.[33] The book focused its attention on the 40 persons who were found to be the top power leaders in the community. He located these 40 people essentially by canvassing those in a position to know within business, government, civic associations, and "society" activities.

Through carefully planned interviews with these leading power figures and through other community-study methods, Hunter was able to

gain a picture of the influence that these individuals wielded, the channels through which they wielded it, the relation of these power figures to each other, and the patterns through which community action in Regional City took place.

Hunter found that these power leaders generally not only knew each other personally but were in frequent interaction with each other, much more so than chance would allow. Their frequent interaction often involved joint efforts in community affairs. This group of leaders was at the top of the power pyramid, and its influence was found to be exerted through organizational positions and through formal and informal connections with a whole group of subordinate leaders who usually did not participate in making major community policy decisions but were active in implementing such decisions. "This pattern of a relatively small decision-making group working through a larger under-structure is a reality, and if data were available, the total personnel involved in a major community project might possibly form a pyramid of power, but the constituency of the pyramid would change according to the project being acted upon."[34] Thus, though major power was exercised by this group of leaders, they were not all necessarily involved in any single action at the same time.

Hunter emphasized two important characteristics of the power system in Regional City. The first was that economic interests tended to dominate it. The second was that the formal leaders of community organizations and institutions were not necessarily the top people.

In the general social structure of community life social scientists are prone to look upon the institutions and formal associations as powerful forces, and it is easy to be in basic

---

[31]*Middletown in Transition,* chap. 3.

[32]W. Lloyd Warner and Paul S. Lunt, *The Social Life of a Modern Community* (New Haven, Conn.: Yale University Press, 1941); August B. Hollingshead, *Elmtown's Youth: The Impact of Social Classes on Adolescents* (New York: John Wiley & Sons, 1949).

[33]*Community Power Structure: A Study of Decision Makers* (Chapel Hill: University of North Carolina Press, 1953), pp. 2–3.

[34]Hunter, *Community Power Structure,* p. 65.

agreement with this view. Most institutions and associations are subordinate, however, to the interest of the policy-makers who operate in the economic sphere of community life in Regional City.

The organizations are not a sure route to sustained community prominence. Membership in the top brackets of one of the stable economic bureaucracies is the surest road to power, and this road is entered by only a few. Organizational leaders are prone to get the publicity; the upper echelon economic leaders, the power.[35]

Hunter found that the understructure of leadership through which top power leaders operate is not a rigid bureaucracy but a flexible system, including people described by top power leaders as first-, second-, third-, and fourth-rate. The first-raters are industrial, commercial, and financial owners and top executives of large enterprises. Second-raters include bank vice-presidents, people in public relations, owners of small businesses, top-ranking public officials, and so on. Third-raters are civic organization personnel, petty public officials, selected organizational executives, and so on, while fourth-raters are ministers, teachers, social workers, small-business managers, and the like.[36] Thus, people who hold office in one or another important civic activity may not be those who actually wield power but may be third- or fourth-raters among their lieutenants.

On community decisions of major importance, actions are considered and developed by top leaders and their immediate followers, or "crowds," and then spread out to a wider group of top leaders and crowds for further support and basic decision-making. Only much later, at the carrying-out stage, are the usual civic organization leaders, the press, and interested citizens' groups brought into the picture.

One of the reasons Hunter's book received so much attention was that it challenged much current thinking in the field of community organization and development, which tended to follow such procedures as "encouraging participation in policy-making by the people who will be affected by the policy," "letting plans arise from the felt needs of community people," "basing programs on grass-roots decisions," and so on. If basic community decisions are not made primarily at city hall or at the community welfare council but at the country club and even more exclusive clubs as well as in informal conferences among a small group of top leaders, then important community actions must be supported and approved by these top groups. Community planning agencies and professional leaders in such fields as public welfare and public health recognize this situation.

Actually, however, like other significant books, Hunter's left a number of important questions unresolved. Their resolution has led to a lot of research activity in the community field, and some of the answers are now beginning to appear in research reports.

One question that can be raised with regard to the concept of community power structure as developed by Hunter is, If the power structure is so important, how does it happen that it so often loses in the contest to determine a public issue? For example, in controversies involving the decision to fluoridate a community's water supply, the "power structure" is usually on the side of fluoridation, yet it often loses. Does the power configuration surrounding any particular community issue invariably take the form that Hunter describes, with top policy being determined by members of essentially the same small power group? Or is it not possible that on some community issues, decisive power is exercised by organizations and minor officials as prime movers, rather than merely as the henchmen of a small power group? There are actually two issues here. One

[35]*Community Power Structure,* pp. 82, 86–87.
[36]*Community Power Structure,* p. 109.

relates to the possible multiplicity of power pyramids, depending on the area of the community activity involved in the issue. The other has to do with the extent to which power on specific issues may fluctuate according to specific organizational campaigns, as against the more or less permanent structure of power wielding that Hunter described.

Turning to the first, a number of studies have been made bearing more or less directly on the question of one versus a number of power structures.[37] With few exceptions, these studies indicate that the picture is much more complex than the one Hunter described, and they indicate a multiplicity of power structures with the power pyramids being much less a tightly knit group of leaders in close interaction than was found in Regional City.

Regarding the more or less flexible aspects of power, as opposed to the concept of a fixed structure, the question would seem to be, To what extent is any particular community issue open to genuine contest, and to what extent is it already determined by the structure of existing power leadership and the attitudes of these leaders with relation to it? Many students of the community are willing to assign much more potential effectiveness to citizen campaigns, organizations promoting particular civic actions, newspaper opinion, and so on, than Hunter would allow. Putting this another way, the power situation surrounding a particular community decision is believed to be influenceable by the organizational activities of various citizens' groups. As Kornhauser asserted, regarding fluoridation controversies, "The antifluoridation forces often win in spite of their general lack of power and prestige, because in many cases they are able to mobilize people who, like themselves, are only poorly attached to the community."[38]

Investigators have also explored other aspects of power than just the making of decisions and obtaining of consent. These other important leadership activities might include initiating formal community proposals, supporting or fighting proposals through such visible means as fund raising, endorsing, public speaking in behalf of an issue, mobilizing extracommunity pressures, articulating, defining, and suppressing issues, and actually making decisions as a community official.[39]

Another question often raised regarding community power structure relates to the "conspiracy" dimension, that is, to what extent the power structure represents a self-consciously functioning group of people in league with each other to control the community and to manipulate subordinates and formal organizations in their own narrow interests. Most community sociologists who have investigated the question do not believe that such a conspirational dimension is operative to any considerable extent. Hunter himself seems to be somewhat ambivalent on this question, but in a later work on which he collaborated there was an excellent example of such cold, self-conscious ma-

[37]See Alexander Fanelli, "A Typology of Community Leadership Based on Influence and Interaction within the Leader Subsystem," *Social Forces,* vol. 34, no. 4 (May 1956); Roland J. Pellegrin and Charles H. Coates, "Absentee-Owned Corporations and Community Power Structure," *American Journal of Sociology,* vol. 61, no. 5 (March 1956); Robert O. Schulze and Leonard U. Blumberg, "The Determination of Local Power Elites," *American Journal of Sociology,* vol. 63, no. 3 (November 1957); Robert O. Schulze, "The Role of Economic Dominants in Community Power Structure," *American Sociological Review,* vol 23, no. 1 (February 1958); Nelson W. Polsby, "The Sociology of Community Power: A Reassessment," *Social Forces,* vol. 37, no. 3 (March 1959), and "Three Problems in the Analysis of Community Power," *American Sociological Review,* vol. 24, no. 6 (December 1959). The literature is, of course, too voluminous to list exhaustively here. Several of the above contain additional references to other studies.

[38]William Kornhauser, *Power and Participation in the Local Community,* Health Education Monographs, no. 6 (Oakland, Calif.: Society of Public Health Educators, 1950), p. 33.

[39]Polsby, "Sociology of Community Power,". 233.

nipulation. The issue involved the transfer of title of some public playground land from the city of Salem to a power company, a proposal that had generated considerable popular opposition. In the words of a leading attorney,

> *In the electric plant situation the city council was on the spot because they had to stand up and be counted before a large group of citizens. To many of them it seemed like political suicide to vote for the land transfer, but the big brass in the community had been working on the city councilmen individually, "reasoning" with them, and they voted for the measure in spite of the fact that most of the civic associations, the veterans organizations, and a good many individual and substantial citizens were against it. One by one they voted as they were told to vote. It isn't very often that we have to have such a test of strength as this, but when the chips are down the interests that I am talking about will throw their weight around.*[40]

A final question appropriate to the present discussion is that of the deliberate development and coming prominence of new sources of power through formal organization of such interest groups as organized labor, Blacks, and other racial or ethnic groups. There is consider-

able indication that officials of these and other voluntary organizations, whether representing special interests or promoting broad planning or health and welfare goals, are exerting increasing power by virtue of their official positions and the strength of the organizations that they represent.[41]

THE COMMUNITY AS A SOCIAL SYSTEM

One of the most promising developments in community studies is the attempt to apply social-system analysis to community phenomena. The social-system concept is based on the idea of structured interaction between two or more units. In sociology these units may be persons or groups. Although the process of interaction among units is basic to the concept, the term social system is not applied to all instances of interaction but to structures of interaction that endure through time and can be recognized as entities in their own right.

Parsons described the social system as "a plurality of individual actors interacting with each other in a situation which has at least a physical or environmental aspect, actors who are motivated in terms of a tendency to the 'optimization of gratification' and whose relation to their situations, including each other, is defined and mediated in terms of a system of culturally structured and shared symbols."[42] Thus, a social system might be an individual family,

---

[40]Floyd Hunter, Ruth Connor Schaffer, and Cecil G. Sheps, *Community Organization: Action and Inaction* (Chapel Hill: University of North Carolina Press, 1956), pp. 104-5.

[41]More recent explorations of the "power" concept have taken three important emphases. The first is the continued pursuit of many of the questions raised by the earlier studies. Claire W. Gilbert made a systematic attempt to summarize the numerous findings in "Community Power and Decision-Making: A Quantitative Examination of Previous Research," in Terry N. Clark, ed., *Community Structure and Decision-Making: Comparative Analyses* (San Francisco: Chandler Publishing Co., 1968). Willis Hawley and Frederick M. Wirt, eds., provide a valuable collection of important articles in this field in *The Search for Community Power* (Englewood Cliffs, N.J.: Prentice-Hall, Inc., 1968, 1974), which also contains an extensive bibliography. There is also recent emphasis on multicity studies of community power configurations, especially as they affect decision-making. Clark, *Community Structure,* has this emphasis. A more recent example is Michael Aiken and

Robert R. Alford, "Comparative Urban Research and Community Decision-Making," *The Atlantis,* vol. 1, no. 2 (Winter 1970). See also Clark's *Community Power and Policy Outputs: A Review of Urban Research* (Beverly Hills: Sage Publications, 1973). A third vein of elaboration has been associated with social action for a transfer of power from existing structures to sectors of the population who exercise little power. A popular example is Stokely Carmichael and Charles V. Hamilton, *Black Power: The Politics of Liberation in America* (New York: Vintage Books, 1967).

[42]Talcott Parsons, *The Social System* (Glencoe, Ill.: Free Press, 1951), pp. 5-6.

an industrial company, a hospital, a football team, or a street-corner gang. All social systems according to Parsons are characterized by the following four coordinates: (1) goal attainment, or the gratification of the units of the system; (2) adaptation, or the manipulation of the environment in the interests of goal attainment; (3) integration, or the attachment of member units to each other; (4) tension, or the malintegration of units seen as themselves systems.[43]

Over a period of years, Parsons has developed a comprehensive theory of social systems. Largely through his influence, social-system analysis has developed in connection with small-group structure and the structure of large organizations and entire societies. Although neither Parsons nor his followers have made a specific application of the theory to communities, they did carry social-system analysis to the point that it is now applied to the community as well.[44]

Meanwhile, Loomis has developed a theory of social systems and a set of tools for their

analysis that he has been applying in rural sociological studies for many years.[45] Loomis pointed out that as interaction persists over a period of time it develops certain orderly and systematic uniformities and thus becomes a social system. "It is constituted of the interaction of a plurality of individual actors whose relations to each other are mutually oriented through the definition and mediation of a pattern of structured and shared symbols and expectations.[46]

For Loomis, social systems can be analyzed in terms of nine elements. These are: (1) *belief* (knowledge)—"any proposition about any aspect of the universe that is accepted as true"; (2) *sentiment*—"sentiments are primarily expressive and represent 'what we feel' about the world no matter why we feel it"; (3) *end, goal, or objective*—"the change (or in some cases the retention of the *status quo*) that members of a social system expect to accomplish through appropriate interaction"; (4) *norm*—"more inclusive than written rules, regulations, and laws; they refer to all criteria for judging the character of conduct of both individual and group actions in any social system"; (5) *status role*—"that which is expected from an actor in a given situation"; (6; *power*—"the capacity to control others"; (7) *rank*—"equivalent to 'standing' and always [has] reference to a specific actor, system or sub-system"; (8) *sanction*—"rewards and penalties meted out by the members of a social system as a device for inducing conformity to its norms and ends"; (9) *facility*—"a means used to attain ends within the system."[47]

[43]Talcott Parsons, Robert F. Bales, and Edward A. Shils, *Working Papers in the Theory of Action* (Glencoe, Ill.: Free Press, 1953), chap. 5. The above statement is taken from a codification of this work by Morris Zelditch, Jr., "A Note on the Analysis of Equilibrium Systems," in Talcott Parsons and Robert F. Bales, *Family, Socialization and Interaction Process* (Glencoe, Ill.: Free Press, 1955).

[44]This statement is probably unfair to Mercer, who applied a modest form of Parsonian analysis in a book written in the 1950s. See Blaine E. Mercer, *The American Community* (New York: Random House, Inc., 1956). More recently, two other books have made direct application of Parsonian analysis to specific communities: Lois R. Dean, *Five Towns: A Comparative Community Study* (New York: Random House, 1967), and Harold Kaplan, *Urban Political Systems: A Functional Analysis of Metro Toronto* (New York: Columbia University Press, 1967). The social-system approach based on general systems theory rather than on Parsonian analysis specifically is beginning to find its way into the urban literature. See, for example, James Hughes and Lawrence Mann, "Systems and Planning Theory," *Journal of the American Institute of Planners,* vol. 35, no. 5 (September 1969), and Robert R. Mayer, "Social System Models for Planners," *Journal of the American Institute of Planners,* vol. 28, no. 3 (1972).

[45]See Charles P. Loomis and J. Allan Beegle, *Rural Social Systems* (New York: Prentice-Hall, 1950), and *Rural Sociology: The Strategy of Change* (New York: Prentice-Hall, 1957). Loomis' recent, most thorough exposition of the social-system concept is to be found in *Social Systems: Essays on Their Persistence and Change* (Princeton: Van Nostrand, 1960), from which the description given here is taken.

[46]Loomis, *Social Systems,* p. 4. Copyright © 1960, D. Van Nostrand Company, Inc., Princeton, N.J.

[47]Loomis, *Social Systems,* pp. 11–29.

These are structural elements. One or more processes corresponds to each one. For example, the first element, belief knowledge), is characterized by the processes of cognitive mapping and validation, while the fourth element, norm, is characterized by the process of evaluation.

In addition, a social system involves certain comprehensive or master processes: (1) *communication*—"the process by which information, decisions, and directives are transmitted among actors and the ways in which knowledge, opinions, and attitudes are formed or modified by interaction"; (2) *boundary maintenance*—"the process whereby the identity of the social system is preserved and the characteristic interaction pattern maintained"; (3) *systemic linkage*— "the process whereby one or more of the elements of at least two social systems is articulated in such a manner that the two systems in some ways and on some occasions may be viewed as a single unit"; (4) *socialization*—"the process through which the social and cultural heritage is transmitted"; (5) *social control*—"the process by which deviancy is either eliminated or somehow made compatible with the functioning of the social groups"; and (6) *institutionalization*—"the process through which organizations are given structure and social action and interaction are made predictable."[48]

With such a set of elements and master processes, any social system can be analyzed and understood, whether it be a small group such as a married couple or a group of friends, an organization such as a ship's company or a retail store, or a nation-state such as the United States or China.

Can communities also be analyzed as social systems? This is a question of great theoretical importance, for if they can, if social-system analysis "fits" communities as well as these other types of social entities, then students of the community do not have to start from scratch,

as it were, and describe communities as though they were unique entities unlike other known social units. Rather, communities can be related to a whole class of other social entities—the class of social systems—and it can be ascertained how structural and processual elements, already known from other social systems, apply specifically to the community. What is known about communities can be related systematically to what is known about other social systems, and further, what is known about other social systems may afford rich hypothetical material for further community research.

This question will receive considerable attention throughout the rest of this book. Meanwhile, it is interesting to note certain ways in which communities tend to differ from other social entities designated as social systems, such as formal organizations. Another sociologist Edward O. Moe describes three important differences:

The community is a system of systems. A community, even a small one, includes a great many different institutions and organizations and the formal and informal subgroups that grow up within them. These organizations and groups are social systems and they are part of the social system of the community.

The community is not structurally and functionally centralized in the same sense as a formal organization. The great range and diversity of the needs, interests, goals and activities of people of the community are met through a variety of separate institutions and groups—no one of which holds a completely dominant position in relation to the others.

The community as a social system is implicit in nature as compared with the explicitness of a formal organization. This is true both of the community system as a totality, as well as of the various elements such as the goals of the people who live in the com-

---

[8]Loomis, *Social Systems,* pp. 30–36.

munity, the prescribed means of achieving goals, and the underlying values.[49]

Strictly speaking, an organization, not only a community, may be a "system of systems."

What distinguishes the community from such formal organizations in this respect is not the existence of subsystems, for both have them, but the fact that in the case of the community, these subsystems are not rationally and deliberately related to each other in centralized fashion, as indicated in the second and third points

---

[49]"Consulting with a Community System: A Case Study," *Journal of Social Issues,* 15, no. 2 (1959): 29.

PERSISTENCE OF LOCAL SENTIMENTS IN MASS SOCIETY

Albert Hunter

As advances are made in history, the organization which has territorial groups as its base (village or city, district, province, etc.) steadily becomes effaced. . . . These geographical divisions are, for the most part, artificial and no longer awaken in us profound sentiments. . . .

They persist, not only through sheer force of survival, but because there still persists something of the needs they once answered. The material neighborhood will always constitute a bond between men; consequently, political and social organization with a territorial base will certainly exist.

[Emile Durkheim, *The Division of Labor in Society,* 1964, pp. 27–28].

Among well-disposed people the necessity or conveniency of mutual accommodation very frequently produces a friendship not unlike that which takes place among those who are born to live in the same family. . . . Even the trifling circumstance of living in the same neighbourhood has some effect of the same kind. We respect the face of a man whom we see every day, provided he has never offended us. . . . There are certain small good offices, accordingly, which are universally allowed to be due to a neighbour in preference to any other person who has no such connection.

[Adam Smith, *The Theory of Moral Sentiments,* 1971, p. 329].

A specter is haunting the rise of modern mass society, the specter of the isolated, alienated urbanite, uprooted, roaming unattached through the streets of the city, a perpetual stranger, fearful but free. The purpose of this chapter is to trace this illusion and to assess its validity in the light of recent research. In the process we will see that the specter may be likened to a cloud: in part it is a wispy light entity full of holes through which rays of sunlight and blue sky pour through, while in part it is what the observer chooses to make of it, an imaginary beast of a benevolent or malevolent mein. We must be careful in observing and interpreting this specter, however, for it carries some of the more emotional concepts in the sociological literature–sentiment and attachment, community and kinship, neighbor and friend. We will have to be careful to maintain the eye of the sociological skeptic, being as neutral as possible, so that we more clearly understand and predict its fate.

Therefore, we must first establish the value positions that too often underlie discussions of this topic. The first centers around a nostalgic yearning for the small community that many feel has been lost in today's world. Intertwined with this yearning is a nostalgia not only of place but also of time, as Kevin Lynch has noted in his book *What Time Is This Place?* (1972). The positive sentiments of past time and place are often juxtaposed with negative sentiments toward the present, and polarities around contrasting the simple with the complex, the innocent with the worldly, and the known with the unknown. The filtered past comes to us as a known pattern, but the raw present presents daily confusions that seem to defy understanding.

A second bias centers around the connotations of the word *community*. There exists an inherent bias not only in the lay conception but more nefariously within social science itself toward viewing community as an unqualified good. The positive connotations of friendliness, warmth, and support are seldom countered with the accompanying characteristics of constraint and conformity, and the loss of privacy, individualism, and freedom. We will not debate these points except insofar as they have assumed a central position in sociological theories or have been explored empirically as variables in sociological research. Instead, we will attempt to describe and define community and to understand more clearly the sentiments associated with it.

Finally, we must not confuse sentiment with sentimentalism. I will paint no romantic or romanticized pictures but rather will treat sentiments as legitimate individual and collective variables in the study of communal life. In short, to study sentiments, we must take care not to be sentimental ourselves.

THEORETICAL LEGACY

The initial visions of the specter I have just alluded to are to be found in the major writings of the classical social theorists, such as Marx, Weber, Durkheim, and Simmel. Their theories have been propagated elsewhere, as in Stein's *The Eclipse of Community* (1960), Nisbet's *The Quest for Community* (1953), and most trenchantly in the often cited article "Urbanism as a Way of Life" by Wirth (1938). To use Stein's categories, the argument simply put is that the major social transformations of the eighteenth and nineteenth centuries, urbanization, industrialization, and bureaucratization, produced a social structure that destroyed the previous local affinities such as kinship and community. It is as if these parochial senti-

ments and attachments were lost in the sheer size and density of cities, clouded over by the smog and smoke from factories and crushed lifeless under the bulk of the bureaucratic forms.

Although each of the classical statements may vary slightly in the specific characteristics emphasized in the emerging "mass society," the effect on local sentiments and attachments is generally interpreted in the same way–they will either be destroyed or lost. However, as the opening quotations in this chapter suggest, the eclipse is partial, the destruction incomplete, and the loss limited.

The opening quotations notwithstanding, we will begin our discussion with the nineteenth-century social theorists who described the transformation of Western society. To Stein's three global processes of urbanization, industrialization, and bureaucratization, we should add the massive immigrations that accompanied these, and the rise of nationalism and the modern nation-state.

For Marx (1956), the rise of capitalism out of and in opposition to the feudal order, based on tradition, land, the estates, and subinfeudation, presented a new social order based on a growing distinction between social classes. The bonds of community were being replaced by market relations just as the market itself became the organizing unit replacing the feudal estate. The growing density of the factors of production in cities during the later stages of industrial capitalism was seen to be a critical factor in the emergence of a new social bond, the bond of the working class with class consciousness that would replace the social bond of the traditional community. The community of land, epitomized in the agricultural peasantry, was seen to be at best a conservative, if not reactionary, force.

For Durkheim (1964), the increasing division of labor in society was seen to be an outcome of the increasing ecological density that in turn arose from the human propensity to aggregate. Out of the ecological density arose a dynamic "moral density," resulting in a diversity of interests and an organic social order based on difference and interdependence. The old mechanical order of similarity and shared interest gave way to diversity exemplified in the increasing division of labor. As in Marx's interpretation, however, the fall of the local community as a basis of social order would not long leave a vacuum, for in its stead one would find the rapid rise of work-related associations of interest. Defining these in occupational rather than in class terms, Durkheim emphasized the job-related homogeneity of interest, which implied a greater number and diversity of social solidarities than did Marx's classes. However, this new solidarity was not totally devoid of communal sentiments, for underlying the diversity of interests expressed in the organic social order would always remain some communal sentiments. However, these would be directed not toward parochial places as in the past but toward the overarching, emerging nation-state, which laid claim to monopolizing (among other things) personal allegiance and collective sentiments. The old local community was replaced by the new community of the nation-state.

For Weber (1958), the central process was one of an increasing rationalization or "demystification" of modern life. Rationality became formally embodied in the bureaucratic structure of organized social life. Like Marx's industrial, capitalistic classes and Durkheim's urbanized, occupational groups, the ideal bureaucracy for Weber became the object of new allegiance that would supersede parochial sentiments. Efficiency and rationality became central values within the new social organization, which viewed the irrationality of sentiments in general and sentiments of community in particular as anathema.

Where Durkheim stressed the *nation* as the communal underpinning of the new nation-state, Weber stressed the *state* as the efficient structure that would maintain social order through its exclusive right to use violence.

A more vivid description of the developing specter of modern urban life was presented by Simmel (1950) in his essay "The Metropolis and Mental Life." Considering the market, the money economy, and the division of labor from the previous theories as key structural characteristics of the modern metropolis, Simmel then spelled out their sociopsychological consequences for individuals. The size, density, and heterogeneity that Wirth (1938) was later to emphasize were seen to lead to a cognitive and psychic overload that required the urbanite to blur distinctions and to become more categorical and less discriminating as well as more objective and less subjective—in short, to develop the aloof, blasé urban attitude. What some might have seen as tolerance for diversity, others saw as indifference. The demands for efficiency, punctuality, and specialization occasioned by the division of labor resulted in a narrowing of personality, a uniqueness that was rightly linked to individualism and freedom but that was objectively and not subjectively defined. People were different, given the diversity and division of labor, but at the price of not developing full personalities or interacting with and experiencing others as full personalities. People become things as their relationships become defined through the money economy and the market: "By being the equivalent to all the manifold things in one and the same way, money becomes the most frightful leveler. . . . All things float with equal specific gravity in the constantly moving stream of money" (Simmel, 1950, p. 414). The result, according to Simmel, is that "the individual has become a mere cog in an enormous organization of things and powers which tear from his hands all progress, spirituality and value" (p. 422).

In summary, the historical legacy presented a picture in which the rise of modern mass society destroyed more parochial communal forms of association. Community was superseded by the overarching, industrial, bureaucratized nation-state, propelling every person toward individualism and freedom with the accompanying isolation, alienation, and anomie. New forms of association developed but did not rest on the broad-based, personal, and territorial sentiments of community; rather, they resulted from the narrow, specific, rational interests of individuals. The world was no longer one of people in communities but rather one of people against society.

COMMUNITY LOST—
THE EMPIRICAL LEGACY

The study of the loss of local community sentiments in mass society is most clearly exemplified by two general empirical traditions: the research of the Chicago School of the 1920s and 1930s, which focused on the disorganization of primary kinship and ethnic bases of solidarity within Chicago's neighborhoods; and research on the transformation of small-town life as a result of the increasing scale of social organization at both the metropolitan and national levels. Exemplary studies of this transformation include Warner's *Yankee City* (1963), the Lynds' *Middletown* (1929) and *Middletown in Transition* (1937), and Vidich and Bensman's *Small Town in Mass Society* (1968).

The Chicago School. The research of the Chicago School has often been interpreted, somewhat inaccurately, as positing a ubiquitous disorganization of urban primary ties of neighbors and kin. This misreading stems largely from the emphasis placed on Wirth's "Urbanism as a Way of Life" (1938), which was considered to be a summary statement of the empirical research of the Chicago School. To be sure, much of the Chicago research did focus on the social problems of the day, such as family disorganization (Mowrer, 1927), as

mental illness (Faris and Dunham, 1939), crime and delinquency (Thrasher, 1926), transient marginal populations like *The Hobo* (Anderson, 1923) and *The Unadjusted Girl* (Thomas, 1927), and institutions that catered to these populations, such as *The Taxi Dance Hall* (Cressey, 1932). However, one must remember that these researchers had a specific social problem orientation often coupled with an ameliorative policy perspective. These studies were, in fact, deviant case analyses and are often inaccurately interpreted as representing the full picture of urban life during this period.

A second series of studies on the ethnic groups that migrated to Chicago and settled in segregated "natural areas" also resulted in declining ethnic and neighborhood sentiments. The invasion-competition-succession sequence that resulted as wave after wave of ethnic groups passed through Chicago's neighborhoods was seen to lead to a decline of such sentiments, either positively as a result of the processes of acculturation and assimilation (Thomas and Znaniecki, 1958; Wirth, 1938) or negatively as a result of the previously mentioned social problems.

Wirth's (1938) essay, which drew on the related theoretical essay by Simmel (1950), failed to document persisting bases of social order and local sentiment that were also a part of the Chicago findings. Especially in the work of Burgess and his students (Burgess, 1972), one finds a careful documenting of the "natural areas" of the city that persist as "symbolic communities" to the present day (Hunter, 1974). Also, the "melting pot" hypothesis of acculturation and assimilation that was largely the basis for the expected decline of ethnic neighborhoods has proven to be questionable, as Glazer and Moynihan (1963) have shown in *Beyond the Melting Pot.* The need to maintain local ethnic and neighborhood sentiments was seen to be critical, for example, to the political processes of aggregating demands and establishing power bases (Gosnell, 1939) and to the governmental process of providing a manageable delivery of urban services (Lineberry, 1977).

Thus, although many of the Chicago School's empirical findings did focus on personal and social disorganization that were linked to a demise of local sentiments toward neighbor, kin, and fellow ethnic, the overemphasis on this perspective was partly a function of a social problem orientation and a selective summary and one-sided interpretation of the Chicago School's empirical work.

Transformation of Small Town Life. The second empirical tradition documenting the decline of local community sentiments focused not on the urban neighborhood but rather on the small towns of America as they were increasingly absorbed by the emerging metropolitan and national scale of modern social organization. Greer, in *The Emerging City* (1962a), described a process that explained this transformation: Technological changes in transportation and communication resulted in a shrinking space/time ratio that increased the geographical mobility of goods, people, and ideas. Socially, this resulted in the rise of nonspatial, large-scale organizations of interest, which replaced the parochial, spatially and temporally bounded social world of the local community. In short, modern man, as Webber (1963) suggested, was able to have "community without propinquity." This general thesis of an "increase in scale" may be seen to summarize the three studies we will briefly examine below.

Warner, in his *Yankee City* study (1963), pointed to the loss of local community sentiments as a function of the increasing metropolitan scale of industrial organization, which turned local, family-owned firms into branch plants of regional and national corporations. Power and control over industry shifted to ever larger corporations located in metropolitan centers, while management of local plants shifted to transient, professional managers. The new managers' interests lay with careers in the corporations. This was in contrast to the previous old family owner/managers who maintained a major interest in the well-being of the social and political life of the community and its residents. This produced a distinction that Merton (1968) described as "locals" versus "cosmopolitans" and that a number of writers documented as a major shift in the nature of political power and control in local communities (Schulze, 1969; Dahl, 1961). As a result of this transformation of industry and shift in power, class interests, both of workers and managers, crosscut and undermined the existing common interests found within the community. Community died, according to Warner, in the violent strikes that ultimately erupted; class conflict replaced common community sentiments.

In their Middletown studies, the Lynds (1929, 1937) also documented a similar loss of local community sentiment and solidarity. The earlier Middletown study documented the degree to which a single extended family dominated the economic, political, and social life of their community, which was relatively stable, parochial, and seemingly self-sufficient and which maintained a set of institutions to satisfy its routine needs. This stability and self-sufficiency were shattered by the Depression, prompting the Lynds to return for their second study. As in Warner's *Yankee City,* Middletown was now comprised of fighting factions of workers versus the commercial and industrial elite. The communal harmony and complacency of the earlier period were replaced by class conflict. However, in contrast to Yankee City, this transformation was brought about not by the displacement of locally owned industry by national corporations but rather by the growing recognition of different groups and classes that the fate of Middletown was inextricably linked to national economic and governmental structures. Middletown, in short, had discovered that it was not an isolated, autonomous, self-sufficient community; the Depression had destroyed this illusion. Rather, it was a community that was a small part of a much larger whole over which Middletowners had relatively little influence. Collective interests assumed a class rather than a community base, and the new scale was national, not local.

A similar loss of small-town autonomy in the face of the large-scale institutions of mass society was studied by Vidich and Bensman (1968) in "Springdale," a farming community in upstate New York. In contrast to the harsh reality thrust upon Middletowners by the Depression, these authors documented the way in which Springdalers clung to the persisting myths about small-town life, which masked the prevailing and at times oppressive reality. For example, the myth of local autonomy was maintained in spite of the fact that farmers' complaints about crop prices did not acknowledge that these prices were set hundreds of miles away in the trading pits of the Chicago Board of Trade. Also, their myth of self-sufficiency prevented them from clearly seeing that for many services, such as highways and schools, they were dependent on the resources and expertise of higher levels of government. Although Springdale, like Middletown and Yankee City, had lost functions and lost control over its own destiny, its residents clung to a set of anachronistic beliefs about the friendly virtues of small-town life in contrast to the wicked ways of the big city. At times the reality crept through and the big city was seen to be awesome as well as awful, which resulted in a debilitating and profound ambivalence on the part of the Springdale residents. As the Whites noted in their little volume *The Intellectual Versus the City* (1962), such attitudes have long been a central part of American social thought. It is ironic, as Vidich and Bensman note, that one of the major sources for perpetuating these contrasting images of rural virtue and urban immorality is the mass media, itself emanating from the metropolitan centers of the mass society.

Thus, the studies of small-town life tended to reinforce the picture of a looming specter that was painted by the Chicago School, namely, that throughout America—in big-city neighborhoods and in small rural towns—the social structure and sentiments of local community were dissolving.

COMMUNITY FOUND: URBAN RESIDUES AND SUBURBAN SELECTIVITY

The rediscovery of local community sentiments in mass society occurred in a series of case studies that have become minor classics within contemporary American sociology. It is noteworthy that most of these were either case studies of ethnic communities in older urban areas or of the emerging post-World War II suburbs. These two empirical traditions were critical in causing a rethinking of the hypothesized loss of local community sentiments. These traditions differed not so much in their findings as in their interpretations. The urban ethnic studies tended to find isolated pockets of residual local sentiments, which were considered carryovers from a previous era. The suburban studies tended to emphasize a more conscious search for community that was a selective merger of the small-town life of the past with the modern requirements of metropolitan America.

Urban Residues

Whyte's *Street Corner Society* (1943) was significant precisely because it documented the degree of social organization and social solidarity that existed in what followers of the Chicago School were more apt to refer to as the disorganized "slum." Although Whyte gave relatively little documentation for a full understanding of the institutional structure of Boston's North End, he presented a very clear picture of the strength of primary ties that existed in Doc's gang "the Nortons" and in Chick's club of upwardly mobile college men. The sentiments and loyalties engendered in these groups served to organize the routine day-to-day life of the community's residents. The one institution that Whyte analyzed in some detail for its linkage to these primary ties was the political machine. Doc's ill-fated political campaign for a local office allowed Whyte to study the almost feudal aggregation of personal loyalty that existed in the ethnic neighborhoods and that constituted the power base of local politicians.

A more comprehensive study by Gans (1962b) in another of Boston's Italian communities, the West End, came to essentially the same conclusions as Whyte's. The persistence of local community sentiments was rooted in the existence of a pervasive "peer group culture." The "urban villagers" able to exist in this seemingly contradictory role because the primary groups (exemplified by the extended family and such male peer groups as childhood gangs and adult social athletic clubs) served to isolate the "villagers" from the larger urban world. Ironically, it was this insularity that rendered the West Enders incapable of dealing with the larger political and economic forces that threatened the destruction of their community through urban renewal.

A more recent study by Suttles (1968) in Chicago's multiethnic Taylor Street neighborhood also emphasized how the sentiments and loyalties of primary relationships formed a basis of social order. Going beyond Whyte and Gans, however, Suttles showed how the primary ties based on the status distinctions of age, sex, and ethnicity, coupled with territorial segregation of specific groups, provided a "segmental social order." This was a social order in which groups that otherwise would have been in frequent conflict instead negotiated a spatial and social ordering that provided a degree of tolerance and acceptance in a generally hostile and untrustworthy environment.

By extending primary ties across these age, sex, and ethnic divisions, a network of knowledge about other persons provided a system of personal accountability, acceptance, and social control.

These are but a few of the studies that have attested to the persistence of residual elements of primary ties and local sentiments in urban neighborhoods within mass society. For the most part, these studies analyzed lower class, ethnic communities in older urban neighborhoods.

These studies emphasized the strength of primary and peer relationships–often linked to extended kin and ethnic loyalties–as the basis for local community sentiments. It should be noted that just as the Chicago School had concentrated its efforts on the social problem area and discovered social disorganization, so too may these studies be criticized as having focused on a somewhat unusual collection of communities. Their representativeness was questioned, and indeed the authors themselves seem not to have fully recognized that the areas they studied were more than anachronistic residues from an earlier era. Local community sentiments, in short, were seen to exhibit a selective persistence–they were surprisingly alive in a world that had earlier considered them extinct.

Suburban Selectivity

At the same time that the researchers were busy discovering the urban residues of local community sentiments, other researchers were leaving the central city to follow their fellow urbanites to the emerging communities of single-family homes and green lawns in suburbia. The size, density, and heterogeneity of the city, with its negative personal and social consequences, were being replaced by this new merger of what was hoped would be the best of both urban and rural worlds. A central motivation in this movement was seen by some to be a conscious search for the personal relations and sentiments of local communities. However, as Rossi (1955) and Abu-Lughod and Foley (1970) have noted, the primary motive for the suburban movement was the linkage of family and child-centered interests with the single-family home.

Whyte (1956), in his study of the new suburban community of Park Forest, a suburb of Chicago; Gans (1967), in his study of Levittown, a suburb of Philadelphia; and Seeley, Sims, and Loosly (1956), in their study of Crestwood Heights, a suburb of Toronto, all documented the emergence of informal and formal associations of neighbors, which often centered on the joint interests of children and home. This family and child centeredness led Whyte to describe the suburban setting as a "filiarchy."

These writers saw the suburban community as a consumption unit, a homogeneous, residential, "bedroom" community linked to the larger metropolitan world primarily through the careers of commuting husbands and fathers. In contrast, then, to the effects of bureaucratization, urbanization, and industrialization that Warner and the Lynds had described earlier, the suburban setting was seen as a partial solution to the maintenance of selective sentiments of local community through a spatial segregation of home and work. As later writers such as Farley (1976) and Wirt and others (1972) began to show, suburbia did not constitute a new spatial and political phenomenon; rather, it was a selective migration—an extension of family- and locality-centered interests that had simply spilled beyond the city's rim as metropolitan areas increased in size and scale. These analysts of the suburban scene were careful to note that this social world did not represent a return to the idyllic small-town life of the past. The relationships with neighbors were more transient and less binding than those of friends and kin, and as Keller (1968) noted, echoing our beginning quotation from

Adam Smith, the neighbor emerged as a differentiated role. What Gans called the "quasi-primary" relationships of suburbia were still significant, however, in generating local sentiments of community.

In summary, both the older urban villagers and the newer suburbanites represented an important corrective to the earlier empirical studies of the loss of local community sentiments in mass society. In both, the family and the primary relationships existing in the residential neighborhood formed the basis for the persisting residues and selective sentiments of community.

MINIMAL VERSUS EMERGENT PERSPECTIVES

In the previous section we saw that in the 1950s American sociologists rediscovered the sentiments of community in urban residues and selective suburban developments. Ensuing research has generally accepted the presence of local sentiments but diverged into two perspectives. The first, or *minimal,* perspective sees local sentiments as persisting residuals that are real but of limited significance in modern social life. By contrast, the second, or *emergent,* perspective sees local sentiments as new social constructions of reality that are not simply holdovers from a previous era. It also sees the significance of local sentiments as varying across space and time.

The Minimal View

The minimal perspective is exemplified in Keller's summary book *The Urban Neighborhood* (1968). The role of neighbor is seen as a limited and sharply circumscribed relationship providing a few residual functions, for example, mutual assistance and emergency aid in times of need. Similarly, the work of Wellman (1976) on "urban networks" suggests that for the most part urbanites engage in social relationships based on interests that transcend the limited scope of the local urban community; instead, contemporary urbanites are seen to operate on a broader metropolitan-wide scale. However, Wellman found that certain functions, such as "helping relationships," are maintained at the scale of the local neighborhood. These include borrowing the proverbial "cup of sugar," watching a neighboring home while the family is on vacation, and providing emergency aid when needed.

A similar minimal argument is presented by Fischer (1976) when he distinguishes between "just neighbors" (people who live nearby) and "real neighbors" (an intimate personal group). The conversion of the former into the latter occurs, according to Fischer, under conditions of functional necessity (such as mutual assistance), prior relationships (as with the ethnic enclaves studied by Whyte, Gans, and Suttles), or lack of alternatives (especially for those with limited mobility, such as carless housewives, children, and the elderly). He concludes that in modern mass society these three factors are of decreasing significance and therefore the neighborhood is reduced from a meaningful social group to a mere happenstance of physical proximity.

The Emergent View

Researchers taking the emergent perspective either see local community sentiments as the product of new and emerging reconstructions or see neighborhoods as occasionally playing a critical role in the organization of modern urban life. It is as if Adam Smith's "small good offices" were small in number but loomed large in their import, or as if Emile Durkheim's persisting neighborly needs were not trivial matters.

One of the earlier versions of this emergent perspective was the "community of limited liability" first proposed by Janowitz (1967) and more fully elaborated in Greer's *The Emerging City* (1962a). The community of limited liability holds that individuals' orientations and attachments to their communities are limited and variable across individuals, communities, and time. Communities, or more specifically local community sentiments, are variables that differ according to a resident's age, sex, social class, family characteristics, and, perhaps most importantly, length of residency. The question becomes not simply whether local sentiments are still significant, but for whom and for what reasons. This limited, variable orientation to community is seen in a sense to be an exchange relationship (Blau, 1967). An individual's investments in the community (emotional, social, and, economic) depend on the degree to which the community provides commensurate rewards. When the local community fails to meet an individual's needs, because of changes in either the individual or the community, the individual will withdraw–if not physically, then socially and emotionally. Conversely, if the local community is seen as an important social unit from which an individual feels he or she derives benefits, then the individual is likely to become involved socially, emotionally, and economically. Community organizers are acutely aware that such involvement may lead to a positive spiral of community development. The effectiveness of the local community in meeting residents' needs will attract new residents and entice fellow residents to become involved, thereby leading to increased resources and increased effectiveness.

Other examples of emergent community sentiments are outlined by Suttles (1972) in his volume *The Social Construction of Communities*. One of the communities that he identifies is the "defended neighborhood," which is basically a local area threatened by external social or ecological change. Such communities tend to become mobilized over issues that threaten the central values of the residents. It is because proximity means a shared or common fate that such mobilization of action and sentiment occurs. The often hostile response to urban renewal programs by local residents (Wilson, 1966) exemplifies the defended community's spontaneous quality, while the Alinsky (1946) "conflict model" of community organizing represents a more conscious manifestation.

A more persistent and stable example of an emergent community is defined by Suttles as the "contrived community." However, this term has a pejorative connotation of being more artificial and more manipulative than what are often assumed to be unplanned, natural, grass roots communities. Therefore, I suggest an alternative, more neutral category of "conscious community" that highlights several critical distinctions. First, conscious communities are positively assertive rather than negatively reactive; second, they are consciously defined and articulated in belief systems that may range from being relatively vague "images" (Lynch, 1960) to highly integrated, utopian world views (Kanter, 1972); and third, conscious communities exhibit a greater temporal/spatial stability.

The primary structural ingredient of the conscious community is the development of a more formal community organization that provides critical internal and external functions for maintaining local solidarity and sentiments. Internally, such groups provide a structure within which primary bonds of neighboring may be developed and within which the common community interests may become expressed and translated into specific organizational goals. Externally, the organization becomes the "legitimate" representative of the community, an identifiable vehicle or corporate body that may more easily interact with outside agencies and institutions (Hunter, 1974). It may even be that such organized local groups are fostered by external agencies and institutions that find it difficult to interact or deal with such a diffuse entity as a community (Taub and others, 1977). An example of the development of a conscious community is seen in the study of an urban neighborhood in Rochester, New York (Hunter, 1975). Responding first as a conflict community to external threats from the local airport and to the "block-busting" tactics of local realtors, the residents developed a local organization that survived by broadening the scope of its activities and developing a conscious ideological position on the community's central values (specifically, commitment to urban living in a racially integrated community). This ideological community may be seen to lie between communities with a vague self-image and utopian communities with a totally encompassing belief system.

A final category of emergent communities that has been identified is what I will call "vicarious communities." Above all others, these exemplify the degree to which people, individually and collectively, may develop parochial sentiments and attachments independently of what are usually considered to be the functional and social bases of such sentiments. In a study of shopping behavior, Stone (1954) found that residents who lacked objective social ties to their local communities, such as formal and informal relationships with local residents, were more likely than those with such ties to transform typical shopping encounters into more personalized relationships. This vicarious primary tie is exemplified by the elderly person holding up the checkout line at the grocery store by engaging in friendly, personal gossip with the cashier. This may occur much to the consternation of those waiting in line, who may feel that this should be nothing more than an efficient market transaction so that they may return to their families and friends more quickly. In short, what Weber (1958) and Simmel (1950) saw as the epitome of the rational urban relationship, the market encounter, is transformed into a more intimate personal relationship. In another study, Stone (1968) found that subjective identification with a community by being a fan at spectator sports was more likely to occur among those people who had the fewest objective social ties to the community. Janowitz (1967) found that avid readers of the local community press in Chicago were often using it as a substitute for personal, first-hand involvement in the local social world.

Finally, in *Symbolic Communities* (Hunter, 1974), I documented the way in which people quite often maintain symbolic attachments to places in which they formerly lived or to the place in which they presently live but as it existed at a previous time in their lives. It should be noted that these vicarious communities are not simply individual aberrations. They may exist within a collective local culture often referring back to a significant historical event or period in the life of the community. This historical symbolism was precisely what Firey (1945) found to be a critical factor in preserving Beacon Hill and the Commons as distinct areas of collective sentiment in downtown Boston. In short, the vicarious community epito-transforming residual communities into reactive communities. The discussion by Suttles of defended neighborhoods constitutes an excellent example.

The third stage is what I refer to as *conscious communities*. The critical distinction between these and emergent communities is the development of a rather clearly articulated set of central values that are positively advanced as defining characteristics of the community and their embodiment in a more formally structured community organization. Represented here are the wide range of activities usually included within the concept of community development. Such positive assertions may involve outside support such as federal funds for model cities or community action programs; but as a general principle, the transition from the second to the third stage requires at least a partial solution to external threats such that the community is not simply defending itself but instead has taken the offensive in promoting central values within the community. The transition also requires the ability to mobilize resources, internally and ex-

ternally, to generate an enduring structure that becomes a legitimate representation of the community's interests in relationships with larger external institutions of mass society. The general range we are proposing here runs the continuum from partial "ideological communities" (Hunter, 1975) to the more extreme and encompassing "utopian communities" (Kanter, 1972).

The final and fourth stage I refer to as *vicarious* or *symbolic communities*. This stage epitomizes the notion of the consciously constructed community, for it may in fact be found even among those who do not overtly and behaviorally participate in the local organized social life of an area but nonetheless symbolically transform their local world into a meaningful unit of personal identification. Examples of this type of community are to be found in the research of Stone (1954) and Janowitz (1967), who found that individuals objectively unintegrated into the social life of a community maintained a vicarious identification through other symbolic activities. Another example is the many elderly residents symbolically identifying with an area because their past was spent within the locale and its institutions. This is perhaps most poignantly noted in Fried's (1969) study of "Grieving for a Lost Home." Such symbolic identification may extend beyond the individual's memory into the "cultural memory" of an area. Vicarious and symbolic identification with an area may stem from historical events and meanings. The sentiments and symbolism of Beacon Hill in Boston as studied by Firey (1945) exemplify this form of vicarious community. This stage of community sentiment requires at a minimum that some supporting institutions from the third stage either currently operate or at one time have operated in the area to provide an objective basis for this symbolic transformation.

In summary, the above stages of residual community, conflict community, conscious community, and vicarious community exemplify a progression in local sentiments that depend primarily on the external structural preconditions existing within the mass society and the relationship of the local community to that mass society, rather than simply the inherent characteristics and composition of the local community itself. Such propositions require that we rethink the nature of mass society and its linkage to local community sentiments.

RETHINKING MASS SOCIETY AND LOCAL SENTIMENTS

Mass society is usually viewed negatively. Kornhauser (1959) has summarized these negative conceptions under two general categories: the aristocratic critique and the democratic critique. The former sees the debasement of central values and institutions to the lowest common denominator; the latter sees a centralization of power and prestige that renders the isolated individual powerless and alienated. Kornhauser sees each of these as partial truths, with the true mass society represented by both high accessibility of elites to the masses (aristocratic critique) and high manipulation of masses by the elite (democratic critique).

Most negative conceptions of mass society have been revised or qualified in the light of subsequent research. For example, the "two-step flow of communication" documented by Katz and Lazarsfeld (1955) in their study of the mass media emphasized the degree to which the media did not impinge directly on isolated individuals but rather was filtered both through "opinion leaders" and the natural social groups to which individuals belonged. In a similar vein, one may view much of the research that has "rediscovered" the existence of local community solidarities within urban society as representing a revision of mass society theories as they apply to urban life. In an important article, "Community Attachments in Mass Society," Kasarda and Janowitz (1974) have shown the degree to which what they call

the "linear perspective" (derived from Wirth)—that size, density, and heterogeneity will lead to a disappearance of local attachments in mass society—is not supported. Instead, they found that local attachments are likely to persist as a function of such variables as family status, personal ties, and length of residence in the local community. This "systemic perspective," they argue, requires a reconception of mass society and local attachments that does not necessarily see the two as antithetical, but as coexisting in a more complex structure of institutions and interests than the previous simplified theories hypothesized. However, little has been done in developing a more systemic revision of mass society and local sentiments that incorporates these new findings. In this section, we will attempt this task, and in the next section we will present some exemplary data.

We will begin by rethinking mass society from the perspective of Shils (1975), one of the few theorists to give a positive interpretation to the social changes covered by the general rubric "mass society." Taking a comparative approach in contrasting modern society with traditional society and using the metaphor of "center and periphery," Shils maintained that "the novelty of 'mass society' lies in the relationship of the mass of the population to the center of the society. The relationship is a closer integration into the central institutional and value systems of the society" (p. 93). Echoing Marx, Durkheim, and Weber, he added that mass society "is vertically integrated in a hierarchy of power and authority and a status order" (p. 93). A society-wide, shared set of values that defines a status order are exemplified empirically in contemporary American society by the two status variables of occupation, or more generally class, and race. A generally shared value system of status ranking implies that within mass society a relatively common set of evaluations will be applied to the social positions and communal contexts within which individuals are located. Shared values, however, do not imply similarity in the outcome of evaluations, especially when comparisons are made between commonly shared standards and the more varied objective realities of given situations. Objective inequalities exist, and evaluations of situations will vary directly as the inequality varies. As Shils said, "Inequalities exist in mass society and they call forth at least as much resentment, if not more, than they ever did. Indeed, there is perhaps more awareness of the diversity of situation and the conflict of sectional aspirations in this society than in most societies of the past" (p. 96).

The "diversity of situation" when applied to the arena of local communities in modern urban societies has been one of the major research concerns of human ecology since its inception. The study of the spatial segregation of populations into different neighborhoods and local communities stems from the early Chicago School through research by the Duncans (1955) and Schnore (1965a) and more recent work by Guest (1971), Hunter (1974), and Berry and Rees (1969). As recent research in "social area analysis" (Shevky and Bell, 1955), or "factorial ecology," has shown, socioeconomic status, racial-ethnic status, and family or life cycle status have repeatedly emerged as the three most important dimensions of social differentiation and spatial segregation within modern industrial cities. It appears that these dimensions selectively distribute the population among homogeneous local communities. Viewing this as a "locational decision process" in which individuals attempt to maximize a complex set of values, Berry and Rees (1969, pp. 460–461) said:

> The inhabitants of the city are faced with a fundamental decision: where to live. The principal determinants of such a housing choice are three in number—the price of the dwelling unit (either in rental or in purchase value terms); its type; and its location both within a neighborhood environment and relative to place of work. These determinants have parallels in the attributes of the individual making the housing choice: the amount he is prepared to pay for housing, which depends on his income; his housing needs, which depend on his marital status and family size, that is, his stage-in-life cycle; his lifestyle preferences, which will affect the type of neighbor he will want; and, finally, the location of his job. When the values of the two sets of characteristics match, a decision to purchase housing will be made.

In short, as Form (1954) and more recently Harvey (1973) have suggested, the various economic, governmental, and status-ranking institutions of mass society operate to determine the spatial distribution of scarce values in local residential communities. The result is a differentiated territorial matrix into which individuals will locate, by choice and by constraint, and which they will differentially evaluate. Mass society, then, has produced a constellation of local communities that exhibits *relative* homogeneity internally. However, externally among communities there is relative heterogeneity and diversity. The result, in Durkheim's terms, is to produce a micro local scale of mechanical solidarity based on similarity and a macro metropolitan-wide scale of organic solidarity based on diversity and interdependence. Given the presence of the mass media and the mobility of the population that are characteristic of mass society, it is likely that individuals, as Shils (1975) suggested, will be very aware of these differential evaluations of local areas and be able to make such judgments independently of actual residence.

As we have seen, many theorists and contemporary investigators of local community sentiments see them minimally as persisting residues of limited significance in modern mass society. However, contrasted with this view is what I refer to as the emergent perspective, which sees such local sentiments not only as a persistent and variable *condition* of mass society, but also in important ways as a unique *product* of mass society.

One may see local sentiments as a condition of mass society from the revisionist research and theories, which suggest that all social action requires some motivational element, some cathexis or sentiment that is rooted in personal relationships. For example, the importance of primary groups in the urban social structure has its parallel in the study of formal organizations (what to Weber constituted the epitome of rationality in mass society). From the research of Mayo (1945), Blau (1955), and Dalton (1959), one sees that formal organizations work not in spite of such primary relationships and sentiments but because of them. Similarly, as Stouffer and others (1949), Janowitz and Shils (1948), and more recently Moskos (1969) have shown, nationalism and patriotism, although significant realities of mass society, are insufficient to explain the behavior and motivations of soldiers in combat. Instead, one must look to the informal relationships and sentiments that inhere within primary groups as they operate within the larger structure.

In countering the view of the alienated individual in mass society, Shils (1975) said that personal attachment and sentiment were not simply residues or conditions of mass society, and more significantly that in mass society "there has been a transcendence of the primordially and authoritatively given, a movement outward toward . . . the experience of other minds and personalities. It gives rise to and lives in personal attachment" (p. 101). From this perspective, mass society has unfettered the growth of volitional personal attachments. Therefore, once located within the ecological matrix of mass society (that is, the *relatively* homogeneous local communities that are differentiated from one another by the central values of mass society), personal primary relationships will then emerge as a *product* of mass society. These in turn will foster personal sentiments

that will be generalized to the setting in which they occur, the collective unit of the local community. It is not simply that local sentiment based on shared space is a residue, but rather, that mass society has permitted propinquity itself to become an important basis for defining relationships. Within mass society the relatively autonomous, functionally and institutionally integrated local community may be lost, but the local sentiments of neighborhood persist and flourish. It is as if in Homans' (1950) model of the human group mass society provides the external *evaluative* system within which the internal *affective* system will emerge.

Thus, I am suggesting not only that local sentiments persist within mass society but that there are unique structural characteristics of mass society that when translated onto the urban landscape permit local community sentiments to develop. They emerge not simply as partial and archaic residues, but in new forms and with new functions that mass society has permitted and perhaps requires. These new forms are only hinted at above, but to be significant such sentiments must be translated into collective social action. The middle class, suburban movement of the 1950s, the inner-city riots of the 1960s, and the ethnic, working class neighborhood movement of the 1970s, along with various ideological and utopian communities that emerged throughout this period, attest to the uneven, faltering, but inexorable attempts to translate local community sentiments into collective political action. The emergence of metropolitan and national federations of local community groups throughout urban America (such as National Neighbors, National Alliance of Neighborhoods, and National People's Action) suggests a new social and political structure based on local community sentiments.

Furthermore, it should be noted that such federations imply that a zero-sum conception of community sentiments often assumed implicitly is questionable. Echoing Durkheim,

Martindale (1958), for example, suggested that in modern mass society the community of the nation-state grows at the expense of the local community. I would suggest rather an additive or multiplicative system in which collective sentiments and attachments, up and down the vertical scale of integration (Warren, 1971; Walton, 1971), serve to reinforce one another. In Shils's (1975) words, mass society is characterized by a closer integration of the periphery with the center, and it appears that local community sentiments may operate as a new critical link in that integration.

Finally, I would caution against a simplification that would see local community sentiments persisting only as the territorial manifestation of class interests. To be sure, these are often of primary importance, but to ignore the other critical dimensions of race, ethnicity, religion, life-style, and life cycle would underrepresent the varied forms that community-based interests may take. It is at the level of the local community that mass society uniquely converges in its myriad forms and from which rises, in the shared fate of propinquity, the multiple and varying forms of community interests and local sentiments.

CONCLUSION

The specter with which we began this chapter has not disappeared magically within the words of these pages. No chants or spells will dispel its looming presence. However, it is hoped that this brief review and recasting of thought about local sentiments in mass society has provided an outline of the various shapes and forms the specter may assume. It is hoped as well that the exaggerated claims of those who see local communities collapsing before the efficient juggernaut of rational large-scale mass society and of those more positively oriented "neighborhood utopians" are equally tempered. I have no desire to discourage thinking of either vein—neither that

which sees individual freedoms emerging out of the demise of such "false conscious" anachronistic attachments nor that which harkens to a reconstituted social order within which individuals in their local communities reassert control over the institutions that affect their daily lives (Altshuler, 1970). However, I would suggest that policy and planning objectives with a more immediate and limited time scale should recognize the upper and lower limits that local communities may play within modern mass society. Therefore in these concluding comments I will attempt to relate our previous discussion to some of the broader policy issues.

Lower Limits of Community

Those who see local communities collapsing assume what I previously referred to as the minimal perspective, and they err by underestimating the degree to which local communities and the sentiments that inhere within them remain as viable bases of collective social action. This limited vision has several interrelated components.

The first of these is an overemphasis on production as opposed to consumption, and as Choldin (1977) has noted, local communities are primarily units of collective consumption. Therefore, in theoretical and empirical studies that emphasize a production orientation—for example, classical human ecology and more recent work in urban political economy—local communities are often slighted as significant units of social organization. At most they are simply seen to be the repositories of differentially distributed economic and class values (Molotch, 1976; Castells, 1977). This, as we have seen, is in fact one of the significant points of intersection between mass society and local communities. However, the consumption and credit markets are significant bases of mobilization of economic and class interests independent of production class relationships. Furthermore, these consumption interests are uniquely centered in local communities in contrast to production interests. For example, the urban riots of the 1960s were defined by some analysts as communal and commodity riots (Kerner and others, 1968). Furthermore, in the 1970s the issue of "redlining" (the denial of mortgage money for housing in older urban neighborhoods) has exemplified the degree to which important political action may arise out of the local neighborhood as an economic unit of commodity and capital consumption. In short, the local neighborhood continues to play a significant economic role in the intersection of mass society and local interests.

Local community sentiments, however, extend beyond the limited sphere of economic and class interests. Life-style and race, though highly correlated with class, continue to operate as powerful and independent bases of collective social action. For example, the life-style dimension exemplifies the degree to which institutions and agencies geared to the family and to child rearing—such as schools, churches, day care centers, and parks and leisure activities—continue to operate at the local level. It is impossible to ignore these local interests, to expect them to disappear, or to translate them solely into class terms. In short, from a policy perspective it becomes imperative to ascertain which among the numerous institutions of modern mass society now operate or will effectively operate in the future at the scale of the local community. Where they now persist or at best emerge sporadically, policies and programs must be developed that recognize the diversity of these interests, their need for a more structured and organized form, and a response to residents' desires for participating in the decision making and control over their functioning.

Upper Limits of Community

Just as the minimalists err by underestimating the significance of local communities, so the neighborhood utopians err by seeing a "community revival" or "neighborhood movement"

as answering most if not all of society's contemporary problems. As has been noted elsewhere (Hunter and Suttles, 1972), their exaggerated expectations are rooted in a misconception of local communities as isolated, relatively self-sufficient, and self-directed units of social organization. Mass society is seen as having usurped functions and activities that local units can and should control. In short, there is in their rhetoric relatively little recognition given to the *limits* of local communities—not simply spatially, but functionally. Certain social problems, such as national defense, perhaps cannot be solved at the local level but are in fact societal problems within the contemporary "world system" (Wallerstein, 1974a). It is ironic, as Barbera (1977) has noted in a parallel argument with respect to the family, that the responsibility for solutions to some social problems is often placed directly on the units of social organization, such as families or communities, that are also seen to be collapsing, or losing functions, as a result of broader and more general social changes. A more limited perspective would suggest that only certain functions and certain problems can be solved by the local community. Again, a central policy question becomes one of ascertaining which problems and which functions.

The idea of an upper limit to local communities points to the direction that future policies and programs should take, namely, providing the links between the sentiments and interests of local communities and the overarching economic and status distributive systems of mass society. This is basically a political problem of providing avenues of collective representation that allow local community interests to affect the larger-scale distributive systems. Linking local community interests with the larger-scale organizations of production directly addresses the older question of home/work separation. This is not simply a spatial separation that is answered by transportation engineers planning routes with shorter commuting times; rather, it is a political and social problem that addresses the divergent interests between geopolitical centers of production and local centers of consumption. The organization of economic interests of production long ago extended beyond the parochial limits of local communities. For example, taxes, corporate interests, capital, and people themselves gravitate to the centers of society, as Shils (1975) would suggest; but it is important that links be maintained so that local community interests may flow in the same direction and so that the central values may as easily flow back to the local communities.

Mass society will not disappear and, as I have suggested throughout this chapter, neither will the local sentiments of community. There must be a concerted effort from both the top and the bottom to establish a working relationship that is realistically within the upper and the lower limits of community. In this way Adam Smith's "small good offices" may continue to be performed within Emile Durkheim's "material neighborhood," and these may in turn continue to humanize modern mass society

TYPES OF INFLUENTIALS:
THE LOCAL AND THE COSMOPOLITAN

Robert K. Merton

The terms "local" and "cosmopolitan" do not refer, of course, to the regions in which interpersonal influence is exercised. Both types of influentials are effective almost exclusively within the local community. Rovere has few residents who command a following outside that community.

The chief criterion for distinguishing the two is found in their *orientation* toward Rovere. The localite largely confines his interests to this community. Rovere is essentially his world. Devoting little thought or energy to the Great Society, he is preoccupied with local problems, to the virtual exclusion of the national and international scene. He is, strictly speaking, parochial.

Contrariwise with the cosmopolitan type. He has some interest in Rovere and must of course maintain a minimum of relations within the community since he, too, exerts influence there. But he is also oriented significantly to the world outside Rovere, and regards himself as an integral part of that world. He resides in Rovere but lives in the Great Society. If the local type is parochial, the cosmopolitan is ecumenical.

Of the thirty influentials interviewed at length, fourteen were independently assessed by three analysts as "cosmopolitan" on the basis of case-materials exhibiting their orientation toward the Rovere community, and sixteen, as "local."

These orientations found characteristic expression in a variety of contexts. For example, influentials were launched upon a statement of their outlook by the quasi-projective question: "Do you worry much about the news?" (This was the autumn of 1943, when "the news" was, for most, equivalent to news about the war.) The responses, typically quite lengthy, readily lent themselves to classification in terms of the chief foci of interest of the influentials. One set of comments was focused on problems of a national and international order. They expressed concern with the difficulties which would attend the emergence of a stable postwar world; they talked at length about the problems of building an international organization to secure the peace; and the like. The second set of comments referred to the war news almost wholly in terms of what it implied for interviewees personally or for their associates in Rovere. They seized upon a question about "the news" as an occasion for reviewing the immediate flow of problems which the war had introduced into the town.

Classifying influentials into these two categories, we find that twelve of the fourteen cosmopolitans typically replied within the framework of international and national problems, whereas only four of the sixteen locals spoke in this vein. Each type of influential singled out distinctively different elements from the flow of events. A vaguely formulated question enabled each to project their basic orientations into their replies.

All other differences between the local and cosmopolitan influentials seem to stem from their difference in basic orientation. From the group-profiles we see the tendency of local influentials to be devoted to localism: they are more likely to have lived in Rovere for a long period, are profoundly interested in meeting many townspeople, do not wish to move from the town, are more likely to be interested in local politics, *etc.* Such items, which suggest great disparity between the two types of influentials, are our main concern in the following sections. There we will find that the difference in basic orientation is bound up with a variety of other differences: (1) in the structures of social relations in which each type is implicated; (2) in the roads they have traveled to their present positions in the influence-structure; (3) in the utilization of their present status for the exercise of interpersonal influence; and (4) in their communications behavior.

STRUCTURES OF SOCIAL RELATIONS

Roots in Rovere

Local and cosmopolitan influentials differ rather markedly in their attachment to Rovere. The local influentials are great local patriots and the thought of leaving Rovere seems seldom to come to mind. As one of them gropingly expressed it:

> *Rovere is the greatest town in the world. It has something that is nowhere else in the world, though I can't quite say what it is.*

When asked directly if they had "ever thought of leaving Rovere," thirteen of the sixteen local influentials replied emphatically that they would never consider it, and the other three expressed a strong preference to remain, although they believed they would leave under certain conditions. None felt that they would be equally satisfied with life in any other community. Not so with the cosmopolitans. Only three of these claim to be wedded to Rovere for life. Four express their present willingness to live elsewhere, and the remaining seven would be willing to leave under certain conditions. Cosmopolitans' responses such as these do not turn up at all among the locals:

> *I've been on the verge of leaving for other jobs several times.*

> *I am only waiting for my son to take over my practice, before I go out to California.*

These basic differences in attitude toward Rovere are linked with the different runs of experience of local and cosmopolitan influentials. The cosmopolitans have been more mobile. The locals were typically born in Rovere or in its immediate vicinity. Whereas 14 of the locals have lived in Rovere for over twenty-five years, this is true for fewer than half of the cosmopolitans. The cosmopolitans are typically recent arrivals who have lived in a succession of communities in different parts of the country.

Nor does this appear to be a result of differences in the age-composition of the local and cosmopolitan groups. The cosmopolitans are more likely to be younger than the local influentials. But for those over forty-five, the cosmopolitans seem to be comparative newcomers and the locals Rovere-born-and-bred.

From the case-materials, we can infer the bases of the marked attachment to Rovere characteristic of the local influentials. In the process of making their mark, these influentials have become thoroughly *adapted to the community* and dubious of the possibility of doing as well elsewhere. From the vantage point of his seventy years, a local judge reports his sense of full incorporation in the community:

> *I wouldn't think of leaving Rovere. The people here are very good, very responsive. They like me and I'm grateful to God for the feeling that the people in Rovere trust me and look up to me as their guide and leader.*

Thus, the strong sense of identification with Rovere among local influentials is linked with their typically local origins and career patterns in this community. Economically and sentimentally, they are deeply rooted in Rovere.

So far as attachment to Rovere is concerned, the cosmopolitans differ from the locals in virtually every respect. Not only are they relative newcomers; they do not feel themselves rooted in the town. Having characteristically lived elsewhere, they feel that Rovere, "a pleasant enough town," is only one of many. They are also aware, through actual experience, that they can advance their careers in other communities. They do not, consequently, look upon Rovere as comprising the outermost limits of a secure and satisfactory existence. Their wider range of experience has modified their orientation toward their present community.

Sociability: Networks of Personal Relations

In the course of the interview, influentials were given an occasion to voice their attitudes toward "knowing many people" in the community. Attitudes differed sharply between the two types. Thirteen of the sixteen local influentials in contrast to four of the fourteen cosmopolitans expressed marked interest in establishing frequent contacts with many people.

This difference becomes more instructive when examined in qualitative terms. The local influential is typically concerned with knowing *as many* people as possible. He is a "quantitativist" in the sphere of social contacts. Numbers count. In the words of an influential police officer (who thus echoes the sentiments of another "local," the Mayor):

> *I have lots of friends in Rovere, if I do say so myself. I like to know everybody. If I stand on a corner, I can speak to 500 people in two hours. Knowing people helps when a promotion comes up, for instance. Everybody mentions you for the job. Influential people who know you talk to other people. Jack Flye [the Mayor] said to me one day, "Bill," he said, "you have more friends in town than I do. I wish I had all the friends you have that you don't even know of." It made me feel good . . .*

This typical attitude fits into what we know of the local type of influential. What is more, it

suggests that the career-function of personal contacts and personal relations is recognized by the local influentials themselves. Nor is this concern with personal contact merely a consequence of the occupations of local influentials. Businessmen, professionals, and local government officials among them all join in the same paeans on the desirability of many and varied contacts. A bank president recapitulates the same story in terms of his experience and outlook:

> *I have always been glad to meet people . . . It really started when I became a teller. The teller is the most important position in a bank as far as meeting people goes. As teller, you must meet everyone. You learn to know everybody by his first name. You don't have the same opportunity again to meet people. Right now we have a teller who is very capable but two or three people have come to me complaining about him. He is unfriendly with them. I told him, you've got to have a kind word for everyone. It's a personal and a business matter.*

This keynote brings out the decisive interest of local influentials in all manner of personal contacts which enable them to establish themselves when they need political, business, or other support. Influentials in this group act on the explicit assumption that they can be locally prominent and influential by lining up enough people who know them and are hence willing to help them as well as be helped by them.

The cosmopolitan influentials, on the other hand, have notably little interest in meeting *as many* people as possible. They are more selective in their choice of friends and acquaintances. They typically stress the importance of confining themselves to friends with whom "they can really talk," with whom they can "exchange ideas." If the local influentials are quantitativists, the cosmopolitans are "qualitativists" in this regard. It is not *how many* people they know but the *kind of people* they know that counts.

The contrast with the prevailing attitudes of local influentials is brought out in these remarks by cosmopolitan influentials:

> *I don't care to know people unless there is something to the person. I am not interested in quantity. I like to know about other people; it broadens your own education. I enjoy meeting people with knowledge and standing. Masses of humanity I don't go into. I like to meet people of equal mentality, learning and experience.*

Just as with the local influentials, so here the basic attitude cuts across occupational and educational lines. Professional men among the cosmopolitans, for example, do not emphasize the importance of a wide and extensive acquaintanceship, if one is to build up a practice. In contrast to a "local" attorney who speaks of the "advantage to me to know as many people as possible," a "cosmopolitan" attorney waxes poetic and exclusive all in one, saying:

> *I have never gone out and sought people. I have no pleasure in just going around and calling. As Polonius advised Laertes,*
> * "Those friends thou hast, and their*
> *   adoption tried,*
> * Grapple them to thy soul with hoops*
> *   of steel,*
> * But do not dull the palm with*
> *   entertainment*
> * Of each new-hatch'd unfledged*
> *   comrade. . . ."*

These diverse orientations of locals and cosmopolitans toward personal relations can be interpreted as a function of their distinctive modes of achieving influence. At the moment, it is sufficient to note that locals seek to enter into manifold networks of personal relations, whereas the cosmopolitans, *on the same status level,* explicitly limit the range of these relations.

Participation in Voluntary Organizations

In considering the "sociability" of locals and cosmopolitans, we examined their attitudes toward informal, personal relationships. But what of their roles in the more formal agencies for social contact: the voluntary organizations?

As might be anticipated, both types of influentials are affiliated with more organizations than rank-and-file members of the population. Cosmopolitan influentials belong to an average of eight organizations per individual, and the local influentials, to an average of six. There is the possibility that cosmopolitans make greater use of organizational channels to influence than of personal contacts, whereas locals, on the whole, operate contrariwise.

But as with sociability, so with organizations: the more instructive facts are qualitative rather than quantitative. It is not so much that the cosmopolitans belong to *more* organizations than the locals. Should a rigorous inquiry bear out this impression, it would still not locate the strategic organizational differences between the two. It is, rather, that they belong to different types of organizations. And once again, these differences reinforce what we have learned about the two kinds of influentials.

The local influentials evidently crowd into those organizations which are largely designed for "making contacts," for establishing personal ties. Thus, they are found largely in the secret societies (Masons), fraternal organizations (Elks), and local service clubs—the Rotary, Lions, and the Kiwanis, the most powerful organization of this type in Rovere. Their participation appears to be less a matter of furthering the nominal objectives of these organizations than of using them as *contact centers.* In the forthright words of one local influential, a businessman:

> *I get to know people through the service clubs; Kiwanis, Rotary, Lions. I now belong only to the Kiwanis. Kiwanis is different from any other service club. You have to be asked to join. They pick you out first, check you first. Quite a few influential people are there and I get to meet them at lunch every week.*

The cosmopolitans, on the other hand, tend to belong to those organizations in which they can exercise their special skills and knowledge. They are found in professional societies and in hobby groups. At the time of the inquiry, in 1943, they were more often involved in Civilian Defense organizations where again they were presumably more concerned with furthering the objectives of the organization than with establishing personal ties.

Much the same contrast appears in the array of public offices held by the two types of influentials. Seven of each type hold some public office, although the locals have an average somewhat under one office per official. The primary difference is in the *type* of office held. The locals tend to hold political posts—street commissioner, mayor, township board, etc.—ordinarily obtained through political and personal relationships. The cosmopolitans, on the other hand, more often appear in public positions which involve not merely political operations but the utilization of special skills and knowledge (*e.g.*, Board of Health, Housing Committee, Board of Education).

From all this we can set out the hypothesis that participation in voluntary associations has somewhat different functions for cosmopolitan and local influentials. Cosmopolitans are concerned with associations primarily because of the activities of these organizations. They are means for extending or exhibiting their skills and knowledge. Locals are interested in associations not for their activities, but because these provide a means for extending personal relationships. The basic orientations of locals and cosmopolitan influentials are thus diversely expressed in organizational behavior as in other respects.

AVENUES TO INTERPERSONAL INFLUENCE

The foregoing differences in attachment to Rovere, sociability, and organizational behavior help direct us to the different avenues to influence traveled by the locals and the cosmopolitans. And in mapping these avenues we shall fill in the background needed to interpret the differences in communications behavior characteristic of the two types of influentials.

The locals have largely grown up in and with the town. For the most part, they have gone to school there, leaving only temporarily for their college and professional studies. They held their first jobs in Rovere and earned their first dollars from Rovere people. When they came to work out their career-pattern, Rovere was obviously the place in which to do so. It was the only town with which they were thoroughly familiar, in which they knew the ins and outs of politics, business, and social life. It was the only community which they knew and, equally important, which knew them. Here they had developed numerous personal relationships.

And this leads to the decisive attribute of the local influentials' path to success: far more than with the cosmopolitans, *their influence rests on an elaborate network of personal relationships.* In a formula which at once simplifies and highlights the essential fact, we can say: *the influence of local influentials rests not so much on what they know but on whom they know.*

Thus, the concern of the local influential with personal relations is in part the product and in part the instrument of his particular type of influence. The "local boy who makes good," it seems, is likely to make it through good personal relations. Since he is involved in personal relations long before he has entered seriously upon his career, it is the path of less resistance for him to continue to rely upon these relations as far as possible in his later career.

With the cosmopolitan influential, all this changes. Typically a newcomer to the community, he does not and cannot utilize personal ties as his chief claim to attention. He usually comes into the town fully equipped with the prestige and skills associated with his business or profession and his "worldly" experience. He begins his climb in the prestige-structure at a relatively high level. It is the prestige of his previous achievements and previously acquired skills which make him eligible for a place in the local influence-structure. Personal relations are much more the product than the instrumentality of his influence.

These differences in the location of career-patterns have some interesting consequences for the problems confronting the two types of influentials. First of all, there is some evidence, though far from conclusive, that the rise of the locals to influentiality is slow compared with that of the cosmopolitans. Dr. A, a minister, cosmopolitan, and reader of newsmagazines, remarked upon the ease with which he had made his mark locally:

> The advantage of being a minister is that you don't have to *prove yourself*. You are immediately accepted and received in all homes, including the best ones. [emphasis inserted]

However sanguine this observation may be, it reflects the essential point that the newcomer who has "arrived" in the outside world, sooner takes his place among those with some measure of influence in the local community. In contrast, the local influentials *do* "have to prove" themselves. Thus, the local bank president who required some forty years to rise from his job as messenger boy, speaks feelingly of the slow, long road on which "I worked my way up."

The age-composition of the local and cosmopolitan influentials is also a straw in the wind with regard to the rate of rise to influence. All but two of the sixteen locals are over forty-five years of age, whereas fewer than two-thirds of the cosmopolitans are in this older age group.

Not only may the rate of ascent to influence be slower for the local than for the cosmopolitan, but the ascent involves some special difficulties centered about the local's personal relations. It appears that these relations may hinder as well as help the local boy to "make good." He must overcome the obstacle of being intimately known to the community when he was "just a kid." He must somehow enable others to recognize his consistent change in status. Most importantly, people to whom he was once subordinate must be brought to the point of now recognizing him as, in some sense, superordinate. Recognition of this problem is not new. Kipling follows Matthew 13 in observing that "prophets have honour all over the Earth, except in the village where they were born." The problem of ascent in the influence-structure for the home-town individual may be precisely located in sociological terms: change of status within a group, particularly if it is fairly rapid, calls for the revamping of attitudes toward and the remaking of relations with the mobile individual. The pre-existent structure of personal relations for a time thus restrains the ascent of the local influential. Only when he has broken through these established conceptions of him, will others accept the reversal of roles entailed in the rise of the local man to influence. A Rovere attorney, numbered among the local influentials, describes the pattern concisely:

> When I first opened up, people knew me so well in town that they treated me as if I still were a kid. It was hard to overcome. But after I took interest in various public and civic affairs, and became chairman of the Democratic organization and ran for the State legislature—knowing full well I wouldn't be elected—they started to take me seriously.

The cosmopolitan does not face the necessity for breaking down local preconceptions of himself before it is possible to have his status as an influential "taken seriously." As we have seen, his credentials are found in the prestige and authority of his attainments elsewhere. He thus manifests less interest in a wide range of personal contacts for two reasons. First, his influence stems from prestige rather than from reciprocities with others in the community. Secondly, the problem of disengaging himself from obsolete images of him as "a boy" does not exist for him, and consequently does not focus his attention upon personal relations as it does for the local influential.

The separate roads to influence traveled by the locals and cosmopolitans thus help account for their diverging orientations toward the local community, with all that these orientations entail.

SOCIAL STATUS IN ACTION: INTERPERSONAL INFLUENCE

At this point, it may occur to the reader that the distinction between the local and cosmopolitan influentials is merely a reflection of differences in education or occupation. This does not appear to be the case.

It is true that the cosmopolitans among our interviewees have received more formal education than the locals. All but one of the cosmopolitans as compared with half of the locals are at least graduates of high school. It is also true that half of the locals are in "big business," as gauged by Rovere standards, whereas only two of the fourteen cosmopolitans fall in this group; and furthermore, that half of the cosmopolitan influentials are professional people as compared with fewer than a third of the locals.

But these differences in occupational or educational status do not appear to determine the diverse types of influentials. When we compare the behavior and orientations of professionals among the locals and cosmopolitans, their characteristic differences persist, even though they have the same types of occupation and have received the same type of education. Educational and occupational differences may *contribute* to the differences between the two types of influentials but they are not the *source* of these differences. Even as a professional, the

local influential is more of a businessman and politician in his behavior and outlook than is the cosmopolitan. He utilizes personal relationships as an avenue to influence conspicuously more than does his cosmopolitan counterpart. In short, *it is the pattern of utilizing social status and not the formal contours of the status itself which is decisive.*

While occupational status may be a major support for the cosmopolitan's rise to influence, it is merely an adjunct for the local. Whereas all five of the local professionals actively pursue local politics, the cosmopolitan professionals practically ignore organized political activity in Rovere. (Their offices tend to be honorary appointments.) Far from occupation serving to explain the differences between them, it appears that the same occupation has a different role in interpersonal influence according to whether it is pursued by a local or a cosmopolitan. This bears out our earlier impression that "objective attributes" (education, occupation, etc.) do not suffice as indices of people exercising interpersonal influence.

The influential businessman, who among our small number of interviewees is found almost exclusively among the locals, typically utilizes his personal relations to enhance his influence. It is altogether likely that a larger sample would include businessmen who are cosmopolitan influentials and whose behavior differs significantly in this respect. Thus, Mr. H., regarded as exerting great influence in Rovere, illustrates the cosmopolitan big-business type. He arrived in Rovere as a top executive in a local manufacturing plant. He has established few personal ties. But he is sought out for advice precisely because he has "been around" and has the aura of a man familiar with the outside world of affairs. His influence rests upon an imputed expertness rather than upon sympathetic understanding of others.

This adds another dimension to the distinction between the two types of influential. It appears that the cosmopolitan influential has a following because *he knows;* the local influential, because *he understands.* The one is sought out for his specialized skills and experience; the other, for his intimate appreciation of intangible but affectively significant details. The two patterns are reflected in prevalent conceptions of the difference between "the extremely competent but impersonal medical specialist" and the "old family doctor." Or again, it is not unlike the difference between the "impersonal social welfare worker" and the "friendly precinct captain." It is not merely that the local political captain provides food-baskets and jobs, legal and extra-legal advice, that he sets to rights minor scrapes with the law, helps the bright poor boy to a political scholarship in a local college, looks after the bereaved—that he helps in a whole series of crises when a fellow needs a friend, and, above all, a friend who "knows the score" and can do something about it. It is not merely that he provides aid which gives him interpersonal influence. It is *the manner in which the aid is provided.* After all, specialized agencies do exist for dispensing this assistance.

Welfare agencies, settlement houses, legal aid clinics, hospital clinics, public relief departments—these and many other organizations are available. But in contrast to the professional techniques of the welfare worker which often represent in the mind of the recipient the cold, bureaucratic dispensation of limited aid following upon detailed investigation are the unprofessional techniques of the precinct captain who asks no questions, exacts no compliance with legal rules of eligibility and does not "snoop" into private affairs. The precinct captain is a prototype of the "local" influential.

Interpersonal influence stemming from specialized expertness typically involves some social distance between the advice-giver and the advice-seeker, whereas influence stemming from sympathetic understanding typically entails close personal relations. The first is the pattern of the cosmopolitan influential; the second, of the local influential. Thus, the operation of these patterns of influence gives a clue to the distinctive orientations of the two types of influential.

II COMMUNITY IN THE MODERN CITY

This section's first three articles relate to community building, providing the reader with tangible steps to making urban communities more livable. Drayton (1996) deals with the special appeal of planting and enjoying gardens in the urban environment. Marcus (2001) pushes the idea on to shared outdoor spaces in the model of "Smart Growth." Both these articles show how to arrange space to bring neighbors together while preserving privacy. Steuteville (2000) shows how the architectural approach found in the "New Urbanism" makes neighborhood life pleasant with many fine ramifications.

Now we turn to several articles that are more quantitative. Academicians often remark on how happy, and nearly proud, people are to state their lack of understanding and appreciation for mathematics. But all of us agree that weighty statistical tables are forbidding. Thus I have deleted almost all of the tables that have the more difficult statistics. These are the parametric statistics such as regression tables. These tables hold a wealth of information, but to a larger degree the authors' discussions of the findings make up for the omissions. That the articles are here in this reader means that the statistical treatments are sound and valuable.

Bridger and Luloff (2001) note that devolution is a major direction in the world today. The argument that issues must be resolved at the largest level possible is not popular these days. The American politician is more likely to say that problems need to be resolved at the most immediate, small-scale level possible. When people use their political capital to solve problems and improve their communities they are building a base that can be sustained the way that the residents prefer. Immigrant communities are famous for starting up neighborhoods (usually "invading" them) using incredible social capital for the betterment of their neighborhoods as discussed here by Raijman and Tienda (2001). African Americans and other minority groups frequently use community development corporations to foster and sustain community initiatives.

Community participation is the subject of some community books that have reached the popular imagination through the literary market. Wuthnow's (1998) chapter from his book, Loose Connections, *says that, "Porous institutions favor civic activities that are more loosely connected" (p. 203, before our selection). What he means here holds promise for a society that no longer has a strong backbone of fraternal "do-good" associations. Lemann's (1996) article is a book review that, as with all of his works, holds more than the basic stuff. What does it mean that we are "kicking in groups," instead of "bowling alone?" Is it true that civic engagement is drifting away, and why are people so prone to agree that it is?*

The story can be unfortunate though as in the case of isolates. People cut off from valuable community support are liable to make unfortunate choices as Sucoff and Upchurch (1998) discuss. In particular Sucoff and Upchurch want to find out if race or income status is more important in explaining high levels of teenage childbearing. Even more particularly, what income levels among blacks are helped the most by living in predominantly white middle-income neighborhoods? Rankin and Quane (2000) discuss how African Americans in poverty neighborhoods are the most liable to live in isolation from valuable social capital. In these unfortunate neighborhoods, family and financial problems are entwined with crime in complex ways that Small and Newman (2001) review.

Communities can be the sites of valuable actions to improve people's lives as found by Mesch and Schwirian (2000). Where there is a decent degree of economic stability people are more likely to be willing to work together, especially if the neighborhood is threatened by environmental or other problems. Etzioni has written extensively on the communitarian perspective arguing that "authentic communities" can meet both individual and collective needs. He argues that community action can be institutionalized and become the main level at which the collective good is sought.

A.
Community Building

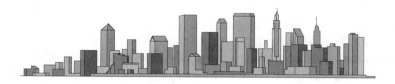

SECRET GARDENS

William Drayton

Everyone bemoans the loss of community in our lives, but a powerful tool for rebuilding it has been overlooked: the creation of private gardens that unify the interiors of city blocks. These are hidden places, but they are also communal—secret squares of green and light and flowers tucked into the hearts of city blocks, invisible to all but those whose back doors open onto the glory of a one-block commons.

One of the earliest and most famous of these secret gardens is the Macdougal-Sullivan Gardens Historic District, in New York City's Greenwich Village. This gorgeous park, hidden from passersby, has for seven decades molded a community spirit in its neighborhood that, if it were duplicated around the country, would make city living far more attractive and also safer. Delicious as it is, however, the garden has had only a few imitators in Manhattan—chiefly the much smaller Bleecker Street Gardens, at Eleventh Street, and the famed Turtle Bay Gardens. For children the Macdougal-Sullivan garden—which measures about forty by

200 feet and occupies the full interior of a city block—is a private playground; for parents it is a godsend; for busy professionals it is a civilized bit of Europe in the concrete jungle. Owners of the twenty-one town-houses surrounding the garden retain small private areas that they can plant as they choose, but fences higher than four and a half feet are prohibited. The private greens merge visually with the common green, a rectangle of grass shaded by tall trees. At one end is a children's play area and a basketball court, at the other end a garden planted with flowers. Here the residents have children's birthday parties, charity cocktail parties, egg hunts, trick-or-treating, visits from Santa (who travels over the garden in a sleigh drawn along a wire, showering candy onto squealing children below), caroling, and ice skating when they decide to flood the green.

Given the obvious attractiveness of these secret gardens, why aren't cities across America filled with blocks of row houses built around a verdant heart? The explanation lies in a quirk of the English property laws that the early Colonists brought with them. These laws were the result of a long struggle by the English to free the country of the tangle of overlapping claims that made it impossible for most property to change hands in the medieval period. American property laws were from the start stacked firmly against multiple claims that might inhibit any property's sale or development.

The political leader and Bank of New York director Nicholas Low bought the Macdougal-Sullivan property in 1796. His heirs built its fashionable Greek Revival townhouses beginning in 1844. Their heirs, rather than demolishing the houses to build tenements, enjoyed the rents and let the properties deteriorate.

The garden was created by one man, William Sloane Coffin, a New York businessman and the heir to W. & J. Sloane & Co., the home-furnishings business, who was disturbed by the decline and by the flight of the middle class from New York. Coffin believed that providing attractive, affordable housing to the middle class through the renovation of old buildings was a solution. He wanted to give homes to "writers, businessmen, artists, actors, and musicians." Coffin's real-estate company, Hearth and Home, bought the block in 1920 from Low's heirs and joined its back yards into one communal garden. Four years later the houses were made available for purchase by the people who were renting them.

Alden Cohen, one resident, told *The New York Times* in 1974 that because it belonged to the community, the garden taught many lessons in cooperation. This spirit began as an "economic necessity," she recalled. "No one had very much money." Residents had to agree on how to plant the garden (a committee still decides each spring, and everyone turns out on Digging Day to touch up paint and to plant flowers and grass). They also had to decide such issues as whether to allow touch football

and whether to give small children bicycle rights. Mothers grew close as their children played together. There have been lapses in neighborliness; once a kid threw a rock through the window of fellow resident Bob Dylan's house and caught hell; once an owner tried to build a wall. However, in general the communal feeling is so strong that sociologists have descended to measure it. The garden's merits are now so clear that houses abutting it sell for several million dollars.

Turtle Bay Gardens, created around the time of Macdougal-Sullivan, is a fancier, Italianate garden with a central fountain, cool shade, and a tree celebrated by E. B. White. Nora Ephron grew up on Turtle Bay and received visits through the garden from Katharine Hepburn. Turtle Bay, between Forty-eighth and Forty-ninth Streets and Second and Third Avenues, was the creation of a Mrs. Walton Martin, who bought the surrounding twenty houses in 1919 and 1920. She altered each one so that all the living rooms faced the garden, tore down fences that separated back yards, and filled in swampy areas for a plan based on group housing she had seen in Italy and France. Rare trees were planted and a central path was set down between low garden walls. Homeowners voluntarily agree to submit to some control over both the houses' exteriors and the upkeep of private terraces; the original covenant stipulates that no fences be built in the rear, no laundry lines or garbage cans be visible, and no building be used as a boardinghouse. Today Turtle Bay is one of New York's most sought after addresses.

Despite the enormous success of these pioneering gardens on every level from human to financial, they haven't multiplied. It is hopelessly expensive to buy twenty houses in a city block in order to tear down their backyard fences. What should be an essential part of cities' ability to compete with the suburbs never came to be. But an urban paradise is surprisingly feasible. All that is required is a modest and relatively simple change in property law. In cities such as Boston, San Francisco, Baltimore, Washington, Chicago, and even Los Angeles thousands of blocks with hollow centers could renew themselves—and in the process strengthen their surrounding neighborhoods. The magnitude of the opportunity is startling, because the housing codes in most cities have long required that the rear walls of homes be set back from the center of their blocks. The resulting hollows make up, in fact, the largest available open space in our cities. Robert Wagner Jr., at one time the chairman of the New York City Planning Commission, estimated in the early eighties that up to three fifths of Manhattan's city blocks (there are approximately 3,200) could have central gardens.

New York's co-op law provides the key. It stipulates that if 51 percent of the tenants in a building that is being transformed from a rental into a cooperative agree to buy their apartments, the minority can be forced to buy or leave. Modern law favors such conversions, even if they create complex patterns of shared ownership, because they advance a number of public goals—including better building maintenance and more homeownership.

The same principle could easily extend to creating co-op gardens. New legislation could make it easy for a majority of a block's owners to negotiate a communal open space. Such an agreement would increase both the value of their property and the quality of their life. The helter-skelter back yards that now divide neighbors would become a crime-stopping, neighborhood-creating common. The new laws could also reward real-estate agents and community organizers with a piece of the action. Thus motivated, these groups would learn how to negotiate attractive designs, speedily resolve problems, ensure that minority rights are protected, and, ultimately, win the required majority support of homeowners.

Once a garden was launched, its beauty and the sense of community it fostered would work their magic. Americans' deep-rooted love of voluntary associations—every bit as distinctive as their individualism—would manifest itself, and everything from new friendships among children to new neighborhood customs to the sharing of names of plumbers and electricians would follow. Disputes could be handled as they are in apartment co-ops—by voting.

Municipal legislatures would have to decide how to balance what a majority of neighbors could mandate for their block and what safeguards were necessary to protect the minority. They might also want to experiment with added incentives—for example, providing reserved on-street parking for residents who give up back-yard garages for the sake of a block garden.

In time, as urban gardens became widespread, the idea could easily be applied to other settings. Owners of lakefront property, for example, could use similar legislation to create or preserve common waterfront access and a green strip. As the world becomes more crowded, people must learn to share limited resources intelligently. Modernizing property laws to enable urban residents to create their own magical gardens would strengthen cities, limit sprawl, and help build communities in a too-divided world.

THE NEIGHBORHOOD APPROACH TO BUILDING COMMUNITY: A DIFFERENT PERSPECTIVE ON SMART GROWTH

Clare Cooper Marcus

"Build Strong Communities" is one of 10 Principles For Smart Growth adopted by the League of California Cities in 2000. Striving for a sense of community is—like motherhood and apple pie—something that few would disagree with, yet just how to bring it about is less clear. One approach is through design—encouraging neighborhood and site layouts that foster safe children's play, casual meetings between neighbors, and feelings of security and identity, thereby sowing the seeds of a strong sense of community.

A basic principle of designing for a strong sense of community is as follows: Residents will tend to casually meet, recognize each other and identify with a group when that group has access to a portion of the physical environment that is walkable and safe, and for which the group feels some sense of responsibility. These criteria are met when residences are clustered around some form of shared outdoor space, whether this be predominantly hard-surfaced (for example, a low-traffic street or cul-de-sac) or predominantly landscaped (for example, the green space in the center of a medium-density housing scheme).

The key issue here is that neighbors have access to shared outdoor space that is neither private (home and yard) nor completely public (through street, public park). Studies of three California housing schemes—each incorporating shared outdoor space—illustrate the significance of this environment.

SHARED SPACE IN SAN FRANCISCO

St. Francis Square is a 299-unit middle-income co-op in San Francisco, completed in 1964. In response to a challenge to create a safe, green, quiet community that would provide an option for middle-income families who wanted to raise their children in the city, the designers created a pedestrian-oriented site plan with parking on the periphery of the three-block site, and three-story apartment buildings facing inwards onto three landscaped courtyards. These courtyards, each serving 100 households, became the shared outdoor space of the development and were critical to the strong sense of community that quickly developed at St. Francis Square and has been characteristic of the development ever since.

The shared outdoor space, owned and maintained by the co-op, is critical to the community in a number of ways. It provides a green, quiet outlook with trees screening the view of nearby apartments, thereby reducing perceived density. It provides an attractive, safe landscape for children's play within sight and calling distance of home. Sitting outside with a small child, walking home from one of the three shared laundries or from a parked vehicle, provides opportunities for adult residents to frequently see each other and stop for a chat. The courtyards at St. Francis Square became, in effect, the family backyard writ large. If these spaces had been the equivalent of a public park, accessible to all, it is very unlikely that they could have supported the strong sense of community that exists at St. Francis Square. Parents would not allow their children to play outside alone, and residents would be less likely to help maintain the space, challenge a stranger, or come out to help a neighbor in need. Such is the success of St. Francis Square that it has served as a model for many comparable schemes in San Francisco and elsewhere, and there is a constant waiting list of people wanting to move in.

CREATING COMMUNITY IN DAVIS

Village Homes is a 240-unit suburban neighborhood on the west side of Davis, California. At the core of Village Homes' success, both aesthetically and socially, is the use of shared outdoor space as the core structure of the neighborhood's design. This space consists of culs-de-sac access and a central common green. The long, narrow, tree-shaded dead-end streets keep the neighborhood cooler in summer, save money on infrastructure, eliminate through traffic, and create quiet and safe spaces for children to play and neighbors to meet. An extensive pedestrian green at the heart of the neighborhood includes spaces for ball games and picnics, community-owned gardens, a vineyard and orchard, and drainage swales taking the place of storm sewers, reducing summer irrigation costs by one third and providing environments for wildlife and children's exploratory play.

This attractive environment, though accessible to outsiders bicycling and walking through, is definitely *not* a public park. Bounded by the inward-facing residences at Village Homes, it provides a green heart to the neighborhood, a safe and interesting area for children's play and adult exercise, and an environment that provides Village Homes with a strong sense of identity lacking in nearby grid-pattern subdivisions.

A SAFE ENVIRONMENT FOR CHILDREN IN PETALUMA

Cherry Hill is a 29-unit development of townhouses for low- and moderate-income families with children in Petaluma, California. A major goal of the site plan was to provide a safe environment for the many children expected to live there and to support a sense of community among the residents. A narrow (22-foot) access road creates a one-way loop around a central green. Off this loop road are four paved courtyards permitting cars to drive up to each house and creating safe hard-surface play areas. Cars and pedestrians coexist safely without sidewalks since cars drive very slowly as they enter the development, their speed regulated by the narrow roadway, speed bumps, and the dead-end nature of the loop-plus-courtyards. Unlike the standard grid, no one enters Cherry Hill except residents or their visitors.

A survey of the residents and observation of outdoor spaces indicate that the dead-end cul-de-sac site plan has been highly successful in facilitating a strong sense of community and providing for children's play. Virtually the only cars entering the site are those of residents, and it is *their* children who are at play, so they are extra careful. It seems reasonable to assume that were this a standard grid pattern neighborhood with through traffic and no shared outdoor space, there would be less of a sense of community and much less outdoor play.

CHARACTERISTICS OF SUCCESSFUL SHARED OUTDOOR SPACE

These three examples suggest that shared outdoor space can be a highly significant component of the neighborhood environment, facilitating a sense of community, if it meets the following criteria:

- It is bounded by the dwellings it serves and is clearly not a public park;
- Entry points into this space from a public street or sidewalk are designed so that it is clear that one is entering a setting which is not public space;
- Its dimensions and the height-to-width ratio of buildings to outdoor space create a human-scaled setting;
- There are clear boundaries and easy access between what is private (dwelling unit, patio, yard) and what is shared; and
- Care and budget is focused on the layout, circulation patterns, planting plan, furnishings, lighting, etc., of the shared outdoor space so that it is attractive and usable, not just a featureless area of grass. In particular, the design needs to focus on children (play equipment, paths for wheeled vehicles, areas for exploratory play, etc.) since research shows that children will comprise more than 80 percent of the users of such spaces if they are designed with the above criteria in mind.

These details are critical. It was the *lack* of many or all of these characteristics that rendered the shared outdoor space of many postwar public housing projects, and many suburban planned unit developments of the 1960s, nonfunctional. Unfortunately, design critics observing that such spaces often became poorly maintained no-man's lands, wrongly assumed that they could never work. There is ample evidence that, appropriately designed, not only do they *work,* but they are actively sought after by people who are able to exercise choice over how they live. And many consumer-preference surveys indicate that suburban house buyers prefer houses that look onto culs-de-sac, rather than those that look onto through streets, because they are safer for children as well as potentially creating a more neighborly context for adults.

SHARED OUTDOOR SPACE AND NEW URBANISM

It is important to reconsider the communities discussed here in view of the current New Urbanist (NU) debate regarding suburban design and public housing redesign. NU principles decry the use of culs-de-sac, favor a return to the grid and emphasize public parks bounded by through streets. While public parks are definitely important in neighborhood design, the social significance of shared outdoor space that is *not* fully public seems to have been overlooked. In NU literature, the only reference to space shared by a group (and not fully public) is the alley, a design device to ensure that curb cuts and garages do not mar the streetscape and that houses can be sited closer together. While these are laudable goals, it seems unlikely that a sense of local identity is facilitated as much by these utilitarian passageways as it is by the provision of common greens bounded by the units they serve. There is no compelling evidence that through streets and large public parks foster a sense of community.

Even more disturbing is the assertion by some NU developers that the ubiquitous alleys are "places for children to play." It doesn't take much imagination to suggest that the play experience (and possibly subsequent environmental values) of children offered play space that doubles as a setting for cars, trash cans, recycling bins and power lines will be vastly different from that of children, such as those at Village Homes, for example, growing up amid creeks, fruit trees, wildlife and gardens. NU-inspired building codes are increasingly being adopted and while many of their goals and principles are undoubtedly positive, the types of site plans that have been unarguably successful, such as those at St. Francis Square, Village Homes and Cherry Hill, are being overlooked, despite the fact that they have certain elements in common with the NU approach, such as the use of front porches and home designs de-emphasizing a dominant garage.

The category of outdoor space that has been defined here as "shared outdoor space" is of great significance in providing a setting for casual social interaction; for strengthening social networks and a sense of community; for children's play; and for enhancing a sense of responsibility and safety in the neighborhood. These findings are particularly pertinent in lower-income settings where residents may not be able to sustain wider social networks or take their children to areas of public recreation.

Let us draw on what we know; what residents who use and value such space have to tell us; and provide shared outdoor settings as green oases in today's newly built and redesigned urban and suburban neighborhoods as we strive towards an era of Smart Growth in California.

REFERENCES

American LIVES Inc. 1995 New Urbanism Study. San Francisco: American LIVES Inc. February 1996.

CoHousing: The journal of the cohousing network. Vol. 13, No. 1. Summer 2000.

Alice Coleman. *Utopia on trial: Vision and reality in planned housing.* London: H. Shipman. 1985.

Cooper Marcus, Clare. Architecture and a Sense of Community: The case of cohousing." Unpublished manuscript, Berkeley, Calif. 1992.

————. St. Francis Square: Attitudes of its residents. *AIA Journal.* December 1971.

————. *Resident attitudes towards the environment at St. Francis Square, San Francisco: A summary of the initial findings.* Institute of Urban and Regional Development, University of California, Working Paper No. 126. July 1970.

Cooper Marcus, Clare, and Wendy Sarkissian. *Housing as if people mattered: Site design guidelines for medium-density family housing.* Berkeley, Calif.: University of California. 1986.

Corbett, Judy, and Michael Corbett. *Designing sustainable communities: Learning from Village Homes.* Washington, D.C.: Island Press. 2000.

Duany, Andres, Elizabeth Plater-Zyberk, and Jeff Speck. *Suburban nation: The rise of sprawl and the decline of the American Dream.* New York: North Point Press. 2000.

Fulton, William. *The new urbanism: Hope or hype for American communities?* Cambridge, Mass.: Lincoln Institute of Land Policy. 1996.

Gehl, Jan. *Life between buildings: Using public space.* New York: Van Nostrand Reinhold. 1987.

Postoccupancy evaluation of Cherry Hill, Petaluma, CA. Berkeley, Calif.: unpublished. 1993.

The promise of New Urbanism. *Places.* Vol. 13, No.2. Spring 2000.

For more information on shared outdoor space as here defined, please see www.communitygreens.org; or contact Rob Inerfeld, Director, Community Greens: Shared Parks in Urban Blocks at rob@communitygreens.org.

THE NEW URBANISM: AN ALTERNATIVE TO MODERN, AUTOMOBILE-ORIENTED PLANNING AND DEVELOPMENT

Robert Steuteville

Through the first quarter of this century, the United States was developed in the form of compact, mixed-use neighborhoods. The pattern began to change with the emergence of modern architecture and zoning and ascension of the automobile. After World War II, a new system of development was implemented nationwide, replacing neighborhoods with a rigorous separation of uses that has become known as conventional suburban development (CSD), or sprawl. The majority of US citizens now live in suburban communities built in the last 50 years.

Although CSD has been popular, it carries a significant price. Lacking a town center or pedestrian scale, CSD spreads out to consume large areas of countryside even as population grows relatively slowly. Automobile use per capita has soared, because a motor vehicle is required for nearly all human transportation.

Those who cannot drive are severely hampered in their mobility. The working poor living in suburbia spend a large portion of their incomes on cars. Meanwhile, the American landscape where most people live and work is dominated by strip malls, auto-oriented civic and commercial buildings, and subdivisions without individuality or character.

The New Urbanism is a reaction to sprawl. A growing movement of architects, planners and developers, the New Urbanism is based on the belief that a return to traditional neighborhood patterns is essential to restoring functional, sustainable communities. Still in its infancy, the trend is beginning to have an impact.

More than 300 new towns, villages and neighborhoods are planned or under construction in the US, using principles of the New Urbanism. Additionally, more than 100 small-scale new urbanist "infill" projects are restoring the urban fabric of cities and towns by reestablishing walkable streets and blocks.

On the regional scale, the New Urbanism has growing influence on how and where metropolitan regions choose to grow. At least 14 large-scale planning initiatives are based on the principles of linking transportation and land-use policies and using the neighborhood as the fundamental building block of a region.

In Maryland and several other states, new urbanist principles are an integral part of smart growth legislation.

Moreover, the New Urbanism is beginning to have widespread impact on conventional development. Just as Starbucks raised the quality of coffee in competing restaurants and cafes, mainstream developers are adopting new urbanist design elements such as garages in the rear of homes, neighborhood greens and mixed-use town centers. Projects which adopt some principles of New Urbanism but remain largely conventional in design are known as hybrids.

The New Urbanism trend goes by other names, including neotraditional design, transit-oriented development, and traditional neighborhood development. Borrowing from urban design concepts throughout history, the New Urbanism does not merely replicate old communities. New houses within neighborhoods, for example, must provide modern living spaces and amenities that consumers demand (and that competing suburban tract homes offer). Stores and businesses must have adequate parking and modern floor plans. The New Urbanism offers parking on the street and to the side and rear of shops and workplaces.

With proper design, large office, light industrial and even "big box" retail buildings can be accommodated in a walkable new urbanist neighborhood.

Another difference between old and new urbanism is the street grid. Historic cities and towns in the US employ a grid that is relentlessly regular. New urbanists generally use a "modified" grid, with "T" intersections and street deflections, to calm traffic and increase visual interest.

That blending of old and new is the basis of the term neotraditional, and represents what is new about the New Urbanism. Successful New Urbanism performs a difficult balancing act by maintaining the integrity of a walkable, human-scale neighborhood while offering the modern residential and commercial "product" to compete with CSD. The difficulty of this balancing act is one reason why many developers choose to build hybrids, instead of adopting all of the principles of the New Urbanism. Some new urbanists think that hybrids pose a serious threat to the movement, because they usually borrow the label and language of the New Urbanism. Other new urbanists believe that hybrids represent a positive step forward from CSD.

PRINCIPLES OF THE NEW URBANISM

The heart of the New Urbanism is in the design of neighborhoods, and there is no clearer description than the 13 points developed by town planners Andres Duany and Elizabeth Plater-Zyberk. An authentic neighborhood contains most of these elements:

1. The neighborhood has a discernible center. This is often a square of a green, and sometimes a busy or memorable street corner. A transit stop would be located at this center.

2. Most of the dwellings are within a five-minute walk of the center, an average of roughly 2,000 feet.

3. There is a variety of dwelling types—usually houses, rowhouses and apartments—so that younger and older people, singles and families, the poor and the wealthy may find places to live.

4. There are shops and offices at the edge of the neighborhood, of sufficiently varied types to supply the weekly needs of a household.

5. A small ancillary building is permitted within the backyard of each house. It may be used as a rental unit or place to work (e.g. office or craft workshop).

6. An elementary school is close enough so that most children can walk from their home.

7. There are small playgrounds near every dwelling—not more than a tenth of a mile away.

8. Streets within the neighborhood are a connected network, which disperses traffic by providing a variety of pedestrian and vehicular routes to any destination.

9. The streets are relatively narrow and shaded by rows of trees. This slows traffic, creating an environment suitable for pedestrians and bicycles.

10. Buildings in the neighborhood center are placed close to the street, creating a well-defined outdoor room.

11. Parking lots and garage doors rarely front the street. Parking is relegated to the rear of buildings, usually accessed by alleys.

12. Certain prominent sites at the termination of street vistas or in the neighborhood center are reserved for civic buildings. These

provide sites for community meetings, education, religion or cultural activities.

13. The neighborhood is organized to be self-governing. A formal association debates and decides matters of maintenance, security and physical change. Taxation is the responsibility of the larger community.

New Urbanist Prototypes

Seaside, Florida, the first new urbanist town, began development in 1981 on 80 acres of Panhandle coastline. Seaside appeared on the cover of the Atlantic Monthly in 1988 when only a few streets were completed, and it since became internationally famous for its architecture, and the quality of its streets and public spaces. Seaside proved that developments that function like traditional towns could be built in the postmodern era. Lots began selling for $15,000 in the early 1980s and, slightly over a decade later, the last lots sold for close to $200,000. The town is now a tourist mecca.

Seaside's influence has less to do with its economic success than a certain magic and dynamism related to its physical form. Many developers have visited Seaside and gone away determined to build something similar.

Since Seaside gained recognition, other neotraditional towns have been designed and substantially built—including Haile Village Center in Gainesville, Florida; Harbor Town in Memphis, Tennessee; Kentlands in Gaithersburg, Maryland; and Orenco Station in Hillsboro, Oregon.

Designers also are using the principles of the New Urbanism to revitalize cities and towns.

The US Department of Housing and Urban Development (HUD) adopted the principles of the New Urbanism in its multibillion dollar program to rebuild public housing projects nationwide. New urbanist projects built in historic cities and towns includes Crawford Square in Pittsburgh, Pleasant View Gardens in Baltimore, Park Du Valle in Louisville, and the downtown of Port Royal, South Carolina.

Meanwhile, leaders in this design trend came together in 1993 to form the Congress for the New Urbanism (CNU), based in San Francisco. The founders are Andres Duany, Elizabeth Plater-Zyberk, Peter Calthorpe, Daniel Solomon, Stefanos Polyzoides, and Elizabeth Moule, all practicing architects and town planners. CNU since has growth to more than 2,000 members and is now the leading international organization promoting new urbanist community design principles.

Disney Builds a Town

In June of 1996, Disney unveiled its town of Celebration, near Orlando, Florida, and it has since eclipsed Seaside as the best-known new urbanist community. Celebration is big—about 5,000 acres, and will eventually have 20,000 residents. Half of the land will remain open space.

In some respects, New Urbanism and Disney have been uncomfortable bedfellows. While using designers and principles closely associated with the New Urbanism, Disney has shunned the label, preferring to call Celebration simply a "town." Meanwhile, the movement has benefited from all of Celebration's publicity and its aesthetic and functional success—but not without a price. Disney has come under attack for what some perceive as heavy-handed rules and management. For those who would attack New Urbanism as insipid nostalgia, Disney is a fat target.

However, Celebration's community design serves most residents well. "The entire focus of our lives has changed," says homeowner Ray Chiaramonte. "Instead of doing everything some place other than close to home, we now can eat, do errands, celebrate special occasions and just hang out near our own home. The changes are most dramatic for our children, who now have a freedom they never had in our old neighborhood."

In the book Edge City, author Joel Garreau wrote that Americans have not built "a single old-style downtown from raw dirt in 75 years." Celebration may be the first real estate project to break that trend, opening its substantially built downtown in October, 1996. Other projects like Seaside, Haile Village Center, Harbor Town, and Redmond Town Center are following suit.

But the new urbanists still have plenty to prove. They must design and build viable retail centers to compete with CSD nationwide—not just in a few projects. They must capture a broad portion of the residential market. New urbanist developers must find ways to offer homes at reasonable prices. New urbanists also must prove, over time, that their ideas are superior for both revitalizing old cities and towns and building new communities.

If they can accomplish those goals—and early projects offer hope that they can—the New Urbanism is poised to become the dominant real estate and planning trend of the next century.

BUILDING THE SUSTAINABLE COMMUNITY: IS SOCIAL CAPITAL THE ANSWER?

Jeffrey C. Bridger
A. E. Luloff

With the emergence of sustainability as the central force behind many new efforts in community development, attention has focused on building the local capacity to create more environmentally friendly and socially equitable places to live. In the course of this search, scholars and policymakers have increasingly embraced the idea that this process depends on increasing a community's available stock of social capital (Coleman 1988, 1990; Putnam 1993; Flora 1998). Unfortunately, the critical linkage between sustainable community development and social capital remains largely unexamined; it is simply assumed that building social capital will enhance efforts to create sustainable communities.

The ensuing discussion examines this assumption in light of what we view as the most important conceptual issues surrounding the relationship between social capital and sustainable community development. To begin, we consider the renewed interest in the local community. This provides a basis for situating the larger discussion. Following this, we turn to the issue of sustainable community development, describe its relationship to the revival of interest in community, define it, and discuss some of the most serious difficulties associated with developing sustainable communities. This leads to a discussion of social capital and the problems involved in trying to link sustainable community development and social capital. The paper concludes with some suggestions for future research.

Sociological Inquiry. Vol. 71, No. 4, Fall 2001, 458–72 © 2001 by the University of Texas Press, P.O. Box 7819, Austin, TX 78713-7819

THE RESURGENCE OF INTEREST IN THE COMMUNITY

After several decades of neglect by academics and policymakers, the local community is once again the focus of attention as an important unit of social organization and locus of action. This emphasis can be seen in a spate of recent books, with titles such as *Changing Places: Rebuilding Community in an Age of Sprawl, Going Local: Creating Self-Reliant Communities in a Global Era,* and *The New Urbanism: Toward an Architecture of Community.* It is also seen in policy recommendations and has made its way into various federal and state agency missions (e.g., USDA's National Research Initiative and the Environmental Protection Agency's new grant programs), and most prominently among the general public in the form of ballot initiatives intended to reduce sprawl and create more livable communities.

Some might argue that this shift can be explained as a manifestation of the recent political climate, especially its rhetoric of individual responsibility and devolution of responsibility to the state and local level. While this may be part of the reason, other factors are involved. First among these is the growing disenchantment and disaffection, on both the right and the left, with the government's typically large-scale, bureaucratic solutions to the nation's most intractable social, environmental, and economic problems. A second, closely related, factor is the deep pessimism about both the national and global political culture—a pessimism that also ignores ideological differences. Indeed, if there is a central force behind the widespread apathy toward national elections it is the pervasive sense that politics at this level is so corrupted by money and special interests that meaningful reform is virtually impossible. Thus, the call for renewal of democratic institutions at the grassroots is a natural and understandable response to this feeling of hopelessness.

Finally, it is arguable that the renewed interest in the local community is one of many, often contradictory, responses to globalization and economic restructuring. As Harvey (1997, p. 297) argues, the advances in transportation and communication that have accompanied these processes have enabled corporations to make locational decisions that were impossible a generation ago:

> When transport costs were high and communication difficult, places were protected from competition by the frictions of distance. Places could depend upon a relatively high degree of monopoly power. But diminished transport costs have made production, merchanting, marketing, and particularly finance capital much more geographically mobile than heretofore. The monopoly power inherent in place is much reduced. This allows much freer choice of location which in turn permits capitalists to take more rather than less advantage of small differences in resource qualities, quantities, costs and amenities between places. *Multinational capital, for example, has become much more sensitive to the qualities of places in its search for more profitable accumulation. (emphasis added)*

This situation has provoked conflicting reactions at the local level. On the one hand, communities find themselves in fierce competition to attract mobile capital. Standard means of industrial and commercial recruitment such as tax abatements and infrastructure improvements are increasingly being supplemented by efforts to "sell" places to potential investors

and consumers through the use of seductive imagery, the commodification of local cultural and historical traditions, and the creation of new amenities (Zukin 1991; Philo and Kearns 1993; Harvey 1997). The logic behind this strategy is not so much to highlight the features that truly distinguish between places as it is to "harness surface differences" (Philo and Kearns 1993, p. 20) that will present a standard set of attractive images to potential investors. As more and more places participate in this process, they end up creating "a kind of serial replication of homogeneity" (Boyer 1988, cited in Harvey 1997, p. 298).

On the other hand, the political and economic processes that commodify and homogenize places have provoked growing resistance and sparked attempts to construct alternative conceptions of community life.[1] In an increasingly fragmented and uncertain world, the search for a geographically based community becomes a means of exerting some control over at least a portion of one's life. It also encourages a means for locals to create an authentic setting in which to live. In our opinion, the central theme behind many of the recent attempts to recapture a sense of community is the recognition that such a task requires alternative constructions of place—symbolic, economic, and physical constructions which reduce the alienation of people from one another and from the environment.

SUSTAINABLE COMMUNITY DEVELOPMENT

Although the concept of sustainable community development is rooted, first and foremost, in the widespread recognition that human activities have placed a serious strain on the earth's carrying capacity, it can also be traced to many of the concerns discussed above. To see this, one need only look at the justifications that are offered for directing sustainability at the local level. For instance, proponents of sustainable community development argue that strategies formulated at the national or global scale tend to prevent "meaningful and concerted political action" (Yanarella and Levine 1992a, p. 764). At such macro levels, the scale of change required is so great that problems of coordination across political units are bound to be enormous (Bridger and Luloff 1999). Attempts to achieve sustainability on a grand scale also tend to be couched in the technocratic language of planning and administration, emphasizing the need for global ecological planners to work with national political elites and multinational corporations to manage environmental crises.

A major problem with such solutions is that relations of domination are left in place. Those who control the resources—and who not surprisingly are responsible for many of the decisions and actions that have caused environmental damage—are generally charged with cleaning up/mitigating their messes (Yanarella and Levine 1992a, p. 766). The result is a crisis mentality that relies on technological solutions for much larger structural problems. From this perspective, sustainable development on a global scale could actually *strengthen* the economic and social conditions which support unsustainable practices, "especially when such 'band-aid' solutions lead to situations where these deeper ecological problems fall below the threshold of public attention and the political momentum for more fundamental change is allowed to dissipate" (Yanarella and Levine 1992a, p. 766).

Alternatively, by focusing on sustainability at the local level, changes can be seen and felt more immediately. Further, discussions of a "sustainable society" or a "sustainable world" are relatively meaningless to most people since they require levels of abstraction not relevant in their daily lives. The community, in contrast, is more conceptually manageable. After all, the consequences of environmental degradation are most keenly felt and the results of intervention most noticeable in one's own backyard. Finally, sustainable community development may ultimately be the most effective means of showing the potential for long term improvement on a broader scale because it places the concept of sustainability "in a context within which it can be validated as a process" (Yanarella and Levine 1992a, p. 769). To the extent that successful intervention becomes a tangible aspect of local life, we increase the likelihood that sustainability will acquire the widespread legitimacy that has thus far proved elusive.

In most models of sustainable community development, successful intervention results from the sort of democratic participation that is not possible in top-down strategies. This reflects the fact that for sustainable community development to occur, the knowledge and efforts of local people are essential. In fact, for some proponents it is precisely this requirement which provides the mechanism for revitalizing our democratic traditions. As Potapchuk (1996, pp. 54–55) puts it,

> This "participatory democracy" becomes the central element in unleashing the power of people to control their own destiny and nurturing the citizen-to-citizen connection that helps build political consensus and will, strengthens neighborhoods, improves intergroup relations, and creates the neighborliness that helps with daily needs.

Obviously, the link between sustainable community development and the search for a more authentic existence is not stated in exactly these terms. Nevertheless, the notion that through the implementation of sustainable practices an authentic relationship to nature and an authentic sense of community will be recovered is a strong undercurrent in much of the literature (Harvey 1997). Wendell Berry probably articulates this relationship more clearly than anyone. In his view, recapturing authenticity depends upon a spiritual connection between people, other creatures, and the land. According to Berry (1993, p. 14):

> *A healthy community is a form that includes all the local things that are connected by the larger, ultimately mysterious form of the Creation. In speaking of community, then, we are speaking of a complex connection not only among human beings or between humans and their homeland but also between the human economy and nature, between forest or prairie and field or orchard, and between troublesome creatures and pleasant ones. All neighbors are included.*

As the preceding discussion illustrates, sustainable community development is hardly a straightforward concept. To develop a more precise definition, it is helpful to begin with the well-known statement of the 1987 World Commission on Environment and Development (also called the Brundtland Commission), which defines sustainable development as "development which meets the needs of the present without compromising the ability of future generations to meet their own needs" (World Commission on Environment and Development 1987, p. 43). Obviously, though, sustainable community development involves a geographic reduction in scope. Broadly speaking, most definitions of sustainable community development stress the importance of striking a balance between environmental concerns and development objectives while simultaneously enhancing local social relationships.

In more specific terms, the ideal typical sustainable community can be defined along five interrelated dimensions (Bridger and Luloff 1999). First, as is the case with standard economic development strategies, there is an emphasis on increasing local economic diversity. Second, virtually all definitions stress the importance of self-reliance, especially economic

self-reliance. This is not to be confused with economic self-sufficiency. Self-reliance entails the creation of local markets, local production and processing of previously imported goods, greater cooperation among local economic entities, and the like. Self-reliant communities would still be linked to larger economic structures, but they would have vibrant local economies that would better protect them from the whims of capital than is currently the case. The third dimension centers around a reduction in energy use coupled to the careful management and recycling of waste products. Ideally, this means that the use of energy and material is in balance with the local ecosystem's ability to absorb waste. The fourth dimension focuses on the protection and enhancement of biological and environmental diversity and wise stewardship of natural resources. Sustainable communities provide a balance between human needs and activities and those of other life forms. Finally, sustainable communities are committed to social justice. Sustainable communities provide for the housing and employment needs of all residents, and they do so without the kind of class and race-based spatial separation that is typical of many localities. As a result, they also ensure equality of access to public services. And perhaps most important, sustainable communities strive to create an empowered citizenry that can effectively participate in local decision-making (Young 1990, p. 251).

Exactly how communities can succeed in all five dimensions is not clear, although it appears that the preferred solution lies in greater local control over a wider range of decisions. The literature is replete with phrases like "devolution of decision-making to the local level" (Gibbs 1994, pp. 106–7), "increased community self-reliance" (Rees and Roseland 1991, p. 17), and "localizing economic production and commerce" (Yanarella and Levine 1992b, p. 305). This language suggests a very active conception of community—one in which communities possess a relatively complete table of social organization and the ability to mobilize for collective, long-term action.

This latter assumption is problematic in several respects. For one thing, studies of community activeness routinely document serious gaps in local social organization and a dearth of locality-oriented actions—especially in rural areas (Wilkinson 1991). Communities do act, but the available evidence suggests that they typically do so in reaction to some perceived crisis (Tilly 1973). Even in communities that can be characterized as active, there is often very little coordination among actors and actions; different interest groups pursue specific objectives largely in isolation from one another (Bridger 1992). Second, the available evidence concerning local economic development—an aspect of community life that occupies a central role in strategies designed to create sustainable communities—suggests that leadership and participation are largely limited to local elites whose interest in development often has much more to do with private gain than community well-being (Molotch 1976; Logan and Molotch 1987; Harvey 1997). A third impediment to local action, as Roland Warren (1972) and others (Berry 1993; Sachs 1995) argue, stems from the increasing reliance on extra-local institutions and sources of income. Decisions and policies may conform in some respects to local needs and wishes, but they are frequently formulated in distant centers with little regard for local social, economic, or environmental consequences. The dependency and consequent vulnerability fostered by this situation leave little room for local maneuvering. Finally, many of the actions that are central to sustainable community development are very different from those found in other kinds of community development initiatives. Here we refer to actions that are intended to protect environmental amenities, balance economic development interests with environmental protection, or manage commonly held natural resources. What makes these actions so different from typical community development activities, such as building a playground or raising funds for a community center, is that they either involve public goods or pit private property rights against the interests of the larger community. In such cases, there will inevitably be conflicts between the common good and what is in the short term best interests of the individual. This is a substantial barrier to successful action. While it is ultimately in everyone's long-term best interest to have clean air, clean water, and a healthy stock of natural resources, it is perfectly rational, at least in the short run, for individuals to become free riders and reap the benefits of a healthier environment without bearing the costs. And, in many, if not most, instances, it is rational to pursue personal profit at the expense of the larger community. In either case, it is difficult to move toward sustainability.

SOCIAL CAPITAL AND SUSTAINABLE COMMUNITY DEVELOPMENT: CONCEPTUAL ISSUES

Taken together, these are powerful arguments that call into question the prospects for meaningful grass-roots action. It is fortunate, therefore, that increased attention is being given to this topic. Scholars from a variety of disciplines are studying the conditions necessary for increased democratic participation and effective decision-making at the local level. One result of this search has been the emergence of a convergence of interest in social capital.

Although the concept of social capital has been around since at least the early 1960s, when Jane Jacobs used the term in her classic work, *The Death and Life of Great American Cities,* it did not gain widespread currency until recently, with the publication of two influential books: *Making Democracy Work* by Robert Putnam and *Trust* by Francis Fukuyama.

What struck reviewers of these books was that although they were written from different ends of the ideological spectrum (Putnam being more liberal and Fukuyama more conservative) they reached the same basic conclusion: successful cooperation for long-term mutual benefit depends on the cultivation of social capital.

The line of reasoning behind this argument is probably most clearly articulated by Putnam, who draws heavily on James Coleman's (1988; 1990) writings on social capital. Putnam conducted a study of twenty regional Italian governments that were created in 1970. The question that motivated his research was—why is it that in some of these regions people were better able to cooperate for the common good? Or, to put things in more specific terms: What factors are associated with successful collective action in cases where the short-term individual benefits are not clear to all participants? In most such instances, even if all parties are predisposed to cooperate, cooperation is nevertheless problematic in the absence of enforceable commitments. This problem is exacerbated by the fact that all parties face the same fundamental predicament. That is, before you are willing to participate in a collective action, you must trust the other participants. At the same time, you have to believe that the other participants trust you. Without this kind of trust between all parties, cooperation is irrational—despite the fact that without it the long-term outcome will be unsatisfactory to everyone. The tragedy of the commons is one of the best known examples of a rational failure to cooperate. In this scenario, "no herder can limit grazing by anyone else's flock. If he limits his own use of the common meadow, he alone loses. Yet unlimited grazing destroys the common resource on which the livelihood of all depends" (Putnam 1993, p. 163).

The classic solution to this problem is third party enforcement, usually by the state (Putnam 1993, p. 165). In the context of sustainable community development, the state is often invoked as the source of a solution to the inability to reach amicable agreements on such thorny issues as environmental protection vs. economic development, natural resource management, and problems associated with urban sprawl. State intervention typically takes the form of new zoning regulations, court imposed orders, the refusal to extend infrastructure improvements, and the like. Clearly, though, there are serious problems with these sorts of remedies. For one thing, state intervention is costly and the solutions tend to be unstable. State intervention can also create animosity between groups, depressing the probability of voluntary collective action in the future. Perhaps the most fundamental problem, however, is that third party enforcement "is itself a public good" (Putnam 1993, p. 165), which means that it is subject to the same dilemmas it is supposed to solve. For third party enforcement to be effective, the third party has to be trustworthy. Who ensures this? There is no guarantee that the state (local or otherwise) will not use its power to pursue agendas at odds with the public interest.

Although this is a dismal scenario, fortunately it has not been the end of the matter. Realizing that we cannot prescribe or enforce rules and laws that will guarantee cooperation for the common good, the search has turned to the forms of social organization that encourage this behavior. Social capital—which depends on such features of social organization as trust, norms, and networks—facilitates collective action (Putnam 1993). As Coleman (1988, p. 98) puts it, "Like other forms of capital, social capital is productive, making possible the achievement of certain ends that in its absence would not be possible." According to this argument, it follows that "voluntary cooperation is easier in a community that has inherited a substantial stock of social capital" (Putnam 1993, p. 176).

To gain a clearer understanding of how social capital facilitates collective action, it is useful to consider its individual components in more detail. Trust is arguably the most important feature of social capital because it increases the likelihood of cooperation, which in turn reinforces trust. Trust is based on intimate familiarity with other individuals, especially in small groups. You trust a specific person because you know her well and have first-hand evidence that she has acted honorably in the past, has made promises and kept them, and so forth. This kind of personal trust, which obviously exists in more complex settings, is not a sufficient basis for collective action; there are typically too many participants, and they simply do not know one another very well. A more impersonal form of trust, what Putnam (1993) calls social trust, is required. Social trust arises from two related sources—norms of reciprocity and networks of civic engagement.

In turn, norms of reciprocity typically take two forms—specific and generalized. Specific reciprocity involves the simultaneous exchange of items of similar or equivalent value. An example of this would be the customary exchange of Christmas gifts by co-workers. Generalized reciprocity, in contrast, involves a continuing relationship of exchange that at any particular time is probably unbalanced. What is important about this type of relationship is that there is a mutual expectation that a favor or benefit performed now will be repaid in the future. When the norm of generalized reciprocity is followed, opportunism can be more easily restrained and the potential for successful collective action enhanced. It works to reconcile self-interest and social solidarity because each act in such a system is characterized by a combination of short-term altruism and long-term self-interest. Generalized reciprocity rests on the expectation that if I help you now, you will return the favor in the future. It is argued that as a result, this combination of short-run altruism and long-term self interest makes everyone better off.

Generalized reciprocity is most likely to be found in dense networks of social exchange. In particular, it is associated with networks in which participants are of roughly equal status and power—what might be called horizontal as opposed to vertical networks. Networks of civic engagement are of central importance at the horizontal level. Groups such as the neighborhood association, the volunteer fire department, and the local legion represent fairly intense patterns of interaction. The more dense these networks, the more likely that residents will be able to cooperate for mutual benefit. The most obvious reason is that dense networks of interaction foster the development of strong norms; when people interact with one another in a variety of contexts, they tend to develop strong norms regarding behavioral expectations.

But there are other reasons as well. Repeated encounters across projects and activities decreases the probability that an individual will engage in opportunistic behavior because this would put at risk the benefits she expects to receive from other current and future transactions.

Networks of engagement also facilitate the flow of communication and provide information about the trustworthiness of people and organizations. If collective action depends in part on accurate information about the trustworthiness of potential participants, then it stands to reason that increased communication would strengthen mutual trust (or, alternatively, it would provide sound information about whom not to collaborate with). Finally, networks of engagement characterized by successful action, increase the probability of future action. This is not surprising. The community action literature has repeatedly documented that one of the best predictors of activeness is previous success (Luloff and Wilkinson 1979; Martin and Wilkinson 1984; Wilkinson 1991).

Social capital, with its emphasis on trust and cooperation, is an attractive concept. After all, it holds out the possibility of developing voluntaristic solutions to problems that have not been solved through market mechanisms, government programs or legislation. Thus it is not surprising that both policymakers and scholars have embraced the idea that sustainable communities depend upon creating a healthy stock of social capital. To date, this belief has received very little scrutiny. This is unfortunate because there are some important conceptual issues that must be resolved before we embrace policies that link sustainable community development and social capital.

First, it is important to acknowledge that social capital is rooted in rational action theory, especially Coleman's (1988, 1990) version of rational action. In this framework, people are viewed as purposive agents who make rational, deliberate choices to maximize their utility. Coleman (1988, p. 95). argues that his version of rational action theory overcomes some of the more individualistic approaches in which the actor is seen as "having goals independently arrived at, as acting independently, and as wholly self-interested." In place of these assumptions, Coleman argues, rational action must be seen in its social context. As he (1988, p. 96) puts it, "persons' actions are shaped, redirected, constrained by the social context; norms, interpersonal trust, social networks, and social organization are important in the functioning not only of society but also of the economy." Despite the inclusion of social organization, the underlying conception of the individual remains unchanged. Individuals maximize their utility by calculating the costs and benefits of pursuing alternative courses of action. In the end, as Alexander (1992, p. 208) points out, Coleman retains "the picture of discrete, separated, and independent individuals."

One of the most serious problems with maintaining this view of the individual is the difficulty it presents in accounting for social structure and collective action. In order to reconcile structure and order with independent individuals, it is necessary that individuals relinquish control over activities and resources for

conscious and calculated reasons that are in their best interests. But this still leaves open the question of how to explain the convergence between short-term self interest, long-term self interest, and long-term collective interest. Presumably this dilemma is resolved by the norm of generalized reciprocity, which reconciles individual self interest and solidarity.

When applied to sustainable community development the limits on long-term rationality make this line of reasoning problematic. If there is an indeterminate gap between some altruistic act and an expected benefit, it is not clear what would motivate an actor to behave altruistically.[2] The norm of generalized reciprocity would only seem to hold when an actor has some expectation that a favor will be repaid within the foreseeable future. In the case of sustainable community development, which is by definition a long-term process, the time frame for repayment is difficult to envision.

Ultimately, rational action theory rests on trust as the means for overcoming short-term limits on rationality. The problem here is that trust itself is the result of a rational, calculated decision. In fact, in Coleman's framework the decision to place trust in an organization or decision when one is not sure about a future payoff is analogous to the decision-making process used when placing a bet. The individual calculates the odds. If the odds favor her, then she would be rational in both trusting the other party and cooperating with it. If the odds are against her, then it would be rational not to cooperate. Coleman puts it this way: "A rational actor will place trust if the ratio of the chance of gain to the chance of loss is greater than the ratio of the amount of potential loss to the amount of potential gain."

This is not a satisfactory solution to many of the issues involved in sustainable community development. In some instances, of course, sustainable community development will involve actions that allow actors to make reasonable predictions about future payoffs.

However, there is another set of actions, including things like the voluntary abrogation of certain property rights and cooperative agreements aimed at reducing externalities associated with production and processing activities, for which future pay-offs are exceedingly difficult to calculate. These involve major concessions, and it is difficult to envision the kinds of long-term benefits that a rational individual could expect to receive which would make up for the losses incurred in the short run. Indeed, in such situations it is difficult to conceptualize how an individual would even begin to calculate odds.

A second issue that must be faced concerns the fungibility of social capital. According to Coleman (1990, p. 302), "Social capital is not completely fungible, but is fungible with respect to specific activities. A given form of social capital that is valuable in facilitating certain actions may be useless or even harmful in others. In short, social capital is not always transferable across networks and domains of action. Thus, it is more than a little misleading to talk about a community's stock of social capital as if the social capital that inheres within particular networks can simply be aggregated to the community level. Consider, for instance, the five dimensions of sustainable community development discussed earlier. In many communities there are networks composed of groups, organizations, and individuals who are active in each of these dimensions. Whether the social capital that facilitates action in one dimension is supportive of action in other dimensions is problematic. What is also problematic is the extent to which social capital cuts across these networks.

This last issue becomes particularly salient when one considers the patterns of stratification that characterize many communities. For instance, in most communities one can find organizations such as volunteer fire departments, the lions club, voluntary service groups, and so forth. Each of these organizations may be char-acterized by dense networks of social exchange, a high level of generalized reciprocity, and strong norms regulating the behavior of members. There may also be a good deal of interaction between these groups. Typically, another set of organizations can be found in the community that are thought of as being more "highbrow"—peopled by the local elite. These include groups like the Chamber of Commerce, professional associations, and the Junior League. Like their more modest counterparts, these groups may contain dense networks of association, strong norms of generalized reciprocity (and the trust associated with these), and strong inter-organizational linkages. The problem is that there tends to be relatively few linkages among elite and non-elite organizations, leading to a situation in which it is exceedingly difficult to develop the level of trust necessary for effective collaboration and successful collective action. In such situations, pockets of social capital, each isolated from one another, tend to exist.

Further, even if mechanisms to increase interaction among stratified organizations existed, it is not clear how a high level of trust would emerge, because as Coleman (1990, p. 307) acknowledges, the development of trust depends on "the actual needs that persons have for help, the existence of other sources of aid . . . and the degree of affluence." Each of these factors is powerfully affected by stratification, regardless of the extent of interaction among groups and individuals.

The problems associated with the fungibility of social capital and stratification point to a more serious gap in the linkage between social capital and sustainable community development. To the extent that social capital exists within a community, it is important that it be situated within this larger context. In our search of the literature, however, we could not find a single study in which the concept of social capital was explicitly connected to a theory of community organization. In most instances, the community seems to serve as little more than a setting or stage. It is not viewed as an important unit of social organization that affects the emergence, maintenance and transformation of social capital. Without bringing a model of community organization firmly into the analysis, creating strategies for sustainable community development on the basis of social capital remains problematic.

CONCLUSION

Despite the conceptual shortcomings identified above, the concept of social capital deserves serious attention because of the political implications associated with its growing acceptance as a solution to the many problems facing communities today. While most advocates of social capital do not argue that it is a replacement for effective public policy, the concept does lend itself to such an interpretation in the political realm—especially given the arguments which trace declines in social capital to the destruction of primordial forms of social organization and the growth of governmental aid programs (Coleman 1993). When appropriated for political purposes, it can be tempting to use this historical account as a justification for policies that focus more on removing constraints to the formation of social capital than on developing local capacity to solve local problems.

The development of effective policies to strengthen social capital is exacerbated by the fact that social capital, as both Coleman and Putnam readily note, is a public good. "As an attribute of the social structure in which a person is embedded, social capital is not the private property of any of the persons who benefit from it" (Coleman 1990, p. 315). Because of this characteristic, "social capital tends to be undervalued and undersupplied by private agents" (Putnam 1993, p. 170). In other words, while social capital benefits all individuals with a particular social structure, many of the benefits are captured by persons other than those who have worked to create it. Such people do not have an incentive to invest in it. What this means is that social capital is often created as a by-product of other actions. It arises without anyone doing anything to consciously bring it into being.

If this description is correct, it seems reasonable to argue that since private agents tend to underinvest in social capital, some form of public investment might be in order. Unfortunately, even if such public investment was possible, it is difficult to gain consensus on where such investments should be placed. That is, while there clearly is agreement that networks of civic engagement are essential, there is no agreement about the types of engagement from which social capital is most likely to emerge. In his study of regional governments in Italy, for example, Putnam correlated good government with voter turnout, newspaper readership, membership in choral societies and literary circles, Lions Clubs, and soccer clubs. Given this hodgepodge of organizations and types of engagement, it is difficult go beyond the vague recommendation that civic engagement, in general, is important.

As we search for ways to create more sustainable communities in an era of declining public resources, social capital will continue to attract attention. But before we endorse it as sound public policy, a great deal of work remains to be done in terms of developing a more precise definition of the concept, situating social capital within extant theories of community organization, constructing better measures of the concept, documenting the kinds of civic organizations and networks of engagement most likely to promote social capital, and gaining an understanding of the forms of social capital that are most important in developing sustainable communities. Without answers to these questions, policy prescriptions in which social capital plays a central role will be more firmly rooted in ideology than empirical evidence.

ENDNOTES

[1]Consider, for instance, the ballot initiatives and referendums aimed at reducing suburban sprawl and limiting growth mentioned above. These can be interpreted as attempts to use the political process to exert control over the physical and symbolic boundaries of the local community. They are, in short, efforts to establish a collective identity in the face of forces that threaten to blur local distinctions.

[2]As Portes (1988, p. 4) observes, the issue of motivation, especially the motivation of donors in "exchanges mediated by social capital," remains poorly understood and undertheorized. As he (1988, p. 4) puts it: "More complex are the motivations of donors, who are requested to make these assets available without any immediate return. Such motivations are plural and deserve analysis because they are the core processes that the concept of social capital seeks to capture."

REFERENCES

Alexander, Jeffrey C. 1992. "Shaky Foundations: The Presuppositions and Internal Contradictions of James Coleman's Foundations of Social Theory." *Theory and Society* 21(2):203–18.

Bender, Thomas. 1978. *Community and Social Change in America.* New Brunswick, NJ: Rutgers University Press.

Berry, Wendell. 1993. *Sex, Economy, Freedom & Community.* New York: Pantheon Books.

Boyer, C. 1988. "The Return of Aesthetics to Community Planning." *Society* 25(4):49–56.

Bridger, Jeffrey C. 1992. "Local Elites and Growth Promotion." Pp. 95–116 in *Research in Community Sociology, Vol. 11,* edited by Dan E. Chekki. Greenwich, CT: JAI Press.

Bridger, Jeffrey C., and A. E. Luloff. 1999. "Toward an Interactional Approach to Sustainable Community Development." *Journal of Rural Studies* 15(4):377–88.

Coleman, James S. 1993. "The Rational Reconstruction of Society." *American Sociological Review* 58(1):1–15.

———. 1990. *Foundations of Social Theory.* Cambridge, MA: The Belknap Press of Harvard University Press.

———. "Social Capital in the Creation of Human Capital." *American Journal of Sociology* 94(Supplement):S95–S119.

Flora, Jan L. 1998. "Social Capital and Communities of Place." *Rural Sociology* 63(4):481–506.

Fukuyama, Francis. 1995. *Trust: The Social Virtues and the Creation of Prosperity.* New York: The Free Press.

Gibbs, D. 1994. "Towards the Sustainable City." *Town Planning Review* 65(1):99–109.

Harvey, David. 1997. *Justice, Nature and the Geography of Difference.* Malden, MA: Blackwell Publishers.

Jacobs, Jane. 1961. *The Death and Life of Great American Cities.* New York: Random House.

Katz, Peter. 1994. *The New Urbanism: Toward an Architecture of Community.* New York: McGraw-Hill.

Logan, John R., and Harvey L. Molotch. 1987. *Urban Fortunes: The Political Economy of Place.* Berkeley: University of California Press.

Luloff, A. E., and Kenneth P. Wilkinson. 1979. "Participation in the National Flood Insurance Program: A Study of Community Activeness." *Rural Sociology* 44(1):137–52.

Martin, Kenneth E., and Kenneth P. Wilkinson. 1984. "Local Participation in the Federal Grant System: Effects of Community Action." *Rural Sociology* 49(3):374–88.

Moe, Richard, and Carter Wilkie. 1997. *Changing Places: Rebuilding Community in the Age of Sprawl.* New York: Henry Holt and Company.

Molotch, Harvey L. 1976. "The City as a Growth Machine." *American Journal of Sociology* 82(2):309–32.

Philo, Chris, and Gerry Kearns. 1993. "Culture, History, Capital: A Critical Introduction to the Selling of Places." Pp. 1–32 in *Selling Places: The City as Cultural Capital, Past and Present,* edited by Gerry Kearns and Chris Philo. New York: Pergamon Press.

Portes, Alejandro. 1988. "Social Capital: Its Origins and Applications in Modern Sociology." *Annual Review of Sociology* 24(1):1–28.

Potapchuk, William R. 1996. "Building Sustainable Community Politics: Synergizing Participatory, Institutional, and Representative Democracy." *National Civic Review* 85(3):54–59.

Putnam, Robert D. 1993. *Making Democracy Work: Civic Traditions in Modern Italy.* Princeton, NJ: The Princeton University Press.

Rees, W.E., and M. Roseland. 1991. "Sustainable Communities: Planning for the 21st Century." *Plan Canada* 31(3):15–26.

Sachs, Wolfgang. 1995. "Global Ecology and the Shadow of Development." Pp. 417–27 in *Deep Ecology for the 21st Century,* edited by George Sessions. Boston: Shambhala.

Shuman, Michael. 1998. *Going Local: Creating Self-Reliant Communities in a Global Age.* New York: The Free Press.

Tilly, Charles. 1973. "Do Communities Act?" *Sociological Inquiry* 43(3/4):209–40.

Warren, Roland I. 1972. *The Community in America, 2nd Edition.* Chicago: Rand McNally.

Wilkinson, Kenneth P. 1991. *The Community in Rural America.* Westport, CT: Greenwich Press.

World Commission on Environment and Development (WCED). 1987. *Our Common Future.* New York: Oxford University Press.

Yanarella, E. J., and R. S. Levine. 1992a. "Does Sustainable Development Lead to Sustainability?" *Futures* (October):759–74.

————. 1992b. "The Sustainable Cities Manifesto: Text, Pretext and Post-Text." *Built Environment* 18(4):301–13.

Young, Iris. 1990. *Justice and the Politics of Difference.* Princeton, NJ: The Princeton University Press.

Zukin, Sharon. 1991. *Landscapes of Power: From Detroit to Disneyworld.* Berkeley: University of California Press.

TRAINING FUNCTIONS OF ETHNIC ECONOMIES: MEXICAN ENTREPRENEURS IN CHICAGO

Rebeca Raijman
Marta Tienda

Previous research in the field of ethnic entrepreneurship has suggested that the ethnic economy functions as a "school for entrepreneurs" (Light et. al. 1994). Presumably, employment in coethnic firms promotes self-employment among coethnic employees by providing opportunities for skill acquisition and importing knowledge about what it takes to start a business (Bailey and Waldinger 1991; Portes and Bach 1985; Portes and Manning 1986; Waldinger 1985, 1986). This view assumes that ethnic economies create business opportunities for immigrant workers by mobilizing ethnic ties in pursuit of market opportunities, whether ties are spatially concentrated in ethnic enclaves or evenly distributed across space (Light and Bonacich 1988; Logan, Alba, and McNulty 1994; Waldinger 1993). However, relatively little empirical evidence has been marshaled to support these claims, dubbed the training function hypothesis. Accordingly, we evaluate the training function hypothesis by drawing on a case study of Mexican business owners in Chicago.

Our focus on Mexicans is novel. Despite the size of the Mexican foreign-born population and its high residential concentration in a few large cities (Greenwood and Tienda 1997), Mexicans have been a neglected group in the field of ethnic entrepreneurship.[1] Previous studies claimed that Mexican immigrants represent a wage labor pool destined to blue-collar and service jobs rather than business owner-

ship (Light and Bonacich 1988:xi; Portes and Bach 1985:167, 297). In fact, most studies of ethnic entrepreneurship focus on groups with high visibility in small businesses (such as Koreans, Cubans, and Chinese), to the relative neglect of Mexicans or other immigrant groups with low rates of self-employment. Little Village, a Mexican immigrant community in Chicago, is an interesting case study for understanding Mexican entrepreneurial activity because the community features a vital business sector dominated by Hispanic entrepreneurs, Mexicans in particular. It thus provides an ideal setting for studying the circumstances conducive to business ownership among recent immigrants.

Based on this community study, we examine the mechanisms through which ethnicity affects access to business ownership to illustrate how ethnic economies stimulate or undermine business activities. Our analysis focuses on one specific training mechanism, namely, the acquisition of skills via employment in a coethnic firm. Specifically, we consider whether current Mexican business owners in Little Village were trained in other coethnic businesses and how the training process differs, depending on whether it occurs within or outside establishments owned and operated by coethnics.

We begin with a theoretical overview that sets the background for understanding entrepreneurship in Little Village. After describing the

Little Village business survey, we profile Mexican business owners and contrast their training experiences according to previous employment in the ethnic versus the open economy. The final section discusses the implications of the ethnic economy's training function for self-employment growth in immigrant communities.

THEORETICAL BACKGROUND

The Ethnic Economy and the Ethnic Enclave: A Conceptual Distinction[2]

For more than two decades, social scientists have tried to understand how different immigrant groups access the world of business ownership, particularly in the context of ethnic and immigrant neighborhoods. Since Portes and associates coined the term "ethnic enclave" to characterize the emergence of a spatially concentrated business sector in Miami (Portes 1987; Portes and Bach 1985; Portes and Manning 1986; Wilson and Portes 1980), there has been highly spirited debate about the necessary and sufficient conditions for an ethnic enclave to emerge, the differences between ethnic economies and enclaves, and the costs and benefits of working in ethnic enterprises. In an effort to bring clarity to the conceptual confusion in the burgeoning entrepreneurship literature, Light and collaborators summarized the theoretical underpinnings of ethnic economies and ethnic enclaves (Light et al. 1994; Light and Gold 2000; Light and Karageorgis 1994). They remind us that the ethnic economy concept derives from a literature about middleman minorities (Bonacich 1973), whereas ethnic enclave economy evolves from writing about labor segmentation (Averitt 1968; Doeringer and Piore 1971; Piore 1975).

Bonacich and Modell (1980) first developed the ethnic economy concept "to differentiate general economy employment from the employment a minority has created for itself" (Light et al. 1994:66). The ethnic economy in-

cludes any ethnic or immigrant persons who are employers, who are self-employed, or who are employees in coethnic firms. The contours of an ethnic economy are defined by race, ethnicity, or national origin, and its defining feature stems from the economic advantages afforded in relations among business owners and between owners and workers of the same national origin (Logan, Alba, and McNulty 1994).

Presumably, ethnic economies operate as sheltered labor markets, because in the absence of competition with natives, immigrants often enjoy job opportunities otherwise denied them (Waldinger 1986). Within the ethnic economy immigrants can avail themselves of job opportunities across the entire occupational hierarchy, including managerial, administrative, and professional positions (Lewin-Epstein and Semyonov 1994). Viewed from an institutional perspective, ethnic economies often function as internal labor markets by protecting (at least partly) immigrant workers from competition in the general labor market while also providing training necessary for future business endeavors (Bailey and Waldinger 1991; Jiobu 1988; Waldinger 1995). However, the ethnic economy concept does not require the locational clustering of firms or coethnic clientele or suppliers (Light et al. 1994). Thus it is possible for any ethnic group to participate in an ethnic economy in the absence of residential concentration.[3]

In the 1980s Portes and associates proposed the concept of an ethnic enclave economy, both to explain the high rates of self-employment among Cubans and to underscore the importance of residential concentration in enhancing the ability of small business owners to capitalize and benefit from coethnic ties (Portes 1981, 1987; Portes and Bach 1985; Portes and Manning 1986; Wilson and Portes 1980). In addition to locational concentration of ethnic firms, ethnic enclaves are distinguished by vertical and horizontal integration of suppliers and distributors and extensive reliance on coethnic employees for labor. Furthermore, enclaves share many features of primary labor markets because they allegedly provide mobility opportunities for employees aspiring to self-employment. Presumably, recent immigrants who enter the U.S. labor market in firms owned and operated by a coethnic (usually an earlier immigrant) are promoted to higher managerial positions when these become available. Under ideal conditions, employees of enclave firms eventually become self-employed, often with the support of their employers, or they move on to better-paying positions outside the enclave (Portes and Bach 1985; Portes and Manning 1986).

Because ideas about the necessary and sufficient conditions to define an ethnic enclave were based on a single group in a single group location, namely, Cubans in Miami, subsequent studies attempted to verify whether parallel residential and economic arrangements are reproduced among other immigrant groups in different locations. Although the Cuban ethnic economy in Miami does not appear to be reproduced exactly elsewhere, similar economic arrangements were identified in New York's Chinatown (Zhou 1992) and in Los Angeles's Koreatown (Light and Bonacich 1988). The common features of these communities are (1) a large and spatially concentrated immigrant population; (2) rapid population growth through continued immigration flows; and (3) a highly visible small business sector. These cases suggest that there now may exist favorable conditions for development of enclaves by groups other than Cubans in Miami and in other parts of the country (Logan, Alba, and McNulty 1994). However, the conditions of vertical and horizontal integration have not been documented for these emergent ethnic enclaves. Therefore, the specific circumstances, nuances, nature, and locales of these new ethnic economic arrangements warrant further scrutiny (Alvarez 1990).

Because most ethnic groups—especially recent immigrants—are associated with some as-

pects of ethnic economies but only a few display an ethnic enclave pattern, many leading scholars in the field of ethnic entrepreneurship have proposed using the *ethnic economy* as a more encompassing concept (Waldinger 1993:450) and the *ethnic enclave* as a special case of the former (Light and Bonacich 1988; Light and Karageorgis 1994; Waldinger 1993; Logan, Alba, and McNulty 1994; Light and Gold 2000:15). Specifically, *ethnic economy* is intended only to distinguish whether work opportunities for a specific group are exclusive or inclusive, irrespective of the residential clustering of interdependent firms, which is a unique attribute of an ethnic enclave. Accordingly, in what follows, we refer to *ethnic economy* as the general concept and *ethnic enclave* as a specific case.

Little Village meets the primary characteristics used to define an ethnic economic enclave as a constellation of residentially concentrated ethnic enterprises with vertical and horizontal linkages among ethnic suppliers, producers, and distributors. Little Village also features a dynamic ethnic business community, a rapidly expanding ethnic consumer market, and a ready supply of new immigrant workers for aspiring entrepreneurs (Portes and Manning 1986). And finally, Little Village is well articulated with a wider Mexican ethnic economy in the city of Chicago. South Chicago, Pilsen, Little Village, Back of the Yards, and the Near West Side are Chicago's largest Mexican neighborhoods. All of these neighborhoods have a continuous flow of new immigrants and feature visible ethnic business communities, the most developed being Little Village (Padilla 1993).

Training in Ethnic Economies and Ethnic Enclaves

According to Bailey and Waldinger (1991:432), ethnic economies are characterized by "an external, informal training system that shapes the employment relationship and increases the availability and quality of information for workers and employers." They define training systems as "the mechanisms by which labor market information is circulated, workers are recruited and skills are obtained" (1991:433). Because recruitment of ethnic workers is facilitated by residential concentration of ethnic-owned and ethnic-operated firms, in the context of an enclave the training functions of ethnic enterprises may serve not only to help new immigrants adapt to the U.S. labor market in a culturally familiar milieu but also to facilitate the proliferation of new firms (Boissevain et al. 1990; Portes and Bach 1985; Portes and Manning 1986; Waldinger 1985, 1993). The latter follows because in ethnic enclaves workers not only can acquire the know-how to start and operate a business, but they also develop contacts among suppliers and distributors that are necessary to establish a firm in a setting that guarantees coethnic workers and consumers.

On-the-job training processes depend on connections to ethnic social networks in which they are embedded, because mutual trust arises more frequently between coethnics than across ethnic boundaries, which putatively facilitates the flow of information and skill acquisition (Bailey and Waldinger 1991; Lee 1999; Zimmer and Aldrich 1987). The web of social relationships that link employees and employers in an ethnic economy reinforces direct family and friendship ties, especially when an atmosphere of mutual obligation prevails (Alvarez 1990; Bonacich 1973; Modell 1985). Therefore, social ties within an ethnic enclave economy widen workers' contacts and hence increase the chances that employees will move through a variety of jobs that develop their firm-specific skills. Several researchers claim that once the training function is in place, the immigrant sector grows via a self-feeding process whereby newcomers start working in ethnic firms and a subset of those who acquire business skills establish their own businesses (Bai-

ley and Waldinger 1991; Light and Karageorgis 1994; Portes and Bach 1985; Portes and Manning 1986; Waldinger 1985, 1986, 1993).

Although residential clustering may be important for securing an ethnic market for consumers and suppliers (Wilson and Martin 1982), locational clustering may not be necessary to guarantee the proliferation of ethnic enterprises among former employees of ethnic-owned and -operated firms. As Waldinger (1993:450) has pointed out, "There is no reason to assume that the particular factors that distinguish the informal training system among immigrant workers and entrepreneurs are uniquely a product of their placement in space. From this perspective the informal training systems operating in concentrated ethnic economies are likely to function in similar ways in ethnic economies which are dispersed across space." Although reasonable on its face, this proposition has not been systematically evaluated.

Portes and Bach (1985) were early claimants that immigrants' employment in enterprises owned and operated by other coethnics, even at low wages, promoted economic incorporation of recent arrivals. They assumed that socioeconomic integration resulted when workers acquired the knowledge and experience either to establish their own enterprises or to compete more effectively in the open labor market as they mastered English and learned how U.S. labor markets operate. This view presumes that low-wage employment in ethnic firms represents on-the-job training rather than exploitation of recent immigrant workers by coethnics. Other studies also claimed that ethnic firms provide substantial opportunities for general skill acquisition, in particular entrepreneurial training. So characterized, ethnic firms operate as training arenas that accord immigrant employees benefits not otherwise available to them in the open market (Bailey and Waldinger 1991; Waldinger 1985; Zhou 1992).

These ideas suggest testable hypotheses that to date have not been subjected to rigorous empirical scrutiny. In fact, case studies provide conflicting conclusions about the nature and consequences of training in ethnic-owned firms. For example, in the Cuban case, Portes and Bach (1985) presented information about ethnicity of employers, but they lack data on training practices within firms. Although they show that working for a coethnic firm at Time 1 is the most important predictor of self-employment at Time 2, this correlation does little to reveal the process (training, resource accumulation, family ties, etc.) that produces the observed outcome. Based on a study conducted in Los Angeles among Asian immigrants, Nee, Sanders, and Sernau (1994) also report that employment in a coethnic firm increases the likelihood of becoming self-employed. However, they recognize that coethnic employers are not always willing to train and encourage their employees to move into business ownership for fear of future competition. Alvarez's (1990:112) case study of the Los Angeles Mexican wholesale produce market and its satellite markets shows that Mexicans actually do experience advancement opportunities in this economic niche and that these experiences are conducive to the development of entrepreneurial activities.

Pessar's (1995) study of Latino business ownership arrives at different conclusions about the training opportunities available in ethnic firms. She finds that the Latino business community in Washington, D.C., does not conform to a pattern of on-the-job training and mentorship. Only one-third of Latino business owners in Washington had been employed by a coethnic. Furthermore, she finds no significant differences with respect to job training and help in establishing businesses between those who did and did not work in a coethnic firm (1995:386). Pessar concludes that Latinos residing in Washington have not achieved an essential precondition for the development of ethnic economies, namely, ethnic solidarity. One possible reason Pessar failed to find a training effect among ethnic firms is the het-erogeneous composition of the Latino business community there. If ethnic solidarity is nationally rather than supranationally defined, then being Mexican, Cuban, or Puerto Rican rather than Hispanic or Latino may be required for mobilizing ethnic solidarity.

The growth of residentially segregated immigrant communities during the 1970s and 1980s, coupled with high rates of self-employment among foreign-born populations, warrants further empirical research to adjudicate conflicting findings about the training hypothesis and to better understand the mechanisms that promote or retard the proliferation of immigrant enterprises. A recent survey of ethnic businesses in Little Village permits a test of the ideas presented above regarding the training functions of ethnic economies and ethnic enclaves. We show that ethnic-owned firms do serve as stepladders to business ownership for ethnic compatriots because previous employment in a coethnic firm increases the likelihood of acquiring skills relevant for running a business. Moreover, Mexican business owners with previous work experience in coethnic firms (whether within or outside Little Village) were exposed to training opportunities that clearly differ from the experiences of their ethnic counterparts who did not acquire job experience in a coethnic firm. Our case study also reveals that business opportunities are transmitted along ethnic lines as former employees of Mexican-operated firms in Little Village subsequently opened their own businesses in similar services or products. Furthermore, we show that Mexican immigrants who currently operate businesses in Little Village received technical and financial help from their previous coethnic employers.

THE LITTLE VILLAGE STUDY

Little Village is the largest Mexican community in the Midwest. Previously a Czech immigrant neighborhood, it experienced considerable social and economic change between 1970 and 1990. In 1970 Mexicans constituted only 30 percent of the neighborhood population, which numbered 62,895 residents. During the next twenty years, Mexicans became the predominant ethnic group, comprising 82 percent of all residents by 1990. The growing Hispanic population in the neighborhood was driven by the exodus of the white population. The process of residential succession generated a crucial market condition for the development of a business sector—that is, a critical mass of ethnic consumers to support ethnic businesses. The pathways to business ownership of Hispanic entrepreneurs in Little Village took the form of a natural succession into vacant storefronts.[4]

Today, the vibrant shopping district on Twenty-sixth Street is populated by small businesses that serve the steady stream of new immigrants. This neighborhood has become the primary magnet for recent immigrants from Mexico who seek employment in the low-wage jobs available within and surrounding the neighborhood. As in other minority neighborhoods, the absence of large retail stores has created a niche for immigrant entrepreneurs (Lee 1999). Merchants and leaders in Little Village's chamber of commerce and in the community proudly talk about West Twenty-sixth Street being the second most successful commercial strip in Chicago, after the Magnificent Mile on Michigan Avenue. Besides formal storefronts, street vendors (Mexican *fruteros* and *eloteros* and Arab cassette vendors) augment the vitality of business activity in the community throughout the year, but especially during the summer months.

For this study we conducted a survey of businesses located in Little Village. The survey is based on a stratified random sample of establishments that were in operation during spring 1994. Our canvassing of the neighborhood yielded approximately one thousand business establishments that were stratified ac-

cording to primary type of industry, product, or service. Relatively uncommon businesses, such as bridal shops, bakeries, iron works products, and factories, were sampled at a rate of 100 percent. Relatively abundant enterprises, like restaurants, bars, auto repair shops, and hair salons, were sampled at a rate of 35 percent. All remaining establishments were sampled at a rate of 50 percent. Weights inverse to the sampling ratio were applied to represent the universe of business enterprises. Professional services (such as lawyers and health services) were *not* sampled for theoretical reasons. Both the process and the formal requirements for self-employment in medicine and law are sufficiently different from those required to establish small business enterprises. Furthermore, most of the clinics located in Little Village actually were part of large HMO networks that were affiliated with one of the major hospitals in the city of Chicago. Thus our sample represents all service industries except for legal and medical services.

The response rate for the business sample was 70 percent. This is a highly successful response rate given that we insisted on interviewing owners and declined to conduct interviews with managers or other employees. Bilingual interviewers conducted all interviews. If a business had multiple owners, only one was interviewed; it was unnecessary (and too costly) to interview all owners because the instrument solicited detailed information about the nature of the partnership and the division of responsibilities among owners. Multiple interviews would have resulted in redundant information. Less than 10 percent of our respondents were partners. Respondents who had multiple businesses were queried about their main business.

A total of 244 interviews were conducted; of these, 162 were Mexican immigrant owners. Although Little Village is predominantly a Mexican residential neighborhood, its business community is ethnically heterogeneous. During the last decade or so, various ethnic groups

(Koreans, Arabs, Chinese, and Pakistanis) joined the white and Mexican business owners in Little Village, thus transforming the neighborhood into a multiethnic business community.[5] Three out of four Little Village owners are of Hispanic origin, the majority of these Mexican and foreign-born. Koreans represented 13 percent of Little Village business owners, and the remaining share consisted of Middle Eastern, other South Asian ethnics (India and Pakistan), and non-Hispanic whites.[6]

The business instrument solicited information about household and respondent characteristics and about employment activity before the current business, which is essential to understand the training process within ethnic firms. Specific questions asked included relationship to previous employer, ethnicity of employer, location of the business, occupation, years/months of work in previous occupation, supervisory functions, and skills acquisition.[7] The originality of the instrument lies in its emphasis on how ethnicity influences the creation and expansion of businesses, through multiple social and economic domains.

Our focus on Mexican immigrants to evaluate the training function of ethnic economies is justified on two grounds. First, the literature on the training function of ethnic economies is based on immigrant populations. Among Hispanic business owners in Little Village, the majority are Mexican and most are foreign-born. This is not so for the non-Mexican business owners.[8] Second, only Mexican business owners display a mixed pattern of employment (ethnic firms vs. nonethnic firms). Other non-Hispanic merchants in Little Village are not included in this analysis because their previous work experiences were either exclusively with coethnic employers (whites and Koreans) or non-coethnic employers (Middle Eastern and other South Asian). Third, our results and conclusions relate only to those Mexican entrepreneurs operating their businesses in the commu-

nity. Our analysis does not include Mexican business owners who live in Little Village but operate firms outside the community.

DATA ANALYSIS

Table 1 displays selected characteristics of the surveyed Mexican foreign-born business owners and their firms. The vast majority (82 percent) were married, in their mid-forties, and they averaged twenty-three years of U.S. residence. Chicago was the first residence for the vast majority. Mexican storefront owners averaged 9.3 years of formal schooling, and despite their long average U.S. tenure (16.3 years), they reported low levels of English proficiency, with nearly one-third reporting they were not proficient in English.

Table 1 also shows the industrial distribution of Mexican-owned business establishments in Little Village. The majority of Mexican immigrant firms operate in retail trade (64 percent), but one-fourth operate business and repair services. Among retailers, Mexican business owners concentrate in clothing and jewelry, but other retail concerns include furniture, music, photo processing, laundromats, and video rentals. Auto repair shops were the model repair services. Restaurants in Little Village were predominantly a Mexican immigrant concern, as were hair salons and barbershops. In these businesses that cater to an ethnic clientele, immigrants from Spanish-speaking countries have a clear competitive advantage.

Mexican businesses in Little Village had been in operation for eight years, on average, although their owners have resided in Little Village for nearly sixteen years. This suggests that these owners worked as salaried employees before opening their own businesses. Approximately half of the immigrant-owned establishments are family businesses, which means that the owner's spouse and/or children worked in the enterprise.[9] Besides providing

TABLE 1   **Selected Characteristics and Prior Employment Experience of Little Village Establishment Owners Means or Percents (Standard deviations)**

	Mexicans Foreign-born
Owner characteristics	
Age	43.4 (9.3)
% Female respondents	30.2
Marital status	
Currently married	82.8
Ever married	12.3
Never married	4.9
U.S. tenure (yrs)	23.6 (9.3)
Tenure in Little Village (yrs)	16.3 (8.4)
English proficiency	
Very proficient	21.6
Moderately proficient	46.9
Not proficient	31.5
Years of formal schooling	9.3 (4.1)
Business characteristics	
Industry distribution of firms	
Construction	1.2
Manufacturing	1.2
Wholesale and retail trade	64.2
Finance-insurance-real estate	1.9
Personal business and repair services	25.3
Entertainment and recreation	2.5
Professional and related services	3.7
Duration of business (yrs)	8.6 (7.2)
% Family business[a]	48.8
% Business with non-family employees	70.2
% Employees residing in Little Village	83.0
% Businesses highly dependent on ethnic clientele	78.0
Activity before starting current business	
Self-employed in another business	25.3
In school	0.6
Worked for someone else in a similar business	21.6
Worked for someone else in other type of business	35.2
Worked for someone else or relative in current business	6.2
Other	11.1
N	162

Source: Little Village Business Survey.

[a] Percent reporting that owner's spouse and/or children worked in the business.

employment to family members, ethnic firms in Little Village also create employment opportunities for other community residents. Approximately 70 percent of all business owners employed at least one non-family member. Moreover, Mexican residents in Little Village benefit most from these employment opportunities, as four out of five jobs created by Mexican entrepreneurs are filled by ethnic coresidents. This is because the majority of Little Village firms hire Mexican workers who reside in the community or in the adjacent Mexican neighborhood of Pilsen. Finally, the business sector in the community is highly dependent on their local coethnic consumers, as 80 percent of business owners so reported.

Responses about the acquisition of know-how relevant to business formation yield insights into the precursors to business formation. Before starting the current business, the modal activity of Little Village business owners was wage and salaried employment. That fully one-fourth of Mexican immigrants worked for another employer in the same line of work suggests that some would-be entrepreneurs acquire knowledge and experience relevant to business practices on the job. Although this is consistent with the training hypothesis, further substantiation, which we provide in the next section, is required. Approximately 25 percent of immigrants and 15 percent of native-born Mexicans reported having been self-employed in another business prior to the current business, which indicates a high turnover rate of immigrant establishments.[10]

Although these tabulations provide insight into the precursors to business formation, they not speak directly to the role of ethnic enterprises as training arenas for business ownership. For our current theoretical concerns, the key questions are whether, how much, and in what ways businesses owned and operated by ethnic compatriots function as a training platform for future immigrant business formation, and to what extent Mexicans rely on ethnic ties

to acquire experience relevant to self-employment. We turn to these issues next.

Training Functions of Ethnic Enterprises

The idea that ethnic economies function as training sectors for future self-employment implies that informal mobility ladders structured along race and ethnic lines are conducive to self-employment (Portes and Bach 1985; Portes and Manning 1986; Waldinger 1985). This would help to explain how immigrants who have limited English proficiency and/or are educationally disadvantaged can establish businesses in their host communities. Claims that working for an ethnic compatriot facilitates entry to self-employment presupposes the existence of ethnically circumscribed opportunity structures to acquire know-how about starting and running a small business. This logic predicts that immigrant minority groups who acquire experience in a particular industry may be more inclined to establish their own business in a similar line of work. More specifically, the training function hypothesis implies that acquisition of work experience either in an ethnic-owned business or in a firm in a related line of work serves to acquaint newcomers with the customs, practices, and regulations governing business ownership in the United States.

Mexican business owners in Little Village differ from non-Mexican entrepreneurs with regard to previous employment in firms of ethnic compatriots.[11] Employment in the ethnic economy is a pathway to business ownership for only 44 percent of foreign-born Mexicans. These figures contrast with those displayed by other ethnic groups who own businesses in Little Village. Specifically, all white and Korean business owners worked for coethnics, while none of the Middle Eastern and Asian business owners did so. However, given that workers secure a job with an ethnic compatriot, what are the chances that they actually acquire relevant training and skills? In other words, does ethnicity of employer facilitate acquisition of skills pertinent to business ownership? Below we examine these ideas in Little Village by comparing the training experiences of Mexican business owners who have worked in coethnic firms and those who have not.

Table 2 illustrates how much acquisition of skills, management experience, and job-specific experience varies according to the ethnicity of the previous employer. These tabulations are based on the subset of business owners who worked for someone else before starting their current businesses. The descriptive results support the idea that working in a coethnic firm influences the likelihood of acquiring skills relevant to establishing a business. For example, Mexican business owners who previously worked for coethnic employers were three times more likely to have held jobs related to their current line of business than their counterparts who did not work for coethnic employers. They also were twice as likely to report having acquired business-relevant skills during previous jobs, and 1.7 times more likely to have had supervisory positions than Mexicans who did not work for coethnic employers.[12]

The data in Table 2 also reveal that employment in the ethnic economy is embedded in family and friendship relationships. More than half of Mexican merchants whose prior employment was in a coethnic firm had a close relationship (either kin or friend) with their previous employer, but none of those who worked for other groups did so. Nearly 53 percent of business owners whose prior employment was in a coethnic business reported that the firm was located in Little Village, compared to only 11 percent of those who did not work for a coethnic boss. Finally, Mexican business owners previously employed by a coethnic are less likely to start their business in the informal economy compared to their counterparts who did not work in a coethnic firm. It would appear that Mexican business owners not employed in the ethnic economy were less likely to benefit from training opportunities in the open economy and hence were more likely to use the informal economy as a venue for acquiring experience and skills before opening a business (see Raijman and Tienda 2000).

Inability to speak the native language constrains the transferability of skills and the type of jobs and tasks an immigrant can perform in the work setting for the firms that do not operate in an ethnic community. However, Spanish proficiency also could be an asset if workers

TABLE 2   Training Functions of the Ethnic Economy: Mexicans in Little Village (Percents)

	Ethnicity of Previous Employer		
	Same	Other	t-test
If prior job related to current business	73.3	26.7	p <.000
If acquired skills relevant to current business	81.3	36.1	p <.000
If held supervisory function in previous job	38.7	22.7	p =.04
Relationship to previous employer			
Family	29.2	—	
Friend	23.6	3.1	p =.000
None	47.2	96.9	
If current business began informally	17.0	36.4	p <.01
N	(53)	(67)	

Source: Little Village Business Survey.

are employed in enterprises that cater to ethnic concerns (Tienda and Neidert 1984). Longer periods of U.S. residence increase the likelihood that immigrants become socially and culturally assimilated, thereby raising the odds that they absorb new skills. Consistent with expectations, tenure in a job increases the likelihood of learning market-relevant skills. Finally, close ties to employers (family or friendship) should also affect training opportunities, because business owners will usually prefer their blood kin in assigning managerial or supervisory responsibilities, other things equal.

Our results (table not shown) clearly support the idea that previous work experiences in ethnic enterprises increase the likelihood of acquiring skills relevant to the current business. The odds of acquiring business-relevant skills are 5.5 times higher for business owners who worked for a coethnic employer before establishing their own business relative to those who worked for others. The results also support the hypothesis that acquiring experience in a particular industry raises Mexicans' probability of establishing a business in a similar line of work. The odds of acquiring skills in the previous job were 3.8 times higher for Mexican business owners who worked in a similar industry compared to those who worked in a different line of business.

The probability of acquiring business-relevant skills was not statistically related to schooling, to U.S. tenure, or to English proficiency. However, it is difficult to comment further about business owners' need for English skills because we lack information about the ethnic composition of the labor force and clientele served in the previous job. If most of the workers or customers are Mexicans, then Spanish becomes an asset, and the lack of English skills may not be a liability because producers and distributors also speak Spanish. That location of previous employment did not influence skill acquisition supports Waldinger's

(1993:450) claim that the spatial concentration per se is not a requisite for mobility processes among immigrant firms, and more specifically for training opportunities.

On balance these findings support the idea that employment in a coethnic firm provides Mexicans with opportunities for skill acquisition that are not reproduced in firms operated by non-coethnics. The ethnic economy serves not only as a channel for the transference of skills and training but also as an arena for stimulating further business activities. In this regard, work in the ethnic economy has also been identified as an ethnic career ladder whereby business owners help their former employees establish their own businesses (Boissevain et al. 1990; Morokvasic, Waldinger, and Phizacklea 1990; Portes and Manning 1986; Werbner 1990). Table 3 shows just how much employers in Little Village help their employees who subsequently opened businesses.

These tabulations suggest that a process of transmission of business opportunities does occur, at least among Mexican business owners operating in Little Village.[13] One-third of Mexican immigrant business owners operating in Little Village reported that a former employee opened a business (mostly in the same product line) after having worked for them, and more than 60 percent of these respondents claimed that they helped their employees in the business start-up phase with technical and financial assistance (60 and 22 percent, respectively). Because we know that virtually all employees of Little Village businesses are of Mexican origin residing within the perimeter of the community or nearby Mexican neighborhoods, these results indicate that the process of transmission of business opportunities—although moderate in its magnitude—is both ethnically and geographically concentrated. However, as several scholars have pointed out, one must be cautious not to depict an idealized vision of coethnic advantages because market concentration can also lead to saturation and sharp competition if too

TABLE 3 Business Characteristics and Transmission of Opportunities for Business Ownership
Means or Percents (Standard deviations)

	Mexican Foreign-Born
Transmission of business opportunities	
% whose previous employees opened a business	34.2
% ex-employees starting business in same line	96.0
% of business owners who helped previous employee	58.0
Type of help provided	
Technical assistance	54.5
Financial assistance	22.7
Other	22.8
N	162

Source: Little Village Business Survey.

many coethnic employees are trained to be their future competitors (Gold 1994:122). In that case ethnic entrepreneurs may be reluctant to hire coethnics and train them for fear of intraethnic competition (Gold 1994; Lee 1999; Nee, Sanders, and Sernau 1994). Because the Mexican ethnic enclave is still in its infancy, these processes may not yet have manifested themselves. It is also conceivable that the terms of cooperation and competition may be different across ethnic groups—but this hypothesis is beyond the scope of our empirical evidence or research objectives.

CONCLUSION

Our results illustrate the relevance of the ethnic economy as a stepladder to business ownership in the Mexican community of Little Village. We argue that working for a coethnic firm increases the likelihood of acquiring business-relevant skills. Specifically, ethnic-owned firms (whether in Little Village or outside it) serve as a stepladder to business ownership for ethnic compatriots because previous employment in a coethnic firm increases the likelihood of acquiring skills relevant for running a business. Our findings show that informal training systems

operating in concentrated ethnic economies function in similar ways to ethnic economies that are dispersed across space (Waldinger 1993). Mexican business owners with previous work experiences in coethnic firms were exposed to opportunities for skill acquisition that apparently differ from the experiences of their ethnic counterparts who lacked job experience in a coethnic firm, and this is true regardless of the location of the coethnic firm. However, Mexicans' chances of entering the business world through employment in a coethnic firm are low, as less than half ever worked for a coethnic boss before opening their current business. Lacking a strong ethnic economy to acquire training and skills, many Mexican immigrants in Little Village (over one-fourth) use the informal sector as another route to business ownership. Informal economic activities allow enterprising immigrants to test the market, accumulate capital or learn about its availability, and acquire skills in a particular line of work. Thus informal self-employment becomes an alternative pathway to business ownership for Mexican immigrants who lack opportunities to acquire business experience in coethnic firms (Raijman and Tienda 2000).

If differences in training systems generate disparate opportunities for self-employment growth within the ethnic community, even though training experiences are available in co-ethnic firms, for Mexicans the multiplier effect that facilitates proliferation of new firms is smaller in the aggregate. Thus the proliferation of Mexican-owned and -operated businesses may remain low, even in the context of high residential concentration, because the minimal base of ethnic businesses that provide training opportunities is relatively small compared to other immigrant groups, such as Cubans or Koreans. To what extent this could explain aggregate differences in self-employment rates is a question that needs to be answered in future research, but our results provide initial insight into this conundrum.

NOTES

[1]For an exception, see Hansen and Cardenas 1988 and the anthropological studies of Alvarez (1990) and Villar (1994).

[2]For a thorough and systematic discussion of ethnic economies, see Light and Gold 2000.

[3]A case in point are Iranian firms in Los Angeles (Light et al. 1994), which are not spatially clustered and where most business owners do not employ coethnics. Koreans who operate businesses in black and Hispanic neighborhoods in Chicago and elsewhere are another example (Yoon 1995).

[4]One of our respondents—who defined himself as one of the first Hispanics (if not the first) to open a business in the community—told us that by the time he opened his business in the mid-1950s, storefronts in Little Village were vacant, as if an epidemic had attacked the community: "Estaba todo vacio. A mi se me hacía que acá había pegado el sarampión."

[5]Little Village houses a Jewish-owned, Korean-operated discount mall that accommodates 120 small booths that are rented by Koreans, Arabs, Asian-Indians, and Mexicans and other Hispanic immigrants.

[6]Non-Hispanic entrepreneurs concentrate in clothing, electronics, jewelry, beauty supply, and laundry services. For a comparative socioeconomic profile of ethnic entrepreneurs in Little Village, see Raijman 1996.

[7]The survey instrument also included a set of questions to measure risk disposition, inputs for business start-up, including sources of capital, use of credit, problems and financial barriers, family members' participation in the business, employees and clients, suppliers, social networks, organizational participation, and current financial status.

[8]Only fourteen business owners were native-born of Hispanic origin.

[9]If we consider all types of relatives, the figures for family participation are much higher.

[10]Business turnover results from various sources: relocation, consolidation of multiple sites, opening of new enterprises, or outright failure.

[11]These tabulations are not shown but are available on request.

[12]These results contrast with those displayed by other non-Hispanic businessmen in the community. For example, all the Korean merchants in our sample had previously worked for a coethnic boss, but only 66 percent reported having acquired relevant skills. For non-Hispanic whites, the figure is 58 percent (see Table 2 in Raijman and Tienda 2000).

[13]One might speculate that because Little Village's businesses have on average only eight years of tenure in the community, as the businesses mature, they will increase their ability to provide assistance to prospective entrepreneurs. This process will be buttressed by continued immigration.

REFERENCES

Alvarez, Roberto, Jr. 1990. "Mexican Entrepreneurs and Markets in the City of Los Angeles: A Case of an Immigrant Enclave." *Urban Anthropology* 19:99–124.

Averitt, Robert T. 1968. *The Dual Economy: The Dynamics of American Industry Structure.* New York: Norton.

Bailey, Thomas, and Roger Waldinger. 1991. "Primary, Secondary, and Enclave Labor Markets: A Training System Approach." *American Sociological Review* 56:432–45.

Boissevain, Jeremy, Jochen Blaaschkee, Hanneke Grotenbreg, Isaac Joseph, Ivan Light, Marlene Sway, Roger Waldinger, and Pnina Werbner. 1990. "Ethnic Entrepreneurs and Ethnic Strategies." Pp. 131–56 in *Ethnic Entrepreneurs: Immigrant Business in Industrial Societies,* edited by R. Waldinger, H. Aldrich, and R. Ward. Newbury Park, CA: Sage.

Bonacich, Edna. 1973. "A Theory of Middleman Minorities." *American Sociological Review* 38:583–94.

Bonacich, Edna, and John Modell. 1980. *The Economic Basis of Ethnic Solidarity in the Japanese American Society.* Berkeley: University of California Press.

Doeringer, Peter B., and Michael J. Piore. 1971. *Internal Labor Markets and Manpower Analysis.* Lexington, MA: Heath.

Gold, Steve. 1994. "Patterns of Economic Cooperation among Israeli Immigrants in Los Angeles." *International Migration Review* 28:104–35.

Greenwood, Michael, and Marta Tienda. 1997. "U.S. Impacts of Mexican Immigration." In *Binational Study: U.S.-Mexico Migration,* chap. 4. Washington, DC: U.S. Commission on Immigration Reform.

Hansen, Niles, and Gilberto Cardenas. 1988. "Immigrant and Native Ethnic Enterprises in Mexican American Neighborhoods: Differing Perceptions of Mexican Immigrant Workers." *International Migration Review* 22:226–42.

Jiobu, Robert M. 1988. "Ethnic Hegemony and the Japanese of California." *American Sociological Review* 53(3):353–67.

Lee, Jennifer. 1999. "Retail Niche Domination among African American, Jewish, and Korean Entrepreneurs: Competition, Coethnic Advantage and Disadvantage." *American Behavioral Scientist* 42:1398–1416.

Lewin-Epstein, Noah, and Moshe Semyonov. 1994. "Sheltered Labor Markets, Public Sector Employment, and Socioeconomic Returns to Education of Arabs in Israel." *American Journal of Sociology* 100:622–51.

Light, Ivan, and Edna Bonacich. 1988. *Immigrant Entrepreneurs: Koreans in Los Angeles, 1965–1982.* Berkeley: University of California Press.

Light, Ivan, and Steve Gold. 2000. *Ethnic Economies.* San Diego, CA: Academic Press.

Light, Ivan, and S. Karageorgis. 1994. "The Ethnic Economy." Pp. 646–71 in *Handbook of Economic Sociology,* edited by N. Smelser and R. Swedberg. New York: Russell Sage Foundation.

Light, Ivan, Georges Sabagh, Mehdi Bozorgmehr, and Claudia Der-Martirosian. 1994. "Beyond the Ethnic Enclave Economy." *Social Problems* 41:65–80.

Logan, John, Richard Alba, and T. McNulty. 1994. "Ethnic Economies in Metropolitan Regions: Miami and Beyond." *Social Forces* 72:691–724.

Modell, Suzanne. 1985. "A Comparative Perspective on the Ethnic Enclave: Blacks, Italians, and Jews in New York City." *International Migration Review* 19:64–81.

Morokvasic, Mirjana, Roger Waldinger, and Annie Phizacklea. 1990. "Immigrant and Minority Business in the Garment Industries of Paris, London and New York." Pp. 157–76 in *Ethnic Entrepreneurs: Immigrant Business in Industrial Societies,* edited by R. Waldinger, H. Aldrich, and R. Ward. Newbury Park, CA: Sage.

Nee, Victor, Jimmy Sanders, and Scott Sernau. 1994. "Job Transitions in an Immigrant Metropolis: Ethnic Boundaries and the Mixed Economy." *American Sociological Review* 59:849–72.

Padilla, Felix. 1993. "The Quest for Community: Puerto Ricans in Chicago." Pp. 129–48 in *In the Barrios: Latinos and the Underclass Debate,* edited by J. Moore and R. Pinder-hughes. New York: Russell Sage Foundation.

Pessar, Patricia. 1995. "The Elusive Enclave: Ethnicity, Class, and Nationality among Latino Entrepreneurs in Greater Washington, DC." *Human Organization* 54:383–92.

Piore, Michael J. 1975. "Notes for a Theory of Labor Market Stratification." Pp. 125–50 in *Labor Market Segmentation,* edited by R. C. Edwards, M. Reich, and D. M. Gordon. Lexington, MA: Heath.

Portes, Alejandro. 1981. "Modes of Structural Incorporation and Present Theories of Labor Immigration." Pp. 279–97 in *Global Trends in Migration: Theory and Research on International Population Movements,* edited by M. Kritz, C. B. Keely, and S. Tomassi. New York: Center for Migration Studies.

———. 1987. "The Social Origins of the Cuban Enclave Economy of Miami." *Sociological Perspectives* 30:340–72.

Portes, Alejandro, and Robert Bach. 1985. *Latin Journey: Cuban and Mexican Immigrants in the United States.* Berkeley: University of California Press.

Portes, Alejandro, and Robert D. Manning. 1986. "The Immigrant Enclave: Theory and Empirical Examples." Pp. 47–68 in *Competitive Ethnic Relations,* edited by S. Olzak and J. Nagel. New York: Academic Press.

Raijman, Rebeca. 1996. "Pathways to Self-Employment and Entrepreneurship in an Immigrant Community in Chicago." Ph.D. dissertation, University of Chicago.

Raijman, Rebeca, and Marta Tienda. 2000. "Immigrants' Pathways to Business Ownership: A Comparative Ethnic Perspective." *International Migration Review* 34(3):681–705.

Tienda, Marta, and Lisa J. Neidert. 1984. "Language, Education and the Socioeconomic Achievement of Hispanic Origin Men." *Social Science Quarterly* 65(2):519–36.

Villar, Maria de Lourdes. 1994. "Hindrances to the Development of an Ethnic Economy among Mexican Migrants." *Human Organization* 53:263–68.

Waldinger, Roger. 1985. "Immigrant Enterprise and the Structure of the Labour Market." Pp. 213–28 in *New Approaches to Economic Life: Economic Restructuring, Unemployment and the Social Division of Labor,* edited by B. Roberts, R. Finnegan, and D. Gallie. Manchester: Manchester University Press.

———. 1986. "Immigrant Enterprise: A Critique and Reformulation." *Theory and Society* 15:249–86.

———. 1993. "The Ethnic Enclave Debate Revisited." *International Journal of Urban and Regional Research* 17:444–52.

———. 1995. "The 'Other Side' of Embeddedness: A Case Study of the Interplay of Economy and Ethnicity." *Ethnic and Racial Studies* 18(3):555–80.

Werbner, Pnina. 1990. *The Migration Process: Capital, Gifts, and Offerings among British Pakistanis.* Oxford: Berg Publications.

Wilson, Kenneth D., and Alejandro Portes. 1980. "Immigrant Enclaves: An Analysis of the Labor Market Experiences of Cubans in Miami." *American Journal of Sociology* 86:295–319.

Wilson, Kenneth L., and W. Allen Martin. 1982. "Ethnic Enclaves: A Comparison of the Cuban and Black Economies in Miami." *American Journal of Sociology* 88(1):135–60.

Yoon, In-Jin. 1995. "The Growth of Korean Immigrant Entrepreneurship in Chicago." *Ethnic and Racial Studies* 18:315–35.

Zhou, Min. 1992. *Chinatown: The Socioeconomic Potential of an Urban Enclave.* Philadelphia: Temple University Press.

Zimmer, Catherine, and Howard Aldrich. 1987. "Resource Mobilization through Ethnic Networks: Kinship Ties of Shopkeepers in England." *Sociological Perspectives* 30:422–45.

NEIGHBORHOOD CHARACTERISTICS, COMMUNITY DEVELOPMENT CORPORATIONS, AND THE COMMUNITY DEVELOPMENT INDUSTRY SYSTEM: A CASE STUDY OF THE AMERICAN DEEP SOUTH

Robert Mark Silverman

SOURCES OF CDC EMERGENCE

The first community development corporations (CDC) were formed in the late 1960's to address poverty and disinvestment in minority communities across the USA. In essence, these organizations were envisioned to have a strong grassroots orientation and address the social and physical development needs of neighborhoods where disenfranchised groups were concentrated. In many respects. CDCs were originally conceived as organizations that would promote alternative development in the United States, and they were designed in a manner that paralleled the structure and function of non-governmental organizations (NGO) in developing nations. In fact, many of the characteristics originally ascribed to CDCs have also been attributed to NGOs engaged in grassroots activities outside of the United States (Anheier and Seibel 1990; Freidmann 1992; McCarthy, et.al. 1992). However, the institutional context in which CDCs are embedded has changed since their inception. The relationship between these organizations, the public sector, private organizations, and grassroots interests has been in flux for decades. Though CDCs operate in an environment where resources and institutional networks are relatively unstable, there has been a general tendency over time for CDCs to become less autonomous and grassroots in their orientation as larger nonprofit or-

ganizations and governmental agencies have increasingly sought to utilize them for policy and program implementation. This trend parallels the experiences of NGOs in developing nations. For instance, Brown and Ashman (1996) identified the conflict between grassroots control and institutional actors in their analysis of NGOs in African and Asian countries. Similarly, Coston (1998) examined the institutional constraints NGOs encounter in her discussion of government-NGO relationships.

In light of these issues, this paper revisits aspects of past research discussing why CDCs emerge and examines the degree to which contemporary organizations are formed in response to structural constraints at the local level and broader institutional pressures. This issue is of interest because past writings in this area remain somewhat equivocal, with most discussions identifying both community activism and institutional intervention as critical in the development of CDCs. For instance, it has been argued that these organizations initially grew out of grassroots movements of the 1960's and 1970's which advocated for greater equity in urban renewal policy, social welfare programs, and civil rights legislation (Perry 1972; Perry 1987; Twelvetrees 1989; O'Connor 1999; Stoutland 1999). Discussions of early CDC emergence focused on a bottom-up approach to building these organizations and their promotion of a more democratic form of community development. This can be distinguished from contemporary accounts of CDC emergence which focus on the expanded role that large institutions from the public, private and nonprofit sectors have in guiding organizational development. In essence, this dialogue identifies a shift toward a greater institutional role in the community development field.

Concern about this shift has fueled several debates related to the role of CDCs in the urban development and policy processes of contemporary American cities: On one side of the issue, scholars have reached an impasse regarding the degree to which CDCs have the capacity to address structural constraints in urban neighborhoods (Bratt 1997; Keating 1997; Stoecker 1997a; Stoecker 1997b). In part, this debate has focused on two issues: the ability of contemporary CDCs to democratize the urban policy process, and the utility of abandoning the current CDC model and adopting an alternative approach to community development that is based on the creation of municipal community development organizations to meet the physical development needs of aging inner-city neighborhoods. To date, disagreement continues concerning the merits of refining the existing CDC model as opposed to developing an alternative.

A related realm of contemporary dialogue concerning these organizations focuses on the extent to which they have recently become more viable due to the development of new institutional relationships in the community development field. In essence, it is proposed that the CDC model has become more resilient in the contemporary period in response to the growth of institutional networks and support for local community development efforts (Clavel, Pitt and Yin 1997; Gittell and Vidal 1998). The cornerstone of this debate is tied to the concept of an emerging community development industry system which links CDCs to local government, corporate philanthropy, and faith-based organizations (Yin 1998). It is argued that this system creates a broader pool of

resources for CDCs, enhancing their capacity to implement social service programs and physical development in urban communities. Despite these apparent gains, questions concerning grassroots participation in the policy formulation process and the extent to which the community development industry system expands decision-making power to disenfranchised groups remain.

This article attempts to explore the degree to which the neighbourhood conditions that promote CDC emergence are subsequently imprinted upon the organizational relationships manifested in the community development industry system. This research is based on a critical case study of organizational development in one city, Jackson, Mississippi. This city was selected as the focus of this study because each of its seven CDCs emerged during the 1990s, a time period corresponding to the rise of the community development industry system. Fortuitously, the timing of CDC emergence in this city also corresponded with the collection of the decennial US Census, allowing for an analysis of the relationship between neighborhood characteristics and subsequent organizational development. This analysis was done in conjunction with ethnographic field research that examined the internal structure of the CDCs in this city and their ties to other institutions in the community development industry system.

Methods and Data

Quantitative and qualitative methods were used to study the relationship between local context, CDC emergence and organizational development. Independent variables measuring neighborhood characteristic were drawn from the 1990 Census of Population and Housing Summary Tape File 3A (US Department of Commerce 1990).

The results from the quantitative analysis were augmented with ethnographic data from a series of formal interviews with CDC directors in the city. These interviews were conducted during October 1998 and November 1998. During the interviews informants were asked a series of open-ended questions drawn from an interview guide that was prepared in advance. The interview guide consisted of thirteen items and nineteen probes. Given the small population under examination, a number of methodological steps were taken to insure that the entire population of CDCs in Jackson was identified. Two lists of community-based organizations were referenced. One was a list of neighborhood organizations registered with the City of Jackson, and the other was a list of community-based organizations compiled by the Mississippi Urban Research Centre at Jackson State University. In addition, individuals active in Jackson's nonprofit community were consulted to ensure that all CDCs were identified. The list of CDCs in the population was also verified by means of snowball sampling. In total, a population of seven CDCs was identified in Jackson. All of the CDCs were established after 1990 and there was

no record of similar organizations existing in the city prior to that date.

The Disenfranchised and Disinvestment

Neighborhoods where CDCs emerge are often characterized as being in physical and social decline. These communities are typically thought to have populations with the following characteristics: numerous female headed households, large concentrations of minorities, low levels of educational attainment, low household incomes, and multiple households receiving public assistance. Similarly, the built environment in these communities is thought to be in a state of deterioration with depressed property values, low rates of home ownership, and high rates of property abandonment. On the surface, the neighborhoods within the boundaries of CDCs in Jackson share several of these characteristics. Table 1 compares various dimensions of population and housing characteristics in the City of Jackson and its CDC neighborhoods.

TABLE 1 Descriptive statistics for city of Jackson and CDC neighborhoods

	City of Jackson	CDC Neighborhoods
Total Populations:	**196,594**	**27,267**
% Female	53.61	54.04
% Black	55.74	94.85
% Age 25 and Above without a High School Diploma	15.09	25.05
Total Households:	**79,352**	**10,535**
Median Income–US$ (1989)	$23,270	$11,639
% Receiving Public Assistance (1989)	10.83	24.80
% Receiving Social Security (1989)	26.94	28.49
Total Housing Units:	**71,492**	**8,533**
Median Value–US$	$53,600	$34,970
% Owner Occupied	51.89	27.89
% Renter Occupied	38.65	54.95
% Vacant	9.46	17.16

Source: U.S. Department of Commerce, Bureau of the Census. (1990) *1990 Census of Population and Housing Summary Tape File 3A.* Washington D.C.: Data User Services Division.

As reflected in Table 1, the city and the CDC neighborhoods present noticeable contrasts along the lines of race, educational attainment, income, public assistance receivership, housing values, and housing tenure. On the surface, it appears that several variables interacted to promote the development of CDCs in this city. In order to identify which factors were correlated with CDC emergence the relationship between neighborhood characteristics and the dependent variable was tested statistically.

Through such an examination it becomes possible to isolate specific neighborhood conditions that promote CDC emergence and use those results to make inferences about the manner in which they impact subsequent organizational relations. The model indicates that there is a significant relationship between the percent of housing units in a neighborhood that are vacant and the emergence of a CDC. In this relationship, each increase in the percentage of vacant housing units increases the odds that a CDC will emerge by 7.57%.

(Parametric statistical table not shown.) Two important characteristics of neighborhoods emerged. These areas have significant numbers of residents who are members of disenfranchised groups and they exhibit significant levels of physical disinvestment. In this specific case, these characteristics are exhibited in terms of a residential population that is 94.85% black and a built environment where 17.16% of the housing units are vacant. Of course, these characteristics may be expressed differently in other settings, but general patterns of disenfranchisement and disinvestment would be expected to be correlated with CDC emergence in other communities. Given the significance of these neighborhood features an examination of the degree to which they are incorporated into the organizational structure of CDCs and the community development industry system becomes incumbent.

COMMUNITY DEVELOPMENT SUBCONTRACTORS

The CDCs examined in this study were imprinted by the neighborhood conditions. In fact, each of the organizations' directors described how these factors influenced the mission of their CDCs. For example, directors of CDCs described how issues related to substandard housing, commercial abandonment, mortage redlining, commercial disinvestment, and deteriorating physical infrastructure shaped organizational goals. For instance, while discussing the decision to form a CDC one director stated:

After a period we started looking at, perhaps we should get involved in economic development activities specifically related to housing. And, that is how the board of directors decided that we should form a community development corporation. . . . It fits pretty neatly into our thinking, because all of the socio-economic conditions that are ripe for housing are also a part of this area.

Similar sentiment was echoed by the other directors. Yet, the physical characteristics of the neighborhoods were not the only factors influencing CDC emergence. These organizations also developed in response to the social structure of the community. In part, this was reflected in some of the CDC's programs dealing with poverty and unemployment. However, it was most clearly illustrated in decisions related to staffing and the appointment of members to the boards of directors of the CDCs. For example, all of the directors expressed the desire to maintain strong black representation in their organizations. As a result, all of the directors and staff members in these organizations were black, and each formed a governing board that was majority black. In essence, actual representation of community members was incorporated into the CDC model.

Despite the incorporation of neighborhood residents and their interests into the goals and structure of the CDCs, the priorities of outside institutions weighed heavily on decision-making. As CDCs planned their development, consideration was given to the relationship between local context and the scope of funding opportunities available through the community development industry system. For example, all of the CDC directors identified external organizations that sponsored their projects and programs. These organizations included a variety of government agencies, nonprofit organizations, private foundations, and private corporations. Although the CDCs were well grounded in the local community, their primary resources came from external organizations. Subsequently, the CDCs had to design their projects and programs in response to the community development goals of these larger external institutions. Moreover, members of the community development industry system were able to imprint on CDCs as they were created, since many of these larger organizations supplied them with funds and played a role in chartering them. For instance, one director described how the parameters of existing funding sources and the power of local government to grant CDC status to an organization influenced decisions surrounding organizational development:

We have a good sense of what kind of money comes into the city for Community Development Block Grant Dollars. We know that there's a specific set-aside for CHD dollars, Community Housing Development dollars, if you are able to get that status. So, we know that the EC community has specific pots of monies for specific kinds of things. We know what those are and the dollars that are allocated to them. Those were considerations, because the agency has to be funded, and it has to be funded yearly.

Another CDC director described similar factors influencing organizational develop-

ment. This CDC depended on a sizeable grant from the United States Department of Housing and Urban Development (HUD) which entailed a number of requirements that governed the organization's design and mission. In accordance with this grant, the CDC was formed to address conditions in neighborhoods surrounding historically black colleges and university (HBCU). As a result, the HUD grant set parameters for activities the CDC pursued and it predetermined the neighborhood in which the CDC would operate. In effect, the scope of organizational activities was determined by HUD guidelines, and additional requirements to collaborate with a local HBCU further constrained the parameters of the organization's community building efforts. In light of these institutional interests, neighborhood participation became more marginalized within the CDC.

In essence, the structure of institutional relationships create a very specific functional role for CDCs in the broader community development industry system. These organizations primarily exist to implement projects and programs for larger institutions. Furthermore, the subordinate position of CDCs makes them susceptible to co-opation and places them in a situation where moderating grassroots activism can result in short-term benefits. Within the context of their position in the community development industry system, CDCs are able to create opportunities for member of disenfranchised groups to become involved in administrative functions at the neighborhood level, and they assist in efforts to redistribute resources in distressed communities. Nevertheless, these roles do not reorganize the distribution of power as it relates to the design of community development policy. In effect, CDCs act as subcontractors in the broader community development industry system. In this capacity they relieve larger public, private and nonprofit organizations of many of the risks associated with neighborhood revitalization efforts and supply these organizations with a flexible environment in which to operate. Consequently, CDCs and the people who work in them are at the bottom of the community development industry system. The irony of this situation is that many of the structural inequalities that CDCs were created to address are rearticulated within the framework of the industry system in which they are embedded.

In terms of the functional role of organizations, the system is divided among policy making organizations and those that focus on implementation. Although there is exchange and feedback between different organizations in the community development industry system, the functional roles that organizations assume create institutional barriers to CDC and neighborhood interests in the policy formulation process. This disadvantage is compounded by inequalities between sectors in the community development industry system. For instance, the organizations identified as primary sector organizations tend to have greater policy-making power, reliable sources of capital, budget allocation authority, and internally developed administrative and technical expertise. In contrast, CDCs, which are identified as secondary sector organizations, tend to have limited access to the policy-making process, unstable sources of capital, limited budget authority, and a dearth of administrative and technical expertise. Hence, CDCs are embedded in an interorganizational environment which maintains their dependence on the subcontracting of neighborhood revitalization projects and social service programs.

Inherent in the structure of the community development industry system is a 'middleman' role for CDCs. These organizations are positioned between neighborhoods and the primary sector institutions that recruit them as subcontractors. This is a precarious position because of the impact of disenfranchisement and disinvestment in CDC neighborhoods, the limited access that residents and CDCs have to the pol-

icy making process, and the resource constraints that CDCs face. Nevertheless, CDCs provide considerable benefits to the community development industry system. Of utmost importance, they buffer primary sector organizations in the community development industry system from criticism when urban policy fails to address structural disadvantages faced by poor communities, while simultaneously serving as model organizations that legitimize the devolution of public sector activity in the area of urban redevelopment.

CONCLUSION

Unquestionably, the role of CDCs in the community development industry system is different than grassroots activists would have predicted several decades ago. The current community development industry system substantially confines CDC and neighborhood interests to the policy implementation arena while allowing grassroots organizations limited voice in the policy formulation process. In a real sense, the CDC model has been unable to promote meaningful participation in the policy formulation process among disenfranchised groups and communities affected by disinvestment. Instead, these groups have received representation by proxy through primary sector organizations in the community development industry system. In exchange, CDCs have been incorporated into this interorganizational network and transformed into subcontractors of public sector services to distressed communities.

The findings from this study mirror the patterns of CDC development identified in the United States as a whole. For instance, Gittell and Vidal (1998), and Rubin (2000) have commented on the growing role of governmental agencies and private foundations in the community development process. However, the findings from this study are distinct, since they suggest that the emerging community development industry system entails more clearly articulated roles for actors within the field of community development. In particular, the redefinition of CDCs as subcontractors within the community development industry system articulates a functional dichotomy between community-based organizations and larger institutions in the public and private sectors. This dichotomy parallels Coston's (1998) discussion of the use of NGO's as independent contractors by governmental and international actors. The implications of this orientation are far reaching. For instance, Petras (1999) points out that the 'sub-contracting' role many NGOs fill results in the moderation of their emphasis on grassroots activism and a reduction in advocacy for the redistribution of wealth and power in society. In essence, NGOs end up serving a similar buffering function for their governmental and international sponsors as CDCs do for primary sector institutions in the American context. Given this potential, more emphasis needs to be placed on expanding the level of access that grassroots organizations have to policy formulation at both the national and international levels.

REFERENCES

Anheier, H. K. and Seivel, W. (1990) *The Third Sector: Comparative Studies of Non-profit Organizations.* Walter de Gruyter, New York.

Bratt, R. (1997) CDCs: Contributions outweigh contradictions, a reply to Randy Stoecker, *Journal of Urban Affairs,* **19**(1), 23–28.

Brown, L. D. (1996) Participation, social capital, and intersectoral problem solving: African and Asian cases, *World Development,* **24**(9), 1467–1479.

Clavel, P. Pitt, J. and Yin, J. (1997) The community option in urban policy, *Urban Affairs Review,* **32**(4), 435–458.

Coston, J. M. (1998) A model and typology of government-NGO relationships, *Nonprofit and Voluntary Sector Quarterly,* **27**(3), 358–382.

Friedmann, J. (1992) *Empowerment: The Politics of Alternative Development.* Blackwell Publishing, Cambridge, MA.

Gittell, R. and Vidal, A. (1998) *Community Organizing, Building Social Capital as a Development Strategy.* Sage Publications, Thousand Oaks, CA.

Glaser, B. G., and Strauss, A. L. (1967) *The Discovery of Grounded Theory: Strategies for Qualitative Research* Aldine De Gruyter, New York.

Jorgensen, D. L. (1989) *Participant Observation: A Methodology for Human Studies.* Sage Publications, Thousand Oaks, CA.

Keating, W. D. (1997) The CDC model of urban development: a reply to Randy Stoecker, *Journal of Urban Affairs,* **19**(1), 29–33.

Mendard, S. (1995) *Applied Logistic Regression Analysis.* Sage Publications, Thousand Oaks, CA.

McCarthy, K.D., Hodgkinson, V.A., Sumariwalla, R. D. and Associates (1992) *The Nonprofit Sector in the Global Community: Voices from Many Nations.* Jossey-Bass Publishers, San Francisco.

Petras, J. (1999) NGOs: in the service of imperialism. *Journal of Contemporary Asia,* **29**(4), 429–440.

O'Connor, A. (1999) Swimming against the tide: a brief history of federal policy in poor communities, pp. 71–137 in R.F. Ferguson and W.T. Dickens, eds, *Urban Problems and Community Development* Brookings Institute Press, Washington, DC.

Perry, S. E. (1972) Black institutions. Black separatism, and ghetto economic development. *Human Organization,* **31**(3), 271–278.

Perry, S. E. (1987) *Communities on the Way: Rebuilding Local Economies in the United States and Canada.* State University of New York Press, Albany.

Rubin, H. J. (2000) *Renewing Hope Within Neighborhoods of Despair: The Community-Based Development Model.* State University of New York Press, Albany.

Stoecker, R. (1997a) The CDC Model of Urban Redevelopment: A Critique and an Alternative, *Journal of Urban Affairs,* **19**(1), 1–22.

Stoecker, R. (1997b) Should we . . . could we . . . change the CDC model? A rejoinder. *Journal of Urban Affairs* **19**(1), 35–44.

Stoutland, Sara E. (1999) Community development corporations: mission, strategy, and accomplishments, pp. 193–240 in R.F. Ferguson and W.T. Dickens, eds., *Urban Problems and Community Development,* Brookings Institute Press.

Twelvetrees, A. (1989) *Organizing for Neighborhood Development: A Comparative Study of Community Development Corporations and Citizen Power Organizations.* Avebury, Brookfield.

US Department of Commerce, Bureau of the Census (1990) *Census of Population and Housing Summary Tape File 3A.* Data User Services Division, Washington, DC.

Yin, J. S. (1998) The community development industry system: a case study of politics and institutions in Cleveland, 1967–1997. *Journal of Urban Affairs,* **20**(2), 137–157.

B.
Community Participation

Social Connections

LOOSE CONNECTIONS
Joining Together in America's Fragmented Communities

Robert Wuthnow

The larger climate in which civic participation can flourish is increasingly conditioned by political and legal initiatives. The health of American democracy depends to a large extent on statutes that promote fairness when personal trust may be lacking, that encourage equitable distribution of economic resources, and that maintain checks and balances among the branches of government. Civic participation appears to be a necessary but not sufficient means of maintaining these political and legal conditions. The porousness of institutions does not in itself imply that these conditions are eroding. But porousness may make governing more complex and create greater opportunities for exploitation: the traditional checks and balances of America's democratic system may not work as well when so many economic transactions take place across national boundaries or when the mass media disseminate heavily edited information to people who have little interaction with their neighbors. It is important that civic participation not focus only on doing good for needy individuals but also on the laws and regulations pertaining to whole populations.

The corporate or for-profit sector will continue to be a major force in shaping the character of civic involvement. Its role is evident in local communities through such organizations as the Chamber of Commerce and Jaycees or in the memberships and meeting places of Rotary, Lions, and Kiwanis. In the 1970s corporate civic responsibility was encouraged through such efforts as the Environmental Defense Fund, Businessmen for the Public Interest, the Council on Economic Priorities, and the Corporate Accountability Research Group. Stockholder initiatives and occasional boycotts were used to raise awareness of corporate responsibility and major firms such as AT&T, General Motors, the Bank of America, and

Boise Cascade introduced public policy committees and community projects as a way of responding to public concerns. Foundations that derive their earnings from corporations have also played an increasing role in financing the work of nonprofit organizations and volunteer efforts.

The corporation has also become one of the major places where people make friends and interact with casual acquaintances (as one woman observes, "It's the prime social aspect of my life"). If civic involvement depends on social ties, the corporation is central in facilitating such involvement. Corporate cultures that reward volunteering and make civic activities more visible have the potential to encourage the relationships that lead to civic involvement.

As people talk about their civic activities, they mention corporations but less often than nonprofit organizations, government agencies, service clubs, and churches. Corporations train people to handle managerial responsibilities and connect them to influential members of the community, both of which prove helpful to the volunteer efforts of employees. Corporations also contribute to service agencies through foundations, in-kind donations (such as leftovers from bakeries and restaurants), direct financing and loans for community housing projects or minority and low-income business initiatives, and participation in community projects such as clean-up days and the Special Olympics.

Compared to the resources at their disposal, the role of corporations in civic activities is relatively small. Funding for nonprofit organizations comes largely from government grants and individual donations rather than from corporate philanthropy, and although many corporations participate in United Way campaigns and encourage employees to do volunteer work, they seldom give employees time during work hours to participate in community projects. Some employees even report taboos

against talking about politics or civic concerns at work. For their part, executives point out that large donations of time or money to civic projects are difficult to reconcile with market pressures that require corporations to keep output at competitive prices. They speak of the need for public programs, laws, and other regulations to ensure that social needs are addressed broadly and fairly.

Corporate leaders need to be aware of the considerable influence of business conditions on the porousness of American life. Much of the looseness of civic participation is linked to the ways in which market capitalism has developed in the United States since World War II. Residential mobility often results from corporate transfers or business closings.

The educational system encourages young people to break ties with their hometowns, develop broad connections, and participate in national labor markets. Divorce is sometimes the outcome of conflicts in two-career families, and is often an option because of dual earnings. Local service organizations are hurt by the divided geographic loyalties of long-distance commuters. Family bankruptcies and leisure time devoted to spectator sports and television are partly a function of the credit-card and entertainment industries and corporate advertising. High unemployment and declining service organizations in inner cities are related to the flight of corporations to suburbs or rural areas, not to mention their quest for cheap labor in overseas markets.

Of these developments, the movement of corporate capital, headquarters, and jobs has probably had the most significant impact on the character of civic involvement; it has also made it harder for nonprofit organizations to work in tandem with corporations. When top decisionmaking roles are transferred to other communities or other countries, local leaders are left with no corporate officials who clearly have local or regional interests as a priority. As one leader complains, "I used to be able to walk into the president's office at [such-and-such corporation] and have an answer when I left; now that they've merged and no longer have a headquarters here, I don't know who's in charge."

The corporate sector is thus deeply implicated in the changing nature of civic involvement. The unraveling of communities, families, and commitment to service organizations is as much attributable to markets as it is to morals. Public discussion about ways to solidify social relationships and restore communities must not be limited to debates about government agencies and individual volunteers. It must also take into account the economic forces to which corporations are subject and the ways in which corporate leaders can respond imaginatively to them.

Religious organizations can help encourage civic participation by taking an active role in their communities. Many people are motivated by religious beliefs, and some have learned about community projects through their churches or synagogues. Many believe their congregations are doing all that is possible, but they wish that more could be done.

If churches are going to do more for their communities, they will have to cooperate with one another. Individual congregations often are too small or are faced with declining finances and thus cannot mount more than token efforts to minister to the wider community. In the past they might have been assisted by denominational bodies or formed alliances with other congregations from the same denomination. These possibilities are less available now because denominational resources and loyalties have weakened. Large congregations may be tempted to keep close control over their own resources rather than working cooperatively with other organizations. Their reach into the community will thus be limited.

Forming loose coalitions and alliances among congregations is a way to amass greater resources, as cooperative food pantries and

homeless shelters illustrate. Interfaith coalitions demonstrate that the members of their various congregations are also members of a single community and are willing to work together for its benefit. As one man (a member of an African American church) puts it: "When you talk about, 'My church is doing something in community X,' that's an isolated effort. Continue doing those isolated things but on a grander scale. Churches, mosques, and synagogues need to combine their efforts, and they need to do like the churches did in the 1950s and 1960s and develop a plan to attack these larger issues."

Religious organizations can also work effectively with nonreligious agencies to address community issues. Development corporations that provide funding and expertise in community planning can cooperate with religious organizations who provide volunteers to serve on oversight boards or to wield hammers at construction sites. Religious organizations sometimes make an important contribution just by providing space for public meetings at which community concerns can be discussed.

Congregations in suburban areas and small towns are often involved in projects that benefit less advantaged communities as well as their own. But it is low-income, inner-city people who voice the strongest pleas for congregations to do more. One inner-city resident characterizes vividly the kinds of work that congregations should be doing: "When you have a church and drug dealers are selling drugs on its corner, the church needs to pull its congregation together and they need to think about an active way to develop a plan of action that solves the problem. That means attacking the issues on a political front, like writing or protesting. It means doing whatever they can on an economic front to empower people so that they don't have the need to sell drugs. It may mean standing on the corner all night themselves to prevent people from doing it. You can't say that it's wrong for people to sell drugs, and not challenge them. Any organization that believes in God can never, never, under any circumstance, justify their inaction with regards to social injustice."

Another relationship that bears close scrutiny in efforts to strengthen civic involvement is that between civic associations and the mass media. In today's world citizens depend heavily on the media for their knowledge about civic issues. This is why some observers are concerned that the media may be eroding the role of community organizations. On the one hand, too much dependence on the media seems to keep people at home watching television rather than participating in their communities. One woman who thinks civic participation is declining in her community explains, "I think television has a lot to do with it; people congregate around their television sets instead of around the village green"—a perception that seems to be confirmed by evidence that those who watch more television are less likely to be involved in civic activities. On the other hand, television has become a way in which people learn about the needs of their communities, and many leaders of civic organizations feel they need to use the media to advertise their work and to help solicit donations and volunteers.

In an era of public relations specialists, one way civic organizations can make use of mass communications is by disseminating information to the media or working with media specialists to publicize a particular message or event. Large bureaucratic organizations relate to the media as one megalith to another, sending out special envoys to control what the media report. Jack Schmidt thinks Rotary should be doing more to cultivate the national newspapers and to get its message on television. Sara Mermel says the same thing about Hadassah: "What we really need is a full-time person working on public relations, getting an article in the paper at least once a week about what's happening; working with the media needs to be done by someone who knows how

to do it; it doesn't just happen." Another community leader has learned by trial and error how to deal with the media; at first she was troubled by the penchant for headlines and sound bites, but now she gives reporters a pithy image within the first two minutes of her conversation with them, and it generally appears as a headline.

The urban partnership in which Jacob Merrick is engaged is a loose network that cannot control the information it disseminates to the media, but its regional base encourages it to work with the press and local television stations to publicize issues that affect the entire region. An organization does not have to be large to do this effectively, as is illustrated by Nancy Fielding's use of the local newspaper to solicit members for the Garden Club and subsequent use of gardening magazines to spread information to interested people across the country. Another organization found it hard to get publicity in newspapers or on television, so it has turned to sending faxes and using the Internet.

Whether large or small, civic organizations need to use their limited resources wisely in dealing with the media. The acid test is how successfully they control their own information. Civic organizations need to communicate a different kind of information from that found in newspapers and on television. Many community leaders have local and specialized knowledge of particular problems that is not suitable for the mass media. It is a more practical form of knowledge, showing them how to tackle community problems instead of simply airing these problems. Civic organizations can be especially effective when they are able to disseminate information that motivates people to take responsibility for social problems, rather than simply feeling despondent about them. Leaders like Jacob Merrick devote a great deal of attention to setting up seminars and providing other occasions for such information to be disseminated.

The strengthening of civic involvement requires above all that people value their role as citizens and the responsibilities of citizenship. It was not without reason that the architects of American democracy looked as much to moral philosophy as to political theory. Good democracy has always depended on the virtue or character of its citizens. And virtue is a kind of strength, an awareness of who one is and what one's capacities are, that transcends simplistic views of citizenship that reduce it to such acts as voting or reading political columns in the newspaper.

In a loosely connected society it is often more difficult for people to know their civic role because their sources of identity are so varied and ephemeral. They are likely to be rewarded for presenting different sides of themselves in different situations. It is for this reason that the self has come to be problematic, taking more time to repair and requiring more effort for reflection. Civic engagement puts people in new situations where they may be forced to think harder about their identities. Personal repair work is likely to go hand in hand with civic engagement, rather than conflicting with it.

Evidence from people who are involved in their communities suggests that personal virtue does not simply precede civic involvement but is an attendant feature of it. People who take an active part in civic organizations typically feel they have grown because of the experience. They gain information that gives them confidence in negotiating with complex political realities, or they learn to muster reserves of courage to speak at meetings. Some who participate in activities that take them out of their own neighborhoods are especially likely to find their self-images recast by these engagements.

People who feel they know themselves and believe they are trying to do what is right generally believe they can trust others to do so as well. Some who have doubts about themselves say they nevertheless try to behave dependably and hope that others will respond by doing the same. Civic organizations can help restore trust by paying more explicit attention to it. When social ties are loose, deliberate effort must be expended to establish expectations about the conditions under which trust is warranted.

Behaving politely and respectfully is a crucial aspect of the interpersonal relations on which trust depends. It is more than a semantic coincidence that has led social theorists to emphasize the integral relationship between civility and civil society. To behave civilly involves showing fundamental respect for the dignity as well as the rights of another human being. Civility is rooted in a prior commitment to the worth of others even if those others have different beliefs or interests from one's own. But civility is also demonstrated in the decorum with which personal relationships are conducted. It includes common etiquette, such as letting others finish speaking, respecting their opinions, and avoiding incendiary language.

Loose connections tempt citizens to behave in a less civil manner because relationships are more likely to be transitory and casual than enduring and dependent on good will. It is precisely for this reason, however, that civility is more important in fluid or sporadic relationships. Adhering to widely acknowledged patterns of decorum becomes a way to signal one's trustworthiness to strangers. Intimate relationships can more easily be repaired when violations of decorum occur. Loose relationships lacking familiar contact need additional behavioral evidence to engender respect and trust. Civility demonstrates respect, a commitment to the humanity of another person that may sustain the relationship despite tension and disagreement.

People who are active in community organizations or in their neighborhoods often mention small manifestations of civility that have impressed them: a mayor who shows up on time to play softball at a community picnic or someone who sends a letter of appreciation to a business that has tried to resolve a community conflict. Sometimes the examples seem trivial, such as paying someone a small compliment as a way of healing a grievance, or staying on the telephone a few minutes longer despite needing to do other things. But they clearly are not trivial to the people involved. They are remembered, not so much as ways people show kindness to one another, but as reasons people believe they can *trust* one another. Often it is the small token of caring, even more than getting the job done, that convinces people it is worthwhile to take part in civic activities.

Because of the porous nature of our society, many people are not attracted to civic organizations and are unlikely to join, no matter how much good these organizations do in their communities. The reasons vary from feeling too busy to believing that the participants in such organizations have a different kind of personality. Individualism, however it is defined, is often a major aspect of these reasons. Yet it is a form of individualism that people see as respectable rather than as a selfish absorption with themselves. As one woman observes when asked why she does not join organizations: "I do not want to be steered along my path. I don't want to be part of a herd. I don't want to be made to feel guilty. I don't want to be part of a social group that I might not enjoy."

It is unlikely that someone like this will overcome her deep antipathy toward membership groups in order to become involved in her community. Indeed, she finds other ways to engage with community needs, such as responding to the call of a neighbor who has been burglarized, keeping in touch with friends and family by phone, donating money to a battered women's shelter, participating in a pick-up musical group, and above all working long hours as a speech pathologist. In any given month she embodies the nonprofit professional, the volunteer, and the soul mate in her practice of civic involvement. She illustrates the diverse ways in which people can play responsible roles in their communities, even when they are not attracted to civic organizations.

That individuals can contribute in so many different ways means that a great deal of responsibility falls on the individuals themselves. This is where moral resolve becomes important. It consists in taking responsibilities seriously, but also in recognizing the social realities with which one is confronted. Nothing in this woman's personal makeup guarantees her continuing involvement in civic affairs or prevents her from becoming so self-absorbed that she ignores the problems that beset the needy in other communities (or her own). She is not drawn out of herself by participating in groups that expose her to people of other races or income brackets, and she is not compelled to listen to speakers talking about unpleasant topics by virtue of obligations to any service organization. Yet several important realities of her life reinforce a certain level of civic participation.

The first reality is her work. As a speech pathologist, she understands something of the contribution of nonprofit organizations, clinics, schools, and government agencies to the well-being of society. She works in a city among people who are quite different from the ones in her suburban neighborhood. Her work puts her in routine contact with a wide variety of organizations, including mental health programs, hospitals, and agencies for the elderly. She is intensely interested in public policies that affect her own and similar organizations; in this she is a self-interested citizen, but one whose interests are also geared toward the provision of social services.

A second is her upbringing. She works in a nonprofit organization partly because her parents taught her the value of caring for other people and her teachers reinforced this value. As a young woman she developed an interest in community needs that continues to be expressed in her work and in some of her leisure activities. Although the daily reinforcement of these values in her work is important, she learned much of what it means to be a good citizen earlier in life.

A third reality is her exposure to the mass media. Being a college-educated professional, she has been trained to keep informed about what is happening in the society. She admits to being uninterested in much of what she reads or sees on television, but she pays attention to the statements of public officials, follows election campaigns, and talks about current events with her friends and family. The media, as well as her job and her upbringing, prompt her with ideas about how to be a responsible citizen.

Critics of contemporary civil society want more than these nominal forms of civic participation. They point out that many people do not work in nonprofit organizations, that those who do may become insular and self-interested, and that having good values and being a media consumer are probably not sufficient for the effective functioning of a spirited democracy. But criticisms of democracy must also take into account the ways in which people do participate in their communities. Rather than calling only for greater personal resolve or for a sweeping cultural reorientation, it may be more useful to work through these existing modes of participation. Nonprofit organizations, schools and families, and the mass media are among the significant institutions through which careful deliberation about public values can take place.

A difficult issue in a society characterized by loose connections is the dilemma of how to make decisions about different levels and kinds of civic involvement. This dilemma has grown in direct proportion to the freedom of choice that is so deeply valued in American culture. Tightly bounded communities and organizations compelled their members to be involved in civic activities. The moral force came from

the outside (from the expectations of other members), rather than having to arise from within. People attended meetings, helped with pancake feeds, or voted because it was customary. They knew that respect, offices, and mutual aid flowed to those who fulfilled these customary expectations. Loose connections in porous institutions depend more on individual deliberation. Sporadic contact is less likely to provide occasions for reflection about enduring values and identity. Messages from competing sources (including internalized messages) provide justifications for alternative responses. For example, helping out, advancing one's career, thinking of oneself as "nonpolitical," being a faithful friend, taking care of one's own needs, pursuing one's interests, and doing what one enjoys can often be found in a single person's language about engaging (or not engaging) in particular civic activities. Even long-term members of service organizations are likely to be faced with conflicting messages from all these moral languages.

It is in relation to the moral dimension of civic involvement that concern about the balance between self-interest and social commitment can best be understood. Moral choices are never made in pure isolation, but are influenced by social context. Contexts that reinforce languages of self-interest, personal happiness, and pleasure are abundant. A consumer economy encourages people to think in these languages in order to sell entertainment, therapy, fast food, expensive automobiles, vacations, and the like. Contexts that reinforce values of service and sharing are often submerged relative to those emphasizing gratification. Thinking seriously about service or about the complexity of public issues is less likely to provide immediate gratification than focusing on the messages of advertising. Participation in volunteer organizations, community service programs, churches, or town meetings is thus important as a way of reinforcing the languages of civic involvement, as much as it is a means of actually contributing to the community.

A popular interpretation of America's social ills blames the newer, more loosely connected forms of civic involvement themselves. Observers who believe traditional membership organizations are the only way to sustain American democracy suggest that any substitute for these organizations inevitably will have undesirable effects. In this view, the increases in crime, drug use, and divorce and the decreases in voting and trust in public officials are evidence that nonprofit professionals, volunteers, and self-help groups are failing to provide vital social bonds or normative commitments that were reinforced by service organizations, fraternal associations, women's clubs, and neighborhoods. But this argument does not take adequate account of broader changes in social institutions. By ignoring these larger changes, it assumes that loose connections are the cause of social problems, rather than recognizing that loose connections and social problems are both results of other developments.

Interpreting current social problems as caused by loosely connected civic involvement implies that the way to solve them is to bring back commitment to membership organizations. These organizations, however, were embedded in a particular set of social arrangements. Loyalties were reinforced in the post-1945 era by (among other things) the memory of a massive war effort and the continuing fear of communist aggression, by segregated neighborhoods and discriminatory club policies that kept memberships homogeneous, and by a virtual taboo on civic organizations open to both men and women. It is unlikely that those who advocate a return to strong membership associations would be willing to promote fears about national security, racial segregation, and gender boundaries in order to bring about such a return.

Failure to understand the ways in which loosely connected forms of civic involvement

are related to one another produces inadequate proposals for addressing social problems. Some critics favor emphasizing volunteerism, viewing it as more effective than the efforts of professionals who work for the so-called welfare establishment or are paid by government programs. This argument implicitly recognizes that people's willingness to volunteer is crucial in social conditions that make it hard to mobilize strong membership associations. But it falters in its insular conception of volunteers. It does not recognize that the appeals that encourage people to volunteer come in large measure from nonprofit organizations.

Another argument emphasizes changing social conditions, stressing not increasing porousness but government bureaucracy and regulatory intervention. In this view, private initiatives have been driven out by public programs. People who depend on welfare checks and people who sit back and wait for the government to solve national problems are both examples of how bureaucracy stifles civic responsibility. This argument ignores all the other changes in American society in the past half-century. New information technologies, corporate downsizing, the relocation of businesses from center cities to suburbs, and rising levels of education, to name a few, have promoted porousness, which has in turn generated some of the social problems to which public and private agencies alike have attempted to respond.

Another popular view attributes worsening social conditions to moral failure on the part of individuals. One variant decries, the immorality of teenagers who become pregnant or use drugs, or that of homeless persons who do not find jobs or families who are on welfare. Another variant blames middle-class Americans who pursue their own interests and seek pleasure rather than participating in civic affairs. These arguments are correct that porous social conditions often give individuals greater discretion about how to lead their lives and thus pose moral questions that individuals need to ponder seriously. But the arguments are overly narrow when they ignore the social conditions that reinforce certain moral choices rather than others. Calls for marriage partners to resist divorce, for example, can be cast in more effective terms if they consider not only the moral resolve of the partners themselves but also ways in which corporate policies on employment and family leave might be altered to lessen the pressures on working couples.

To acknowledge that loose forms of civic involvement are embedded in porous social conditions is not to deny the weaknesses of these arrangements. It is fair to say that many social problems have increased *despite*—not because of—the efforts of volunteers, nonprofit organizations, and public agencies. Nevertheless, it is also fair to say that these kinds of civic involvement perpetuate certain responses to social problems and perhaps preclude consideration of others. Nonprofit professionals are often the first to admit that having to submit grant proposals to more than a dozen sources of funding is inefficient, even though they may recognize that competition and decentralization are preferable to depending on a single government agency. Volunteers

observe that their efforts are often ineffective, compared to those of paid professionals, if only because they do not have the requisite skills. Discussion is needed of ways in which civic organizations can adapt to these conditions.

American democracy continues to be a frustrating endeavor, just as its architects expected. As the twentieth century moves to its end, social observers are right to worry about the health of democracy and to question whether or not civic involvement is declining. As the society has become more diverse, the need for active engagement in our communities has increased. But it is also helpful to note that civic involvement has been changing. Despite the persistence of many clubs and service organizations from an earlier era, millions of Americans are experimenting with new ways of reaching out to their communities. The new forms of civic involvement have been shaped by the information technologies, the market forces, and the cultural redefinitions that have made our society more fluid. Part of the challenge confronting all civic-minded Americans is to understand these changes so that efforts to promote civic involvement can be both realistic and effective.

KICKING IN GROUPS

Nicholas Lemann

IN 1958 Edward Banfield published *The Moral Basis of a Backward Society,* a study of underdevelopment in a village at the southern tip of Italy—"the extreme poverty and backwardness of which," he wrote, "is to be explained largely (but not entirely) by the inability of the villagers to act together for their common good." Banfield called the prevailing ethos of the village "amoral familism": "Maximize the material, short-run advantage of the nuclear family; assume that all others will do likewise." The best way to improve the village's economic condition, he said, would be for "the southern peasant to acquire the ways of the north."

Ten years later, in *The Unheavenly City,* Banfield applied a similar line of argument to American inner-city black ghettos, without benefit of the kind of firsthand research he had done in Italy. This time he identified "present-mindedness" as the quality that caused the communities' problems. Whereas *The Moral Basis of a Backward Society* had been respectfully received, *The Unheavenly City* was so controversial that for years Banfield required police protection when he spoke in public. The lesson seems to be that studying the difference between northern and southern Italy is a safe way of addressing a question still very much on Americans' minds: Why is there such a wide variation in the social and economic health of our neighborhoods and ethnic groups and, for that matter, of different societies all over the world?

Robert Putnam, a professor of government at Harvard, has to decide whether to confront just this issue. In 1993 Putnam published a book called *Making Democracy Work: Civic Traditions in Modern Italy.* Though its main text is only 185 pages long, *Making Democracy Work* is the fruit of immense labor. In 1970 Italy created local governments in its twenty regions and turned over many of the functions of the central government to them. Putnam and a team of colleagues almost immediately embarked on a study of the new governments' performance, covering the entire nation and focusing particularly on a few localities, including a town quite near the one where Banfield researched his book. The finding that leaped out at Putnam was that the governments in the prosperous north of Italy outperformed the ones in the benighted south. Through a variety of statistical exercises he tried to demonstrate that their success was not simply a case of the rich getting richer. For example, he showed that regional government officials are less well educated in the north than in the south, and that in the northern provinces economic-development levels are not especially predictive of government performance. He found the north's secret to be a quality that Machiavelli called *virtu civile* ("civic virtue")— an ingrained tendency to form small-scale associations that create a fertile ground for political and economic development, even if (especially if, Putnam would probably say) the associations are not themselves political or economic. "Good government in Italy is a by-product of singing groups and soccer clubs," he wrote. Civic virtue both expresses and builds trust and cooperation in the citizenry, and it is these qualities—which Putnam called "social capital," borrowing a phrase from Jane Jacobs—that make everything else go well.

Putnam was arguing against the conventional wisdom in the social sciences, which holds that civic virtue is an appurtenance of a traditional society—"an atavism destined to disappear" with modernization, which replaces small organizations that operate by custom with big ones that operate by rules. Instead, he said, even the biggest and most modern societies can't function well if the local civic dimension is weak. He hinted here and there that it was actually the large bureaucratic overlay that was going to wind up being obsolete.

What causes some societies to become more civic-minded than others? In Italy, Putnam said, the north-south difference dates from the 1100s, when the Normans established a centralized, autocratic regime in the south, and a series of autonomous republics arose in the north. The southern system stressed what Putnam called "vertical bonds": it was rigidly hierarchical, with those at the bottom dependent on the patronage of landowners and officials rather than on one another. In the north small organizations such as guilds and credit associations generated "horizontal bonds," fostering a sense of mutual trust that doesn't exist in the south. Putnam continually stressed the "astonishing constancy" of the north-south difference: it survived the demise of the independent northern republics in the seventeenth century and the Risorgimento in the nineteenth. "The southern territories once ruled by the Norman kings," he wrote, "constitute exactly the seven least civic regions in the 1970s." We shouldn't expect the situation to change anytime soon, because "where institution building . . . is concerned, time is measured in decades."

Social science has become a statistical art, overwhelmingly concerned with using correlation coefficients to express the effect of one thing on another—or, to use the jargon, to dis-cover and isolate the independent variable that has the greatest influence on the dependent variable. Civic virtue can be understood as Putnam's contribution to an ongoing quest for the magic independent variable that will explain economic development; he belongs to an intellectual tradition that tries to locate it in intrinsic cultural tendencies. In this sense civic virtue is a descendant of Max Weber's Protestant ethic, and is the opposite of Oscar Lewis's culture of poverty and Banfield's amoral familism. The venerability of the tradition and its powerful commonsense appeal shouldn't obscure the fact that all such independent variables are, necessarily, artificial constructs. Civic virtue is measured (to three decimal places!) by cobbling together such indices as newspaper-readership figures, voter turnout, and the abundance of sports clubs, and is not, as Putnam admitted, all-powerful as a predictor. Even in parts of northern Italy "the actual administrative performance of most of the new governments"—the subject under study, after all—"has been problematical."

Nonetheless, when Putnam tentatively brought his theory home to the United States, it created a sensation—of exactly the opposite kind from the one Banfield created a quarter century ago with *The Unheavenly City*. An article called "Bowling Alone," which Putnam published in the January, 1995, issue of the *Journal of Democracy*, had an impact far, far beyond the usual for academic writing. In the wake of "Bowling Alone," Putnam has been invited to Camp David to consult with President Bill Clinton. His terminology has heavily influenced the past two State of the Union addresses: *Making Democracy Work*, initially ignored by the general-interest press, was reviewed on the front page of *The New York Times Book Review;* Putnam was prominently mentioned in the musings of Senator Bill Bradley about his disillusionment with politics; and, unlikeliest of all, he was the subject of a profile in *People* magazine.

The thesis of "Bowling Alone" is that "the vibrancy of American civil society"—the magic variable—"has notably declined over the past several decades." Putnam gets his title from the finding that from 1980 to 1993 league bowling declined by 40 percent while the number of individual bowlers rose by 10 percent. The rest of his evidence is less whimsical: voter turnout, church attendance, and union membership are down. The percentage of people who trust the government and who attend community meetings has dropped. The leading indicator for Putnam—membership in voluntary associations—is down. Look at the Boy Scouts, the Lions, the Elks, the Shriners, the Jaycees, the Masons, the Red Cross, the Federation of Women's Clubs, and the League of Women Voters: "Serious volunteering declined by roughly one-sixth" from 1974 to 1989. The logic of *Making Democracy Work* would suggest that the true import of these changes is not that they are inherently unfortunate so much as that they predict a broader decline in our society's economic vitality—since, according to Putnam, that vitality rests on a cultural bedrock of local associational strength.

Putnam is scrupulously careful in "Bowling Alone" not to push his theory too hard. Earlier this year, though, he stated the thesis more firmly, in an article in *The American Prospect* called "The Strange Disappearance of Civic America," and offered an explanation for it: Americans who were born after the Second World War are far less civic-minded than their elders, and the main reason is that they grew up after the introduction of television, which "privatizes our leisure time." Putnam is now working up a book on the subject.

"Bowling Alone" struck a nerve in part because it provided a coherent theory to explain the dominant emotion in American politics: a feeling that the quality of our society at the everyday level has deteriorated severely. An economic statistic like the "misery index" doesn't match the political mood; Putnam's

theory does. It is especially appealing to liberal politicians, who see in it the possibility of a rhetoric they can use to address an issue that has been owned by conservatives. Also, if Putnam is right that as local associations go, so goes the nation, his work suggests the possibility of solving our problems through relatively low-cost association-strengthening local initiatives that don't require higher taxes. This makes a wonderful message for Democrats, who want to offer a positive program that is not vulnerable to anti-tax rhetoric. Foundation executives, who want to believe that the limited grants they make can reap large social benefits, also tend to be Putnam fans. Even people whose interests aren't directly affected have eagerly subscribed to the theory of "Bowling Alone," partly because of its apparent validity and partly for reasons I'll discuss later.

It must be said, however, that the talk about "Bowling Alone," and to a lesser extent the article itself, directly contradict the logic of *Making Democracy Work*. In Putnam's Italian model the kind of overnight deterioration of civic virtue that he proposes regarding America would be inconceivable—once civic virtue is in place it is incredibly durable over the centuries. Putnam heartily endorses a theory from economic history called "path dependence," which he has summarized this way: "Where you can get to depends on where you're coming from, and some destinations you simply cannot get to from here." In "Bowling Alone" he quotes Tocqueville's view that "nothing . . . deserves more attention" than Americans' amazing associational predilections: by the standards of *Making Democracy Work,* these ought to have held us in good stead well into the next century. Putnam plainly believes that we were in pretty good associational shape as recently as 1960. How can a tendency toward civic engagement vanish in a single generation?

Not only was Putnam in *Making Democracy Work* insistent upon the lasting good effects of civic virtue, but he was elaborately pessimistic about the possibility of establishing civic virtue where it doesn't already exist. He predicted disaster in the former Communist dictatorships of Europe, because of their weakness in the local-associational area: "Palermo may represent the future of Moscow." Putnam drew this lesson from a comprehensive survey of Third World development efforts:

Unhappily from the point of view of social engineering . . . local organizations 'implanted' from the outside have a high failure rate. The most successful local organizations represent indigenous, participatory initiatives in relatively cohesive local communities.

If Putnam was right the first time, and civic virtue is deeply rooted, then it's worth wondering whether the United States might actually still have as much of it as ever, or nearly. If that is the case, the dire statistics in "Bowling Alone" reflect merely a mutation rather than a disappearance of civic virtue, because civic virtue has found new expressions in response to economic and social changes. From bowling leagues on up, many of the declining associations Putnam mentions are like episodes of *The Honeymooners* seen today—out of date.

I spent a couple of days phoning around in search of examples of new associations that have sprung up to take their place. Putnam mentions several of these in "Bowling Alone" in order to dismiss them as real replacements for the lost bowling leagues, either because they don't involve regular face-to-face contact (the many associations in cyber-space; the 33-million-member American Association of Retired Persons) or because they don't encourage people to build lasting ties based on mutual strength (Alcoholics Anonymous and other support groups). The most dramatic example I could find—and a nicely apposite one, too—is U.S. Youth Soccer, which has 2.4 million members, up from 1.2 million ten years ago and from 127,000 twenty years ago.

As a long-standing coach in this organization, I can attest that it involves incessant meetings, phone calls, and activities of a kind that create links between people which ramify, in the manner described by Putnam, into other areas.

Another intriguing statistic is the number of restaurants in the United States, which has risen dramatically, from 203,000 in 1972 to 368,000 in 1993. True, this probably means that fewer people are eating a family dinner at home. But from Putnam's perspective, that might be good news, because it means that people who are eating out are expanding their civic associations rather than pursuing amoral familism. (If you've ever visited northern Italy, the connection between restaurants and *virtu civile* seems obvious.) The growth in restaurants is not confined to fast-food restaurants, by the way, although it is true that the number of bars and taverns—institutions singled out for praise in "Bowling Alone"—has declined over the past two decades.

The number of small businesses—what the Internal Revenue Service calls "non-farm proprietorships"—has about doubled since 1970. These can be seen as both generators and results of civic virtue, since they involve so much personal contact and mutual trust. A small subset, Community Development Corporations (organizations that are often explicitly Putnam-like schemes to promote association locally in the hope of a later economic payoff), have grown in number from 500 to 2,200 over the past twenty years. Individual contributions to charity, which are still made by more than three quarters of Americans, grew from $16.2 billion in 1970 to $101.8 billion in 1990. Although church attendance is, as Putnam says, down, the Pentecostal denominations are booming: their domestic membership has burgeoned over the past quarter century. Little League membership has increased every year. Membership in the PTA has risen over the past decade or so, though it's still far below its peak, which occurred in 1962–1963. Home-ownership is high and steady, and, as Putnam admits in "Bowling Alone," Americans move less frequently now than they did in the 1950s and 1960s.

Weighed against all this, the statistics in "Bowling Alone" are still impressive, and no doubt Putnam will nail down his case in his book. Let's say, however, for the sake of argument, that Putnam's thesis that civic virtue is rapidly collapsing in America isn't true. What would account for its being so widely and instantly accepted as gospel?

Bowling leagues, Elks and Lions, and the League of Women Voters are indisputably not what they used to be. Large internal population shifts have taken place since the 1960s: to the Sunbelt and, within metropolitan areas, to the suburbs. Birth rates dropped substantially and then rose again. Most mothers now work. All these changes could have resulted in atrophied forms of association that are culturally connected to older cities and to old-fashioned gender roles (bowling leagues are a good example), while other forms more oriented to open space and to weekends (like youth soccer) have grown.

I have lived in five American cities: New Orleans, Cambridge, Washington, Austin, and Pelham, New York. The two that stand out in my memory as most deficient in the Putnam virtues—the places where people I know tend not to have elaborate hobbies and not to devote their evenings and weekends to neighborhood meetings and activities—are Cambridge and Washington. The reason is that these places are the big time. Work absorbs all the energy. It is what people talk about at social events. Community is defined functionally, not spatially; it's a professional peer group rather than a neighborhood. Hired hands, from nannies to headmasters to therapists, bear more of the civic-virtue load than is typical.

To people living this kind of life, many of whom grew up in a bourgeois provincial environment and migrated to one of the capitals, the "Bowling Alone" theory makes sense, because it seems to describe their own situation so well. It is natural for people to assume that if their own life trajectories have been in the direction of reduced civic virtue, this is the result not of choices they have made but of a vast national trend. I wonder if the pre-presidential Bill Clinton—the man who spent the morning after Election Day in 1992 wandering around Little Rock engaging in front-porch visits with lifelong friends—would have found "Bowling Alone" so strongly resonant.

A second reason for the appeal of "Bowling Alone" is that it avoids the Banfield problem. A true application of the line of thinking in *Making Democracy Work* would require searching the United States for internal differences in civic virtue and then trying to explain those differences. One inevitable result would be the shining of a harsh spotlight on the ghettos, with their high rates of crime, welfare dependency, and family breakup. In an article that appeared in *The American Prospect* in 1993 Putnam made a point of saying, "It would be a dreadful mistake, of course, to overlook the repositories of social capital within America's minority communities." This doesn't mean that the spotlight wouldn't still fall on the ghettos, because Putnam was clearly referring to minority communities most of whose members are not poor. But with this caveat he demonstrates at least that he is aware of the sensitive areas into which his Italian inquiry could lead in the United States. So far he has resolutely kept his examples of the decline of civic virtue in America in the realm of middle- or even upper-middle-class culture.

In the 1993 *American Prospect* article Putnam wrote,

Classic liberal social policy is designed to enhance the opportunities of individuals, *but if social capital is important, this emphasis is partially misplaced. Instead we must focus on community development, allowing space for religious organizations and choral societies and Little Leagues that may seem to have little to do with politics or economics.*

With respect to the United States, the opposite of Putnam's theory would be this: There has been relatively little general decline in civic virtue. To the extent that the overall civic health of the nation did deteriorate, the dip was confined mainly to the decade 1965 to 1975—when, for example, crime and divorce rates rose rapidly—and things have been pretty stable since then. The overwhelming social and moral problem in American life is instead the disastrous condition of poor neighborhoods, almost all of which are in cities.

The model of a healthy country and needy ghettos would suggest a program much closer to the "liberal social policy" from which Putnam wants us to depart. Rather than assume, with Putnam, that such essential public goods as safety, decent housing, and good education can be generated only from within a community, we could assume that they might be provided from without—by government. If quite near the ghettos are working-class neighborhoods (and not insuperably distant are suburbs) of varying ethnic character and strong civic virtue, then the individual-opportunity model might be precisely the answer for ghetto residents—opportunity, that is, to move to a place that is part of the healthy American mainstream.

The difficulty with such a program is that it is politically inconvenient. It would involve, by contemporary standards, far too much action on the part of the government, with the benefits far too skewed toward blacks. The model of an entire United States severely distressed in a way that is beyond the power of government to correct is more comforting.

B.
Community Participation

Social Isolation

NEIGHBORHOOD CONTEXT AND THE RISK OF CHILDBEARING AMONG METROPOLITAN-AREA BLACK ADOLESCENTS

Clea A. Sucoff
Dawn M. Upchurch

We focus on the intersection of two important social problems: The concentration of poverty and racial segregation in urban neighborhoods, and high rates of premarital adolescent childbearing. Previous studies find that black adolescents from the most impoverished and segregated neighborhoods experience significantly higher rates of premarital childbearing than do their peers in neighborhoods at any other socioeconomic level (Brewster 1994a; Brewster, Billy, and Grady 1993; Brooks-Gunn et al. 1993; Crane 1991; Hogan and Kitagawa 1985). These findings imply that black adolescents living in poor, segregated neighborhoods experience normative environments that do not discourage premarital adolescent childbearing. However, theorists disagree over whether neighborhood socioeconomic status or racial composition is the key structural neighborhood characteristic that accounts for the association between living in a poor, segregated neighborhood and experiencing a high risk of premari-

tal adolescent childbearing (Massey and Denton 1993; Wilson 1987, 1996).

An ecological perspective provides additional insight into the nature of the relationship between neighborhood factors and individual outcomes (Aneshensel 1996; Aneshensel and Sucoff 1995). The ecological orientation examines "person-environment fit"—how individuals in a given neighborhood respond to the neighborhood differently depending on their individual characteristics or their social position in the neighborhood. Two ecological models are relevant for explaining the risk for premarital childbearing: potentiator and protective models (Kupersmidt et al. 1995). The potentiator model focuses on the fit between affluent families and affluent neighborhoods, suggesting that teens from affluent families will benefit more from living in affluent neighborhoods than will teens from low socioeconomic status families. The protective model focuses on the fit between affluent families and poor, segregated neighborhoods, suggesting that more affluent families buffer their daughters from the neighborhood environment, thereby reducing the negative effect of those neighborhoods on affluent youths compared with other families in the neighborhood.

We draw on these two research traditions—the structural and ecological orientations—to test whether neighborhood socioeconomic status or racial composition is a more important predictor of premarital adolescent childbearing among blacks in metropolitan areas. We also examine whether the effects of a given neighborhood's socioeconomic status and racial composition vary according to the adolescent's socioeconomic status. These two perspectives, taken together, provide new information on the relationship between neighborhood factors and premarital childbearing among blacks.

NEIGHBORHOOD CONTEXT AND ADOLESCENT CHILDBEARING

The structural and ecological perspectives explore the connection between neighborhood and individual outcomes. The structural orientation focuses on how modal neighborhood characteristics shape adolescent outcomes (Aneshensel 1996). Structural models posit that living in an extremely poor neighborhood uniformly increases the risk of a premarital first birth for all adolescent girls in the neighborhood. Young women who grow up in ghetto neighborhoods—in which many adolescent girls have babies, most households are headed by women, and the predominant source of income is public assistance—may choose early childbearing and participation in welfare as the most viable pathway to adulthood (Burton 1990). Their latent socialization differs from that of young women who grow up in affluent neighborhoods and who witness the rewards of higher education and delayed childbearing in the lifestyles of their neighbors.

Within the structural perspective, two explanations predominate. Wilson (1987, 1996) argues that the increases in concentrated poverty and in related forms of social dislocation in inner-city black neighborhoods result from the shift of industrial production out of urban centers and the concomitant out-migration of middle-class blacks. As jobs become increasingly scarce in inner-city neighborhoods, many residents lose access to the formal labor market. Middle-class families move out of the inner city to better jobs and better neighborhoods. The black youths left behind grow up in an environment in which they do not witness the rewards of education and employment in the lifestyles of their neighbors because work is no longer a regulating force of adult life.

Wilson (1996) asserts that the cross-cutting pressures of poverty and joblessness, combined with the allure of the streets, result in short-lived male-female relationships. Young men are not interested in marriage because they cannot earn steady incomes that will support a family. Instead, they seek sexual conquests to gain status among their peer group (Anderson 1990). For young women, pregnancy and childbirth become a rite of passage to adulthood, a way to achieve adult status and economic independence via Aid for Families with Dependent Children that is not attainable through the labor market. In addition, for some young women pregnancy may bring the hope of a stable future with a husband, children, and a home (Anderson 1990).

Massey and Denton (1993) agree with Wilson that macroeconomic shifts, out-migration, and joblessness undermined economic supports for urban blacks. However, they assert that in the absence of racial segregation, these macroeconomic shifts would not have produced the social and economic deprivation found in inner-city black neighborhoods. Massey and Denton propose a threshold model for how residential segregation concentrates poverty and leads to neighborhood decline.

Once blacks in a neighborhood reach a certain percentage, whites' tolerance for their black neighbors is surpassed and whites move out of the neighborhood. Because blacks tend to be poorer, they are not as likely to invest in their properties, and the neighborhood deteriorates. Cities reduce services to these neighborhoods as they become increasingly segregated. Massey and Denton (1993) contend that once a threshold of neighborhood deterioration is crossed, the process becomes irreversible. They describe an alternative status system or "culture of segregation" that has evolved in inner-city black neighborhoods as a collective psychological defense mechanism against white racism. Like Wilson (1996), they describe how pregnancy and childbirth become a way for young women to achieve independence and status not attainable through mainstream options such as employment and marriage.[1]

We test whether poverty and joblessness or racial composition is the more important predictor of premarital adolescent childbearing. If poverty and joblessness are the driving neighborhood-level forces behind high rates of premarital adolescent childbearing, as Wilson (1987, 1996) suggests, premarital childbearing should be strongly associated with neighborhood socioeconomic status and less strongly related to the racial composition of the neighborhood. Conversely, if racial composition is the key structural mechanism, the risk of premarital adolescent childbearing should be strongly associated with neighborhood racial composition and less strongly associated with neighborhood socioeconomic status.

Research has not attempted to disentangle the effects of neighborhood racial composition and socioeconomic status. Brooks-Gunn et al.

(1993) found that a neighborhood's racial composition was not associated with adolescent childbearing. However, the effects of racial composition were examined for blacks and whites jointly, which assumes that blacks and whites respond to segregation similarly, a problematic assumption. They also assumed a linear relationship between racial composition and premarital childbearing, although other studies suggest that only the poorest, most segregated neighborhoods increase the risk of adolescent pregnancy and childbearing (Crane 1991; Hogan and Kitagawa 1985).

Three studies have examined blacks separately (Brewster 1994a; Crane 1991; Hogan and Kitagawa 1985). Crane (1991) did not include racial composition variables in his analysis. Brewster (1994a) found that variables measuring neighborhood socioeconomic status were more strongly associated with the timing of first sexual intercourse than was racial composition. Hogan and Kitagawa (1985) found that in low-quality neighborhoods, which were on average 99 percent black and had a poverty rate of 45 percent, pregnancy rates were one-third higher than in the medium-quality neighborhoods, which averaged 87 percent black and 25 percent in poverty, or the high-quality neighborhoods, which averaged 64 percent black and 10 percent in poverty. Their neighborhood typologies, however, did not allow them to disentangle the effects of race and socioeconomic status because the low-quality neighborhoods had both a higher percentage of blacks and a higher percentage in poverty than the other neighborhood types. We compare neighborhood typologies that hold the percentage of blacks constant and vary by socioeconomic status.

The structural perspective underscores the uniformly harmful effects of ghetto neighborhoods on adolescents' risk of a premarital first birth. In contrast, the ecological perspective focuses on how the impact of neighborhood is conditional on individual and family character-

---

[1]Although we focus on premarital motherhood during adolescence, becoming a mother is an important marker of adulthood for women generally.

istics, particularly why some youths in high-risk settings demonstrate negative outcomes while others have positive outcomes (Bronfenbrenner 1986; Jencks and Mayer 1990; Jessor 1993). While the structural approach focuses on the main effects of neighborhood, the ecological perspective highlights the interaction between neighborhood and individual factors (Aneshensel 1996).

We test two ecological models representing different types of "person-environment fit" (Kupersmidt et al. 1995). The potentiator model relates the effects of living in a "low-risk" environment on "low-risk" individuals. This model hypothesizes that middle-class neighborhoods influence high socioeconomic status adolescents more than lower socioeconomic status adolescents. According to this hypothesis, young black women who economically mirror their middle-class neighbors and can afford the neighborhood's middle-class lifestyle are more likely to fit in with their neighborhood peer group. As a result, middle-class teens are more likely to adopt local middle-class norms discouraging early childbearing. Less advantaged teens do not receive the same benefit because they do not have the personal social or economic resources to capitalize on their neighborhood advantage.

The protective model suggests that although high-risk neighborhoods adversely affect most youths, certain families are able to protect their adolescents from these negative effects. This model hypothesizes that economically advantaged families have the resources to counteract a neighborhood social climate that fosters early childbearing. For example, relatively advantaged families may have the social and economic resources to help their daughters secure well-paying jobs or undertake higher education, both attractive alternatives to early premarital childbearing.

In her study of the transition to first intercourse among black women, Brewster (1994a) tested statistical interactions between neighborhood socioeconomic status and two family characteristics—mother's education and family structure. She found that the responsiveness of teenagers' sexual behavior to neighborhood environment was not conditional on their family characteristics. Mayer (1990) examined whether the association between school socioeconomic status (rather than neighborhood) and female students' likelihood of having a baby was conditioned by family socioeconomic status. She found that the effects of school socioeconomic status were larger for low-status students than for high-status students, indicating that attending a high-status school has a greater benefit for low-status students than for high-status students. However, she did not control for the school's racial or ethnic mix.

In sum, previous research has not disentangled the potentially unique effects of neighborhood racial composition and socioeconomic status on adolescent fertility-related behaviors. Nor has it examined ways in which family characteristics moderate neighborhood contextual effects.

ANALYTIC STRATEGY

Structural Neighborhood Effects

Our primary goal is to determine whether racial composition or neighborhood socioeconomic status is the more important predictor of the risk of adolescent childbearing. Ideally, we would like to include separate measures of racial composition and socioeconomic status in a multivariate model to isolate their effects. However, treating socioeconomic status and racial composition as distinct factors with independent effects does not accurately reflect the stratification of neighborhoods in this sample. In particular, it neglects the absence of certain combinations of neighborhoods, such as underclass white communities or affluent black neighborhoods (Aneshensel and Sucoff 1996).[2]

The stratification of neighborhoods by race and socioeconomic status poses analytical problems distinct from the problems posed by high correlations between race and socioeconomic status at the individual level. While there are affluent black families and extremely poor white families in our nationally representative sample, we do not find this same range for neighborhoods. In other words, there is greater heterogeneity among individuals than among neighborhoods.

Several researchers studying neighborhood effects have recognized that selection into neighborhoods is based jointly on race and socioeconomic status, and they have developed measurement strategies to take this into account. These strategies include principal components analysis (Duncan and Aber 1997; Hogan and Kitagawa 1985) and creating an indicator variable based on cut-off points on multiple factors (Kupersmidt et al. 1995). Neither of these strategies allows us to distinguish between the effects of race and of socioeconomic status. For example, principal components analysis of our sample produced a single factor that contains both racial composition and socioeconomic status measures (Sucoff 1995).

We create neighborhood typologies using cluster analysis to distinguish the independent effects of neighborhood racial composition and socioeconomic status. Cluster analysis groups together cases with similar profiles across variables. It is particularly suitable for our analysis because it assumes no particular distribution of the data and therefore allows for the fact that only certain combinations of neighborhood characteristics exist (Aldenderfer and Blash-

field 1984). For example, in our sample cluster analysis identifies poor black neighborhoods, working-class black neighborhoods, working-class racially mixed neighborhoods, and middle-class white neighborhoods. These are the prevalent types of neighborhoods in our sample.

We test the structural hypotheses suggested by Wilson (1987; 1996) and Massey and Denton (1993) by comparing rates of childbearing across neighborhood types, controlling for family characteristics. A finding that the relative risk of adolescent childbearing in segregated black neighborhoods compared with racially mixed neighborhoods is the same, regardless of neighborhood socioeconomic status, would indicate that racial composition, rather than socioeconomic status, is the key neighborhood-level predictor of early premarital childbearing. Conversely, a finding that the relative risk of adolescent childbearing in impoverished neighborhoods compared with that in working-class neighborhoods is the same, regardless of neighborhood racial composition, would indicate that poverty and joblessness are the key neighborhood-level determinants of premarital adolescent childbearing.

Any attempt to understand the impact of neighborhood context on premarital first births must control for family-level determinants of early childbearing because these family-level variables affect where a family lives and also contribute their own independent effects. Our analytic model includes three categories of family characteristics that are associated with the risk of adolescent premarital childbearing: (1) family socioeconomic status (measured as mother's education, parental employment, and family income); (2) family structure and size; and (3) number of residential moves, which is both an independent risk factor for adolescent childbearing and a measure of length of exposure to neighborhood environment (An,

---

[2]The poorest white neighborhoods are considerably more affluent than the poorest black neighborhoods; the most affluent black neighborhoods do not match the affluence of the richest white neighborhoods (Brewster 1994b; Massey, Gross, and Shibuya 1994).

Haveman, and Wolfe 1993; Michael and Tuma 1985; Wu and Martinson 1993). We also include birth cohort, to account for any changes in societal norms regarding premarital childbearing between 1966 and 1988.

Ecological Interactions between Family and Neighborhood Contexts

We hypothesize that high-status families "buy" either neighborhood (the potentiator model) or more advantaged (the protective model) cultures and opportunities, thereby moderating neighborhood effects. We test whether neighborhood effects vary across two measures of family socioeconomic status: the income-to-needs ratio and mother's education. For the potentiator model, the income-to-needs ratio represents the economic resources available to the adolescent that enable her to be part of the local peer culture in middle-class neighborhoods (e.g., recreational activities, clothing, and so on). Similarly, young black women with more highly educated mothers may have the social language and skills necessary to conform in middle-class white neighborhoods. Both measures also serve as indicators for unmeasured attitudes and values.

For the protective model, a high family income-to-needs ratio represents parents' ability to purchase better schools and after-school activities than can their more disadvantaged peers in the disadvantaged neighborhoods in which they live. Young women who attend better schools or participate in educational activities outside the neighborhood have increased educational and employment opportunities. Their calculus of the costs and benefits of childbearing may differ from those of their more impoverished neighbors. Similarly, better-educated mothers serve as role models and may instill values in their daughters that encourage them to choose pathways to adulthood other than early premarital childbearing.

DATA AND METHODS

Data

The data for this study come from a special release of the Panel Study of Income Dynamics (PSID) that appends 1970 and 1980 census-tract measures to the individual records through the 1988 interview year.

We then merged data from the 1989 PSID file with the geocoded dataset.

The outcome is time to premarital first birth, measured as the risk each month of having a premarital birth given that the young woman has not already had a first birth. This measure captures changes over time in the risk of having a premarital first birth. Table 1 indicates that the rate of premarital childbearing was low during the early adolescent years and increased with age. By age 16, 6.6 percent of the young women have had a premarital first birth. This figure rises to 22.8 percent by age 18 and to 37.7 percent of the young women by age 20. Although the neighborhood characteristics vary widely, the young women tend to live in black neighborhoods that are predominantly poor.

Family Covariates

Table 1 presents descriptive statistics for the variables used in the analysis. Mother's education is measured as a dichotomous variable indicating whether the young woman's mother completed high school. Parental employment consists of two dichotomous variables indicating whether the household head and wife, if present, worked full-time (defined as 30 or more hours per week). Family income is operationalized as the family income-to-needs ratio, defined as total family income divided by its food needs, in the interview year following the young woman's fourteenth birthday. The income-to-needs ratio was divided into quartiles, and a dichotomous variable indicates whether the young woman's income-to-needs ratio is in the upper quartile or otherwise. In this way, we

TABLE 1 Descriptive Statistics for Variables Used in the Analysis: Black Women in the Panel Study of Income Dynamics, 1985 to 1988

Variable	Value
Family Socioeconomic Status	
Percentage of mothers with less than a high school education	62.0
Percentage with education data missing	3.2
Income-to-needs ratio	10.5
	(10.0)
Percentage of household heads working over 30 hours per week	56.2
Percentage of wives working over 30 hours per week[a]	29.6
Family Structure	
Percentage who lived in a single-parent household at age 14	50.7
Percentage who experienced family disruption at ages 11–16	17.1
Number of children in the home at respondent's age 14	3.9
	(2.0)
Residential Mobility	
Percentage with one residential move at ages 11–16	28.6
Percentage with two or more residential moves at ages 11–16	20.2
Percentage with mobility data missing	2.9
Birth Cohort	
Percentage born in 1953–1957	29.8
Percentage born in 1958–1962	36.1
Percentage born in 1963–1968	34.1
Outcome[b]	
Had premarital first birth:	
By age 15	1.8
By age 16	6.6
By age 17	14.4
By age 18	22.8
By age 19	30.3
By age 20	37.7
Number of cases	940

Note: All family characteristics are measured in the year the respondent turned age 14, unless otherwise noted. Numbers in parentheses are standard deviations. All means and percentages are unweighted.

[a] Calculated if wife is present in the household N = 463).

[b] Cumulative percentage, calculated using Kaplan-Meier survival curves.

allow for a nonlinear association between family poverty and time to premarital first birth.

Overall, the sample represents extremely disadvantaged young black women. As adolescents, these young women lived with constrained economic and educational resources: Sixty-two percent of their mothers did not complete high school, one-half of the sample lived in single-parent households at age 14, and only 56 percent of household heads worked full time. Moreover, these women's parents had limited time available because they were single parents, were working, or had many other children.

Table 2 shows one large cluster of working-class black neighborhoods containing 463 young women and three smaller clusters containing neighborhoods of 146, 176, and 155 women. The underclass black neighborhoods are characterized by extreme segregation and extreme poverty: The median neighborhood in this cluster is 95 percent black and has a poverty rate of 53 percent. The working-class black neighborhoods are also highly segregated but are less poor (27 percent below the poverty line); working-class racially mixed neighborhoods are, on average, 52 percent black and have a poverty rate of 24 percent; middle-class white neighborhoods are predominantly white (17 percent black) and relatively affluent (13 percent in poverty). The results from the cluster analysis highlight the interdependence of neighborhood socioeconomic status and racial composition: Few

blacks in this sample live in well-off black neighborhoods or extremely poor white neighborhoods.

Test of Competing Structural Hypotheses: Racial Composition or Socioeconomic Status?

Model 1 in Table 3 presents the zero-order association between neighborhood type and the ratio of the rate of a premarital first birth for young women. Model 1 shows that neighborhood racial composition and socioeconomic status are associated with the risk of a premarital first birth in the expected pattern: Young women living in the poorest, most segregated neighborhoods (underclass black neighborhoods) have the highest rates of premarital first births (1.68 times the rate of women in the working-class, racially mixed neighborhoods). In other words, adolescent women in these neighborhoods have premarital first births at younger ages than do teens in the working-class, racially mixed neighborhoods.

TABLE 2   Median Characteristics of Neighborhood Types at Age 14: Black Women in the Panel Study of Income Dynamics, 1985 to 1988

Neighborhood Type	Number of Women	Percentage	Median Characteristics		
			Percentage Below the Poverty Line	Mean Income (in $1,000s 1980)	Percentage Black
Underclass black	146	15.5	53.2	10.1	94.8
			(33.7–80.0)	(6.0–23.0)	(57.5–100.0)
Working-class black	463	49.2	26.6	15.8	94.0
			(7.0–46.0)	(10.0–27.1)	(66.0–100.0)
Working-class racially mixed	176	18.7	23.8	17.0)	52.4
			(6.0–42.4)	(11.5–25.0	(29.0–65.0)
Middle-class white	155	16.5	13.4	20.2	16.8
			(2.6–32.4)	(12.6–44.6)	(0–34.0)
Total	940	100.0	25.8	15.9	83.0
			(2.6–80.0)	(6.0–44.6)	(0–100.0)

Note: Numbers in parentheses show ranges of values.

TABLE 3   Proportional-Hazards Regression Parameters Predicting the Risk of a Premarital First Birth from Neighborhood Context and Family Background Variables: Black Women in the Panel Study of Income Dynamics, 1985 to 1988

Independent Variables	Model 1		Model 2		Model 3	
	Coefficient	Risk Ratio	Coefficient	Risk Ratio	Coefficient	Risk Ratio
Neighborhood Type						
Underclass black	.52**	1.68	.41*	1.51	.43*	1.54
	(.19)		(.19)		(.19)	
Working-class black	.32*	1.38	.39*	1.47	.37*	1.45
	(.16)		(.17)		(.17)	
Middle-class white	.26	1.30	.22	1.25	.38	1.47
	(.20)		(.20)		(.21)	
Family Socioeconomic Status						
Mother has less than high school education	—	—	.50***	1.65	.50***	1.64
			(.13)		(.13)	
Mother's education data missing	—	—	−1.07	.34	−1.08	.34
			(.59)		(.59)	
Top income-to-needs quartile	—	—	−.44**	.64	−.28	.75
			(.17)		(.18)	
Household head works 30+ hours per week	—	—	.03	1.03	.04	1.04
			(.12)		(.12)	
Wife works 30+ hours per week	—	—	.23	1.26	.24	1.27
			(.19)		(.19)	
Family Structure						
Single-parent household at age 14	—	—	.36**	1.43	.37**	1.44
			(.14)		(.14)	
Four or more children in household at age 14	—	—	.23*	1.26	.23*	1.26
			(.12)		(.12)	
Family disruption at ages 11–16	—	—	−.08	.92	−.05	.95
			(.15)		(.15)	
Residential Mobility						
One residential move at ages 11–16	—	—	.19	1.21	.20	1.23
			(.13)		(.13)	
Two or more residential moves at ages 11–16	—	—	.45**	1.56	.44**	1.56
			(.15)		(.15)	
Mobility/disruption data missing	—	—	.47	1.60	.47	1.60
			(.29)		(.29)	

(continued)

TABLE 3   Proportional-Hazards Regression Parameters Predicting the Risk of a Premarital First Birth from Neighborhood Context and Family Background Variables: Black Women in the Panel Study of Income Dynamics, 1985 to 1988 (Continued)

Independent Variables	Model 1		Model 2		Model 3	
	Coefficient	Risk Ratio	Coefficient	Risk Ratio	Coefficient	Risk Ratio
Birth Cohort						
Born in 1953–1957	—	—	.13	1.14	.12	1.13
			(.14)		(.14)	
Born in 1963–1968	—	—	.03	1.03	.03	1.03
			(.14)		(.14)	
Middle-class white neighborhood × Top income-to-needs quartile	—	—	—	—	−1.00*	.37
					(.47)	
−2 Log-likelihood	4,418.8	—	4,339.5	—	4,334.0	—
X^2	7.78*	—	87.08***	—	92.61***	—
Degrees of freedom	3	—	16	—	17	—

*$p<.05$
**$p,.01$
***$p,.001$

Young women who lived in working-class black neighborhoods at age 14 also have significantly higher rates of a premarital first birth than do their peers in the working-class racially mixed neighborhood type. These findings suggest that both racial composition and socioeconomic status matter, because as neighborhoods become progressively socioeconomically better off and more racially mixed, the risk of a premarital first birth declines.

Controlling for family-level characteristics reveals a different pattern of neighborhood effects (Model 2). Young women in the two black neighborhood types experience rates approximately 1.5 times as great as those in the working-class racially mixed neighborhoods, despite the fact that the underclass black neighborhoods are more impoverished than the working-class black neighborhoods.

Residential racial segregation is a more important structural determinant of adolescent childbearing than is neighborhood socioeconomic status. The improvement in status between the impoverished underclass black cluster and the working-class black cluster does not substantially reduce a teenager's risk of having a premarital birth. The rate of a premarital first birth in the working-class black neighborhoods is 1.5 times the rate in the working-class racially mixed neighborhood type, despite the similar socioeconomic status composition of the two neighborhood types.

Model 2 also presents the effects of family characteristics on the risk of a premarital birth. Most associations are in the expected direction: Young black women who at age 14 lived in low-status households, lived with one parent, had many siblings, or had moved frequently experience higher rates of a premarital first birth before age 20 than do young women without these attributes. Experiencing a family disruption as an adolescent (between ages 11 and 16) and parental employment status are not significantly related to the risk of a premarital first birth.

Test of the Ecological Models: Potentiator and Protective Effects

The potentiator model focuses on the differential effect on high-status and low-status young women of living in middle-class white neighborhoods. Model 3 tests the potentiator model by including the interaction between middle-class white neighborhood and the top quartile of the income-to-needs ratio. The log-likelihood ratio test for Model 3 indicates that the effect of living in middle-class white neighborhoods varies according to the family income level of the young women in the neighborhood (Allison 1984). Thus, we find some support for the potentiator hypothesis—the negative coefficient for the interaction term indicates that the protective effect of being in the top income-to-needs quartile is greater in the middle-class white neighborhoods than it is in the other neighborhood types. In middle-class white neighborhoods, young black women whose families were in the top income-to-needs quartile are only .28 times as likely to have a premarital first birth as are their neighborhood peers with incomes in the lower three quartiles.

A model containing the interaction term for the middle-class white neighborhood by mother's education did not improve the fit of the model (results not shown), indicating that the effect of living in a middle-class white neighborhood on the risk of a premarital first birth does not depend on mother's education. Together, these findings partially support the potentiator model and suggest that in middle-class white neighborhoods, the more affluent teens adopt a norm discouraging adolescent childbearing, and this norm differs from the norms adopted by their less affluent black peers. Family income rather than mother's education appears to be the key family characteristic that invokes the potentiating effect of the neighborhood.

The protective model focuses on the effect of highly segregated black neighborhoods (the "high-risk" neighborhood types) on high-status and low-status young women. Family socioeconomic status does not condition the effect of living in a segregated neighborhood. Thus, we find no support for our hypothesis that living in a segregated neighborhood presents less of a risk for families with more resources.

DISCUSSION

We have drawn from two research traditions—the structural and ecological orientations—to test whether neighborhood socioeconomic status or racial composition is a more important predictor of premarital adolescent childbearing among metropolitan blacks, and whether family socioeconomic status potentiates or buffers these neighborhood effects. We have found that living in a highly segregated neighborhood is associated with an elevated rate of premarital first births, regardless of the neighborhood's economic affluence. This suggests that segregation directly impacts adolescent childbearing by sealing off participation in mainstream social and economic arenas, as hypothesized by Massey and Denton (1993). In contrast, our findings fail to support the hypothesis that concentrated poverty in the absence of segregation produces norms sanctioning premarital adolescent childbearing in black neighborhoods.

We also hypothesized that families moderate neighborhood effects through two individual-environment interactions: the potentiator and protective models. Our research provides some evidence for the potentiator model, which predicts that in middle-class white neighborhoods, relatively affluent black teens adopt neighborhood norms that discourage premarital adolescent childbearing. In contrast, we find no support for the protective model: High-status and low-status teens respond similarly to structural conditions in highly segregated neighborhoods. Relatively affluent families do not change the perceived costs and benefits of premarital childbearing associated with living in highly segregated neighborhoods.

These findings extend previous research in several ways. Although earlier studies documented the association between "low-quality" neighborhoods and fertility-related behaviors among metropolitan blacks (Crane 1991; Hogan and Kitagawa 1985), they did not distinguish the unique effects of neighborhood socioeconomic status and racial composition. Our finding that racial composition appears to be the key neighborhood variable predicting high rates of premarital first births in poor neighborhoods corroborates and refines the interpretations of these studies.

The series of fertility-related decisions that precedes child-bearing—initiation of sexual activity, contraception, pregnancy, and abortion—systematically sorts out women. The subset of adolescents who choose to become mothers are more disadvantaged and live in more disadvantaged neighborhoods than does the larger group of teens who decide to become sexually active. A normative culture that promotes adolescent childbearing may have a relatively powerful effect on childbearing but a more diffuse influence on sexual initiation. Using a methodology similar to the one used here, we found that living in a highly segregated black neighborhood is unrelated to the timing of first sexual intercourse among a sample of female adolescents in Los Angeles County (Upchurch et al. 1997). These divergent findings across dependent variables point to the importance of identifying general and specific neighborhood influences.

Our findings in partial support of the potentiator model are also not consistent with Brewster's finding that family socioeconomic status does not moderate neighborhood effects on the timing of first sexual intercourse. Again, this could be because Brewster examined a different outcome. Or it could be because we tested one particular person-environment fit—high-status adolescents in high-status neighborhoods—whereas Brewster tested the interaction across all types of families and all levels of neighborhood socioeconomic status.

Mayer's (1990) finding that low-status students benefit *more* than high-status students from attending high-status schools also appears to contradict our findings that high-status blacks benefit more than do low-status blacks from living in middle-class white neighborhoods. This difference could stem from the different social contexts studied—schools and neighborhoods. The extent to which school and neighborhood effects overlap is difficult to disentangle (Tienda 1991). In addition, Mayer did not control for the school's racial composition and therefore could not determine if low-status black students benefit from attending high-status white schools. Our apparently contradictory findings point to the importance of incorporating measures of both racial composition and socioeconomic status measures into person-environment fit hypotheses.

Our research speaks to the debate over whether between-group differences in rates of premarital adolescent childbearing result from differences in socioeconomic status or from cultural differences (Brewster 1994b; Furstenberg et al. 1987; Lauritsen 1994). Our finding, that neighborhood racial composition is associated with adolescent childbearing regardless of the neighborhood socioeconomic status, provides indirect evidence that cultural norms are an important explanation for variation in rates of childbearing. Age-specific norms, such as those regarding adolescent childbearing, evolve when members of a given cohort develop common responses to shared experiences (Marini 1984; Riley, Foner, and Waring 1988). The shared experience of social isolation in segregated black neighborhoods may engender norms sanctioning (or at least not proscribing) premarital adolescent childbearing. In contrast to much previous research that attributes unexplained variation in rates of childbearing to cultural differences, our work suggests that norms develop in response to specific structural conditions. Moreover, our study emphasizes the variation in norms *within* a single racial group. Typically, cultural norms are studied in the context of explaining inter-group differences in fertility-related behaviors (Brewster 1994b; Furstenberg et al. 1987; Lauritsen 1994).

The results suggest that reducing segregation is an important policy goal, and that programs like the Gautreaux project in Chicago, which offered residents of inner-city black neighborhoods the opportunity to move to predominantly white suburbs (Rosenbaum and Kaufman 1991), show promise and could be adopted in other large cities in which residential segregation is high. However, our finding from the ecological model that only relatively affluent black teens benefit (i.e., have a decreased risk of an adolescent premarital birth) from living in middle-class white neighborhoods undermines this conclusion. Over time, of course, newly arrived poor black residents of middle-class white neighborhoods may improve their economic status by taking advantage of the increased availability of jobs. Thus, their relative risk of a premarital first birth may decline over time.

Although modeling neighborhoods as typologies allowed us to differentiate the impacts of neighborhood racial composition from those of socioeconomic status to a greater degree than had been done previously, the approach does result in loss of information. The neighborhood socioeconomic status effect was estimated from a single comparison—underclass black neighborhoods versus working-class black neighborhoods. Similarly, the segregation effect was estimated from a comparison of working-class black and working-class racially mixed neighborhoods. Although these types of neighborhoods are the most prevalent types of neighborhoods in which blacks lived at the

time of data collection, they cannot answer all the pertinent questions. We cannot, for example, determine the effect of a unit change in racial composition on the risk of a premarital first birth as we could if we had conceptualized the neighborhood variables linearly. Moreover, neighborhood composition has changed since the young women in this sample completed their adolescence between 1974 and 1988. Poor segregated black neighborhoods have become even more impoverished, while the number of middle-class black neighborhoods has increased (Wilson 1996).

A second limitation of our study is our use of a single dependent variable. Neighborhood context affects multiple domains of adolescent well-being, and the effects of a particular neighborhood characteristic may vary across adolescent behaviors and outcomes (e.g., see Aneshensel and Sucoff 1996; Brooks-Gunn et al. 1993; Sampson and Groves 1989). Although we found that neighborhood socioeconomic status is a less important predictor of a premarital first birth than is racial composition, neighborhood socioeconomic status may be a more important factor influencing other adolescent outcomes. Our focus on a single outcome provides potentially misleading conclusions about the general consequences of neighborhood structure for adolescent well-being (Aneshensel, Rutter, and Lachenbruch 1991).

Future research should elaborate on the mechanisms through which neighborhood structure influences adolescent well-being, and determine how these mechanisms operate differentially depending on the adolescent's socioeconomic position relative to his or her neighbors. Neighborhood conditions do not directly affect adolescents' decisions about fertility and marriage. Rather, neighborhood conditions are perceived and incorporated into a youth's calculus about the benefits and opportunities that are lost or gained through certain actions.

REFERENCES

Aldenderfer, Mark S. and Roger K. Blashfield. 1984. *Cluster Analysis.* Sage University Paper Series on Quantitative Applications in the Social Sciences. Beverly Hills, CA: Sage.

Allison, Paul D. 1984. *Event History Analysis: Regression for Longitudinal Event Data.* Sage University Paper Series on Quantitative Applications in the Social Sciences. Beverly Hills, CA: Sage.

An, Chong-Bum, Robert Haveman, and Barbara Wolfe. 1993. "Teen Out-of-Wedlock Births and Welfare Receipt: The Role of Childhood Events and Economic Circumstances." *The Review of Economics and Statistics* 75:195–208.

Anderson, Elijah. 1990. "Neighborhood Effects on Teenage Pregnancy." Pp. 375–408 in *The Urban Underclass,* edited by C. Jencks and P. E. Peterson. Washington, DC: The Brookings Institution.

Aneshensel, Carol S. 1996. "The Neighborhood As a Context for Social Stress." Paper presented at the International Stress Conference, May 27–29, Paris, France.

Aneshensel, Carol S., Carolyn M. Rutter, and Peter A. Lachenbruch. 1991. "Social Structure, Stress, and Mental Health: Competing Conceptual and Analytic Models." *American Sociological Review* 56:166–78.

Aneshensel, Carol S. and Clea A. Sucoff. 1995. "Neighborhood and Adolescent Mental Health: Structure and Experience. Paper presented at the NIMH-sponsored conference Social Stressors, Personal Resources, and Their Health Consequences, August 17–19, Washington, DC.

———. 1996. "The Neighborhood Context of Adolescent Mental Health" *Journal of Health and Social Behavior* 37:293–310.

Brewster, Karin. 1994a. "Neighborhood Context and the Transition to Sexual Activity among Young Black Women." *Demography* 31:603–14.

———. 1994b. "Race Differences in Sexual Activity among Adolescent Women: The Role of Neighborhood Characteristics." *American Sociological Review* 59:408–24.

Brewster, Karin, John O. G. Billy, and William Grady. 1993. "Social Context and Adolescent Behavior: The Impact of Community on the Transition to Sexual Activity." *Social Forces* 71:713–40.

Bronfenbrenner, Urie. 1986. "Ecology of the Family as a Context for Human Development." *Developmental Psychology* 22:723–42.

Brooks-Gunn, Jeanne, Greg J. Duncan, Pamela Kato Klebanov, and Naomi Sealand. 1993. "Do Neighborhoods Influence Child and Adolescent Behavior?" *American Journal of Sociology* 99:353–95.

Burton, Linda M. 1990. "Teenage Childbearing as an Alternative Life Course Strategy in Multigeneration Black Families." *Human Nature* 1:123–43.

Crane, Jonathon. 1991. "The Epidemic Theory of Ghettos and Neighborhood Effects on Dropping Out and Teenage Childbearing." *American Journal of Sociology* 96:1126–59.

Duncan, Greg J. and Larry Aber. 1997. "Neighborhood Models and Measures." Pp. 62–78 in *Neighborhood Poverty: Context and Consequences for Children,* edited by G. J. Duncan, J. Brooks-Gunn, and L. Aber. New York: Russell Sage Foundation.

Furstenberg, Frank F., Philip S. Morgan, Kristin A. Moore, and James L. Peterson. 1987. "Race Differences in the Timing of Adolescent Intercourse." *American Sociological Review* 52:511–18.

Hogan, Dennis P. and Evelyn M. Kitagawa. 1985. "The Impact of Social Status, Family Structure, and Neighborhood on the Fertility of Black Adolescents." *American Journal of Sociology* 90:825–55.

Jencks, Christopher and Susan E. Mayer. 1990. "The Social Consequences of Growing Up in a Poor Neighborhood." Pp. 111–86 in *Inner-City Poverty in the United States,* edited by L. E. Lynn, Jr. and M. G. H. McGeary. Washington, DC: National Academy Press.

Jessor, Richard. 1993. "Successful Adolescent Development among Youth in High-Risk Settings." *American Psychologist* 48:117–26.

Kupersmidt, Janis B., Pamela C. Griesler, Melissa E. DeRosier, Charlotte J. Patterson, and Paul W. Davis. 1995. "Childhood Aggression and Peer Relations in the Context of Family and Neighborhood Factors." *Child Development* 66:360–75.

Lauritsen, Janet L. 1994. "Explaining Race and Gender Differences in Adolescent Sexual Behavior." *Social Forces* 72:859–83.

Marini, Margaret M. 1984. "Age and Sequencing Norms in the Transition to Adulthood." *Social Forces* 63:229–44.

Massey, Douglas S. and Nancy A. Denton. 1993. *American Apartheid: Segregation and the Making of the Underclass.* Cambridge, MA: Harvard University Press.

Massey, Douglas S., Andrew B. Gross, and Kumiko Shibuya. 1994. "Migration, Segregation, and the Concentration of Poverty." *American Sociological Review* 59:425–45.

Mayer, Susan E. 1990. "How Much Does a High School's Racial and Socioeconomic Mix Affect Graduation and Teenage Fertility Rates?" Pp. 321–41 in *The Urban Underclass,* edited by C. Jencks and P. E. Peterson. Washington, DC: The Brookings Institution.

Michael, Robert T. and Nancy Brandon Tuma. 1985. "Entry into Marriage and Parenthood by Young Men and Women: The Influence of Family Background." *Demography* 22:515–44.

Riley, Matilda White, Anne Foner, and Joan Waring. 1988. "Sociology of Age." Pp. 243–20 in *Handbook of Sociology,* edited by N. J. Smelser. Newbury Park, CA: Sage.

Rosenbaum, James E. and Julie Kaufman. 1991. "Educational and Occupational Achievements of Low-Income Black Youth in White Suburbs." Paper presented at the annual meeting of the American Sociological Association, August 23–27, Cincinnati, OH.

Sampson, Robert J. and W. Byron Groves. 1989. "Community Structure and Crime: Testing Social-Disorganization Theory." *American Journal of Sociology* 94:774–802.

Sucoff, Clea A. 1995. *Neighborhood Context and the Risk of Adolescent Childbearing among African-American Women.* Ph.D. dissertation, School of Public Health, University of California, Los Angeles, CA.

Survey Research Center (SRC). 1984. *Panel Study of Income Dynamics: User Guide.* Ann Arbor, MI: University of Michigan Institute for Social Research.

———. 1991. *Preliminary Documentation for PSID Young Women Dataset.* Ann Arbor, MI: University of Michigan Institute for Social Research.

Tienda, Marta. 1991. "Poor People and Poor Places: Deciphering Neighborhood Effects on Poverty Outcomes." Pp. 244–62 in *Macro-Micro Linkages in Sociology,* edited by J. Huber. Newbury Park, CA: Sage.

Upchurch, Dawn M., Carol S. Aneshensel, Clea A. Sucoff, and Lené Levy-Storms. 1997. "The Influences of Neighborhood and Familial Contexts on the Timing of Onset of Sexual Activity." Paper presented at the Annual Meeting of the Population Association of America, March 27–29, Washington, DC.

Wilson, William J. 1987. *The Truly Disadvantaged: The Inner City, the Underclass, and Public Policy.* Chicago, IL: University of Chicago Press.

———. 1996. *When Work Disappears: The World of the New Urban Poor.* New York: Alfred A. Knopf.

Wu, Lawrence L. and Brian C. Martinson. 1993. "Family Structure and the Risk of a Premarital Birth." *American Sociological Review* 58:210–32.

Yamaguchi, Kazuo. 1991. *Event History Analysis.* Applied Social Research Methods Series, vol. 28. Newbury Park, CA: Sage.

NEIGHBORHOOD POVERTY AND THE SOCIAL ISOLATION OF INNER-CITY AFRICAN AMERICAN FAMILIES

Bruce H. Rankin
James M. Quane

The economic devastation experienced by many inner-city neighborhoods over the last several decades has fueled interest in the impact of concentrated neighborhood poverty on individual life chances. While relatively abundant research on the relationship between individual behavior and residence in poor neighborhoods exists, especially as it relates to youth (see Brooks-Gunn et al. 1997; Jencks & Mayer 1990), very little has been done to specify the intervening mechanisms (Tienda 1991). It has been argued that social isolation, which refers to "the lack of contact or of sustained interaction with individuals and institutions that represent mainstream society" (Wilson 1987:60), is a mechanism that plays a major role in the disadvantaged status of the ghetto poor (see also Wilson 1996). The significance of the social isolation concept is that it serves as a "critical link between macro-level social and economic processes and the behavior of poor people" (Fernandez & Harris 1992:257). Conceptually, it represents a structural alternative to cultural explanations of so-called ghetto behavior that is often assumed to be rooted in the intergenerational transfer of deviant norms and values (see Mead 1986; Murray 1984).

However, despite claims that social isolation is an important factor in explaining the problems plaguing many inner-city communities, thus far there have been few empirical tests of the social isolation thesis. The purpose of this research is to reassess the role of neighborhood poverty in the social isolation of inner-city residents—in particular, the relative importance of individual and family characteristics and neighborhood poverty in the type of social networks and organizations that individuals are exposed to. A central concern is to determine the extent to which the social isolation of poor ghetto residents is due to the fact that they are poor and otherwise disadvantaged and the extent to which it is due to the fact that they live in poor neighborhoods where opportunities for interaction with socially connected persons and access to institutional resources are limited.

LITERATURE REVIEW

Poor Neighborhoods and Social Isolation

In the past thirty years conditions in many inner-city neighborhoods have dramatically declined. The loss of low-skill manufacturing jobs during the 1970s and the shift toward jobs that require more education and higher skill levels produced a sharp rise in the concentration of poverty in many inner-city neighborhoods. The growth of poverty and increasing levels of social disorder in ghettos also helped fuel the outmigration of middle-class and stable working-class families, thus deepening the impoverishment of these neighborhoods. Together these factors have radically altered the class composition of today's ghetto neighborhoods. Whereas earlier inner-city neighborhoods were characterized by a mix of poor working-class and middle-class blacks, the new urban ghetto has a much higher concentration of poor and otherwise disadvantaged residents (Jargowsky 1997; Jargowsky & Bane 1991; Wilson 1987).

Concurrent with this structural transformation were increasing social problems in many of America's inner cities, as levels of crime, gang activity, chronic joblessness, welfare dependency, and teenage pregnancy soared during the 1970s and 1980s. Early attempts by social scientists to explain these trends centered on the behavior of the poor, typically some variant of the "culture of poverty" thesis, where the behavior of the urban poor is thought to be rooted in a cultural milieu of deviant norms and values (Mead 1986; Murray 1984). This view, however, has not gone unchallenged by urban social scientists. Gans (1982) argued for a "situational conception of culture" that explains the behavior of the urban poor as "a response to the constraints and incentives with which people must deal" (283). Similarly, Ogbu (1985) argued that ghetto culture is first and foremost an adaptation to economic, political, and informational exclusion.

The emphasis on the structural underpinnings of cultural life, especially the deleterious effects of social exclusion, is also a centerpiece of Wilson's work. Drawing on the insights of classical and contemporary urban ethnographies on the importance of social networks for community social integration and cohesion (e.g., Anderson 1990; Liebow 1967; Rainwater 1970), Wilson argues that the social process behind "ghetto culture" is not the intergenerational transmission and internalization of an autonomous and persistent nonnormative subculture. Rather, the structural consequences of concentrated poverty and the social isolation it engenders foster adaptive strategies that are often at odds with the norms of the broader society (Wilson 1987, 1996).

This approach, recalling the classical work on the social ecology of neighborhoods (Shaw & McKay 1942), implies that the urban poor are doubly disadvantaged—by the individual experience of poverty and by the concentrated poverty of the neighborhoods in which they reside. Trapped in economically devastated neighborhoods where few employed adults or stable families remain, individuals and families often lack contact with persons with the knowledge, experience, and, most important, the valuable social connections to aid them in their efforts to improve their life circumstances.

Furthermore, concentrated poverty disrupts social organization such that important institutional resources often found in more affluent neighborhoods are lacking in many poor inner-city neighborhoods. The vitality of a community's institutional structure depends to a large extent on the economic support and involvement of working people, especially the more affluent middle class. When a critical mass of this social stratum is lacking, as it is in many high-poverty neighborhoods, key community institutions—businesses, schools, churches, social clubs, voluntary associations, and community organizations—decline and often disappear, leaving residents cut off from institutional resources and the benefits they can have for families with few resources of their own (Wilson 1996). Indeed, a weak institutional resource base may be a critical mechanism behind the deleterious effects of neighborhood disadvantage on the life chances of poor inner-city residents (Tienda 1991).

The concept of social isolation and the more general formulations of social disorganization theory are complemented by Coleman's (1988, 1990) work on social capital. Several forms of social capital, defined as social-network resources that support individuals in their efforts to realize their goals, are thought to be lacking in high-poverty, socially disorganized neighborhoods. First, weakly organized neighborhoods often suffer from a deficit of effective community norms, such that residents are exposed to cultural socialization and role modeling that reinforces nonnormative attitudes and behavior. In this climate, not only are youth and adults alike less likely to internalize conventional attitudes toward education, steady employment, and family stability, but the lack of normative reinforcement also weakens social control, allowing criminal activity, gangs, teen pregnancy, and drug use to flourish in the community (Sampson & Wilson 1995; Wilson 1987, 1996). Socially connected network members are also an important source of informational social capital about finding jobs, learning the norms and habits of a regular work life and how to move up the occupational ladder (Campbell 1988; Granovetter 1973; Wilson 1987, 1996), and accessing available community programs and services (Briggs 1998).

Furthermore, adaptive strategies for coping with neighborhood disadvantage hamper the creation of a form of social capital critical to the collective life of the community. Distrust and fear of victimization lead residents of socially disorganized neighborhoods to avoid social contact outside their own kin and close friends (Furstenberg 1993; Rainwater 1970; Stack 1974). Better-off residents minimize involvement with their poorer neighbors and maintain friendship ties that are more geographically dispersed (Anderson 1990; Hannerz 1969). These strategies, while functional for individual families, lower the density of obligations and expectations necessary to actuate neighborhood social cohesion (Coleman 1990). With low levels of trust and expectation of reciprocity, residents of poor neighborhoods are also less likely to come to the aid of their neighbors and, consequently, have fewer people they can turn to for social support, especially in times of crisis and financial need (Orthner 1996; Pedder 1991). Weak and less dense social networks mean that the symmetrical relations of obligations and expectations between family members, parents, and neighbors is attenuated. While this reduces the available social capital to all members of the network, the collective supervision of children is particu-

larly compromised (Coleman 1988; Sampson et al. 1997).

In short, the social organization of disadvantaged inner-city neighborhoods exacerbates the social isolation of poor families by limiting the amount of social capital available in community networks. The lack of normative reinforcement and of useful information and the low levels of trust and mutual obligation mean that families have few local social resources to aid them in their efforts to accomplish socially desired ends—labor-market success, family stability, and responsible child-rearing.

Past Research on Social Isolation

The literature reviewed above suggests that residents of poor neighborhoods are more isolated by virtue of residing in areas with more unemployed persons and families on welfare, fewer opportunities for community participation, and a greater propensity to restrict social contacts. Critics, however, have pointed out that much of the evidence in support of the link between neighborhood poverty and social isolation is based on inferences drawn from census measures of the class composition of neighborhoods and not on existing social networks, activities, and patterns of community involvement among the urban poor (Newman 1992).

While empirical research on social isolation using actual social networks and activities is scant, some support for the neighborhood poverty–social isolation hypothesis can be found. It has long been known that communities influence the pattern of social relations by virtue of the types of people encountered in their social environment (Blau & Schwartz 1984). Individuals who reside in neighborhoods where one social class predominates tend to have friends from that social class, regardless of their own (Huckfeldt 1983). This principle also seems to apply to ghetto residents, who are less likely to come into contact with affluent neighbors than are nonresidents of ghettos (Johnstone 1978). Fernandez and Harris (1992) report that both male and female residents of poorer neighborhoods in Chicago had more publicly assisted and less educated friends and that women in these communities also had more unemployed friends. They also report that some types of organizational participation are lower in poorer neighborhoods. Additional evidence of social-network isolation comes from ethnographic interviews with poor residents of Chicago inner-city neighborhoods, whose social networks tend to be restricted to similarly disadvantaged residents of their neighborhoods (Smith 1996).

However, existing research findings are not universally supportive of the neighborhood poverty–social isolation relationship. Using the same data as Fernandez and Harris, Sosin (1991) found no evidence that neighborhood poverty affects the number of workers in the social networks of poor black adults. Furthermore, both Sosin (1991) and Pedder (1991) report that organizational participation is uncorrelated with neighborhood poverty, and both found that low levels of participation were evident across all Chicago study neighborhoods.

In addition to work that explores the link between neighborhood poverty and social isolation, a related literature demonstrates that social-network and neighborhood associational outcomes are strongly influenced by individual and family characteristics. Life cycle, demographic, and social-status factors have long been known to affect friendship networks and involvement in community activities.

DATA AND METHODS

Data

The primary source of the data is the Youth Achievement and the Structure of Inner City Communities study, a project funded by the MacArthur Foundation Research Program on Successful Adolescent Development in High Risk Areas. Face-to-face interviews using a structured questionnaire were completed in June 1991. The sample is made up of African American mothers and up to two of their adolescent children (aged 11 to 16) living in 62 poor and middle-class inner-city tracts with high concentrations of African American residents.[1] Since the focus is on the social isolation of adults, we use data only from the mothers' interviews in the analyses that follow. In all, 383 mothers from poverty tracts and 163 mothers from middle-class tracts were interviewed. Additional data were obtained from the 1990 Census of Population and Housing (STF3A file) (U.S. Bureau of the Census 1992). Using census tracts as a proxy for neighborhoods, tract-level poverty figures are attached to the survey data for use as an indicator of neighborhood disadvantage.

Our sample neighborhoods are highly representative of those neighborhoods where black families in Chicago were likely to reside in the early 1990s. Using 1990 census data and the closest comparable child-age categories, we estimate that the population of census tracts represented in our sample includes 86% of all black families residing in Chicago. We do, however, have to exercise caution in generalizing to other black households, since families with children under 18 years old account for only 35% of all black households. The sample is more representative of black families—52% of all black families in these types of neighborhoods have children between the ages of 5 and 17. Our respondents are quite similar to those in the universe of Chicago inner-city census tracts on those characteristics that could be compared using census data (see discussion of descriptive statistics).

The Youth Achievement Study provides a unique opportunity to assess neighborhood effects. First, in contrast to many national studies where the residential locators are typically large geographical areas (e.g., counties), and therefore not useful for studying neighborhoods, this study identifies census tract of residence. The hierarchical structure of the data, where study respondents are grouped within neighborhoods (i.e., census tracts), facilitates multilevel analyses. Furthermore, a cluster design was implemented to help ensure that neighborhoods would contain enough respondents to satisfy the statistical requirements of hierarchical linear modeling necessary for reliable estimates of neighborhood effects. The study also gathered information on a variety of social isolation indicators, including social networks, neighborhood associations, and community resource use, as well as important individual and family characteristics.

Social Isolation Measures: Network Composition and Organizational Participation

Two types of social isolation are explored in this article—network composition and organizational participation. Following past research, we use the employment, public aid, and educational status of the respondent's friends to measure network composition isolation (Fernandez & Harris 1992; Sosin 1991). Respondents whose friendship networks contain more unemployed, welfare-dependent, and less educated persons are believed to be more socially isolated. Three items are taken from detailed information collected on noncoresiding close friends.[2] Employed friends is the number of friends who have steady jobs. The measure of friends on public aid is the number of friends who receive public aid. College graduate friends is the number of friends who are college graduates.[3]

To test for isolation from community organizations, we use two measures. The first is the mother's community organizational participation, which is a count of the number of times in the past year she has participated in block clubs, neighborhood or tenant groups, and

other community organizations. This measures the level of involvement of the mother in adult-centered voluntary associations and organizations. We also created a measure of the community involvement of families. The level of family participation is a count of the number of times the respondent indicated that someone in the respondent's family ever participated in the following: community watch, summer recreation, community center, youth group, organized sports, or local politics. These organizational measures were selected because these organizational types facilitate contact with more socially connected, resourceful community residents and integrate adults and their families into the broader society (Berger & Neuhaus 1977; Sosin 1991; Wilson 1987). Youth-oriented organizational activities were included because children are also subject to the effects of social isolation.

RESULTS

Table 1 contains the descriptive statistics of our sample of African American mothers residing in the selected Chicago neighborhoods. The average age of the mothers is around 39 years, and the average number of children ever born to them is slightly over 3. About half the mothers have partners whom they are either married to or cohabiting with. Mean educational attainment is around a high school degree (i.e., slightly over 12 years of schooling). Nearly half the mothers were employed (48%) at the time of the survey, while 36% were receiving public assistance (i.e., Aid to Families with Dependent Children). The average length of residence in their current neighborhood is about 12 years. The rate of poverty (i.e., the percentage of families who are poor) in the 62 neighborhoods ranges from 3% to 87%, with an average rate of 35%. About a third of the neighborhoods ($N = 20$) are high-poverty neighbor-

TABLE 1   **Sample Means and Standard Deviations**

	Mean	**S.D.**
Individual/family measures		
Age (in years)	38.82	7.98
Education (in years)	12.62	2.56
AFDC (1 = current recipient)	.36	.48
Partner (1 = married or cohabiting)	.52	.50
Employed (1 = yes)	.48	.50
Number of children (ever born to respondent)	3.21	1.87
Time in neighborhood (in years)	11.67	8.83
Neighborhood measures		
Percentage of families in poverty	34.73	20.74
High poverty (1 = 40% or more in poverty)	.32	.47
N = 507		

hoods, that is, have poverty rates of 40% or more. Differences between the demographics of our sample and comparable census figures for the universe of poor and middle-class inner-city neighborhoods from which our neighborhoods were drawn are relatively minor.[4]

The means and standard deviations for the social isolation measures are presented in Table 2 and are also broken down to illustrate neighborhood variation by level of poverty— low (0–19%), moderate (20–39%), and high (40–100%). For the most part, average levels of social isolation are higher in high-poverty neighborhoods and lower in low-poverty neighborhoods. The pattern is strongest for the social-network measures. Residents of high-poverty neighborhoods, on average, report having fewer close friends who are employed (2.02) or college-educated (.58) and more on public assistance (1.57) than residents of low-poverty neighborhoods (3.79, 2.19, and .19, respectively). Respondents in moderate-poverty neighborhoods fall somewhere between. Scheffe tests comparing group means-indicate that all network mean differences are statistically significant, except the difference

between moderate- and high-poverty college graduate means.

Poverty group differences in organizational isolation are much less apparent. The participation of our adult respondents in community-related organizations is about the same in low and high-poverty neighborhoods. (2.79 compared to 2.69 times per year), with residents of moderately poor neighborhoods having the lowest attendance (2.08). However, none of the differences reaches statistical significance. On the other hand, family participation in organizations and youth programs is significantly lower in moderate- and high-poverty neighborhoods than in low-poverty neighborhoods. We conclude that average levels of social isolation are higher in poorer neighborhoods, especially with respect to the composition of social networks and, to a lesser extent, family participation in community organizations and programs. (Parameteric statistical table not shown.)

Welfare receipt among network members in the high-poverty neighborhood is nearly three times the rate in the low-poverty neighborhood. If we were to stop at this point we might conclude that poverty is a highly significant predictor of social-network outcomes and ex-

TABLE 2   Average Social Isolation Outcomes by Level of Neighborhood Poverty

| | All Neighborhoods | | Neighborhood Poverty[a] | | |
	Mean	S.D.	Low	Moderate	High
Social-network isolation					
Number of employed friends	2.94	1.55	3.79	3.00	2.02[b]
Number of AFDC recipient friends	.88	1.34	.19	.911	.57[b]
Number of college graduate friends	1.26	1.63	2.19	.97	.58[c]
Organizational isolation					
Community participation	2.55	7.99	2.79	2.08	2.69[d]
Family participation	1.39	1.65	1.87	1.11	1.15[c]
N = 507					

[a] Low = 0–19% poor; moderate = 20–39% poor; high = 40% or more poor

[b] All poverty group mean differences are statistically significant, $p \leq .05$.

[c] Moderate- and high-poverty group mean differences are not statistically significant.

[d] No poverty group mean differences are statistically significant.

plains much of their variation by neighborhood—74% for employment, 45% for public assistance, and 34% for college education.

The results (parametric statistical table not shown) show that much of the observed relationship between neighborhoods and social-network isolation outcomes is due to the clustering of similar types of families and individuals in the neighborhood. We find that mothers who are more educated, employed, and not receiving welfare have more higher-status network members, thereby confirming past findings that link socioeconomic status and network composition (see Campbell 1988; Campbell, Marsden & Hurlbert 1986; Fernandez & Harris 1992; Marsden 1987). The results suggest that most of the between-neighborhood variance in the status measures of network members is explained by the individual-level characteristics— 91% of employment, 79% of network public assistance, and 72% of college education.

High-SES mothers have about twice as many employed friends and 3.5 times as many college graduate friends as low-SES mothers who reside in neighborhoods with the same level of poverty. The differences are even greater for the number of friends receiving public aid. Figures for the low-SES group are five times those of the high-SES group. Comparisons provide additional evidence of the relatively greater impact of socioeconomic status. For all outcomes, a low-SES mother residing in a low-poverty neighborhood is more isolated than a high-SES mother residing in a high-poverty neighborhood.

Our findings on organizational isolation were similar to those of Pedder (1991); we found no evidence that neighborhood poverty has a *linear* effect on organizational isolation. (Parameteric statistical table not shown.) However, even the full models explain only a small amount of the between-neighborhood variance in community-related organization participation and family participation, 13% and 6%, respectively. Thus, despite the lack of a linear relationship with neighborhood poverty, other neighborhood characteristics may be important determinants of participation. As for individual-level determinants of participation, mothers' socioeconomic characteristics, especially having more education and not receiving welfare, are important factors associated with greater involvement and participation in community organizations (Woodward 1988). Mothers who have resided in the neighborhood for longer periods have families with greater community participation. We speculate that longer-term residents participate more because they are more aware of community organizational activity and have greater attachment to the area than short-term residents (Kasarda & Janowitz 1974). Not surprisingly, family participation is higher in larger families. The presence of children motivates participation in organizations that supply resources to families (Janowitz 1967).

Following previous research showing nonlinear neighborhood disadvantage effects, Figure 1 presents those isolation outcomes that were found to have statistically significant nonlinear relationships to neighborhood poverty. The figures compare the predicted outcomes for both the linear and nonlinear models. There is little or no poverty effect on the number of employed friends in low- to moderate-poverty neighborhoods, but a more sharply negative one in high-poverty neighborhoods. The results support the argument that those residing in a high-poverty neighborhood are much less likely to come into contact with employed adults (Wilson 1987).

Nonlinear poverty effects were also found for family participation. While participation decreases as poverty increases, it does so only in low- and moderate-poverty neighborhoods. For residents of high-poverty neighborhoods, participation actually increases as poverty worsens. We speculate about the reasons for this unexpected finding below.

DISCUSSION AND CONCLUSION

Social isolation has been posited as a key element in the reduction of life chances of the inner-city poor (Wilson 1987, 1996). Disadvantaged both by the individual experience of poverty and by residence in poor neighborhoods, ghetto residents are thought to be isolated from valuable social contacts that promote social mobility in American society. The purpose of this research has been to reexamine the link between neighborhood poverty and social networks and community involvement in a manner that disentangles the individual and neighborhood causes of social isolation. We briefly summarize the major findings and their implications, and follow with a discussion of the limitations of the study and avenues for further research.

The strongest support for the link between neighborhood poverty and social isolation comes from the analysis of social-network composition. Similar to Fernandez and Harris (1992), we found that residents of poorer neighborhoods had fewer friends who were stably employed or college-educated and more who were on public assistance. Residence in neighborhoods with the highest poverty concentrations is especially deleterious for the prospects of having stably employed network members. Confirmation of this is crucial to the social isolation thesis, given Wilson's contention that residents of high-poverty neighborhoods are deprived of conventional role models and important social-network resources, particularly access to informal job networks.

In contrast to the social-network findings, our results raise new questions about the role of neighborhood poverty in organizational isolation. First, the hypothesized linear relationship—lower levels of organizational participation in poorer neighborhoods—was not supported for community organization participation among our adult respondents (parameteric statistical table not shown). Second, we found evidence of an unexpected nonlinear relationship, in which families are more likely to participate when they reside in the poorest neighborhoods. This was somewhat surprising, since we assumed poorer neighborhoods would have both fewer opportunities for community involvement, as the result of a weaker institutional resource base (see Tienda 1991), and a lower propensity among residents to participate if social avoidance behaviors predominate (see Furstenberg 1993).

While there are many possible explanations for these unexpected findings, we believe that greater family involvement among residents of the poorest neighborhoods is precipitated by attempts on the part of residents and communities to deal with the ecological effects of neighborhood disadvantage. This argument recalls the notion of the "community of limited liability," wherein community involvement is generally limited but can be activated by a perceived threat (Janowitz 1967; Suttles 1972). Higher levels of family participation in the poorest neighborhoods may reflect the fact that these families and neighborhoods take proactive measures to defend themselves against the forces of disorder and deterioration. Others have observed that families attempt to counter these forces by reaching out to more advantaged family and friends both inside and outside their community, forming strong social ties with neighbors and utilizing community resources (Wilson 1996). Higher involvement may indicate greater efforts on the part of parents to manage risk by seeking out safe and supervised activities for their children (Furstenberg et al. 1999).

Moreover, the goals and functions of similar types of organizations are likely to differ by neighborhood contexts in ways that may affect participation. For example, a neighborhood watch program in a poor, gang-infested neighborhood may inspire high levels of involvement because of critical issues related to personal safety, whereas the neighborhood watch program in a more affluent, crime-free neighborhood may receive only tepid interest. Finally, opportunities for community involvement may also be greater than expected if mobilization in poor neighborhoods results in new institutional and organizational resources, including those that come from extracommunity sources. As to the latter, successful political pressure at the municipal level for investment in inner-city community resources may have resulted in greater opportunities for participation in some poor inner-city Chicago neighborhoods (e.g., the construction of a community center or funding of a summer youth program).

Our findings of rather modest neighborhood effects, similar to those in much of the research on the effects of neighborhood disadvantage on other outcomes (e.g., on youth outcomes see Brooks-Gunn et al. 1997; Jencks & Mayer 1990), seem to suggest that individual life circumstances are much more important than residential location. Most of the neighborhood differences in social isolation, particularly isolation from higher-status friends, can be attributed to the neighborhood clustering of family and individual characteristics. Class-related indicators of family socioeconomic status were the strongest predictors of social-network composition and affected both types of organizational participation (Campbell 1988; Campbell, Marsden & Hurlbert 1986; Marsden 1987). Put another way, the networks of those residing in high-poverty neighborhoods contain fewer high-status friends mainly because the residents of these neighborhoods are more likely to be poor and otherwise disadvantaged. Those individual factors that reduce the chances of forming friendships with high-status individuals are much more important than simply residing in a poor neighborhood. We caution, however, that more research is needed and highlight ways to improve studies of social isolation.

In specifying our models we have tried to address criticism of previous research that neighborhood selection factors are not adequately controlled for (see Jencks & Mayer 1990; Tienda 1991). In doing so, an implicit assumption of our models is that individual selection traits are causally prior to the neighborhood. However, to the extent that those traits are themselves a result of neighborhood disadvantage, as theorizing about the consequences of social isolation suggests and as previous research shows (e.g., see Crane 1991 on dropping out of high school), the neighborhood poverty effect is underestimated. Better estimates await a solution to this thorny problem of endogenous neighborhood selection factors.[5]

Refinements in the measurement of social isolation are also needed, especially since conventional measures may underrepresent neighborhood differences in isolation. The social-network composition measures used in our study, as well as in most of the previous research, capture only crude differences in the social status of network members and organizational participation of respondents. Measures are needed that are more sensitive to subtle differences in, for example, the occupational status and educational credentials of network members and the types of activities and social contacts that occur as a result of participation in various community activities. Moreover, the presence of higher-status network members or participation in particular community activities does not by itself confer social and cultural resources. Ideally, we would like to have more direct measures of the type of resources (e.g., job networks) that help poor families cope with disadvantage. Finally, network measures are usually drawn from the respondent's close friends, whereas "weakly tied" relationships involving casual friendships and acquaintances that give individuals access to larger and more diverse social circles are also important to social mobility (Campbell, Marsden & Hurlbert 1986; Granovetter 1973). These types of relationships should be incorporated into studies of social isolation.

Progress in social isolation research also depends on better theorizing about how neighborhoods influence social isolation. The literature on social isolation has centered on the role of poverty as the key neighborhood determinant of isolation outcomes. However, other dimensions of neighborhood disadvantage may be important to consider for future research. Sampson (1988) reports that fear of crime, residential mobility, racial composition, and public housing residence also affect some aspects of social ties and participation. Public transportation systems that are both costly and inconvenient also contribute to the isolation of inner-city residents by segregating them from other areas of the city (Wilson 1996).

Our understanding of the influence of neighborhoods would also benefit from remembering that there is substantial variation in institutional resources and social networks across poor neighborhoods (Elliot et al. 1996; Furstenberg 1993; Newman 1992). While many impoverished neighborhoods suffer from weak social organization, others are characterized by relatively effective police, decent schools, strong community organizations, and dense and cohesive social networks of people that embrace the basic norms and values of the broader society. Residents of such neighborhoods are better able to cope with disadvantage because the neighborhood social organization facilitates access to social capital and institutions that integrate residents into the broader society (Coleman 1990). In short, theory and research about the causes of social isolation need to include an understanding of how patterns of inner-city social life and community involvement are affected not only by the level of disadvantage but also by the structure of social and institutional resources.

Although we have argued above that a focus on African American mothers of adolescent children is warranted given our interest in the social isolation in inner-city neighborhoods, research would benefit from racial and ethnic and gender comparisons. We know, for example, that some social-network characteristics vary by gender (Campbell 1988; Fernandez & Harris 1992; Rainwater 1970) and by race (Lee & Campbell 1999; Lee, Campbell & Miller 1991). Racial and ethnic comparisons are especially needed, since high levels of segregation experienced by African Americans (Jargowsky 1997; Massey & Denton 1993) mean that racial and individual outcomes are confounded by the unique community contexts experienced by different racial and ethnic groups (Sampson & Morenoff 1997).

Finally, neighborhood influences should be greater for those who work, socialize, and worship in neighborhoods they reside in. However, social interaction in workplaces, churches, and other social groupings increasingly takes place outside the neighborhood (Taub et al. 1977). Studies indicate that the number of residents who do not know their neighbors is growing and, aided by advances in telecommunications and transportation, network members increasingly reside outside the neighborhood (Sampson 1999; Wellman 1999). Thus, while the neighborhood continues to be thought of as a critical context, especially for children and adolescents, neighborhoods seem to be declining in relevance as a site of adult social integration. A more complete understanding of the factors affecting social isolation outcomes would require incorporating salient social contexts that are more spatially dispersed.

NOTES

[1]Poverty census tracts are 20% or more in poverty and at least 50% African American; nonpoor tracts are census tracts with a median income of $30,000 or more and at least 30% African American. Household selection in the poverty stratum involved random sampling using a listing of Chicago poverty tract households provided by the National Opinion Research Center. Since no listing of households in middle-class tracts was available, a block quota selection method was used on randomly selected census blocks in all Chicago census tracts fitting the middle-class stratum criteria.

[2]The names of friends were generated using the following prompt: "The next few questions are about your relations with friends and relatives. I'll be asking for first names and initials of some of these people, just so we can keep the list straight. I'll leave the list of names with you when we're finished. Please give me the first names of friends you have, who are not related to you." Respondents were then asked to provide information on each friend's race, neighborhood residence, gender, supportiveness, employment status, public aid receipt, and educational attainment, as well as the number of years the respondent has known each friend named.

[3]We considered combining the three network compositional items into a single socioeconomic status scale but decided against it after exploratory analysis indicated that the use of a combined scale masked important relationships between neighborhood poverty and the constituent measures.

[4]Based on aggregated 1990 census data, we estimate that in the tracts from which our neighborhoods were selected about a third of all African American couples with children between the ages of 12 and 17 were married, compared to 31% for our study respondents. Slightly fewer members of the general population of black adults were high school graduates (62% compared to 67% of the respondents), but this may reflect the inclusion of males and older persons in the census breakdowns. Employment rates for black females with children between the ages of 12 and 17 are similarly close (51% compared to 48% of the respondents). Not surprisingly, since our sample is composed of families with chil-

dren, the rate of public assistance is somewhat higher—35% of our sample, compared to 28% of the population of households in this type of neighborhood.

[5]A partial remedy suggested by one reviewer is to use measures of the respondent's family background (i.e., that of her parent's) in place of the respondent's measures and let the respondent's social isolation be jointly the result of the respondent's family background attributes and the neighborhood. Due to data limitations, the option was unavailable to us.

REFERENCES

Anderson, Elijah. 1990. *Streetwise: Race, Class, and Change in an Urban Community.* University of Chicago Press.

Berger, Peter, and John Neuhaus. 1977. *To Empower People.* American Enterprise Institute.

Blau, Peter, and Joseph Schwartz. 1984. *Crosscutting Social Circles.* Academic Press.

Briggs, Xavier de Souza. 1998. "Brown Kids in White Suburbs: Housing Mobility and the Multiple Faces of Social Capital." Housing Policy Debate 9:177–221.

Brooks-Gunn, Jeanne, Greg J. Duncan, Tama Leventhal, and J. Lawrence Aber. 1997. "Lessons Learned and Future Directions for Research on the Neighborhoods in Which Children Live." Pp. 279–98 in *Neighborhood Poverty: Context and Consequences for Children,* edited by Jeanne Brooks-Gunn, Greg J. Duncan, and J. Lawrence Aber. Russell Sage Foundation.

Bryk, Anthony, and Stephen Raudenbush. 1992. *Hierarchical Linear Modeling: Applications and Data Analysis Methods.* Sage Publications.

Campbell, Karen E. 1988. "Gender Differences in Job-Related Networks." *Work and Occupations* 15:179–200.

Campbell, Karen E., Peter V. Marsden, and Jeanne S. Hurlbert. 1986. "Social Resources and Socioeconomic Status." *Social Networks* 8:97–117.

Coleman, James. 1988. "Social Capital in the Creation of Human Capital." *American Journal of Sociology* 94:S95–120.

———. 1990. *Foundations of Social Theory.* Harvard University Press.

Crane, Jonathan. 1991. "The Epidemic Theory of Ghettos and Neighborhood Effects on Dropping Out and Teenage Childbearing." *American Journal of Sociology* 96:1226–59.

Elliott, Delbert S., William J. Wilson, David Huizinga, Robert J. Sampson, Amanda Elliott, and Bruce Rankin. 1996. "The Effects of Neighborhood Disadvantage on Adolescent Development." *Journal of Research on Crime and Delinquency* 33:389–426.

Fernandez, Roberto, and David Harris. 1992. "Social Isolation and the Underclass." Pp. 257–93 in *Drugs, Crime, and Social Isolation,* edited by Adele V. Harrell and George E. Peterson. Urban Institute Press.

Fischer, Claude S. 1982. *To Dwell among Friends: Personal Networks in Town and City.* University of Chicago Press.

Furstenberg, Frank F., Jr. 1993. "How Families Manage Risk and Opportunity in Dangerous Neighborhoods." Pp. 231–58 in *Sociology and the Public Agenda,* edited by William J. Wilson. Sage Publications.

Granovetter, Mark S. 1973. "The Strength of Weak Ties." *American Journal of Sociology* 78:1360–80.

Guo, Guang. 1996. "Negative Multinomial Regression Models for Clustered Event Counts." *Sociological Methodology* 26:113–32.

Hannerz, Ulf. 1969. *Soulside: Inquiries into Ghetto Culture and Community.* Columbia University Press.

Hogan, Dennis P., and Everlyn M. Kitagawa. 1985. "Social and Environmental Factors Influencing Contraceptive Use among Black Adolescents." *Family Planning Perspectives* 17:165–69.

Huckfeldt, R. Robert. 1983. "Social Contexts, Social Networks, and Urban Neighborhoods: Environmental Constraints on Friendship Choice." *American Journal of Sociology* 89:651–69.

Janowitz, Morris. 1967. *The Community Press in an Urban Setting.* University of Chicago Press.

Jargowsky, Paul A. 1997. *Poverty and Place: Ghettos, Barrios, and the American City.* Russell Sage Foundation.

Jargowsky, Paul A., and Mary J. Bane. 1991. "Ghetto Poverty in the United States, 1970–1980." Pp. 235–73 in *The Urban Underclass,* edited by Christopher Jencks and Paul E. Peterson. Brookings Institution.

Jencks, Christopher, and Susan E. Mayer. 1990. "The Social Consequences of Growing Up in a Poor Neighborhood." Pp. 111–86 in *Inner-City Poverty in the United States,* edited by Laurence E. Lynn Jr. and Michael McGreary. National Academy Press.

Johnstone, John. 1978. "Social Class, Social Areas, and Delinquency." *Sociology and Social Research* 63:49–72.

Kasarda, John D., and Morris Janowitz. 1974. "Community Attachment in Mass Society." *American Sociological Review* 39:328–39.

Lee, Barrett A., and Karen E. Campbell. 1999. "Neighbor Networks of Black and White Americans." Pp. 119–46 in *Networks in the Global Village,* edited by Barry Wellman. Westview Press.

Lee, Barrett A., Karen E. Campbell, and Oscar Miller. 1991. "Racial Differences in Urban Neighboring." *Sociological Forum* 6:525–50.

Marsden, Peter V. 1987. "Core Discussion Networks of Americans." *American Sociological Review* 52:122–31.

Massey, Douglas S., and Nancy A. Denton. 1993. *American Apartheid: Segregation and the Making of the Urban Underclass.* Harvard University Press.

Mead, Lawrence. 1986. *Beyond Entitlement: The Social Obligations of Citizenship.* Free Press.

Murray, Charles. 1984. *Losing Ground: American Social Policy, 1950–1980.* Basic Books.

Newman, Katherine S. 1992. "Culture and Structure in the Truly Disadvantaged." *City and Society* 6:3–25.

Olsen, Marvin, Harry Perlstadt, Valencia Fonseca, and Joanne Hogan. 1989. "Participation in Neighborhood Associations." *Sociological Focus* 22:1–17.

Orthner, Dennis K. 1996. "Families in Poverty: Key Issues in Research." *Journal of Family Issues* 17:588–92.

Pedder, Sophie. 1991. "Social Isolation and the Labor Market: Black Americans in Chicago." Paper presented at the Chicago Urban Poverty and Family Life Conference, October 10–12, Chicago.

Peeples, Faith, and Rolf Loeber. 1994. "Do Individual Factors and Neighborhood Context Explain Ethnic Differences in Juvenile Delinquency?" *Journal of Quantitative Criminology* 10:141–58.

Rainwater, Lee. 1970. *Behind Ghetto Walls.* Aldine.

Sampson, Robert J. 1988. "Local Friendship Ties and Community Attachment in Mass Society: A Multilevel Systemic Model." *American Sociological Review* 53:766–79.

———. 1999. "What 'Community' Supplies." Pp. 241–92 in *Urban Problems and Community Development,* edited by Ronald F. Ferguson and William T. Dickens. Brookings Institution Press.

Sampson, Robert J., and Jeffrey Morenoff. 1997. "Ecological Perspectives on the Neighborhood Context of Urban Poverty: Past and Present." Pp. 1–22 in *Neighborhood Poverty: Policy Implications in Studying Neighborhoods,* edited by Jeanne Brooks-Gunn, Greg Duncan, and Lawrence Aber. Russell Sage Foundation.

Sampson, Robert J., and William J. Wilson. 1995. "Toward a Theory of Race, Crime, and Urban Inequality." Pp. 37–54 in *Crime and Inequality,* edited by John Hagan and Ruth Peterson. Stanford University Press.

Smith, Sandra S. 1996. "Poverty Concentration and Social Networks: Implications for Joblessness." Paper presented at the annual meetings of the American Sociological Association, Washington, D.C., August 19–23.

Sosin, Michael. 1991. "Concentration of Poverty and Social Isolation of the Inner-City Poor." Paper presented at the Chicago Urban Poverty and Family Life Conference, October 10–12, Chicago.

Stack, Carol. 1974. *All Our Kin: Strategies for Survival in a Black Community.* Harper and Row.

Suttles, Gerald D. 1972. *The Social Construction of Community.* University of Chicago Press.

Taub, Richard P., George P. Surgeon, Sara Lindholm, Phyllis Betts Otti, and Amy Bridges. 1977. "Urban Voluntary Associations, Locality Based and Externally Induced." *American Journal of Sociology* 83:425–42.

Tienda, Marta. 1991. "Poor People, Poor Places: Deciphering Neighborhood Effects on Poverty Outcomes." Pp. 244–62 in *Macro-Micro Linkages in Sociology,* edited by Joan Huber. Sage Publications.

U.S. Bureau of the Census. 1992. Census of Population and Housing, 1990: Summary Tape File 3 on CD-ROM [computer file]. Washington, D.C.: Census Bureau [producer and distributor].

Wellman, Barry. 1999. "The Network Community: An Introduction." Pp. 1–48 in *Networks in the Global Village,* edited by Barry Wellman. Westview Press.

Wilson, William Julius. 1987. *The Truly Disadvantaged: The Inner City, the Underclass, and Public Policy.* University of Chicago Press.

———. 1996. *When Work Disappears: The World of the New Urban Poor.* Knopf.

Woodward, Michael D. 1988. "The Effects of Social Class on Voluntary Association Membership among Urban Afro-Americans." *Sociological Focus* 21:67–80.

URBAN POVERTY AFTER *THE TRULY DISADVANTAGED:* THE REDISCOVERY OF THE FAMILY, THE NEIGHBORHOOD, AND CULTURE

Mario Luis Small
Katherine Newman

THE NEIGHBORHOOD

Perhaps no single question in urban inequality has produced more research than whether neighborhood poverty affects the life chances of the poor. Wilson (1987) argues that the concentration of poverty results in the isolation of the poor from the middle class and its corresponding role models, resources, and job networks; more generally, he argues that being poor in a mixed-income neighborhood is less damaging than being poor in a high poverty neighborhood. Concentration effects increase the likelihood of being unemployed, dropping out of school, taking up crime, and becoming pregnant out of wedlock. A large body of empirical research has tested for neighborhood effects on unemployment (Vartanian 1999, Elliott 1999), dropping out of school (Crane 1991), crime (Sampson & Groves 1989), out-of-wedlock births (Crane 1991, Anderson 1991, 1999, South & Crowder 1999), and cognitive development (Brooks-Gunn et al 1997a, 1997b). The body of research is large enough to require its own separate review, and indeed, several of them exist (Jencks & Mayer 1990b, Gephart 1997). Instead of repeating the work of these reviewers, we (*a*) discuss the most important methodological problems with measuring whether neighborhoods have these hypothesized effects; (*b*) report the latest findings on whether neighborhood poverty affects life chances; and (*c*) examine what we argue is the

most pressing unresolved question with respect to neighborhood effects: how they work.

Much of the literature on neighborhood effects has been methodological, and with good reason. It is extremely difficult to test the hypothesis that, everything else being equal, an individual living under any particular neighborhood condition is worse off than in the absence of that condition. Several problems are related to this difficulty, such as the need for longitudinal data, the challenge of disentangling neighborhood from school effects, and the possibility of nonlinear effects (for extended discussions, see Duncan et al 1997, Tienda 1991, Jencks & Mayer 1990b). But two problems are particularly important.

First, people are not randomly distributed across neighborhoods. People live in neighborhoods as a result of both observable and unobservable characteristics that may themselves, independently of neighborhoods, affect life outcomes. For example, parents with little education are more likely to live in poor neighborhoods, and they are also more likely to have children who drop out of high school. By neglecting to control for the parents' low educational attainment, researchers may overstate the impact of living in a poor neighborhood. Most published studies of neighborhood effects deal with this question in a perfunctory fashion, adding a small number of controls for parental education and income. There are exceptions, such as Duncan et al (1997), who control for a battery of typically unmeasured variables; Duncan et al (1997) and Cutler & Glaser (1997), who make use of instrumental variables; and Rosenbaum & Popkin (1991), who, via the Gautreaux program, approximate a randomized experiment (see also Spencer et al 1997). But the bottom line is that most neighborhood studies are unable to make causal links and can only point to strong associations.

Second, how do we define and measure neighborhoods? The problem involves three interrelated issues: conceptualizing neighborhoods, drawing their geographic boundaries, and determining which neighborhood characteristics should be used to measure disadvantage. Most sociologists conceptualize neighborhoods in terms of informal relationships or social networks among persons living in a geographic space; thus, when we use the term "neighborhood" we tend to mean "community" (Wellman 1988, Chaskin 1997, Sampson 1999). But geographic location and social networks are separate and distinct attributes that may have different effects on individuals. Failing to account for this and for the many possible ways neighborhoods may be defined will result in an increasingly muddled discourse on the effects of neighborhoods on people. A few recent scholars have proposed that we conceive of neighborhoods in terms of several separate and complementary dimensions, such as (a) a social space, (b) a set of relationships, (c) a set of institutions, and (d) a symbolic unit (Chaskin 1997); or that we think of neighborhoods alternatively as (a) sites, (b) perceptions, (c) networks, and (d) cultures (Burton et al 1997). These works, though still in their conceptual infancy, push us toward the important task of developing greater clarity over what is meant by neighborhoods.

Even if we sharpen our thinking about neighborhoods in terms of nongeographic concepts, we still have to determine their geographic boundaries if we want to test whether they matter for poverty outcomes. This task is not straight-forward. Most sociologists resort to the census tract, but, depending on how we think neighborhoods matter, census tracts may be woefully inadequate proxies. For example, the perceptions of local residents regarding the boundaries of their neighborhoods may be important determinants of how the neighborhoods affect them; in that case, census-tract operationalizations will be of little use. Some scholars suggest replacing census tracts with the smaller block groups (a practice common in the fields of demography and public health), which allow for a narrower geographic area of socialization (C Jencks, personal communication). A few recent studies (Sampson et al 1997, Sampson & Groves 1989) employ "neighborhood clusters" or "localities," which are neighborhood boundaries drawn by researchers explicitly for the purpose of studying neighborhood effects. The advantage of these clusters is that they are often drawn with an eye to local perceptions about what constitutes the end of one neighborhood and the beginning of another. The disadvantage is that the more accurately they reflect local perceptions of neighborhood boundaries, the more costly and time-consuming it is to draw them.

Finally, what characteristics should we employ to measure disadvantage (Gephart 1997, Mincy 1994, Elliot et al 1996)? There are many possibilities: neighborhood poverty, segregation, the unemployment rate, and the level of educational attainment. Consequently, some researchers have combined these measures into composite "disadvantage" or "risk factor" indexes that encompass race, class, and other variables (e.g., Brooks-Gunn et al 1997a,b, Duncan & Aber 1997, South & Crowder 1999). These indexes have the advantage of statistical parsimony, especially since many of these variables tend to be correlated. Yet indexing makes replication cumbersome, especially when the index employs survey data. Furthermore, that solution does not help us discern which neighborhood characteristics affect people and which do not. The substantively important question is whether neighborhood unemployment or racial homogeneity or resource-deprivation affects life chances. A composite index that lumps all of these variables obscures which factors are creating the effect (see Massey 1998).

Methodological difficulties notwithstanding, several major recent studies have collected copious and increasingly sophisticated data that suggest neighborhoods matter with respect to certain variables. In an early release of the findings from the Gautreaux program. Rosenbaum & Popkin (1991) report that low-income black families who moved from public housing to the suburbs were more likely to be employed than similar families who remained in the inner city. Brooks-Gunn et al (1997a,b,c), employing data from the Working Group on Communities and Neighborhoods. Family Processes, and Individual Development, find that neighborhood conditions are often predictors of children's development, that the effect is strongest during early childhood and late adolescence, and that affluent or middle-class neighborhoods increase children's development and improve adolescents' achievement. After interviewing 500 families in Philadelphia, Furstenberg et al (1999) uncovered the fact that neighborhood conditions affect parents' family management practices (e.g., the more dangerous the neighborhood, the more restrictive the parents), but not achievement among early adolescents. Relying on data compiled in Chicago, Denver, and Philadelphia by the Neighborhood Project. Elliott et al (1996) find that neighborhood disadvantage affects successful behavioral development and delinquency among adolescents, but only via the mediating effect of informal social control (a concept encompassing many of the variables of social organization and collective efficacy, which we discuss below). Using data from the Multi-City Study of Urban Inequality, Tigges et al (1998) find that neighborhood poverty

significantly increases social isolation and decreases access to resources. The ambitious Moving to Opportunity study is preparing early findings at the time of this writing. We should reiterate that most of these studies, though they may point to strong correlations, cannot make causal statements. Still, if these studies are any indication, future, more sophisticated work will probably show that (*a*) neighborhoods affect life chances during early childhood and late adolescence, that (*b*) most neighborhood effects are not as strong as family effects, and that (*c*) social networks, which sometimes are linked to neighborhoods but often transcend them, are critical.

The Mechanisms Behind Neighborhood Effects

How does neighborhood poverty produce its negative effect? Surprisingly few studies have tackled this question seriously, although many researchers have argued that we need to do so (Jencks & Mayer 1990b, Tienda 1991, Furstenberg & Hughes 1997). Based on the works that have addressed this question (Wilson 1987, 1996, Jencks & Mayer 1990b, Massey & Denton 1993), we identify two general categories of models: socialization mechanisms, which describe how neighborhoods socialize those who grow up in them, and instrumental mechanisms, which describe how individual agency is limited by neighborhood conditions.

Socialization mechanisms tend to conceive of individuals as (relatively passive) recipients of powerful socializing forces, suggesting that neighborhoods mold those who grow up in them into certain behavioral patterns. For this reason, these mechanisms tend to focus on children and adolescents. There are six socialization mechanisms. The epidemic model (Jencks & Mayer 1990b, Wilson 1987) argues that when many of a child's neighborhood peers engage in a certain type of behavior, the child will be socialized into engaging in such behavior. The collective socialization model (Jencks & Mayer 1990b, Wilson 1987) argues that having a scarcity of successful role models in their neighborhood makes children less likely to envision success for themselves (see also Cutler & Glaeser 1997, Newman 1999). The institutional model (Jencks & Mayer 1990b) argues that non-resident adults (such as teachers and police officers) attached to institutions in the neighborhood will treat young people worse if the neighborhood is poor (thus either teaching them poorly or treating them as criminals). A fourth, the linguistic isolation model, refers to the socialization of African-American children in poor, segregated neighborhoods (Massey & Denton 1993, also Labov & Harris 1986). It argues that black children under such circumstances become isolated from Standard American English, absorb only Black English Vernacular, and therefore do poorly in school and when interviewing for jobs. The fifth, relative deprivation, model argues that poor children will be worse off in rich than in poor neighborhoods (Jencks & Mayer 1990b). Because people judge their economic position by comparing themselves to those around them, poor children will develop more unfavorable opinions of themselves the richer the neighborhoods they live in, resorting (in many cases) to deviance as a maladaptive response. The sixth is the oppositional culture model (Massey & Denton 1993 and Jencks & Mayer 1990b call this the cultural conflict model), which argues that either segregation or neighborhood poverty causes residents to develop a culture opposed to mainstream norms and values.

Whereas socialization models explain how neighborhood environments socialize individuals, instrumental models focus on how individual agency is limited by neighborhood environment. Here, the mechanisms tend to focus on adults, rather than children and adolescents. The most prominent of these is the networks

isolation model, which argues that being in a poor, or extensively unemployed, neighborhood will disconnect individuals from social networks of employed people, making it difficult for them to obtain information about job opportunities (Wilson 1987, 1996, Elliott 1999, Tigges et al 1998). The resource model argues that poor neighborhoods, deprived of institutional resources such as schools, churches, recreational areas, and daycare centers, make it difficult for parents to raise their children effectively (Wilson 1987, Brooks-Gunn et al 1997a,b). (See Jencks & Mayer 1990b for a variant of this model.) The final one is the limitation of political alliances model. Massey & Denton (1993), focusing not on neighborhood poverty but on neighborhood segregation, argue that blacks have a difficult time developing political alliances across racial lines because, in conditions of segregation, no neighborhood-specific benefits accrued to blacks will accrue to members of other races. Consequently, they are unable to attract the public resources that will undergird decent schools, playgrounds, and business investment.

Most of these models have received little or no theoretical or empirical attention (Newman 1992; but see Rankin & Quane 2000, Fernandez & Harris 1992, Huckfeldt 1983, Elliott 1999, Tigges et al 1998). Most of them require observational and interview data that students of urban poverty have not collected systematically. Students have also spent little time thinking through these explanations, some of which rely on tenuous assumptions about how much time people spend in their neighborhoods, how much they interact with their neighbors, and how attitudes and values develop (see Wellman 1988, 1999, Fischer 1982).

There is one more model of how neighborhood effects work, one that focuses on the effects not on individuals but on neighborhood crime. Building on the foundation laid by the works of Shaw & McKay (1942), Sampson and his colleagues argue that a major cause of delinquency is social disorganization or the lack of collective efficacy (Sampson 1988, 1999, Sampson & Groves 1989, Sampson & Raudenbush 1999, Sampson & Wilson 1995, Sampson et al 1997). In empirical papers, both terms have referred to (*a*) the density of social networks in a neighborhood, (*b*) the extent of neighbors' involvement in voluntary associations, and (*c*) the degree to which neighbors are willing to supervise the young and inter-

vene in social situations for the collective good; the term collective efficacy has tended to refer in greater degree to the latter attribute. Sampson and his colleagues have collected a wide array of evidence to demonstrate that neighborhoods with a high level of social organization and collective efficacy have lower crime rates, regardless of their poverty level. Since poor neighborhoods tend to be lower on these factors, their crime rates tend to be high.

C.
Community Action

THE EFFECTIVENESS OF NEIGHBORHOOD COLLECTIVE ACTION

Gustavo S. Mesch
Kent P. Schwirian

Urban redevelopment forces have created major and complex issues for residents of local areas. As redevelopment has proceeded, both city and suburban neighborhoods have had to face forces of change that threaten their physical and social environments. Land development pressures, housing deterioration, population change, and crime have become threats to the physical integrity of local areas, to the web of social relations among neighborhood residents, and to the reputations and images of the neighborhoods in the community's galaxy of social worlds.

Faced with such threats, many neighborhoods have become proactive and have attempted to control and shape their own destiny through both collective organization and social action (Logan and Rabrenovic 1990; Heskin 1991; Hogan 1986). However, the sheer fact that neighborhood organizations are established and that they engage in change-driven social action does not guarantee the ability to solve local problems. Simply put, when it comes to social action, some neighborhood organizations are effective and some are not (Schwirian and Mesch 1993; Austin 1991). This paper investigates the factors that contribute to effective neighborhood social action. We place special emphasis on the role of three general factors in attaining local success: local ecology, organizational complexity, and coalitional embeddedness.

BACKGROUND

Neighborhood organization has become a central theme in urban research (Sampson 1991; Haberle 1989; Berry, Portney, and Thompson 1993). The main agents of neighborhood action are neighborhood associations. They are civic associations whose goals are to maintain and improve neighborhood quality of life and to protect common economic and social interests (Logan and Rabrenovic 1990). Neighborhood associations are place-specific, volunteer-driven, shaped by the direct participation of members, and defined by problem-solving as their principal reason for existence (Florin and Wandersman 1990).

In recent years the activities of neighborhood associations have become visible as local organizations confront public and private agents that pose threats to the social and physical well-being of the neighborhood (Hogan 1986; Graham and Hogan 1990). Neighborhood residents have learned that there are limited prospects for outside political or economic help in their struggle against the large-scale agents of change—city hall, the growth machine, and big development interests (Schwirian and Mesch 1993).

A number of factors have prompted neighborhood organization and action. The first is gentrification. Gentrifiers are joiners; they are much more likely than other newcomer middle-class city residents to contact and join neighborhood organizations. In general, these gentrifier organizations are aggressive in taking steps to regulate land use, reduce crime, and to improve municipal services (Crenshaw and St. John 1990). Their degree of social action prompts other non-gentrified inner-city neighborhoods to organize and become active, for fear that their lack of organization and inaction will result in an exacerbation of their major political and economic disadvantage vis-à-vis the gentrifiers.

Urban redevelopment is an additional factor prompting current neighborhood organization and action. Even though metropolitan areas continue to expand at their periphery, the redevelopment of the city core has continued in most places. Redevelopment has become more complex for all parties—redevelopers, financial institutions, city government, and neighborhood groups—in recent years because the scale of urban redevelopment has expanded. The number of projects going on at any one time has increased so that many projects are at various stages of planning or completion; the result is that redevelopment becomes a continuous process rather than a single event. The de-

velopment game has come to be played city-wide and has become intertwined with the total web of city politics. Government resources invested in one project drain resources available for others. Thus, redevelopment projects have become the focus of city politics, in which the city's administration must demonstrate both "vision" and fiscal responsibility in order to ensure electability (Davis 1991; Filion 1987; Heskin 1991). Redevelopment has become international in scope. With the emergence of the global city and the internationalization and mobility of development capital, the whole process of redevelopment has become more volatile (Mollenkopf 1983; Savitch 1988; Sassen 1991). This has raised the level of uncertainty for urban core residents, thereby prompting them to adopt a permanent "on guard" mentality and motivating them to organize for self-protection.

The third factor prompting neighborhood action is participation inducements issued by local governments (Berry, Portney, and Thompson 1993). Some urban administrations have attempted to reach out to the neighborhoods through empowering local groups in such matters as zoning changes. Typically, neighborhoods form advisory councils that are officially recognized by the city's government. The advisory body meets regularly and reviews matters referred to it by the city's administration. Through regular meetings and regular contacts with city hall, the neighborhood council comes to be recognized by city hall as the "voice" of its neighborhood (Mesch 1993).

The fourth major factor is the urban drug war. In most large cities the drug war is totally out of control and the police and cities' administrations must rely on local support to enhance their operations. Block watch groups, anti-drug marches, and neighborhood councils provide the police a neighborhood base for their efforts in identifying and arresting dealer suspects, in closing crack houses, and monitoring gang activity and violence (Skogan 1992).

The net effect of these factors is a high level of neighborhood organization and activity in today's cities. In this paper we attempt to identify the factors that contribute to perceptions of successful neighborhood organizations.

SUBSTANTIVE MODEL AND HYPOTHESES

We argue that there are three general factors that are important for effective neighborhood social action. These are neighborhood ecology, the organizational complexity of neighborhood associations, and the coalition embeddedness of neighborhood associations. We approach this research problem through the Neighborhood Political Ecology Model (Schwirian and Mesch 1993). First we discuss the model in general terms and then we present the hypotheses about organizational effectiveness in terms of the model.

The Neighborhood Political Ecology Model

The Neighborhood Political Ecology model (NPE) is concerned with neighborhood response to potential changes in the environment, population, or sociocultural system of the area. The NPE model focuses on both the processes of social organization within the neighborhood as it prepares to deal with important local issues and with the social action of the neighborhood in pursuit of local goals for neighborhood structure and change.

From the standpoint of the NPE model, the traditional ecological conception of neighborhood as population is expanded to include environmental and social actors. The neighborhood is an open system that is affected by forces, processes, and groups operating in the larger community milieu. It is this very openness that results in the neighborhood system being attuned to both external and internal triggers for potential changes.

In addition to being ecological, the NPE model is also political. Major urban issues and programs today have important implications for the stability or change in neighborhoods ecological systems. The political economy of cities results in neighborhoods becoming political actors either by their own design or by the design of local political institutions. Neighborhood associations enter the development-redevelopment fray as their interests become entangled with those of other action-oriented political actors.

The NPE model recognizes that change often is generated by varied interests and organizations in the larger community's political economy. Consequently, the local neighborhood is potentially influenced by impulses for change from three social contexts: within the neighborhood, from the larger city system of which the neighborhood is a part, and from the larger world urban system in which the city is networked.

From the perspective of the NPE model, the neighborhood is a system of social action that consists of the interests and ideologies held by the neighborhood's residents; the associations, institutions, and organizations within the neighborhood, and their goals and patterns of organization; and the conflictual and coalitional relations among these organizations. Action may be either reactive or proactive—that is, prompted by threats to the neighborhood environment (NIMBY—Not In My Back Yard), or by aggressive attempts to achieve internally established goals for enhancements of some or all of the neighborhood's interests (Heskin 1991).

The NPE model argues that planning is an important activity for organizational actors. Planning is the process through which social actors lay out their course of action and assess their resource needs. Action alternatives are weighed, selected, and prioritized in terms of their relative utilities for obtaining a favorable action outcome (Burt 1982). Planning is a political process in which different local interests and ideologies contend with each other in the formation of proposed social action. Planning success is enhanced by the inclusion of the concerns of the various interests, social origin groups, and ideologies in the neighborhood (Laumann and Pappi 1986).

Successful planning requires skill in resource mobilization. Money and talent are resources that enhance the likelihood of successful social action. Another important resource is information. Neighborhood groups that have information as to how the city's political economy works, how issues may be successfully attacked, and where outside help may be secured are much more likely to engage in effective social action than are those groups that do not know about such things.

Sources of neighborhood resources may be internal to the neighborhood, external, or both. Internal resources include money, people, institutions, organizations, knowledge, and leadership skills that are available among the locals. External resources come from the social system beyond the neighborhood. An example of an external resource is the city, state, or federal government program package—such as a block grant or demonstration project—that underwrites neighborhood activities.

Thus the NPE model argues that neighborhood social action results from the combination of people and organization. To act, local organizations must secure resources, engage in effective planning, and form coalitions with other organizations that serve to magnify their own efforts. Some populations are better at this than others because their more favorable position in the social system gives them access to powerful contacts, information, and insights into the overall functioning of the system.

Hypotheses

According to the NPE model three sets of factors contribute to effectiveness in the social action of neighborhood associations: neighborhood social ecology, organizational complexity, and coalitional embeddedness. Local ecology refers to the demographic and environmental conditions of the neighborhood. Urban research has shown that three variables measure the basic demographic dimensions of neighborhoods. They are socioeconomic status, neighborhood investments, and ethnic composition (Schwirian 1983). Each dimension is predicted to have an independent connection to effectiveness in local social action.

Local ecology: Socioeconomic status. H1: The higher the neighborhood's socioeconomic status, the more effective the neighborhood association in social action.

The first hypothesis is predicated on the idea that socioeconomic status may be either an asset or a liability in community social action. It is an asset for the upper class. Past research has shown that upper-class and upper middle-class neighborhoods have an advantage in dealing with the urban bureaucracy in resolution of issues and in heading off unwanted land use and demographic changes in the neighborhood or adjacent areas (Schwirian and Mesch 1993). But socioeconomic status is a liability for lower-class populations. These populations are at a disadvantage and often must rely on help from outside agencies and leaders to organize effectively (Hogan 1986; Oropesa 1989).

Local ecology: Neighborhood investments. H2: The greater the proportion of residents with interest in locale the greater the effectiveness of local action.

Local organization is an instrumental response by those with economic and social stakes in the locality. In the Community of Limited Liability Model, individuals are believed to rationally calculate ends that may be obtained by residence in specific territories; political activity is seen as a logical way to achieve desirable goals for the territory. Among the most important investments are home ownership and a traditional family lifestyle (Schwirian 1983). It reflects the degree of investment in neighborhood continuity (Davis 1991). Residential stability provides opportunities for interaction between neighbors and provides the confidence in others that is required for cooperative action through neighborhood associations. Populations with high investment in the neighborhood have a high level of motivation to act effectively in issues affecting the area (Oropesa 1992).

Local ecology: Racial composition. H3: Neighborhood associations located in predominantly white neighborhoods are likely to be more effective in social action than neighborhood associations located in predominantly African American neighborhoods.

African American neighborhoods traditionally have been portrayed as being at the edge of the city's political economy. They have been viewed as areas besieged by problems but lacking in sufficient resources to confront them (Suttles 1968, 1972). Consequently, it has been argued that most African American neighborhoods have been caught in the downward slide predicted by the neighborhood life cycle model (Hoover and Vernon 1959). People in these neighborhoods have a difficult time confronting the local government and agents of growth in seeking solutions to their problems.

Local ecology: Environmental threat. H4: The greater the number of environmental-threat issues with which a neighborhood association must deal, the greater its effectiveness in social action.

In addition to the population characteristics of the neighborhood, the nature of the neighborhood's environment is part of local ecology. Some environments are free of threats, while others contain many threats. This hypothesis deals with environmental threats but it also reflects both efficiency

and social learning (Crenshaw and St. John 1989). It argues that, net of other factors such as socioeconomic status and minority population concentration, as neighborhood associations confront a larger number of issues and engage increasingly in social action on those issues, they become more knowledgeable and more able to acquire the resources they need and to form the linkages to other organizations that will help them achieve their action goals (Mesch 1993). Thus, environmental threats motivate social action; as threats multiply, so too do social action and effectiveness in dealing with the threats.

Organizational complexity. H5: The more organizationally complex the neighborhood association, the greater its effectiveness in social action.

Complexity is an important dimension of organizational structure. It refers to the degree of task differentiation among roles in the organization (Drabeck and Haas 1974; Blau 1981). It has been argued that structural complexity allows an organization to deal better with an unstable resource base by formally delegating responsibilities and activities (Austin 1991). Neighborhood associations with more complex structures are more likely to define more tasks and to undertake a wider range of social actions.

Coalitional embeddedness. H6: The greater the extent to which a neighborhood association is embedded in coalitions with other associations, institutions, and organizations, the greater its effectiveness in social action.

In the context of the urban political economy, neighborhoods must confront organizations with resources. This means a clear resource disadvantage for the typical neighborhood association. This disadvantage can be compensated through coalition formation with other organizations. Through coalition building, resources can be pooled or exchanged, thereby enhancing the association's chances of social action success. Indeed, Wiewel and Hunter (1985) report that organizational success is associated with the neighborhood's density of interorganizational networks.

Coalition formation with organizations external to the neighborhood can also provide the resources to enhance social action. This is more difficult than coalition embeddedness within the neighborhood since it requires both a thorough knowledge of the city's social action field (organizations, interests, leadership, ideologies, and plans) and a *quid pro quo* to motivate other organizations to engage in coalition building with the neighborhood association. An example of such coalitions today are the councils of associations active in some cities. These councils bring together associations from the spectrum of the city's neighborhoods. The purpose of these councils is to provide a united front against the city in matters of physical redevelopment and social programs (Schwirian and Mesch 1993).

The Neighborhood Political Ecology Model attributes a central place to forces and actors in the large community as triggers of neighborhood change. In the next section we elaborate on the city context of neighborhood social action.

The City Context

This study was conducted in the City of Columbus, Ohio, and surrounding suburbs. Unlike other old cities, the metropolitan area is growing very fast. During the last decade the population increased 12 percent and the number of housing units almost doubled. The city's economic base is diverse and shaped by its position as state capital. Local employment is concentrated in the service sector, health and education, finance and insurance, and retail trade.

African Americans represent about 23 percent of the population and are highly residen-

tially concentrated. Although the residential segregation of African Americans decreased in Columbus during the '70s from .81 to .71, this level is above the national average. Predominantly African American neighborhoods report higher levels of environmental threats—such as housing deterioration, lack of adequate services, unwanted business establishing in the area, and land use change—than predominantly white neighborhoods.

Like many other cities in the process of development and expansion, Columbus experiences tension between development forces and neighborhood residents. As new areas develop and old areas change, conflicts emerge between developers interested in intensifying land use, politicians' interest in expanding the number of available jobs and the tax base, and residents' interest in conserving and improving their neighborhoods.

Since the late 1970s Columbus has worked to create a body of advisory neighborhood representatives. In 1981 the City Code was changed and some neighborhood associations were recognized to

> *afford additional voluntary citizen participation in decision making in an advisory capacity and to facilitate communication, understanding, and cooperation between neighborhood groups, city officials and developers (The City Bulletin 1981).*

The recognition of neighborhood associations was designed to solve the problems of representation and accessibility to the political center. However, recent studies have shown that structured participation is detrimental to neighborhood collective action. Recognition and technical and material support are allocated to neighborhood associations in wealthy and stable areas (Mesch 1993). Thus, the structure of community participation underrepresents minorities and residents of low socioeconomic status and predominantly African American neighborhoods; these are the neighborhoods that suffer the most from environmental problems such as land-use change and commercial development.

Other organized areas influence the decision-making process while avoiding being officially tied to the city government. In the mid-1980s some groups started organizing in area coalitions. Currently there are six area coalitions and each claims to represent an average of 10 neighborhood organizations. Area coalitions are a forum where leaders of neighborhood associations share their experience and knowledge, enhancing their leadership skills. Area coalitions are umbrella organizations that address a broad range of issues from zoning to services in a geographically bounded area. Their creation was a reaction to the government initiative to recognize neighborhood associations. Their goal is to make sure that the concerns of areas not represented on the officially recognized advisory boards are heard.

Columbus, then, is an appropriate setting for the study. First, it is a growing city experiencing conflicts over land use in which private interests, the government, and neighborhood groups are involved. Second, the inner-city neighborhoods are confronted with serious housing and crime problems. Third, together with rapid growth, the number of neighborhood associations has increased. The result is a city where conflicts over land use and new developments are common and neighborhood groups are active.

METHOD

Sample

Data were collected by a survey of the neighborhood associations in the Columbus, Ohio, metropolitan area. The universe of existing organizations was defined with the assistance of the Department of Human Services of the City of Columbus and the departments of community relations in the suburban communities. Those agencies provided lists of civic associa-

tions that defined as their goals the maintenance or improvement of the quality of life in their geographically delimited residential area, and that were known to be active in the last three years.

The final list included a total of 184 neighborhood associations. In addition, in the process of data collection, informants were asked for the names of other neighborhood organizations with which they were familiar. No new names surfaced, so there is strong reason to believe that the list of 184 is comprehensive.

Given our goal of studying the determinants of collective action and its success, an effort was made to contact only active organizations. The choice of active organizations follows the theoretical model that places a prominent role to organizational complexity and coalition building. Overall, 41 neighborhood associations reported being inactive or defunct. Hence 143 organizations were currently active.

Data Collection

The data were collected during the winter of 1993. The primary source was a questionnaire that requested presidents of neighborhood associations to provide information about the organizational structure and resources of the association, problems affecting the neighborhood, actions taken to solve these problems, relationships with other neighborhood organizations, and perceptions of the nature of their relationship with city government.

Previous studies of neighborhood associations report a medium to low level of response to surveys (Crenshaw and St. John 1989). To increase this study's response rate as compared with others, the final list of 143 active associations was divided into two subsamples. A random sample of 50 organizations was selected, and data from 41 were collected in face-to-face interviews in which the questionnaire was administered as an interview schedule. The data from the remaining 93 organizations were collected by mailed survey using the same instrument. This twofold strategy for collecting data yielded 105 completed questionnaires, 41 from face-to-face interviews and 64 from the mailed survey. Thus, the overall response rate was 73 percent, which is the highest reported in recent research.

VARIABLES AND MEASURES

Dependent Variable

In recent years there has been a growing interest among sociologists in the effectiveness of voluntary associations. The study of effectiveness presents problems of conceptualization and operationalization. At the conceptual level different organizational perspectives define effectiveness in different ways. The rational system perspective assumes that organizational goals can be identified. Therefore measures of effectiveness take the specific goals of the organization as the basis for generating effectiveness criteria (Scott 1992). This perspective has been criticized since different constituencies have different ideas about what the goals of the organization should be (Anspach 1991). The natural systems model views organizations as collectivities that engage in activities required to maintain themselves as a social unit. This perspective emphasizes internal organizational processes that are required to evoke participants' time, energy, and skills. Effectiveness of voluntary associations has often been operationally measured by a single item that asked informants how effective their association is (Oropesa 1989; Knoke 1990). This approach is limited because it relies on a single measure and the use of an item that measures goal attainment.

Following Scott (1992), we argue that effectiveness provides an answer to the question of how well an association is doing. Neighborhood associations engage in collective action to influence policymaking. A necessary condi-

tion for the achievement of these goals is the development of sufficient capacity to participate in political actions. Thus the effectiveness of a neighborhood association should be measured by studying process and outcomes. Outcomes refer to the results of any operation performed by the association. In social-influence associations the major outcome is the solution of major problems affecting the area and influence on the decision makers in matters of importance for the residents. Process measures assess effort rather than effect. Regarding neighborhood associations, we argue that process involves residents' awareness of common problems and their increased organization to monitor and react to issues that might threaten their neighborhood.

An additional problem is that various participants and external constituencies have interests in the functioning of an association and may be expected to attempt to impose their own effectiveness criteria on the organization. A recent study shows that performance assessed by these varying criteria results in a pattern of low and often negative correlation: To do well on a criterion preferred by one constituency is to do poorly on a criterion favored by another (Anspach 1991). In the case of neighborhood associations that operate in a city with a structured participation system, where some associations are tied to the city political structure and others are not, governmental reputational measures will be higher for associations that participate in the organizational field defined by the city government. We follow previous work and focus on the assessment of organizational process and outcomes as reported by presidents of neighborhood associations because of their high level of involvement and information (Logan and Rabrenovic 1990; Oropesa 1989; Knoke 1990). The respondents were asked to indicate their extent of agreement/disagreement on a four-point scale with each of four statements. Following our discussion of the concept two statements were presented to measure organization process: 1) "As a result of the activities of the neighborhood association, the residents are more aware of neighborhood issues," and 2) "The residents of our area are well organized in the neighborhood." Two statements were presented to measure organization outcomes: 1) "The neighborhood association has solved major neighborhood problems," and 2) "The neighborhood association has an influence in major decisions affecting the neighborhood."

Independent Variables

Local ecology. Local ecology measures the neighborhood's demographic composition and ecological characteristics. Four variables were used to measure local ecology. Three of them were drawn from the literature of neighborhood factorial ecology (Schwirian 1983). In order to establish the ecological characteristics of the neighborhood a factor analysis was conducted introducing six variables: percent of population with college education; median home value; median household income; percent of families with young children; percent of owner occupied housing; and proportion of residents living in the same house in the last five years.

The second variable was an index of social and economic investments. It measures the extent to which people have structural commitments to the neighborhood. Items and their loadings include: percent of families with children under 18 years of age (.728); percent of owner-occupied housing (.689); proportion of residents who lived in the same house from 1985 to 1990 (.922). Cronbach's alpha was .82.

The third variable was a measure of the ethnic composition of the neighborhood. It was measured using a series of three dummy variables: White, African American, and racially heterogeneous. The cutting points were defined after data were examined. Following the work of Lee and Wood (1991) on neighborhood change, predominantly white neighborhoods have between 0 to 15 percent African Americans. Racially heterogeneous areas were defined as neighborhoods in which the proportion of African Americans is between 30 percent to 60 percent. Twelve percent of the neighborhood associations were located in these heterogeneous areas. African American homogeneous areas were defined as neighborhoods where more than 60 percent of the residents were African Americans. Thirteen percent of the neighborhood associations were located in these African American neighborhoods.

Respondents were asked to rate the extent to which several environmental problems affected their neighborhood. The three specific issues were: new developments such as shopping centers; land-use change such as from residential use to commercial or industrial; and the presence of unwanted businesses such as noxious metal processing facilities or automobile impound lots.

Organizational complexity. A necessary condition for a neighborhood association to influence policy making is the ability to participate in political actions. An association's political capacity is determined by the number of specialized roles and programs it maintains that are responsible for monitoring and intervening in important policy decisions (Knoke 1990).

The number of specialized roles was measured by an item that asked how many internal committees exist in the associations. The existence of internal committees allows the association to deal with an unstable resource base by delegating responsibility to others. The ability to perform certain tasks, such as the publication of a newsletter, is another measure of organizational complexity; it requires the coordination of technical tasks on a regular basis and the existence of a number of members who specialize in raising residents' awareness of local issues. Newsletter publication was measured by response to the question. "How many times a year does your neighborhood association publish a newsletter?"

Active members are an important resource that determines the ability of an association to have specialized roles and programs. Organizations with a large number of active members were viewed as having more human resources than organizations with a small number of active members. Active members are sources of help in carrying out organizational tasks (such as attending city council meetings or picketing unwanted activities). This variable was measured by the response to the question, "How many people usually attend a general meeting to which all members of your association are invited?"

Coalitional embeddedness. Coalitional embeddedness refers to the extent to which the neighborhood association forms linkages with other organizations through which information and resources are exchanged and assistance is rendered. There are two aspects of coalitional embedding. One is resource exchanges with other neighborhood-based organizations, and the other is direct membership in formally established neighborhood coalitions. Resource exchange was measured by the number of organizations listed in response to this question: "In dealing with local issues, neighborhood associations sometimes ask for technical advice, moral support, provision of meeting places or other material support from other community organizations. Which of the following organizations would you say provide that kind of support to your organization?" A check list was provided with the following possible responses: local churches, local business association, community development corporations, educational organiza-

tions (schools, colleges), other community organizations (Kiwanis, Rotary, etc.), local hospital, local library branch, other.

The second aspect of coalitional embedding is direct and formal membership in coalitional bodies. We measured this as a dummy variable by response to the question "Does your association participate in any coalition, federation or any umbrella organization of neighborhood associations?"

RESULTS

Descriptive Findings

We begin our discussion of the results by providing some important background information about the neighborhood organizations. In terms of location, neighborhood associations were located in areas that were residentially stable with a high percentage of home owners. Associations were located in areas in which, on average, 43 percent of the residents had lived five years or more, and an average of 57 percent of the residents were home owners. Neighborhood associations were more linked to other neighborhood-based associations than to area coalitions representing broad areas. A majority of the associations (78 percent) reported that they had received material, technical, or other support from other neighborhood associations. Only 47.6 percent of the neighborhood associations reported that they were members of area coalitions.

There are a variety of types of social action that neighborhood associations take. Table 1 shows that when they acted, most associations contacted public officials by phone or mail (96.2 percent). They also organized or participated in public hearings (91.4 percent) and organized programs dealing with crime, neighborhood clean-up or beautification (87.6). They were least likely to organize petition drives, although 64.8 percent of the organizations did petition drives in the year of study.

TABLE 1 Percent of Organizations Taking Various Types of Social Action

Type of Action	Percent
Negotiation	67.0
Organize/Participate in Public Hearings	91.4
Formed Ad-Hoc Coalitions	71.4
Contacted Public Official by Phone or Mail	96.2
Organized Petitions	64.8
Organized Crime, Clean Up or Beautification Program	87.6

(Parametric statistical table not shown.) Significant positive correlations were found between neighborhood socioeconomic status and all the measures of effectiveness. The higher the socioeconomic status of the neighborhood the higher the perception that residents were aware of local issues, were well organized, had solved major problems affecting the area, and that the association was able to influence the city government.

As expected, neighborhood racial composition was negatively related to all the measures of effectiveness. The higher the percent of African Americans in the neighborhood the lower the perception that neighborhood residents were aware of local issues, were well organized, were able to solve major problems affecting the area, and were able to influence government decisions. Land use changes were positively related to all the measures of effectiveness. At the bivariate level, there was a positive correlation between the circulation of newsletters and the number of active members.

An interesting finding is that the bivariate correlation between the number of actions taken by the neighborhood association to improve the area and perception of effectiveness was not significant. Effectiveness was positively related to socioeconomic status and land use changes. On the other hand, action was negatively related to socioeconomic status and positively related to environmental threats (land-use change, commercial developments, and unwanted businesses). It seems that neighborhoods located in wealthy areas were effective in influencing policymakers and solving problems without the need to rely on intensive action. By contrast, neighborhoods located in low-income areas suffered the most from environmental threats, lacked access to the government, and therefore relied on intensive action.

Multiple Regression Analysis

The six hypotheses were tested by the multiple regression analysis whose results are set out in Table 2.

Greater effectiveness in social action was associated with higher socioeconomic status, higher neighborhood investments, higher environmental threat, greater newsletter production, greater membership attendance at meetings, and more linkages with other neighborhood-based organizations. Membership with social actors outside the community was not related systematically to organizational effectiveness.

The regression models for each of the components of the combined effective measure show that the effect of socioeconomic status and neighborhood investments was significant for the solution of problems affecting the area and influencing governmental policy. In other words, neighborhood associations located in wealthy and stable areas perceived

TABLE 2 Results of the Multiple Regression Analysis of Organizational Effectiveness on Neighborhood Ecology, Organizational Complexity, and Coalitional Embedding

Variable	Effectiveness	Aware	Organized	Problem Solution	Influence
Neighborhood Ecology:					
SES	.212**	.132	.060	.288**	.213**
Family Investments	.165**	.042	.144	.133	.196**
White Neighborhoods	.215	.153	.199	.153	.174
Mixed Neighborhoods	.161	.019	.205	.151	.116
Threats:					
Commercial Developments	−.005	−.006	−.140	.107	.051
Land-Use Changes	.285*	.209**	.128	.155	.171**
Unwanted Business	.042	.070	.035	.003	.026
Organizational Complexity:					
Internal Committees	.014	.052	−.160	.157	.037
Newsletter	.295*	.298*	.331*	.013	.278*
Member Participation	.287*	.166**	.365*	.188**	.161*
Coalitional Embeddness:					
Resources Exchange	.176**	.179**	.106	.110	.174**
Coalition Membership	.004	−.044	−.033	.043	.053
$R^2_{ADJ} =$	.336	.215	.246	.251	.251

Notes:

* Sig. at .01 ** Sig at .05

Entries are Standard Coefficients (Beta's).

themselves as more able to solve problems and influence the city government than neighborhood associations located in low-income areas.

Regarding environmental threats, the existence of problems related to changes in land use increased residents' awareness of local issues and neighborhood associations' ability to influence city government. The existence of environmental threats such as major commercial developments and unwanted businesses did not affect perception of effectiveness.

Organizational complexity affected the effectiveness of the neighborhood association. The higher the number of active members and the publication of newsletters, the more aware the residents were of local problems and the better they were organized. The higher the number of active members, the higher the perception that the neighborhood association was able to solve major problems and to exert influence on the city government.

Regarding coalitional embeddness, resources exchange with other neighborhood-based organizations had a positive effect. The higher the number of neighborhood-based organizations providing material and technical support to the neighborhood association, the higher the perception that residents were aware of local issues, were well organized, were able to solve local problems and to influence the city government. Area coalitions were created to facilitate the process of policy influence for associations that were not part of the city structure of participation. The effect of coalition membership on effectiveness is not significant.

DISCUSSION

The purpose of this study is to examine the factors associated with the perception of effectiveness of neighborhood social action. We expanded previous studies on neighborhood associations in that the concept was studied using multiple measures of organizational process and outcomes. In addition, a Neighborhood Political Ecology Model concerned with neighborhood collective responses to potential changes in the environment was tested. The empirical evidence provides partial support for the model.

In terms of local ecology, we found that the higher the socioeconomic status of the neighborhood the more effective the association. Previous studies found a positive relationship among socioeconomic status, neighborhood social organization (Sampson 1991), and residents' participation in neighborhood associations (Thomas 1986; Haberle 1989). Studies using a global measure of effectiveness explained this finding as the result of an inability of low-income neighborhoods to recruit individuals with political experience and communication skills (Oropesa 1989). In this study we used multiple measures and found that leaders of neighborhood associations located in wealthy and stable neighborhoods did not report that residents were more aware and organized than residents in low-income and unstable neighborhoods. However, the higher the socioeconomic status of the residents and the more stable the neighborhood, the higher the perception that the neighborhood association was able to solve major problems and to influence the government. This finding is more consistent with the elitist perspective on city politics that argues that inequalities in city politics are the result of a bias towards wealthy and stable neighborhoods (Berry, Portney, and Thompson 1993).

Contrary to expectations, the racial composition of the neighborhood did not affect the ef-

fectiveness of neighborhood social action. At the bivariate level we found a negative correlation. However, once socioeconomic status of the neighborhood, organizational complexity, and coalition embeddness were controlled the effect of racial composition was not significant. In other words, residents of neighborhood associations located in predominantly Black areas were no less aware of local issues and no less organized than residents located in predominantly white areas. In addition, they did not perceive that they were less able to influence the city government. This finding suggests that city inequalities in access to and influence on the city government are related to socioeconomic status and not to race. However a note of caution is needed here. Only 13 percent of the associations were located in predominantly African American neighborhoods.

Resources that local associations were able to mobilize significantly influence the effectiveness of their actions. The complexity of the association—measured as newsletter circulation and active membership—reflects the resources that the association recruits from its constituency. Complex associations are more effective because through the newsletter they communicate relevant information to their members and have a number of active and committed members who routinely contribute their time and energy to the goals of the association (Austin 1991).

The greater the links with other neighborhood-based organizations the higher the effectiveness of collective action. Other neighborhood-based associations, such as the local business association and the local church, may have provided essential material and human resources. Meeting places, office facilities, and skilled leaders allowed the association to regularize and extend the actions to a larger number of issues. Links with other organizations provided legitimacy to the association and its activities, both inside and outside the neighborhoods. Our data do not allow us to understand exactly how effectiveness was enhanced by links with other neighborhood-based organizations. This issue requires further research.

A finding that requires further elaboration is that, contrary to expectations, membership in area coalitions did not affect the perception of effectiveness. This finding is consistent with previous studies that show that coalitions formed by the association are not related to effectiveness (Oropesa 1989). Area coalitions were created to facilitate the process of policy influence for associations that were not part of the city structure of participation. We interpret this non-significant effect as evidence that associations that are not part of the city structure are no less or more effective than associations that are part of the city structure of participation.

Regarding environmental threats, only land-use changes significantly affected effectiveness. Previous studies have shown that land-use changes are related to neighborhood action and effectiveness (Logan and Rabrenovic 1990; Oropesa 1989). In this study we found that threats of land-use change increased the awareness of local problems and the perception that the association was able to influence the local government. The non-significant effect of threats related to large commercial developments and unwanted business points to the limited ability of neighborhood associations to influence the government on issues in which large economic interests are involved.

At this point we may ask about the connection between social action and effectiveness. In other words, does activity breed success? The answer is "Not necessarily." We found a non-significant bivariate correlation between the two of only -.08. When the variable action was introduced in the regression models (analysis not shown) the effect on the global measure

and each of the individual components was not significant. This finding can be explained in terms of inequalities of access. Effectiveness is positively related to socioeconomic status and land-use changes. On the other hand, action is negatively related to socioeconomic status and positively related to environmental threats (land-use change, commercial developments, and unwanted business). It appears that neighborhoods located in wealthy areas are effective in influencing policymakers and solving problems. On the other hand, neighborhoods located in low-income areas suffer the most from environmental threats, lack access to the government, and therefore rely on taking more actions.

Finally, studies of the social action success of neighborhood associations need to be expanded in two dimensions. The first is longitudinal. A panel study of several organizations needs to be conducted in which a closer week-to-week observation of activities and success can be made. Such a longitudinal series of case studies would indeed require a large amount of resources, but it would yield invaluable information on the specifics of planning and resource mobilization.

The second dimension of expansion had to do with the measurement of effectiveness of collective action. The use of multiple measures represents an improvement relative to other studies because it facilitates understanding the effect of different variables on different dimensions of effectiveness. However, the question remains as to whether the perception of association leaders represents actual ability to influence. Future research should include measures of policy implementation, which will make it possible to test whether the perception of presidents of neighborhood associations reflects the actual ability to exert an influence on the city agenda.

REFERENCES

Anspach, Renee R. 1991 "Everyday methods for assessing organizational effectivenss." Social Problems 38:1–19.

Austin, Mark, D. 1991 "Community context and complexity of organizational structure in neighborhood associations." Administration and Society 22:516–531.

Berry Jeffrey, Kent Portney, and Ken Thomson 1993 The Rebirth of Urban Democracy. Washington, D.C.: The Brookings Institution.

Blau, Peter 1981 "Interdependence and hierarchy in organizations." In the Sociology of Organizations: Basic Studies, eds. Oscar Grusky and George A. Miller. New York: Free Press.

Bollen, K.A., and R.W. Jackman 1985 "Regression diagnostics." Sociological Methods and Research 13:510–542.

Burt, Ronald S. 1982 Toward a Structural Theory of Action. New York: Academic Press.

City Bulletin 1981 "Changes in 1981 Columbus City Code." The City of Columbus, Ohio, 875–878.

Crenshaw, Edward, and Craig St. John 1989 "The organizationally dependent community." Urban Affairs Quarterly 24:412–434.

Davis, John Emmeus 1991 Contested Ground: Collective Action and the Urban Neighborhood. Ithaca, N.Y.: Cornell University Press.

Drabek, Thomas, and J. Eugene Hass 1974 Understanding Complex Organizations. Dubuque, IA: William C. Brown.

Fillon, Pierre 1987 "Core redevelopment, neighborhood revitalization and municipal government motivation: Twenty years of urban renewal in Quebec City." Canadian Journal of Political Science 20:131–148.

Florin, Paul, and Abraham Wandersman 1990 "An introduction to citizen participation, voluntary organization and community development." The American Journal of Community Psychology 18:41–54.

Graham, Laurie, and Richard Hogan 1990 "Social class and tactics: Neighborhood opposition to group homes." Sociological Quarterly 31:513–529.

Haberle, Steven 1989 Planting the Grassroots: Structuring Citizen Participations. New York: Praeger Press.

Heskin, Alan David 1991 The Struggle for Community. Boulder, Col.: Westview.

Hogan, Richard 1986 "Community opposition to group homes." Social Science Quarterly 67:442–449.

Hoover, Edgar M., and Raymond Vernon 1959 Anatomy of a Metropolis. Boulder, Col.: Westview.

Knoke, David 1990 Organizing for Collective Action. Hawthorne, N.Y.: Aldine de Gruyter.

Laumann, Edward O., and Franz U. Pappi 1976 Networks of Collective Action: A Perspective on Community Influence Systems. New York: Academic Press.

Lee, Barrett A., and Peter Wood 1991 "Is neighborhood racial succession place specific?" Demography 28:21–40.

Logan, John, and Gordana Rabrenovic 1990 "Neighborhood associations, their issues, their allies and their opponents." Urban Affairs Quarterly 26:68–94.

Mesch, Gustavo S. 1993 "The political, ecological, and organizational determinants of neighborhood action." Unpublished doctoral dissertation. Columbus. OH: The Ohio State University.

Mollenkopf, John H. 1983 The Contested City. Princeton, N.J.: Princeton University Press.

Oropesa, R.S. 1989 "The social and political foundations of effective neighborhood associations." Social Science Quarterly 70:723–743.

1992 "Social structure, social solidarity and involvement in neighborhood improvement associations." Sociological Inquiry 62:107–118.

Sampson, Robert 1991 "Linking the micro and macro dimensions of community social organization." Social Forces 70:43–64.

Sassen, Saskia 1991 The Global City. Princeton, N.J.: Princeton University Press.

Savitch, H.V. 1988 Post-Industrial Cities. Princeton, N.J.: Princeton University Press.

Schwirian, Kent P. 1983 "Urban spatial arrangements as reflections of social reality." In Remaking the City: Social Science Perspectives on Urban Design, eds. John S. Pipkin, Mark E. LaGory, and Judith R. Blau, 121–147. Albany: State University of New York Press.

Schwirian, Kent P., and Gustavo S. Mesch 1993 "Embattled neighborhoods: The political ecology of neighborhood change." In Research in Urban Sociology, ed. Ray Hutchinson, 3:83–110. Greenwich, Conn.: JAI Press.

Scott, W. Richard 1992 Organizations Rational, Natural, and Open Systems. Englewood Cliffs, N.J.: Prentice-Hall, Inc.

Skogan, Wesley 1992 "The correlates of community antidrug activism." Crime and Delinquency 38:510–521.

Suttles, Gerald 1968 The Social Order of the Slum. Chicago, Ill.: University of Chicago Press.

1972 The Social Construction of Communities. Chicago, Ill.: University of Chicago Press.

Thomas, John Clayton 1986 Between Citizen and City. Lawrence, Kan.: University Press of Kansas.

Wiewel, Wim, and Albert Hunter 1985 "The interorganizational network as a resource: A comparative case study on organizational genesis." Administrative Quarterly 44:1–34.

THE RESPONSIVE COMMUNITY:
A COMMUNITARIAN PERSPECTIVE

Amitai Etzioni

My thesis is that sociology can provide a compelling answer to an age-old problem, an exit from an entrapping dilemma: how to maintain both social order and personal autonomy in one and the same society; in other words, how to construct a society that protects its members from one another—from civil war to violent crime—and does so without oppressing them.[1] This dilemma, which in one form or another has occupied social philosophers and sociologists from the first days of the discipline, still confronts contemporary societies, from Russia to Iran to the United States.

The quest for such a peaceful society is significant. Yet major social thinkers have argued that the concept is too narrowly framed. Simply seeking to prevent hostilities will not guarantee social justice to members of the society, other than indirectly, when it is argued that the absence of justice leads to violence. And, aiming at peace alone will not reveal the ways a society can reduce alienation or enable its members to grow as persons without becoming highly dependent on the state.

Only a community that is responsive to the "true needs" of all its members, both in the substance of its core/shared values and in its social formation, can minimize the penalties of order and the dangers of autonomy. I refer to such a community as an *authentic community* and to all others as *partial* or *distorted commu-*

nities. While a fully authentic community might well be a utopian vision, it is a vision that can guide the personal and collective efforts of social actors and one that can be approximated.

Responsiveness is the cardinal feature of authentic communities. If the values the community fosters and the form of its structure (allocation of assets, application of power, shapes of institutions, and mechanisms of socialization) do not reflect its members' needs, or reflect only the needs of some, the community's order will be ipso facto imposed rather than truly supported. And in the long run, imposed order is unstable (indeed ultimately disorderly) and threatens the autonomy of individual members and subgroups.

Thus far, then, I assume that (1) there is a strong measure of built-in contradiction between the common good and the needs of community members; (2) as the community's responsiveness is enhanced, the scope of this fundamental contradiction can be significantly reduced (but not eliminated); and (3) the ways a community can be made more responsive can be specified.

I draw on previously advanced ideas strictly as markers to indicate the intellectual place of my presentation and, more generally, of communitarian thinking. I stress that when I refer to Talcott Parsons, Sigmund Freud, or Karl Marx, I make no attempt to summarize their positions, let alone to do justice to the rich complexity of their theories; I reference their theories merely to place the discussion in a context.

---

[1]The concepts of order and autonomy have parallels in the concepts of civility and piety as examined by Selznick in *The Moral Commonwealth* (1994:387–427)

RESPONSIVE COMMUNITIES: BEYOND PARSONS, MARX, AND FREUD

Sociological theories vary greatly in their assumptions as to how difficult it is to provide order and maintain autonomy for community members. Parsons's ideas are at the optimistic side of a continuum. He sees societies as having a set of collective needs and a core of shared values. These values are internalized through socialization, so society members voluntarily seek to accomplish what the society needs. Social control mops up recalcitrant deviants. Wrong (1961) has captured this implied notion of the pliability of human nature (also see Wrong 1994).

The underlying idea is that one can bring members of a community to truly affirm their societal formation. Little attempt is made to assess the particular societal regime or to examine whether the society could or should adapt to the members, at least to some extent. For example, according to this Parsonian view, a traditional society that expects all its members to marry and labels women who do not do so in derogatory terms, such as "spinsters," would not be expected to change to accommodate the needs of women who do not seek marriage.

Marx approaches the issue rather differently; surprisingly, he largely defines away the dilemma. Within history, Marx views the notion of a social order that serves all members of a society as a false conception advanced by one class of members to hold the others at bay. There is no one society. Existing class consciousness and organization do not reflect the objective needs of "the people" as a whole; at best they reflect the needs of the oppressors. In short, in the terms I use here, there is no one order into which society members fit or that can be modified to meet members' needs part of the time. At the "end of history," though, this basic contradiction will be resolved, and the society and its members will live in basic harmony.[2] Marx's prescription, hence, advances conflict, to hurry society to the end of history.

Freud approaches the order/autonomy dilemma with much less optimism, and at the same time he shows greater respect for these two cardinal elements of the human condition. Disregarding differences among his various writings and conflicting interpretations, he argues that while order (civilization) can be attained, such as order exacts considerable costs from the individual. Moreover, individuals can only be partially socialized; the veneer of civilization is thin and troubled. Although Freud moves us forward by not defining away the problem of order and autonomy, he too fails to seriously entertain the possibility of recasting society to reduce the distance between the societal needs for order, the claims on individuals that such order poses, and the needs of the members of the society.

A review of sociological evidence—the recent collapse of communist regimes, the high level of alienation in capitalist countries, the disaffection and restlessness in social democratic societies, the rise of religious fundamentalism in Islamic nations—strongly indicates that there are indeed limits to the extent to which members of a society can be fully socialized. From a normative viewpoint, I find this conclusion rather reassuring. If people could be successfully socialized, using a Soviet, Madison Avenue, or some other propaganda technique, one could make slaves sing with joy in their galleys or teach the oppressed to cheer their oppressors. This hardly seems a commendable world.

I put forth, then, that *there is a fundamental contradiction between the society's need for order and the individual's quests for autonomy.* I use the term autonomy rather than liberty be-

---

[2]Marx does see the possibility for some limited individual antagonism even in a communist society (Marx and Engels 1970:183).

cause much more than individual rights is involved—including opportunities to follow one's own subculture, for individual self-expression Maslow-style, and for creativity—all of which are diminished when the pressure to maintain order is unduly high.

I maintain that *this fundamental contradiction can be reduced by means other than fitting people into social roles—namely, by rendering the social order more responsive to the members' true needs.*

I digress briefly here to explain "true" versus "false" needs. One can empirically determine whether the wants a people express reflect their true nature or have been falsely implanted. One indication is the direction that human behavior moves when mechanisms of socialization and social control slacken: Does a behavior persist or decrease? For example, the "true need" for many women to work outside the home is supported by the observation that women seek to work even when they are well-off and are not under economic pressure. On the other hand, the fact that rich people do not line up to work on assembly lines tells us volumes about the compatibility of assembly-line jobs with true human needs (Etzioni 1968a, 1968b). Another indication of true needs is that, generally, people's behavior reveals what they truly believe. The fact that practically all smokers try strenuously to stop smoking suggests that they are addicted to cigarettes and do not truly prefer to smoke (Goodin 1991; Wolfe 1991).

To return to my main argument, I choose my words carefully: I suggest that a society can be made "more responsive" rather than fully responsive, because evidence strongly suggests that the built-in contradictions can be significantly reduced but not eliminated. Even the Israeli *kibbutzim,* communal settlements, which in their heyday, were highly responsive, have been unable to bring their social formation and their members' needs into full harmony. Again, behavior offers evidence: For every person who stayed in a *kibbutz,* several left, and frequently there have been internal pressures to dismember many *kibbutz* institutions. In short, I conclude that while the order/autonomy contradiction built into the human condition can be eased by enhancing responsiveness (not merely through more socialization and social control), it cannot be eliminated.

THE PROCESSES OF RESPONSIVENESS

Libertarians,[3] whose influence has been rising in social science, law, philosophy, and society over the last two decades, take a highly voluntaristic and individualistic approach to both the basic issue of reconciling the order/autonomy dilemma and to finding ways to reduce the built-in contradiction. Expressions of libertarian thinking are found in the Chicago School, especially in the works of Richard Epstein, Richard Posner, and Terry Eastland; it is reflected in the works of rational-choice sociologists; and it has roots in the earlier texts of Robert Nozick, Ronald Dworkin, and John Rawls, although the latter two have moved toward a partial recognition of some elements of communitarian thinking.

The libertarian perspective, put succinctly, begins with the assumption that individual agents are fully formed and their value preferences are in place prior to and outside of any society. It ignores robust social scientific evi-

[3]The terms "liberals," "classical liberals," "contemporary liberals," and "libertarians" have all been used to characterize the critics of communitarians. These labels are confusing; for instance, many readers do not realize that the labels are not confined to or even necessarily inclusive of those who are called liberals in typical daily parlance. Most importantly, because the defining element of the position is the championing of the individual, "libertarian" seems both the less obfuscating term and the one that is substantively most appropriate.

dence about the ill effects of isolation, the deep-seated human need for communal attachments, the social anchoring of reasoning itself, and the consistent interactive influence of society members on one another. Much of the communitarian writing in the 1980s by nonsociologists focused on remaking this basic sociological point: There are no well-formed individuals bereft of social bonds or culture.[4]

Most important for the point at hand is that libertarians actively oppose the notion of "shared values" or the idea of "the common good." They argue that once a community defines certain behaviors as virtuous, all members who do not live up to the standards are judged inferior. The only principled way to avoid discrimination is to have no collective judgments at all (Nozick 1974:28–35, 153–55). Libertarians "solve" the problem of order and provide maximum responsiveness in one and the same way: by denying the need for collective goals (other than defense and a few others) and by relying on the aggregation of individual preferences. To reiterate, these are preferences that libertarians assume are formed by individuals *on their own,* without membership in, influence from, or regard for a community. These aggregated individual choices occur when people vote, which is said to guide the polity; when individuals voluntarily form contracts and craft agreements; and when consumers apply their purchasing power to "vote" for products with currency.

While individual choices and the aggregation of choices enhance responsiveness somewhat, the main features of these processes are: (1) Individuals' actions are often deeply affected by groups and communities of which they are members and by the dysfunctional effects of being denied group membership; (2) much relevant social action takes place when

groups act in unison, rather than when individuals act alone; (3) individual choices and actions reflect affect and values more than do "evidence" and "reasoning"; and (4) the mobilization of groups and coalition-building among them are among the most powerful factors that affect final societal outcomes—the extent to which a society's responsiveness is enhanced or diminished (for details, see Etzioni 1968a, 1988).

RESPONDING TO CRITICS

While other social sciences and branches of social philosophy have recently begun to acknowledge the importance of the concept of community and are pondering what defines an authentic community, the concept of community has been a cornerstone of sociological thinking for nearly two centuries—note, for example, the works of Durkheim, Tönnies, and Marx. Sociologists have established the pivotal role of authentic communities as a major antidote to alienation and tyranny and as a key element of a "good society." Neoclassical economists, rational choice political scientists, law-and-economics legal scholars, and various laissez-faire conservatives and libertarians have continued to draw on a social model describing masses of individuals who act as free agents, ignoring the concept of community, indeed society in toto (Bentham [1935:8] and Margaret Thatcher [1993:626] declared the concept a fiction), or conceiving of community as a social contract, deliberately crafted and rationally constructed by individuals. The importance of shared culture, history, social bonds, and social structure is typically overlooked.

During the early 1990s, tribal wars have frayed the social fabric in a score of countries, formerly communist countries have sought new civic cultures, and individualism has increased in the West. All of this, combined with some social activism led by sociologists, has

---

[4]This observation was made by Philip Selznick during a session on communitarian thinking at the 1995 meeting of the American Sociological Association.

accorded the language of community a new currency in the public discourse. This, in turn, has strengthened academic interest in the concept of community.[5]

In reaction, both old-timers and newcomers to the sociological concept of community have posed several questions about the empirical validity and normative implications of the concept—questions that deserve systematic attention. Can community be clearly defined? What can be determined about the forces that seek to diminish order versus those that seek to curtail autonomy? Under what conditions do communities cease to be exclusive, and instead become encompassed in communities of communities.

WHAT IS COMMUNITY?

Several critics have argued that the concept of community should be avoided because it is too ill-defined. Margaret Stacey (referenced in Bell and Newby 1973:49) argues that the problem of defining community can be solved by avoiding the term all together. Bell and Newby (1974) argue, "There has never been a theory of community, nor even a satisfactory definition of what community is" (p. xliii). In another text, Bell and Newby (1973) write, "But what is community? . . . [I]t will be seen that over ninety definitions of community have been analyzed and that the one common element in them all was man!" (p. 15).

It should first be noted that many widely used terms are not readily definable. The concept of a chair seems much simpler to define than almost any sociological term, let alone community. However, what is a chair? A place on which to sit? So are benches and sofas. A piece of furniture that has four legs? Some

chairs have three of legs. And so on. Yet, we have little difficulty using such a term.

Moreover, community can be defined with reasonable precision. Community is defined by two characteristics: (1) A community entails a web of affect-laden relations among a group of individuals, relations that often crisscross and reinforce one another (rather than merely one-on-one relations or chains of individual relations); and, (2) community requires a commitment to a set of shared values, norms, and meanings, and a shared history and identity—in short, a shared culture. This definition recognizes that there are collective, historical actors and not merely grand individuals. Communities are not only aggregates of persons acting as free agents, but also collectives that have identities and purposes of their own and can act as a unit. In effect, these very communities often drive history and set the contexts for individual actions in society.

I suggest that a third characteristic further defines community: (3) Communities are characterized by a relatively high level of responsiveness. This third characteristic excludes social entities that oppress their members: It defines as partial communities those that are responsive to some members or sub-groups, but not to all; it characterizes as unauthentic those communities that respond to the false needs of members rather than to their true needs.

BASIC FORCES AND THE COMMUNITARIANS

The notion that communities share a culture has raised the hackles of those who are opposed to any community-based definition of the common good and of shared values as having a role in social life and history. Libertarians are correct in saying that if a community undergirds a norm (e.g., community members ought to attend church on Sunday), those who

---

[5]Coughlin (forthcoming) provides a chart of the increase in the number of articles, both general circulation and academic, about communitarianism.

violate the norm (as distinct from being exempt for an accepted reason, e.g., they are ill) will come under some measure of community censure. However, while libertarians are troubled by such outcomes, most sociologists recognize community censure as a major way that communities uphold members' commitments to shared values and service to the common good—community order. And indeed community censure reduces the reliance on the state as a source of order, a matter libertarians consider of utmost importance.

Put differently, communities command *centripetal forces* that seek to pull in members' commitments, energies, time, and resources for what the community as a collectivity endorses as its notion of the common good. Communities do so by taxing members' income and demanding that they make contributions in-kind or provide sweat equity, defining which activities members may pursue as individuals versus those that the community abhors (e.g., nursing patients versus dealing crack) (Goode 1978). In this sense, communities are anti-individualistic (although not necessarily, and often not, anti-individual). That is, they oppose excessive withdrawal into self and self-centered projects, but do not oppose individual endeavors that might be compatible with, or contribute to, the common good.

Surprisingly, many discussions of community leave the matter at this point. Perhaps because it is self-evident or because they subscribe to the assumptions of sanguine sociologists who presume that most individuals can be deeply socialized, these discussions ignore the reality that community members do have needs of their own that cannot be served by merely being part of their community. These individual needs are deeply rooted—members of any one community have different needs, while the community definition of the common good is often, at least in part, applied to all members. (For instance, the expectation a century ago that all people retire by a given age, while today millions of people who reach that age are able and anxious to continue working.)[6] Also, community members have a need for self-expression, although Maslow (1954: 180–83) may be correct in suggesting that it is activated only after more basic human needs, such as security and creature comforts, are relatively sated.

To reiterate, while not all quests for autonomy are anti-communal (e.g., many scientific projects are not), attempts to extend the realm of individual autonomy generate centrifugal forces, forces that, if they reach high levels, undermine the communal bonds and culture.

What is the relationship between the concepts of centripetal and centrifugal community forces and the concepts of order and autonomy? Order and autonomy are community needs; centripetal and centrifugal forces either exacerbate or ease the fulfilling of these needs. The relationship between these forces and needs are like those between a new crime wave and the means employed to maintain public safety: They affect each other, but they are hardly identical.

First, to reiterate a key observation that should guide social theory: *All social entities are subject to both centrifugal and centripetal forces. Communities have social formations that protect the community from being pulled off balance by either of these forces.* For instance, national service, to the extent that it fosters social bonds and shared normative conceptions, serves as an antidote to excessive individualism, and the Bill of Rights serves as an antidote to excessive collectivism. This perspective leaves behind the libertarian-communitarian debate that dominated the 1980s: whether a group of individuals should have a

---

[6]Some anthropologists have observed tribes in which the members are reported not to have a concept of an "I," of an individual. But in all complex societies this concept or its equivalent seems to exist and reflects the need for personal autonomy.

shared concept of the common good. Instead, this view focuses on the scope, power, and content of such concepts, taking for granted that they are, and ought be, defining elements of communities.[7]

Second, *the basic centripetal and centrifugal forces vie with one another continually, pulling the community in opposite directions:* centripetal forces pull toward higher levels of community service, regulation, and mobilization; centrifugal forces pull toward higher levels of differentiation, individualization, self-expression, and subgroup liberty. This tug of war between contradictory forces is not accidental, encountered under some special sociological or historical conditions, but should be assumed to influence all communities.

Third, and most important, *authentic communities require that the two basic forces be in balance,* as opposed to allowing one force to gain a decisive upper hand.[8]

THE INVERTING SYMBIOTIC RELATIONSHIP

I turn next to discuss the peculiar relationship between centripetal and centrifugal forces— one that is rather different from relationships we are more familiar with. Some forces cancel each other out. For instance, bases neutralize acids. Some forces support one another—go hand in hand—such as loans from the World Bank combined with the reduction of trade barriers by First World nations. There are also symbiotic relations, when two forces enrich one another rather than merely work well together. Plover birds, for example, stand in the mouths of crocodiles, eating worms and leeches. The crocodiles get their teeth cleaned, and the plovers get a ready supply of choice food. We rarely, though, encounter a combination of forces that enhance one another up to a point—forming a balanced symbiotic relationship—but become antagonistic if either force gains too much strength.[9] I refer to this unusual relationship as *inverting symbiosis* (cf. schismogenesis in Bateson 1958:175).

The relationship between centripetal and centrifugal community forces is one of inverting symbiosis: The two forces are mutually enhancing up to a point, and then they can turn antagonistic. To assess this hypothesis, let us engage in a mental experiment. Let us start with a low level of community, say residents in a recently completed high-rise building, and assume that some social agents (maybe some community organizers) start to build social bonds and foster a culture among the new residents. Up to a point, *both* the common good and the individual members' autonomy will be enhanced by these centripetal forces.[10] The common good, such as tending a shared garden or dealing as a group with the building's service providers, will be richer for them. The high-rise residents, getting to know one another as persons, will feel less isolated and will have a stronger sense of self and feel secure in their autonomy.

However, if the newly found community lays ever increasing claims on its members, eventually both community order and personal autonomy will be threatened. Thus, if the centripetal forces grow too strong, not only will

---

[7]Many overviews of the 1980s debates on this topic exist (Bell 1993; Avineri and de-Shalit 1992; Sandel 1984).

[8]We need also to take into account whether the levels of both forces and the responsive formations they encounter are low or high; the said balance can be achieved on several force levels (Bell 1995).

[9]Note that this relationship is different from relationships that are described as dialectical, or as having a declining marginal utility, and from those that are curvilinear. For instance, some studies suggest that if people consume alcohol in moderation it will enhance their health, but beyond a certain point health will diminish. But this holds only one way—alcohol to body and not vice versa—hence, it is not inverting symbiosis.

[10]This point has been made with regard to China (Bell 1995:41).

the members' autonomy shrivel, but the communal bonds will fray—social responsibilities will turn into imposed duties, and opposition to the community will grow. This is what happens in totalitarian regimes: While initial calls for new social responsibilities are rather warmly accepted, as these regimes escalate their demands, alienation grows.

On the other hand, if centrifugal forces grow too strong, not only will service to the community become deficient (as would happen if residents had to arrange for their own garbage pick up), but the autonomy of high-rise residents who depend in varying degrees on the community for basic needs will be diminished. In the terms used here, the relation between the two forces in this community will have moved from being mutually enhancing to antagonistic.

Once one recognizes these relations between centrifugal and centripetal forces and their respective formations in communities, many arguments in this realm can be disentangled by applying the concept of inverting symbiosis. Take, for example, the argument that individualism is a basic feature of American society, and hence, criticisms of individualism constitute attacks on the core value of the American society, versus the notion that individualism is a form of societal malaise.[11] If one views such arguments as misleadingly dichotomous and applies the concept of inverting symbiosis, both claims are off the mark: The American tradition is a mixture of the two formations and of a quest for "corrections" when one formation becomes too strong. The fact that both individualization and communal bonds are part of the American experience is well reflected in our founding documents. The Declaration of Independence and the U.S. Constitution contain statements such as "[W]e mutually pledge to each other our Lives, our

Fortunes and our sacred trust"; "We have appealed to their [the British] native justice and magnanimity, and we have conjured them by the ties of our common kindred to disavow these usurpations"; and "We the people of the United States, in order to form a more perfect union, . . . promote the general welfare. . . .'"

Moreover, when seen in this context, calls for more individual autonomy when communal bonds are very strong or even oppressive, as they were in the early colonies or states, are, in effect, calls to move from antagonistic relations back to the mutually enhancing relations of inverting symbiosis—not to a system based on individualism (or high centrifugal and low centripetal formations). This also was the socio-historical context of the Britain in which John Locke and Adam Smith were writing. However, when prescriptions for more individualism are applied to contemporary and highly individualistic Western societies, especially to the United States, they have the opposite effect: Such prescriptions move society deeper into the antagonistic zone.

In the same vein, recent statements by communitarians pointing to the need for increased emphasis on community in the United States have been misconstrued as antithetical to individuation. To the extent that these statements are made in a context seen as excessively individualistic, they point to a need to move from the antagonistic zone toward the mutually enhancing one, one in which order and autonomy sustain one another, and both are well served.

The same confusion is particularly evident in the debate between individual rights (a legal expression of the centrifugal formations) and the call for personal and social responsibility (for stronger centripetal formations). Again, this confusion is resolved when the concept of inverting symbiosis is applied. Libertarians have distorted arguments by communitarian Mary Ann Glendon and others (myself included), who argue that individual rights have been overemphasized, interpreting these argu-

---

[11]This issue is discussed elsewhere in greater detail (Bellah et al. 1985).

ments as if they suggest that individual rights should be curtailed, if not suspended (McClain 1994:1032).

The concept of inverting symbiosis allows one to see that rights and responsibilities enhance one another up to a point. This can be demonstrated both regarding specific rights and on a more generic level. For instance, the right to free speech, if one looks at it sociologically, presumes that those subjected to it (as distinct from those who exercise it) must tolerate speech that they find offensive. If individuals are intolerant, the right to free speech is at best contested, and ultimately not sustainable.

Similarly, the majority of Americans have believed for decades that they have a right to numerous government services, but they refuse to assume the duty to pay for them. The communitarian argument here is that we are in a mutually enhancing zone: greater government services to individuals presumes a willingness of individuals to assume responsibility by paying taxes.

More generally, libertarians have long feared that any recalibration of legal rights will cause a sociological phenomenon widely referred to as the "slippery slope." The fear is that once a limited change is made in an institution or tradition, uncontrollable social forces are unleashed that widen and extend the change and lead to the destruction of that institution or tradition (Schauer 1985: 361–62). Hence, for example, the argument that we should refrain from making changes in the U.S. Constitution. The fear of a slippery slope has been one reason that activists from rather varied political backgrounds oppose having a constitutional assembly of the states in Philadelphia in 1996. I have suggested elsewhere that one can make sociological "notches" on the slope, formatting social arrangements that can prevent social avalanches (Etzioni 1993: 177–90).

A more profound point: Historically, governments that provide rich legal rights to their citizens have been endangered, not when the community demanded that those who have rights also live up to their social responsibilities, but when this was *not* done. The link is that *rights, which impose demands on community members, are effectively upheld only as long as the basic needs of those community members are attended to.* Thus, during the first third of this century when the needs of the Soviet and German peoples were denied, they supported those who would replace democratic governments with tyrannies. In short, the sociological protection for a regime of individual rights (of liberty) is to ensure that the basic needs of the community members are served. This in turn requires that community members live up to their social responsibilities—they must pay taxes, serve in neighborhood crime watches, and attend to their children and their elders. We see here that there exists at the core of civil democratic societies a proud mutuality between individual rights and social responsibilities.

However, if a society legitimizes ever more individual rights or imposes ever more social responsibilities, there will come a time when the balance is uneven. This occurs, for instance, when, as a result of bestowing ever more legal rights on a people, individuals move from attempting to resolve conflicts through negotiations, bargaining, and mediation to relying on the courts (a phenomenon often referred as litigiousness) (Glendon 1991). Or, when imposing ever more taxes on a people leads to a tax rebellion (as many states saw in the 1980s following California's Proposition 13), if not a full-blown political rebellion, like that faced by King George III. In short, while up to a point individual rights and social responsibility are mutually enhancing, they turn antagonistic if the level of either increases after that point.

I am the first to grant that the exact point at which mutually enhancing relations turn antagonistic is not clearly marked. One can establish, however, when a society passes from one zone to the other: The term anarchy is often applied when excessive individualism prevails, and collectivism when social duties are excessive.

WITHIN HISTORY

So far I have depicted the relationship between the two core elements of community in largely analytical terms: A balanced combination makes for a good alloy called "community." I first posed the question in static terms: Which combinations are most conducive to community? I then pointed out that in an historical perspective communities are perpetually subjected to centrifugal or centripetal forces.[12] These varying forces push the communities and other social entities either toward collectivism or toward individuation. Thus, even if a community reaches the best possible balance based on its organizing principles—the ultimate symbiosis—it cannot be stable for long because the dynamic constellation of historical forces will change.

Therefore, for a community to maintain an overarching pattern, to be metastable (the specific formation of the community will change, but not the basic balance between order and autonomy), the community must respond like a person riding a bicycle; it must continually correct tendencies to lean too far in one direction or the other, as it moves forward over a changing terrain. Thus, forces in the United States in the early 1990s that are pushing for a reemphasis on social responsibility and of which the communitarian movement has been a significant part, can be viewed as a move to

counterbalance a period of unduly high centrifugal forces.

Communities in which no balancing forces are activated lose their overarching pattern through tribal wars, revolutions, or an accumulation of smaller changes that lead to a fundamentally different pattern. Japan, for instance, changed in this way during Western occupation after World War II: It became a constitutional democracy in which individual rights are recognized and protected, albeit less than in the West. And, of course, the U.S.S.R. experienced a major breakdown in 1990, moving to a drastically different formation in terms of its balance of order and autonomy.

Those who seek to maintain the basic existing societal pattern must cast themselves on the other side of history. They must try to pull against the forces that are tilting the society off balance at that particular time. Those who seek to destroy a particular societal pattern often cast themselves in support of forces that push the existing societal formations even further out of kilter, out of the zone in which the particular pattern can be maintained.

COMMUNITY OF COMMUNITIES: RELATIONS TO NONMEMBERS

Even communities that are responsive and well-balanced will be particularistic, having identities that separate and a sense of sociological boundary that distinguishes members from nonmembers. These features render even these communities potentially hostile, if not dangerous, to nonmembers. Communities can be exclusive—they can take positions against immigrants or persons of different economic, racial, or ethnic backgrounds, or sexual orientations; they can seek to break up societies in order to gain greater autonomy for their members (e.g., Quebec); they can engage in tribal warfare against other communities that were once members of their own society (Afghanistan,

---

[12]I cannot discuss their origins, but suffice it to say that some forces are externally generated, for instance due to the spread of American culture on worldwide television, and some forces are internally generated, for instance, when an oppressed group mobilizes itself for social action (Etzioni 1968a).

Bosnia, Sri Lanka, India, and the former U.S.S.R.).

Some see these potential failings of communities as sufficiently damning to oppose community as a normatively approved sociological formation and seek to replace it with a "world-wide family," of which all individuals are members, or with a "universal state," in which all are citizens (Schlesinger 1992). But there is no reason to expect that such developments will take place or can even be engineered, or if they were to develop, that members of existing communities would find these mega-societal entities responsive to their needs.

A more realistic and normatively acceptable position lies in developing those social processes that foster what I call *layered loyalties* in members of various communities. As a result, members see themselves as, and act as, members of more than one community. People who have a loyalty to a region (for example, the South in the United States, or Scotland in the United Kingdom), but also to their nation, are a case in point. Attempts to develop supra-national communities, for instance, in Western Europe, reflect attempts to develop new layered loyalties. To the extent that layered loyalties evolve, they discourage exclusivity and tribal wars.

I note, though, that the mere existence of layered loyalties will not suffice. When normative conflicts occur between the layers of communities on some select issues concerning order and autonomy, loyalty by all member communities to the overarching community must take precedence over loyalty to the immediate community. This ensures that the "community of communities" will be responsive to member communities' needs and not merely be imposed on them or be of only marginal significance. For instance, only if all the various Canadian provinces have a higher commitment to the Canadian society than to their provinces will they be willing to make the sacrifices needed to make Canada responsive to all member communities. Such levels of loyalty seem natural when they are in place in highly integrated nations, yet in other nations they are difficult to attain. Note, though, that quite a few communities of communities did evolve out of separate communities, including the United States, Germany, and Italy.

At the same time, one must acknowledge that until these layered loyalties encompass the ultimate community of communities, that *of all people,* intercommunity dangers will not be overcome, although they may be curtailed.

IN CONCLUSION

The need for order and the need for autonomy cannot be fully reconciled. Moreover, communities are subject to centrifugal forces that strain efforts to maintain order, and to centripetal forces that undermine autonomy. Hence, communities must constantly endeavor to balance both, or be thrown off into social anarchy or collectivism.

The order of an authentic community is based on social formations that are continually reshaped in response to the members' true needs rather than relying only, or even mainly, on socializing the members to accept the community's demands or on utilizing control processes. This is not to deny that, when all is said and done, communities do face tragic choices. They cannot meet all the demands of all members, but they can reduce the distance between the demands on members for order and what the members seek through a process of resocializing the members.

A common mistake is to view order and autonomy either as antagonistic (a zero-sum relationship, so that the more we have of one the less we have of the other) or as mutually enhancing. They are complimentary up to a point, after which they grow antagonistic. It is the role of those who care to fashion authentic communities to pull their communities into the highly responsive zone, into one in which mutuality between the basic elements of order and autonomy is high and antagonism low.

While communities are by nature limited in terms of the number of members they encompass and have separatist tendencies, they often do become parts of still more encompassing communities. Under the proper conditions, these overarching communities can maintain order among communities without suppressing autonomy (Etzioni 1965).

REFERENCES

Avineri, Shlomo and Avner de-Shalit. 1992. *Communitarianism and Individualism.* New York: Oxford University Press.

Bateson, Gregory: 1958. *Naven: A Survey of the Problems Suggested by a Composite Picture of the Culture of a New Guinea Tribe Drawn from Three Points of View.* Stanford, CA: Stanford University Press.

Bell, Daniel A. 1993. *Communitarianism and Its Critics.* Oxford, England: Clarendon Press.

———. 1995. "A Communitarian Critique of Authoritarianism." *Society* 32:38–44.

Bell, Colin and Howard Newby. 1973. *Community Studies: An Introduction to the Sociology of the Local Community.* New York: Praeger Publishers.

———. 1974. *The Sociology of Community: A Selection of Readings.* London, England: Frank Cass.

Bellah, Robert, Richard Madsen, William M. Sullivan, Ann Swidler, and Steven M. Tipton. 1985. *Habits of the Heart: Individualism and Commitment in American Life.* Berkeley, CA: University of California Press.

Bentham, Jeremy. 1935. *An Introduction to the Principles of Morals and Legislation.* New York: Doubleday, Doran and Company.

Coughlin, Richard. Forthcoming. "Whose Morality? Which Community? What Interests? Socio-Economic and Communitarian Perspectives." *Journal of Socio-Economics.*

Etzioni, Amitai. 1965. *Political Unification: A Comparative Study of Leaders and Forces.* New York: Holt, Rinehart, and Winston.

———. 1968a. *The Active Society.* New York: Free Press.

———. 1968b. "Basic Human Needs, Alienation, and Inauthenticity." *American Sociological Review* 33:870–84.

———. 1988. *The Moral Dimension.* New York: Free Press.

———. 1993. *The Spirit of Community: The Reinvention of American Society.* New York: Simon and Schuster.

Goode, William J. 1978. *The Celebration of Heros: Prestige as a Social Control System.* Berkeley, CA: University of California Press.

Goodin, Robert. 1991. "Permissible Paternalism: In Defense of the Nanny State." *The Responsive Community* 1:42–51.

Glendon, Mary Ann. 1991. *Rights Talk: The Impoverishment of Political Discourse.* New York: The Free Press.

Marx, Karl and Frederick Engels. 1970. *Selected Works.* New York: International Publishers.

Maslow, A. H. 1954. *Motivation and Personality.* New York: Harper and Brothers.

McClain, Linda. 1994. "Rights and Irresponsibility." *The Duke Law Journal* 43:989.

Nozick, Robert. 1974. *Anarchy, State, and Utopia.* New York: Basic Books.

Sandel, Michael. 1984. *Liberalism and Its Critics.* New York: New York University Press.

Schauer, Frederick. 1985. "Slippery Slopes." *Harvard Law Review* 99:361.

Schlesinger, Arthur, Jr. 1992. *The Disuniting of America.* New York: Norton.

Selznick, Philip. 1994. *The Moral Commonwealth.* Berkeley. CA: University of California Press.

Thatcher, Margaret. 1993. *The Downing Street Years.* New York: HarperCollins.

Wolfe, Alan. 1991. "The Right to Welfare and the Obligation to Society." *The Responsive Community* 1:12–22.

Wrong, Dennis. 1961. "The Oversocialized Concept of Man." *American Sociological Review* 26:183–93.

———. 1994. *The Problem of Order: What Unites and Divides Society.* New York: The Free Press.

III MODERN ECOLOGICAL VIEWS OF THE CITY

Urban ecology looks at how components of a city relate to each other—basically, how are they interdependent. The urban ecologist conceptualizes these units (e.g., neighborhoods) at the macrosociological level and studies them in relation to one another or in relation to the community, which is usually viewed as being composed of neighborhoods. So too, studying how the communities of a city, or of cities more generally, take collective actions or have similar problems may be in the ecological mode. Urban ecologists make great use of demographic variables and view them in relation to space, i.e., areas, boundaries, and nodal points; so it is not surprising that geographers and demographers, whether or not they are also sociologists, make great use of the ecological perspective.

The section begins with the Socio-Geographic View in which the spatial dimension is paramount and is usually studied in relation to aggregated data. Mitchell, Thomas, and Cutter (1999) study the issue of "environmental racism." They study the question of whether black communities were singled out as recipients of environmental hazards. This question is answered by longitudinal use of Geographic Information Systems a computer method that provides a range, density, and specificity of data and analysis unknown to the social sciences until just several several ago (Martin and McDonald 1995). Through the use of GIS, Mitchell, Thomas, and Cutter are able to determine if black communities in South Carolina were the victims of discriminatory placement of hazardous facilities. Kunstler (1996) focuses on space and architecture and finds that urban governments commonly have unfortunate zoning policies that cause them to have unattractive business areas? Kunstler notes that changing zoning is terribly difficult and time consuming. Kaplan (1998) looks at "The Spatial

227

Structure of Urban Ethnic Economies." How an enclave is clustered may be important for the success of its businesses and its residents. The spatial distributions of entrepreneurs, customers, and workers are critical to business success and hence to a successful ethnic enclave.

Socio-Demographic Views begin with Myers' (2000) article on children and spatial mobility. Certainly people who are never long in one place never become attached to any place. But is the impact more far-reaching? Maybe marriage seems less of a goal if a young adult was moved frequently as a child. Charles (2000) uses the interview technique where little stick-house drawings are used to illustrate little neighborhoods with houses occupied by members of one's own race and houses with another race. Race is still important and so is money: so, who wants to live where? When the issue is made more complex by the presence of multiple groups, a pecking order becomes rather clear, but is any group an outlier?

Many of the articles in this section are steeped in statistical tables, but yet again, these have been excised for your convenience.

A.
Socio-Geographic Views

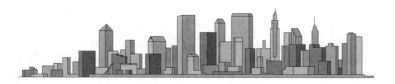

DUMPING IN DIXIE REVISITED:
THE EVOLUTION OF ENVIRONMENTAL
INJUSTICES IN SOUTH CAROLINA

Jerry T. Mitchell
Deborah S. K. Thomas
Susan L. Cutter

The South has been tagged as a "sacrifice zone" for the rest of America's toxic waste (Schueler, 1992; Bullard, 1990). More pointedly, the assertion is that racial minorities and the lower-income classes within this sacrifice zone bear a disproportionate burden of the region's environmental problems. A serious research effort has been undertaken to legitimize this claim, nationally and regionally, with results ranging from an unequivocal "yes" (United Church of Christ, 1987; Bullard, 1990; Mohai and Bryant, 1992; Pollock and Vittas, 1995) to several more recent studies suggesting "maybe" or "maybe not" (Yandle and Burton, 1996; Anderson et al., 1994; Been, 1994; Been and Gupta, 1997; Cutter et al., 1996; Cutter and Solecki, 1996). Past scholarly efforts, however, have focused on *current* outcomes with little regard to *process*—how the inequitable situation came into existence in the first place. Been (1994) notes that in some instances poor and minority residents living near locally unwanted land uses came to the area after the land-use siting decision had been made. Regardless of process or outcome mechanisms, blanket statements of environmental racism, certainly as applied to an entire region such as the South, demand critical review.

This article thus addresses the ambiguities in environmental justice research by examining the question of which came first: Did the residents come to the nuisance or was the nuisance imposed on them? In other words, were the sources of environmental threats (e.g., hazardous waste or Toxic Release Inventory sites) located in communities because they were poor, minority, or politically weak? Or were the facilities originally placed in communities with little reference to race or economic status, and, over time, did the composition of the area change due to migration, market dynamics, or some other factor? We present a systematic appraisal of process inequity in South Carolina and use this research as an illustration of some of the difficulties common to equity studies, such as geographic scale, population migration trends, economic development, and the uncertainties associated with data sources.

DETERMINING PROCESS INEQUITY

A longitudinal review of the circumstances that led to today's environmental picture requires the consideration of several factors. First and perhaps most troublesome is the scale of inquiry—that is, identifying the appropriate geographic unit of analysis (Cutter et al., 1996; Perlin et al., 1995). The United Church of Christ (UCC) study (1987) utilized zip-code areas, while others have used minor civil divisions (Zimmerman, 1993) or census tracts (Anderton et al., 1994; Been and Gupta, 1997; Burke, 1993). Inherent within all these studies is the assumption of a spatially uniform population distribution. In addition, the enumeration units inform us only about "night" conditions—where people sleep—but provide little insight into daytime risk. This is important in considering those who benefit from employment at a site but who may not carry the environmental burden because they reside elsewhere. (Still, census tracts remain attractive due to their relatively stable nature, availability, and comparability of population size [Been, 1995].) A third assumption is that tracts reflect the area around the facility, and that the area closest to the facility will therefore bear the worst impact. Although Pollock and Vittas (1995) discuss exposure as a function of distance, people living closest to a facility do not always face greater exposure than people further away. This assumption neglects the importance of toxicity and magnitude, method of pollutant dispersal, and the physical dispersal processes themselves, all of which contribute to the potential exposure (Glickman, 1994).

The utility of census tracts for longitudinal analysis is helpful only so far as 1980 for South Carolina (when the delineation first appeared statewide, not just in selected urban

areas). This is a significant limitation. If we are to follow the premise established by Bullard (1994), that the present risk landscape, or riskscape, results from the past social and economic "backwardness" of the region, limiting our investigation to dates based on census-tract availability misses several opportunities. Environmental threats in the South did not just appear on the scene after 1960 with the rise of the "New South" and its accompanying rapid industrialization, but may have manifested themselves much earlier. To fully appreciate the injustice process, then, we must explore older established facilities, accepting that census-tract enumeration, while optimal as a spatial unit of analysis, should not be the limiting factor in our investigation. This research thus uses incorporated areas and counties as the spatial unit of analysis.

METHODS

To conduct a statewide historical analysis, we selected Toxic Release Inventory (TRI) sites in South Carolina as our risk indicator. Although considerable controversy surrounds the reporting accuracy of industrial emissions in general (Air and Waste Management Association, 1997), and TRI releases specifically (Lynn and Kartez, 1994), TRI data are used widely in equity analyses (Perlin et al., 1995; Cohen, 1997). In using TRI data, we can compare results to existing studies and also replicate our methods for other places.

The TRI facilities included in this study met three criteria: 1) emissions were reported by the facility for each of the six years of the study (1987–1992); 2) facility emissions exceeded an average of 100,000 pounds for the six-year period; and 3) income and racial demographic data were available for the area in which the facility was located. Between 1987 and 1992 89 facilities in South Carolina reported more than 100,000 pounds of annual emissions; 17 of these reported more than 1,000,000 pounds of emissions. Census data were not available for the areas surrounding 7 facilities, so the total number of TRI facilities serving as point sources of environmental threats in this research is 82.

Establishing Accurate Locations and Facility Start Dates

Thirty of South Carolina's 46 counties (about 65%) host at least one of the 82 facilities used in this analysis. Our previous research found that almost half (48%) of the locations of South Carolina's TRI facilities were in the wrong block group, which required correction (Scott et al., 1997).

Facility establishment dates were confirmed using *The South Carolina Industrial Directory* (South Carolina Department of Commerce, 1941–1996). Entries in this directory include the following information: establishment dates, locations, employment totals, and product descriptions. The 1996 edition contains listings for more than 3,600 manufacturers with Standard Industrial Codes of 20 to 39. Determining plant start dates was a little more problematic than expected as several facilities changed corporate ownership or were renamed under another division; often the establishment dates on record reflected the time of that corporate change, not the date the plant was originally opened.

To maintain quality control over the establishment-date identification, we implemented a four-step date-confirmation procedure that included cross-checking earlier directories and local newspapers, consulting local economic development boards for host towns and counties, and contacting the companies directly. First, industrial directories were compared against each other to detect changes or inconsistencies in listings. Then local newspapers were researched for articles pertaining to plant openings. When establishment-date confirmation was unavailable using these sources, economic development boards were contacted for tax information that could point to a facility opening date. Direct firm contact was initiated as the last option if the other sources were unsuccessful. The industrial directory provided confirmation for 59 start dates, and 5 more were identified through researching newspaper articles and making calls to economic development boards. The remaining 18 facility start dates were confirmed via direct contact with the firms.

Demographic Characteristics

We collected data for incorporated areas and counties from the U.S. Census of Population and Housing in order to have a consistent geographic unit across all decades. The facility point locations and political boundaries were georeferenced and entered into a geographic information system (GIS). A one-mile buffer was constructed around each incorporated area (1990 boundary), so we could examine facilities located on the fringes of towns that might potentially affect those towns' populations. The incorporated areas were labeled as urban locations in our analysis. Suburban locations were defined by the one-mile buffer around the incorporated area, but did not include the urban core (i.e., the incorporated area). Rural locations were defined as everything beyond the one-mile buffer. Twenty-five sites were defined as urban, 28 as suburban, and 29 as rural. Data for incorporated areas were used for both the urban and suburban locales and county data were used for the rural places. The demographic data were collected for the period from the decade preceding the earliest establishment date of the facility through 1990. For example, if a facility start date was 1961, we collected socioeconomic data for that location starting with 1950.

The variable percentage Black is used in this analysis since the state populace has been overwhelmingly either African American or White. The 1990 census reflects this, as 98.8%

of the state's population is either African American or White. In other words, to speak of this state's racial minorities in a historical sense is synonymous with discussing its African American population. Median family income was used as the economic variable because of its availability in the historic censuses.

Data Source Limitations

Creating a historical profile using census data posed several challenges. First, the variables reported in the census were not always uniform over time or geographic space. For example, the definition of certain variables changed, or they were reported differently from decade to decade—such as percentage Negro changing to percentage Black, changing to percentage Non-White—with subtle definitional changes. Also, we were unable to collect data for towns with populations smaller than 1,000 people for any decade. Finally, the geographic boundaries of incorporated areas changed over time. Facilities that were located in rural areas at start-up may now be located within a town boundary (e.g., in an urban area) because of population growth, annexation, or suburbanization. Unfortunately, most of the earlier incorporated boundaries are unavailable, a casualty of the large number of small towns in this investigation and the lack of historic geographic data about them. As such, the incorporated areas described in this article refer to the 1990 boundaries.

Using the TRI as a measure of environmental threat also presents some limitations. First, the TRI represents only one of many potential environmental risks that communities face. Furthermore, it could be viewed as both an economic good (a source of jobs) and an environmental bad (a source of toxic releases). In addition, it is impossible to ascertain the quantity and toxicity of emissions prior to the implementation of the TRI reporting. Thus, we have made an assumption in our analysis that toxic chemicals were produced from the establishment date forward.

A final data concern is the establishment of a baseline with which to compare demographic changes in the TRI host communities over time. At least two possible solutions exist: paired community comparisons or comparisons to a larger standardized unit. Paired comparisons would allow changes to be followed between TRI and non-TRI host communities. This requires, however, a level of comparability between places that is difficult to achieve in South Carolina due to the varied spatial distribution of its population, economy, and industry. Instead, we have chosen to analyze demographic changes using the state means for each decade in which a facility has been operating.

RESULTS

The census data and the information on the TRI facilities were input into a geographic information system (GIS) for management, analysis, and display purposes. We examined three relationships: 1) regional variations in facilities' locations and start-up dates; 2) racial and economic differences between the state and the facility host area at the time of the facility's establishment; and 3) racial and economic differences between the state and the facility host area in 1990.

Regional Variations

Most of South Carolina's largest emitters were established in the 1960s and 1970s, a period coinciding with the rapid industrialization of the state as well as the South in general. Notable exceptions include a number of facilities established in old mill towns at the turn of the century. The oldest facility in our study (a phosphate producer) was founded in 1880 in Charleston. In contrast, the three newest facilities were built in 1987.

The geographic distribution of TRI facilities closely follows the historical industrial development of South Carolina (Kovacik and Winberry, 1987). Facilities are concentrated in the upstate region around the cities of Spartanburg and Greenville, both along the Interstate 85 corridor. Smaller clusters exist in Columbia, which is the state capital, and Charleston. The facilities established earliest are scattered throughout the state and are located primarily within incorporated or urban areas. Beginning in the 1950s and continuing through the 1960s, most facilities were located in the upstate region. Also during this period a transition occurred in the location of the facility relative to the town (see Table 1). Beginning in the 1950s, the location of greater numbers of facilities shifted to the periphery of incorporated areas. By 1960, many were being situated in rural areas. This trend continued into the 1980s. The average facility establishment date for each category—urban (1952), suburban (1962), and rural (1969)—further demonstrates this trend of locating facilities farther from incorporated areas over the last few decades.

Race and Income of Facility Host Area at Establishment

Generally, the host areas with facilities in the upstate region were predominantly White. In the coastal plain, however, the reverse was true. These communities tended to be above the state average for the black population. The Midlands region was mixed. These demographic patterns in racial composition parallel both the historic and contemporary social geography of the state.

The average minority-population percentage for each host area by establishment decade was compared to the state minority-population percentage for the same decade. For instance, ten facilities were established in rural host areas in the 1970s, with an average minority population of 35.9% compared to the state's average minority population of 30.7%. The differences between minority-population averages for host areas and the minority-population average for the state were analyzed through a t

TABLE 1 Average Establishment Dates of TRI Facilities, by Type of Area

Decade Est.	Average Est. Date No. of facilities		
	Urban (within incorporated area)	Suburban (within one mile of incorporated area)	Rural
1880s	1880 (1)	*	*
1890s	*	1899 (1)	*
1900s	1904 (1)	*	*
1910s	*	*	*
1920s	1920 (1)	*	1928 (1)
1930s	1936 (4)	1937 (2)	*
1940s	1944 (3)	1948 (2)	*
1950s	1953 (3)	1954 (5)	1959 (1)
1960s	1963 (5)	1964 (6)	1964 (12)
1970s	1975 (5)	1974 (8)	1975 (10)
1980s	1986 (2)	1983 (4)	1982 (5)
N = 82	1952 (25)	1962 (28)	1969 (29)

* No facilities established.

test. No significant differences were found to exist for urban or rural host-area minority populations at establishment date as compared to the overall state minority average. Only in the suburban host areas in the 1950s and 1960s do we find minority percentages that differ significantly from the state mean. In this instance, however, the relationship is negative, indicating that on average, the populations of host facility areas were significantly more White than the state average.

The average income level for each host area by establishment decade was also compared to the state average income level for the same decade (table not shown). For example, ten facilities established in rural host areas in the 1970s had an average income level of $6,000, compared to a state average income level of $7,621. The differences between the average income levels of the host areas and the average income level for the state were also analyzed through a *t* test. The average income levels for urban host areas in the 1960s and for suburban host areas in the 1950s, 1960s, and 1970s were found to be significantly higher than the state averages at those times. Only for rural host areas in the 1960s and 1970s were the average income levels significantly lower than the state

average. Both Tables 2 and 3 only portray those instances where significance testing was possible; the absence or small number of facilities in previous decades precluded their analysis. It appears that for South Carolina, TRI facilities were located quite equitably so that low-income and minority populations bore no disproportionate burdens.

Race and Income of Facility Host Area in 1990

There were few significant differences in income levels or minority-population percentages between host areas and the state at the time the facilities were established. In all but two instances the differences that are significant point to the establishment of facilities in host areas that had higher income levels and a smaller minority-population percentage than the state.

In examining the same host areas in 1990, however, we see that demographic patterns have changed dramatically. By 1990, all urban and suburban host areas had minority-population percentages that were significantly higher than the statewide average. In contrast, minority-population percentages for rural host areas

TABLE 2 South Carolina Black Population Change

Census Year	Black Population	Total Population	% Black
1880	604,472	995,577	60.7%
1890	689,141	1,151,149	59.8
1900	782,509	1,340,316	58.3
1910	836,239	1,515,400	55.1
1920	865,186	1,683,724	51.3
1930	794,725	1,738,765	45.7
1940	815,496	1,899,804	42.9
1950	823,622	2,117,027	38.9
1960	831,572	2,382,594	34.9
1970	796,086	2,590,516	30.7
1980	974,596	3,121,820	31.2
1990	1,079,729	3,486,703	30.9

continued to show no significant differences when compared with the state average in 1990.

Regarding income levels, by 1990 suburban host areas had income levels significantly lower than the state average. These same host-area income levels either were not significantly different or were significantly higher than the state average at the time the facilities were established. Overall, rural host-area income levels remained significantly lower than the state average in 1990; urban host-area income levels showed no significant changes.

DISCUSSION

We began this article addressing the following question: Did the residents come to the nuisance or was the nuisance imposed on them? Our results seem to indicate the former. When these facilities were established, there was no significant differentiation in host communities by race or income. It would appear that these facilities were not located in communities because they were poor or minority but instead were situated with little reference to race or economic status. Yet over time the socioeconomic composition of the areas in which they were located changed. Admittedly, however, the scale used here is too coarse to determine whether facilities are situated within predominantly minority neighborhoods in the host areas.

Several broad processes help to explain these changes. First, the percentage of the overall population that is Black has decreased substantially over time. Additionally, while Black populations in urban and suburban areas are growing, the reverse is taking place in rural areas. Lastly, the economics associated with the siting of industrial facilities influenced a shift of facility locations from urban areas to more rural locales.

While utilizing the local level as the scale of analysis is important for examining environ-

mental equity, each area has unique characteristics that may create ambiguities in the analysis, thus making environmental equity claims more difficult. For example, contextual factors like statewide and regional migration and economic factors add to our understanding of the racial composition of areas around environmental threats. Simply relying on a time-series census analysis overlooks these important factors.

South Carolina's Racial Migration Trend

The shifts in the demographic composition of incorporated areas from White to Black likely has more to do with statewide migration trends than the actual siting of TRI facilities. South Carolina experienced a steady decline in its Black population relative to the total population as a consequence of a mass exodus of Blacks during the 1960s. This decline slowed beginning in the 1980s. The initial Black migrants were from the rural farm areas, with most leaving South Carolina for perceived better employment and social equality in northern cities. Apparent dissatisfaction with the North and a changing political and economic climate in South Carolina caused a reversal of the migration trend. Blacks were not returning to rural areas, however, but rather turning toward urban centers for work. The shift of more Blacks into metropolitan areas (such as Charleston) and the rapid suburbanization of Whites (as in Berkeley and Dorchester Counties, adjacent to Charleston) dramatically altered the demographic profiles of host areas. Thus, the racial composition of TRI host areas with large Black populations may have been caused by state and regional migration trends, not necessarily by environmental injustices.

Inequity or Economic Development?

Although TRI represents facilities releasing toxic chemicals into the environment, arguably benefits exist as well. Depressed local economies can be uplifted by employment generated by the plants and strengthened by an increase in corporate tax dollars. Lobbying by local areas for these plants can be intense even when it is known that hazardous by-products are part of the deal (Bourke, 1994). Indeed, the promise of financial benefits arising from the establishment of new facilities may have led to siting facilities closer to White communities in order to provide jobs. The pattern of facility siting in the predominantly White upstate region during the 1950s and 1960s potentially reflects this goal. The subsequent siting of post-1960 facilities in rural areas—those areas with an average income level significantly lower than the rest of the state—attempted to reverse this trend by bringing economic development to impoverished areas; this effort was a response to changing racial and social attitudes within South Carolina.

Familiarity with the Local Context

Broad-based state, regional, or national studies of empirically based indicators designed to uncover inequity patterns make attractive, neat packages to hand policymakers, but they neglect several issues related to the local context. One example of the importance of understanding local factors is the Baxter Healthcare facility in Kingstree, South Carolina, which was established in 1961 and closed in 1996. Census data for 1990 shows Kingstree's population to be 64% Black with an income level only 60% of the state average. On the surface, the site of the Baxter Healthcare facility appears to be a strong candidate for an equity investigation. The facility, however, is actually removed from the town and its residents and instead is situated among vast acreages of farmland; the company only uses an Kingstree address. Thus Kingstree residents may not be at risk when compared to another community downwind from the facility. Further, the composition of the plant's workforce and the location of work-

ers' residences would determine whether those who live near the facility actually benefit from employment by its location. Only through this type of individual, local investigation can we truly understand the context and processes that produce inequities.

CONCLUSION

This research examined the issue of which came first: Were toxic facilities initially located in areas irrespective of racial or economic factors, and over time did community demographics change so that inequities appear to exist in 1990? Or were the facilities located in communities that were initially poor or minority and remained so during the intervening years? Our results suggest that the former mechanism was true for the state of South Carolina. The outcome of inequity that we see manifested in 1990 reflects sociodemographic processes of population change and not inequitable siting practices, at least at this scale of analysis. It appears that larger economic and social processes such as land cost and migration are more likely determinants of the current outcomes visible today than when the industrial facilities were initially sited.

While this study cannot provide indisputable answers to the question of environmental equity, it does point to the necessity of undertaking process-equity analyses in order to substantiate current claims of environmental inequity. It suggests three directions for future research. First, it would be useful to develop paired comparisons of communities with and without facilities to test for differences in sociodemographic changes. A second line of inquiry should detail the siting process as much as possible, including minutes from public hearings, tax records, government incentives, and a review of property values and changes over time. Finally, a third important research area involves differentiating between emission types, toxicity, magnitude, and disposal methods. An example of the utility of such research is provided by the following case: a particular social group resides near few facilities, and yet those facilities adjacent to it have the highest emission rate of toxic releases. It should be understood, however, that since the present research only examined one type of environmental threat, these conclusions therefore address only one part of the equity debate.

REFERENCES

Air and Waste Management Association. 1997. "Are Inaccurate Emission Measurements Clouding Pollution Control Planning?" *EM* (September):16–17.

Anderson, Andy B., Douglas L. Anderton, and John Michael Oakes. 1994. "Environmental Equity: Evaluating TSDF Siting over the Past Two Decades." *Waste Age* 25:83–100.

Anderton, Douglas L., Andy B. Anderson, John Michael Oakes, and M. R. Fraser. 1994. "Environmental Equity: The Demographics of Dumping." *Demography* 31:229–248.

Been, Vicki. 1994. "Locally Undesirable Land Uses in Minority Neighborhoods: Disproportionate Siting or Market Dynamics?" *Yale Law Journal* 103:1383–1422.

———. 1995. "Analyzing Evidence of Environmental Justice." *Journal of Land Use and Environmental Law* 11:1–36.

Been, Vicki, and Francis Gupta. 1997. "Coming to the Nuisance or Going to the Barrios? A Longitudinal Analysis of Environmental Justice Claims." *Ecology Law Quarterly* 24:1–56.

Bourke, Lisa. 1994. "Economic Attitudes and Responses to Siting Hazardous Waste Facilities in Rural Utah." *Rural Sociology* 59:485–496.

Bullard, Robert D. 1990. *Dumping in Dixie: Race, Class, and Environmental Quality.* Boulder, Colo.: Westview Press.

———. 1994. "Overcoming Racism in Environmental Decisionmaking." *Environment* 36 (4):10–20, 39–44.

Burke, Lauretta M. 1993. "Race and Environmental Equity: A Geographic Analysis in Los Angeles." *Geo Info Systems* 3 (October):44–50.

Cohen, Maurie J. 1997. "The Spatial Distribution of Toxic Chemical Emissions: Implications for Nonmetropolitan Areas." *Society and Natural Resources* 10:17–41.

Cutter, Susan L., Danika M. Holm, and Lloyd Clark. 1996. "The Role of Geographic Scale in Monitoring Environmental Justice." *Risk Analysis* 16:517–526.

Cutter, Susan L., and William D. Solecki. 1996. "Setting Environmental Justice in Space and Place: Acute and Chronic Airborne Toxic Releases in the Southeastern United States." *Urban Geography* 17:380–399.

Glickman, Theodore S. 1994. "Measuring Environmental Equity with Geographical Information Systems." *Resources* 116:2–6.

Kovacik, Charles F., and John J. Winberry. 1987. *South Carolina: The Making of a Landscape.* Columbia: University of South Carolina Press.

Lynn, Frances, and Jack Kartez. 1994. "Environmental Democracy in Action: The Toxic Release Inventory." *Environmental Management* 18:511–521.

Mohai, Paul, and Bunyan Bryant. 1992. "Environmental Racism: Reviewing the Evidence." Pp. 163–176 in Bunyan Bryant and Paul Mohai, eds., *Race and the Incidence of Environmental Hazards: A Time for Discourse.* Boulder, Colo.: Westview Press.

Perlin, Susan A., R. Woodrow Setzer, John Creason, and Ken Sexton. 1995. "Distribution of Industrial Air Emissions by Income and Race in the United States: An Approach Using the Toxic Release Inventory." *Environmental Science and Technology* 29:69–80.

Pollock, Philip H., and M. Elliot Vittas. 1995. "Who Bears the Burdens of Environmental Pollution? Race, Ethnicity, and Environmental Equity in Florida." *Social Science Quarterly* 76:294–310.

Schueler, Donald G. 1992. "Southern Exposure." *Sierra* 77 (6):42–49.

Scott, Michael S., Susan L. Cutter, Charmel Menzel, Minhe Ji, and Daniel F. Wagner. 1997. "Spatial Accuracy of the EPA's Environmental Hazards Databases and Their Use in Environmental Equity Analyses." *Applied Geographic Studies* 1:45–61.

South Carolina Department of Commerce. 1941–1996. *South Carolina Industrial Directory.* Columbia: South Carolina Department of Commerce.

United Church of Christ. Commission for Racial Justice. 1987. *Toxic Wastes and Race in the United States: A National Report on the Racial and Socioeconomic Characteristics of Communities with Hazardous Waste Sites.* New York: United Church of Christ.

Yandle, Tracy, and Dudley Burton. 1996. "Reexamining Environmental Justice: A Statistical Analysis of Historical Hazardous Waste Landfill Siting Patterns in Metropolitan Texas." *Social Science Quarterly* 77:477–492.

Zimmerman, Rae. 1993. "Social Equity and Environmental Risk." *Risk Analysis* 13:649–666.

HOME FROM NOWHERE

James Howard Kunstler

Americans sense that something is wrong with the places where we live and work and go about our daily business. We hear this unhappiness expressed in phrases like "no sense of place" and "the loss of community." We drive up and down the gruesome, tragic suburban boulevards of commerce, and we're overwhelmed at the fantastic, awesome, stupefying ugliness of absolutely everything in sight—the fry pits, the big-box stores, the office units, the lube joints, the carpet warehouses, the parking lagoons, the jive plastic townhouse clusters, the uproar of signs, the highway itself clogged with cars—as though the whole thing had been designed by some diabolical force bent on making human beings miserable. And naturally, this experience can make us feel glum about the nature and future of our civilization.

When we drive around and look at all this cartoon architecture and other junk that we've smeared all over the landscape, we register it as ugliness. This ugliness is the surface expression of deeper problems—problems that relate to the issue of our national character. The highway strip is not just a sequence of eyesores. The pattern it represents is also economically catastrophic, an environmental calamity, socially devastating, and spiritually degrading.

It is no small irony that during the period of America's greatest prosperity, in the decades following the Second World War, we put up almost nothing but the cheapest possible buildings, particularly civic buildings. Compare any richly embellished firehouse or post office built in 1904 with its dreary concrete-box counterpart today. Compare the home of a small-town bank president of the 1890s, with its massive masonry walls and complex roof articulation, with the flimsy home of a 1990s business leader, made of two-by-fours, Sheetrock and fake fanlight windows. When we were a far less wealthy nation, we built things with the expectation that they would endure. To throw away money (painfully acquired) and effort (painfully expended) on something certain to fall apart in thirty years would have seemed immoral, if not insane, in our great-grandparents' day.

The buildings our predecessors constructed paid homage to history in their design, including elegant solutions to age-old problems posed by the cycles of weather and light, and they paid respect to the future in the sheer expectation that they would endure through the lifetimes of the people who built them. They therefore embodied a sense of chronological connectivity, one of the fundamental patterns of the universe: an understanding that time is a defining dimension of existence—particularly the existence of living things, such as human beings, who miraculously pass into life and then inevitably pass out of it.

Chronological connectivity lends meaning and dignity to our little lives. It charges the present with a vivid validation of our own aliveness. It puts us in touch with the ages and with the eternities, suggesting that we are part of a larger and more significant organism. It even suggests that the larger organism we are part of *cares* about us, and that, in turn, we should respect ourselves and our fellow creatures and all those who will follow us in time, as those preceding us respected those who followed them. In short, chronological connectivity puts us in touch with the holy. It is at once humbling and exhilarating. I say this as someone who has never followed any formal religious practice. Connection with the past and the future is a pathway that charms us in the direction of sanity and grace.

The antithesis to this can be seen in the way we have built things since 1945. We reject the past and the future, and this repudiation is manifest in our graceless constructions. Our residential, commercial, and civic buildings are constructed with the fully conscious expectation that they will disintegrate in a few decades. This condition even has a name: "design life." Strip malls and elementary schools have short design lives. They are expected to fall apart in less than fifty years. Since these things are not expected to speak to any era but our own, we seem unwilling to put money or effort into their embellishment. Nor do we care about traditional solutions to the problems of weather and light, because we have technology to mitigate these problems—namely, central heating and electricity. Thus in many new office buildings the windows don't open. In especially bad buildings, like the average Wal-Mart, windows are dispensed with nearly altogether. This process of disconnection from the past and the future, and from the organic patterns of weather and light, done for the sake of expedience, ends up diminishing us spiritually, impoverishing us socially, and degrading the aggregate set of cultural patterns that we call civilization.

DESTROYING THE GRAND UNION HOTEL

The everyday environments of our time, the places where we live and work, are composed of dead patterns. These environments infect the patterns around them with disease and ultimately with contagious deadness, and deaden us in the process. The patterns that emerge fail to draw us in, fail to invite us to participate in the connectivity of the world. They frustrate our innate biological and psychological needs—for instance, our phototropic inclination to seek natural daylight, our need to feel protected, our need to keep a destination in sight as we move about town. They violate human scale. They are devoid of charm.

Our streets used to be charming and beautiful. The public realm of the street was understood to function as an outdoor room. Like any room, it required walls to define the essential void of the room itself. Where I live, Saratoga Springs, New York, a magnificent building called the Grand Union Hotel once existed. Said to have been the largest hotel in the world in the late nineteenth century, it occupied a six-acre site in the heart of town. The hotel consisted of a set of narrow buildings that lined the outside of an unusually large superblock. Inside the block was a semi-public parklike courtyard. The street sides of the hotel incorporated a gigantic verandah twenty feet deep, with a roof that was three stories high and supported by columns. This façade functioned as a marvelous street wall, active and permeable. The hotel's size (a central cupola reached seven stories) was appropriate to the scale of the town's main street, called Broadway. For much of the year the verandah was filled with people sitting perhaps eight feet above the sidewalk grade, talking to one another while they watched the pageant of life on the street. These verandah-sitters were protected from the weather by the roof, and protected from the sun by elm trees along the sidewalk. The orderly rows of elms performed an additional architectural function. The trunks were straight and round, like columns, reiterating and reinforcing the pattern of the hotel façade, while the crowns formed a vaulted canopy over the sidewalk, pleasantly filtering the sunlight for pedestrians as well as hotel patrons. All these patterns worked to enhance the lives of everybody in town—a common laborer on his way home as well as a railroad millionaire rocking on the verandah. In doing so, they supported civic life as a general proposition. They nourished our civilization.

When I say that the façade of the Grand Union Hotel was permeable, I mean that the building contained activities that attracted people inside, and had a number of suitably embellished entrances that allowed people to pass in and out of the building gracefully and enjoyably. Underneath the verandah, half a story below the sidewalk grade, a number of shops operated, selling cigars, newspapers, clothing, and other goods. Thus the street wall was permeable at more than one level and had a multiplicity of uses.

The courtyard park that occupied the inside of the six-acre block had winding gravel paths lined with benches among more towering elm trees. It was a tranquil place of repose—though sometimes band concerts and balls were held there. Any reasonably attired person could walk in off the street, pass through the hotel lobby, and enjoy the interior park. This courtyard had even-more-overt characteristics of a big outdoor room than the street did. It was much more enclosed. Like the street façade, the courtyard façade featured a broad, permeable verandah with a high roof. The verandah functioned as a mediating zone between the outdoor world and the world of the hotel's interior, with its many public, semi-public, and private rooms. One passed from public to private in a logical sequence, and the transition was eased at each stage by conscious embellishment. The order of things was, by nature, more formal than what we are accustomed to in our sloppy, clownish, informal age. The layers of intersecting patterns at work in this place were extraordinarily rich. The patterns had a quality of great aliveness, meaning they worked wonderfully as an ensemble, each pattern doing its

job while it supported and reinforced the other patterns. The hotel was therefore a place of spectacular charm. It was demolished in 1953.

Although nothing lasts forever, it was tragic that this magnificent building was destroyed less than a hundred years after it was completed. In 1953 America stood at the brink of the greatest building spree in world history, and the very qualities that had made the Grand Union Hotel so wonderful were antithetical to all the new stuff that America was about to build. The town demolished it with a kind of mad glee. What replaced the hotel was a strip mall anchored by, of all things, a Grand Union supermarket. This shopping plaza was prototypical for its time. Tens of thousands of strip malls like it have been built all over America since then. It is in every one of its details a perfect piece of junk. It is the anti-place.

What had been the heart and soul of the town was now converted into a kind of mini–Outer Mongolia. The stripmall buildings were set back from Broadway 150 feet, and a parking lot filled the gap. The street and the buildings commenced a nonrelationship. Since the new buildings were one story high, their scale bore no relation to the scale of the town's most important street. They failed to create a street wall. The perception that the street functioned as an outdoor room was lost. The space between the buildings and the street now had one function: automobile storage. The street, and consequently the public realm in general, was degraded by the design of the mall. As the street's importance as a public place declined, townspeople ceased to care what happened in it. If it became jammed with cars, so much the better, because individual cars were now understood to be not merely personal transportation but personal home-delivery vehicles, enabling customers to haul away enormous volumes of merchandise very efficiently, at no cost to the merchandiser—which was a great boon for business. That is why the citizens of Saratoga Springs in 1953 were willing to sacrifice the town's most magnificent building. We could simply throw away the past. The owners of the supermarket that anchored the mall didn't live in town. They didn't care what effect their design considerations had on the town. They certainly didn't care about the town's past, and their interest in the town's future had largely to do with technicalities of selling dog food and soap flakes.

What has happened to the interrelation of healthy, living patterns of human ecology in the town where I live has happened all over the country. Almost everywhere the larger patterns are in such a sorry state that the details seem irrelevant. When Saratoga Springs invested tens of thousands of dollars in Victorian-style streetlamps in an effort to create instant charm, the gesture seemed pathetic, because the larger design failures were ignored. It is hard to overstate how ridiculous these lampposts look in the context of our desolate streets and the cheap, inappropriate new buildings amid their parking lots in what remains of our downtown. The lamppost scheme was like putting Band-Aids on someone who had tripped and fallen on his chainsaw.

The one-story-high Grand Union strip-mall building must be understood as a pattern in itself, a dead one, which infects surrounding town tissue with its deadness. Putting up one-story commercial buildings eliminated a large number of live bodies downtown, and undermined the vitality of the town. One-story mall buildings became ubiquitous across the United States after the war, a predictable byproduct of the zoning zeitgeist that deemed shopping and apartment living to be unsuitable neighbors.

CREATING SOMEPLACE

Almost everywhere in the United States laws prohibit building the kinds of places that Americans themselves consider authentic and traditional. Laws prevent the building of places that human beings can feel good in and can af-

ford to live in. Laws forbid us to build places that are worth caring about.

Is Main Street your idea of a nice business district? Sorry, your zoning laws won't let you build it, or even extend it where it already exists. Is Elm Street your idea of a nice place to live—you know, houses with front porches on a tree-lined street? Sorry, Elm Street cannot be assembled under the rules of large-lot zoning and modern traffic engineering. All you can build where I live is another version of Los Angeles—the zoning laws say so.

This is not a gag. Our zoning laws are essentially a manual of instructions for creating the stuff of our communities. Most of these laws have been in place only since the Second World War. For the previous 300-odd years of American history we didn't have zoning laws. We had a popular consensus about the right way to assemble a town or a city. Our best Main Streets and Elm Streets were created not by municipal ordinances but by cultural agreement. Everybody agreed that buildings on Main Street ought to be more than one story tall; that corner groceries were good to have in residential neighborhoods; that streets ought to intersect with other streets to facilitate movement; that sidewalks were necessary, and that orderly rows of trees planted along them made the sidewalks much more pleasant; that roofs should be pitched to shed rain and snow; that doors should be conspicuous, so that one could easily find the entrance to a building; that windows should be vertical, to dignify a house. Everybody agreed that communities needed different kinds of housing to meet the needs of different kinds of families and individuals, and the market was allowed to supply them. Our great-grandparents didn't have to argue endlessly over these matters of civic design. Nor did they have to reinvent civic design every fifty years because no one could remember what had been agreed on.

Everybody agreed that both private and public buildings should be ornamented and embellished to honor the public realm of the street, so town halls, firehouses, banks, and homes were built that today are on the National Register of Historic Places. We can't replicate any of that stuff. Our laws actually forbid it. Want to build a bank in Anytown, USA? Fine. Make sure that it's surrounded by at least an acre of parking, and that it's set back from the street at least seventy-five feet. (Of course, it will be one story.) The instructions for a church or a muffler shop are identical. That's exactly what your laws tell you to build. If you deviate from the template, you will not receive a building permit.

Therefore, if you want to make your community better, begin at once by throwing out your zoning laws. Don't revise them—get rid of them. Set them on fire if possible and make a public ceremony of it; public ceremony is a great way to announce the birth of a new consensus. While you're at it, throw out your "master plan" too. It's invariably just as bad. Replace these things with a traditional town-planning ordinance that prescribes a more desirable everyday environment.

The practice of zoning started early in the twentieth century, at a time when industry had reached an enormous scale. The noisy, smelly, dirty operations of gigantic factories came to overshadow and oppress all other aspects of city life, and civic authorities decided that they had to be separated from everything else, especially residential neighborhoods. One could say that single-use zoning, as it came to be called, was a reasonable response to the social and economic experiment called industrialism.

After the Second World War, however, that set of ideas was taken to an absurd extreme. Zoning itself began to overshadow all the historic elements of civic art and civic life. For instance, because the democratic masses of people used their cars to shop, and masses of cars required parking lots, shopping was declared an obnoxious industrial activity around which people shouldn't be allowed to live. This tended to destroy age-old physical relationships between shopping and living, as embodied, say, in Main Street.

What zoning produces is suburban sprawl, which must be understood as the product of a particular set of instructions. Its chief characteristics are the strict separation of human activities, mandatory driving to get from one activity to another, and huge supplies of free parking. After all, the basic idea of zoning is that every activity demands a separate zone of its own. For people to live around shopping would be harmful and indecent. Better not even to allow them within walking distance of it. They'll need their cars to haul all that stuff home anyway. While we're at it, let's separate the homes by income gradients. Don't let the $75,000-a-year families live near the $200,000-a-year families—they'll bring down property values—and for God's sake don't let a $25,000-a-year recent college graduate or a $19,000-a-year widowed grandmother on Social Security live near any of them. There goes the neighborhood! Now put all the workplaces in separate office "parks" or industrial "parks," and make sure nobody can walk to them either. As for public squares, parks, and the like—forget it. We can't afford them, because we spent all our funds paving the four-lane highways and collector roads and parking lots, and laying sewer and water lines out to the housing subdivisions, and hiring traffic cops to regulate the movement of people in their cars going back and forth among these segregated activities.

The model of the human habitat dictated by zoning is a formless, soul-less, centerless, demoralizing mess. It bankrupts families and townships. It disables whole classes of decent, normal citizens. It ruins the air we breathe. It corrupts and deadens our spirit.

The construction industry likes it, because it requires stupendous amounts of cement, asphalt, and steel and a lot of heavy equipment and personnel to push all this stuff into place.

Car dealers love it. Politicians used to love it, because it produced big short-term profits and short-term revenue gains, but now they're all mixed up about it, because the voters who live in suburban sprawl don't want more of the same built around them—which implies that at some dark level suburban-sprawl dwellers are quite conscious of sprawl's shortcomings. They have a word for it: "growth." They're now against growth. Their lips curl when they utter the word. They sense that new construction is only going to make the place where they live worse. They're convinced that the future is going to be worse than the past. And they're right, because the future has been getting worse throughout their lifetime. Growth means only more traffic, bigger parking lots, and buildings ever bigger and uglier than the monstrosities of the sixties, seventies, and eighties.

So they become NIMBYs ("not in my back yard") and BANANAS ("build absolutely nothing anywhere near anything"). If they're successful in their NIMBYism, they'll use their town government to torture developers (people who create growth) with layer upon layer of bureaucratic rigmarole, so that only a certified masochist would apply to build something there. Eventually the unwanted growth leapfrogs over them to cheap, vacant rural land farther out, and then all the new commuters in the farther-out suburb choke the NIMBYs' roads anyway, to get to the existing mall in NIMBYville.

Unfortunately, the NIMBYs don't have a better model in mind. They go to better places on holiday weekends—Nantucket, St. Augustine, little New England towns—but they think of these places as special exceptions. It never occurs to NIMBY tourists that their own home places could be that good too. *Make Massapequa like Nantucket? Where would I park?* Exactly.

These special places are modeled on a pre-automobile template. They were designed for a human scale and in some respects maintained

that way. Such a thing is unimaginable to us today. We must design for the automobile, because . . . because all our laws and habits tell us we must. Notice that you can get to all these special places in your car. It's just a nuisance to use the car while you're there—so you stash it someplace for the duration of your visit and get around perfectly happily on foot, by bicycle, in a cab, or on public transit. The same is true, by the way, of London, Paris, and Venice.

The future will not allow us to continue using cars the way we've been accustomed to in the unprecedented conditions of the late twentieth century. So, whether we adore suburbia or not, we're going to have to live differently. Rather than being a tragedy, this is actually an extremely lucky situation, a wonderful opportunity, because we are now free to re-design our everyday world in a way that is going to make all classes of Americans much happier. We do not have to come up with tools and techniques never seen before. The principles of town planning can be found in excellent books written before the Second World War. Three-dimensional models of the kinds of places that can result from these principles exist in the form of historic towns and cities. In fact, after two generations of architectural amnesia, this knowledge has been reinstalled in the brains of professional designers in active practice all over the country, and these designers have already begun to create an alternate model of the human habitat for the twenty-first century.

What's missing is a more widespread consensus—a cultural agreement—in favor of the new model, and the will to go forward with it. Large numbers of ordinary citizens haven't heard the news. They're stuck in old habits and stuck in the psychology of previous investment; political leadership reflects this all over America. NIMBYism is one of the results, a form of hysterical cultural paralysis. *Don't build anything! Don't change anything!* The consensus that exists, therefore, is a consensus of fear, and that is obviously not good enough. We need a consensus of hope.

In the absence of a widespread consensus about how to build a better everyday environment, we'll have to replace the old set of rules with an explicit new set—or, to put it a slightly different way, replace zoning laws with principles of civic art. It will take time for these principles to become second nature again, to become common sense. It may not happen at all, in which case we ought to be very concerned. In the event that this body of ideas gains widespread acceptance, think of all the time and money we'll save! No more endless nights down at the zoning board watching the NIMBYs scream at the mall developers. No more real-estate-related lawsuits. We will have time, instead, to become better people and to enjoy our lives on a planet full of beauty and mystery. Here, then, are some of the things citizens will need to know in order to create a new model for the everyday environment of America.

THE NEW URBANISM

The principles apply equally to villages, towns, and cities. Most of them apply even to places of extraordinarily high density, like Manhattan, with added provisions that I will not go into here, in part because special cases like Manhattan are so rare, and in part because I believe that the scale of even our greatest cities will necessarily have to become smaller in the future, at no loss to their dynamism (London and Paris are plenty dynamic, with few buildings over ten stories high).

The pattern under discussion here has been called variously neo-traditional planning, traditional neighborhood development, low-density urbanism, transit-oriented development, the new urbanism, and just plain civic art. Its principles produce settings that resemble American towns from prior to the Second World War.

1. The basic unit of planning is the neighborhood. A neighborhood standing alone is a hamlet or village. A cluster of neighborhoods becomes a town. Clusters of a great many neighborhoods become a city. The population of a neighborhood can vary depending on local conditions.

2. The neighborhood is limited in physical size, with well-defined edges and a focused center. The size of a neighborhood is defined as a five-minute walking distance (or a quarter mile) from the edge to the center and a ten-minute walk edge to edge. Human scale is the standard for proportions in buildings and their accessories. Automobiles and other wheeled vehicles are permitted, but they do not take precedence over human needs, including aesthetic needs. The neighborhood contains a public-transit stop.

3. The secondary units of planning are corridors and districts. Corridors form the boundaries between neighborhoods, both connecting and defining them. Corridors can incorporate natural features like streams and canyons. They can take the form of parks, nature preserves, travel corridors, railroad lines, or some combination of these. In towns and cities a neighborhood or parts of neighborhoods can compose a district. Districts are made up of streets or ensembles of streets where special activities get preferential treatment. The French Quarter of New Orleans is an example of a district. It is a whole neighborhood dedicated to entertainment, in which housing, shops, and offices are also integral. A corridor can also be a district—for instance, a major shopping avenue between adjoining neighborhoods.

4. The neighborhood is emphatically mixed-use and provides housing for people with different incomes. Buildings may be various in function but must be compatible with one

another in size and in their relation to the street. The needs of daily life are accessible within the five-minute walk. Commerce is integrated with residential, business, and even manufacturing use, though not necessarily on the same street in a given neighborhood. Apartments are permitted over stores. Forms of housing are mixed, including apartments, duplex and single-family houses, accessory apartments, and outbuildings. (Over time streets will inevitably evolve to become less or more desirable. But attempts to preserve property values by mandating minimum-square-footage requirements, outlawing rental apartments, or fomulating other strategies to exclude lower-income residents must be avoided. Even the best streets in the world's best towns can accommodate people of various incomes.)

5. Buildings are disciplined on their lots in order to define public space successfully. The street is understood to be the pre-eminent form of public space, and the buildings that define it are expected to honor and embellish it.

6. The street pattern is conceived as a network in order to create the greatest number of alternative routes from one part of the neighborhood to another. This has the beneficial effect of relieving traffic congestion. The network may be a grid. Networks based on a grid must be modified by parks, squares, diagonals, T intersections, rotaries, and other devices that relieve the grid's tendency to monotonous regularity. The streets exist in a hierarchy from broad boulevards to narrow lanes and alleys. In a town or a city limited-access highways may exist only within a corridor, preferably in the form of parkways. Cul-de-sacs are strongly discouraged except under extraordinary circumstances—for example, where rugged topography requires them.

7. Civic buildings, such as town halls, churches, schools, libraries, and museums, are placed on preferential building sites,

such as the frontage of squares, in neighborhood centers, and where street vistas terminate, in order to serve as landmarks and reinforce their symbolic importance. Buildings define parks and squares, which are distributed throughout the neighborhood and appropriately designed for recreation, repose, periodic commercial uses, and special events such as political meetings, concerts, theatricals, exhibitions, and fairs. Because streets will differ in importance, scale, and quality, what is appropriate for a part of town with small houses may not be appropriate as the town's main shopping street. These distinctions are properly expressed by physical design.

8. In the absence of a consensus about the appropriate decoration of buildings, an architectural code may be devised to establish some fundamental unities of massing, fenestration, materials, and roof pitch, within which many variations may function harmoniously.

Under the regime of zoning and the professional overspecialization that it fostered, all streets were made as wide as possible because the specialist in charge—the traffic engineer—was concerned solely with the movement of cars and trucks. In the process much of the traditional decor that made streets pleasant for people was gotten rid of. For instance, street trees were eliminated. Orderly rows of mature trees can improve even the most dismal street by softening hard edges and sunblasted bleakness. Under postwar engineering standards street trees were deemed a hazard to motorists and chopped down in many American towns.

ACCOMMODATING AUTOMOBILES

The practice of maximizing car movement at the expense of all other concerns was applied with particular zeal to suburban housing subdivisions.

Suburban streets were given the characteristics of county highways, though children played in them. Suburban developments notoriously lack parks. The spacious private lots were supposed to make up for the lack of parks, but children have a tendency to play in the street anyway—bicycles and roller skates don't work well on the lawn. Out in the subdivisions, where trees along the sides of streets were often expressly forbidden, we see those asinine exercises in romantic landscaping that attempt to recapitulate the forest primeval in clumps of ornamental juniper. In a setting so inimical to walking, sidewalks were often deemed a waste of money.

In the new urbanism the meaning of the street as the essential fabric of the public realm is restored. The space created is understood to function as an outdoor room, and building façades are understood to be street walls.

Thoroughfares are distinguished by their character as well as by their capacity. The hierarchy of streets begins with the boulevard, featuring express lanes in the center, local lanes on the sides, and tree-planted medians between the express and local lanes, with parallel parking along all curbs. Next in the hierarchy is the multilane avenue with a median. Then comes a main shopping street, with no median. This is followed by two or more orders of ordinary streets (apt to be residential in character), and finally the lane or alley, which intersects blocks and becomes the preferred location for garages and accessory apartments.

Parallel parking is emphatically permitted along the curbs of all streets, except under the most extraordinary conditions. Parallel parking is desirable for two reasons: parked cars create a physical barrier and psychological buffer that protects pedestrians on the sidewalk from moving vehicles; and a rich supply of parallel parking can eliminate the need for parking lots, which are extremely destructive of the civic fabric. Anyone who thinks that parallel parking "ruins" a residential street should take a look at some of the most desirable real estate in America: Georgetown, Beacon Hill, Nob Hill, Alexandria, Charleston, Savannah, Annapolis, Princeton, Greenwich Village, Marblehead. All permit parallel parking.

Residential streets can and should be narrower than current specifications permit. In general, cars need not move at speeds greater than 20 m.p.h. within a neighborhood. Higher speeds can be reserved for boulevards or parkways, which occupy corridors. Within neighborhoods the explicit intent is to calm and tame vehicular traffic. This is achieved by the use of corners with sharp turning radii, partly textured pavements, and T intersections. The result of these practices is a more civilized street.

Even under ideal circumstances towns and cities will have some streets that are better than others. Over time streets tend to sort themselves out in a hierarchy of quality as well as size. The new urbanism recognizes this tendency, especially in city commercial districts, and designates streets A or B. B streets may contain less-desirable structures—for instance, parking-garage entrances, pawnshops, a homeless shelter, a Burger King—without disrupting the A streets in proximity. This does not mean that B streets are allowed to be deliberately squalid. Even here the public realm deserves respect. Cars are still not given dominion. A decent standard of detailing applies to B streets with respect to sidewalks, lighting, and even trees.

PROPERTY VALUES AND AFFORDABLE HOUSING

Zoning required the artificial creation of "affordable housing," because the rules of zoning prohibited the very conditions that formerly made housing available to all income groups and integrated it into the civic fabric. Accessory apartments became illegal in most neighborhoods, particularly in new suburbs. Without provision for apartments, an unmarried sixth-grade schoolteacher could not afford to live near the children she taught. Nor could the housecleaner and the gardener—they had to commute for half an hour from some distant low-income ghetto. In many localities apartments over stores were also forbidden under the zoning laws. Few modern shopping centers are more than one story in height, and I know of no suburban malls that incorporate housing. In eliminating arrangements like these we have eliminated the most common form of affordable housing, found virtually all over the rest of the world. By zoning these things out, we've zoned out Main Street, USA.

The best way to make housing affordable is to build or restore compact, mixed-use, traditional American neighborhoods. The way to preserve property values is to recognize that a house is part of a community, not an isolated object, and to make sure that the community maintains high standards of civic amenity in the form of walkable streets and easy access to shops, recreation, culture, and public beauty.

Towns built before the Second World War contain more-desirable and less-desirable residential streets, but even the best can have income-integrated housing. A $350,000 house can exist next to a $180,000 house with a $600-a-month garage apartment (which has the added benefit of helping the homeowner pay a substantial portion of his mortgage). Such a street might house two millionaires, eleven professionals, a dozen wage workers, sixteen children, three full-time mothers, a college student, two grandmothers on Social Security, and a bachelor fireman. That is a street that will maintain its value and bring people of different ages and occupations into informal contact.

DENSITY, NOT CONGESTION

"Congestion" was the scare word of the past, as "growth" is the scare word of our time. The fear of congestion sprang from the atrocious conditions in urban slums at the turn of the century. The Lower East Side of Manhattan in 1900 is said to have contained more inhabitants per square mile than are found in modern-day Calcutta. If crowding had been confined to the slums, it might not have made such an impact on the public imagination. But urban congestion was aggravated by the revolutionary effects of the elevator, the office skyscraper, the sudden mass replication of large apartment buildings, and the widespread introduction of the automobile. These innovations drastically altered the scale and tone of city life. Within a generation cities went from being dynamic to being—or at least seeming—frighteningly overcrowded. Those with the money to commute were easily persuaded to get out, and thus in the 1920s came the first mass evacuation to new suburbs, reachable primarily by automobile. The movement was slowed by the Great Depression and then by the Second World War.

The memory of all that lingers. Tremendous confusion about density and congestion persists in America today, even though most urban areas and even many small towns (like my own) now suffer from density deficits. Too few people live, and businesses operate, at the core to maintain the synergies necessary for civic life. The new urbanism proposes a restoration of synergistic density, within reasonable limits. These limits are controlled by building size. The new urbanism calls for higher density—more houses per acre, closer together—than zoning does. However, the new urbanism is modeled not on the urban slum but on the traditional American town. This is not a pattern of life that should frighten reasonable people. Millions pay forty dollars a day to walk through a grossly oversimplified version of it at Disney World. It conforms exactly to their most cherished fantasies about the ideal living arrangement.

Houses may be freestanding in the new urbanism, but their lots are smaller than those in sprawling subdivisions. Streets of connected row houses are also deemed desirable. Useless front lawns are often eliminated. The new urbanism compensates for this loss by providing squares, parks, greens, and other useful, high-quality civic amenities. The new urbanism also creates streets of beauty and character.

This model does not suffer from congestion. Occupancy laws remain in force—sixteen families aren't jammed into one building, as in the tenements of yore. Back yards provide plenty of privacy, and houses can be large and spacious on their lots. People and cars are able to circulate freely in the network of streets. The car is not needed for trips to the store, the school, or other local places. This pattern encourages good connections between people and their commercial and cultural institutions.

The crude street pattern of zoning, with its cul-de-sacs and collector streets, actually promotes congestion, because absolutely every trip out of the single-use residential pod must be made by car onto the collector street. The worst congestion in America today takes place not in the narrow streets of traditional neighborhoods such as Georgetown and Alexandria but on the six-lane collector streets of Tysons Corner, Virginia, and other places created by zoning. Because of the extremely poor connectivity inherent in them, such products of zoning have much of the infrastructure of a city and the culture of a backwater.

COMPOSING A STREET WALL

In order for a street to achieve the intimate and welcoming quality of an outdoor room, the buildings along it must compose a suitable street wall. Whereas they may vary in style and expression, some fundamental agreement, some unity, must pull buildings into alignment. Think of one of those fine side streets of row houses on the Upper East Side of New York. They may express in masonry every historical fantasy from neo-Egyptian to Ruskinian Gothic. But they are all close to the same height, and even if their windows don't line up precisely, they all run to four or five stories. They all stand directly along the sidewalk. They share materials: stone and brick. They are not interrupted by vacant spaces or parking lots. About half of them are homes; the rest may be diplomatic offices or art galleries. The various uses co-exist in harmony. The same may be said of streets on Chicago's North Side, in Savannah, on Beacon Hill, in Georgetown, in Pacific Heights, and in many other ultra-desirable neighborhoods across the country.

Similarly, buildings must be sized in proportion to the width of the street. Low buildings do a poor job of defining streets, especially overly wide streets, as anyone who has been on a postwar commercial highway strip can tell. The road is too wide and the cars go too fast. The parking lots are fearsome wastelands. The buildings themselves are barely visible—that is why gigantic internally lit signs are necessary. The relationship between buildings and space fails utterly in this case. In many residential suburbs, too, the buildings do a poor job of defining space. The houses are low; the front lawns and streets are too wide. Sidewalks and orderly rows of trees are absent. The space between the houses is an incomprehensible abyss.

The new urbanism advances specific solutions for these ills—both for existing towns and cities and to mitigate the current problems of the suburbs. Commerce is removed from the highway strip and reassembled in a town or neighborhood center. The buildings that house commerce are required to be at least two stories high and may be higher, and this has the additional benefit of establishing apartments and offices above the shops to bring vitality, along with extra rents, to the center. Buildings on designated shopping streets near the center are encouraged to house retail businesses on the ground floor.

A build-to line determines how close buildings will stand to the street and promotes regular alignment. Zoning has a seemingly similar feature called the setback line, but it is intended to keep buildings far away from the street in order to create parking lots, particularly in front, where parking lots are considered to be a WELCOME sign to motorists. When buildings stand in isolation like this, the unfortunate effect is their complete failure to define space: the abyss. In the new urbanism the build-to line is meant to ensure the opposite outcome: the positive definition of space by pulling buildings forward to the street. If parking lots are necessary, they should be behind the buildings, in the middle of the block, where they will not disrupt civic life.

Additional rules govern building height, recess lines according to which upper stories may be set back, and transition lines, which denote a distinction between ground floors for retail use and upper floors for offices and apartments. (Paris, under Baron Haussmaan, was coded for an eleven-meter-high transition line, which is one reason for the phenomenal unity and character of Parisian boulevards.)

In traditional American town planning the standard increments for lots have been based on twenty-five feet of street frontage, which have allowed for twenty-five-foot row houses and storefronts, and fifty-, seventy-five-, and 100-foot lots for free-standing houses. Unfortunately, the old standard is slightly out of whack with what is needed to park cars efficiently. Therefore, under the new urbanism lot size will be based on the rod (sixteen and a half feet), a classic unit of measurement. This allows for a minimum townhouse lot of sixteen and a half feet, which has room for parking one car in the rear (off an alley) plus a few feet for pedestrians to walk around the car. The 1.5-rod townhouse lot permits two cars to park in the rear. The two-rod lot allows for a townhouse with parking for two cars plus a small side yard. Three rods allows for a standard detached house with on-site parking in

different configurations. The four-rod lot provides room for a very large detached building (house, shops, offices, or apartments) with parking for as many as ten cars in the rear. The issue of a standard increment based on the rod is far from settled. Some new-urbanist practitioners recommend an adjustable standard of twelve to eighteen feet, based on local conditions.

The new urbanism recognizes zones of transition between the public realm of the street and the semi-private realm of the shop or the private realm of the house. (In the world of zoning this refinement is nonexistent.) Successful transitions are achieved by regulating such devices as the arcade, the store-front, the dooryard, the ensemble of porch and fence, even the front lawn. These devices of transition soften the visual and psychological hard edges of the everyday world, allowing us to move between these zones with appropriate degrees of ease or friction. (They are therefore at odds with the harsh geometries and polished surfaces of Modernism.)

The arcade, for instance, affords shelter along the sidewalk on a street of shops. It is especially desirable in southern climates where both harsh sunlight and frequent downpours occur. The arcade must shelter the entire sidewalk, not just a portion of it, or else it tends to become an obstacle rather than an amenity. Porches on certain streets may be required to be set back no more than a "conversational distance" from the sidewalk, to aid communication between the public and private realms. The low picket fence plays its part in the ensemble as a gentle physical barrier, reminding pedestrians that the zone between the sidewalk and the porch is private while still permitting verbal and visual communication. In some conditions a front lawn is appropriate. Large, ornate civic buildings often merit a lawn, because they cannot be visually comprehended close up. Mansions merit setbacks with lawns for similar reasons.

ARCHITECTURAL CODES

The foregoing presents the "urban code" of the new urbanism, but architectural codes operate at a more detailed and refined level. In theory a good urban code alone can create the conditions that make civic life possible, by holding to a standard of excellence in a town's basic design framework.' Architectural codes establish a standard of excellence for individual buildings, particularly the surface details. Variances to codes may be granted on the basis of architectural merit. The new urbanism does not favor any particular style.

Nowadays houses are often designed from the inside out. A married couple wants a fanlight window over the bed, or a little octagonal window over the Jacuzzi, and a builder or architect designs the room around that wish. This approach does not take into account how the house will end up looking on the outside. The outside ceases to matter. This is socially undesirable. It degrades the community. It encourages people to stay inside, lessening surveillance on the street, reducing opportunities for making connections, and in the long term causing considerable damage to the everyday environment.

The new urbanism declares that the outside *does* matter, so a few simple rules re-establish the necessary design discipline for individual buildings. For example, a certain proportion of each exterior wall will be devoted to windows. Suddenly houses will no longer look like television sets, where only the front matters. Another rule may state that windows must be vertical or square, not horizontal—because horizontal windows tend to subvert the inherent dignity of the standing human figure. This rule reinstates a basic principle of architecture that, unfortunately, has been abandoned or forgotten in America—and has resulted in millions of terrible-looking houses.

Likewise, the front porch is an important and desirable element in some neighborhoods. A porch less than six feet deep is useless except for storage, because it provides too little room for furniture and the circulation of human bodies. Builders tack on inadequate porches as a sales gimmick to enhance "curb appeal," so that the real-estate agent can drive up with the customer and say, "Look, a front porch!" The porch becomes a cartoon feature of the house, like the little fake cupola on the garage. This saves the builders money in time and materials. Perhaps they assume that the street will be too repulsive to sit next to.

Why do builders even bother with pathetic-looking cartoon porches? Apparently Americans need at least the idea of a porch to be reassured, symbolically, that they're decent people living in a decent place. But the cartoon porch only compounds the degradation of the public realm.

In America today flat roofs are the norm in commercial construction. This is a legacy of Modernism, and we're suffering because of it. The roofscapes of our communities are boring and dreary as well as vulnerable to leakage or collapse in the face of heavy rain or snow. An interesting roofscape can be a joy—and a life worth living is composed of many joys. Once Modernism had expanded beyond Europe to America, it developed a hidden agenda: to give developers a moral and intellectual justification for putting up cheap buildings. One of the best ways to save money on a building is to put a flat roof on it.

Aggravating matters was the tendency in postwar America to regard buildings as throwaway commodities, like cars. That flat roofs began to leak after a few years didn't matter; by then the building was a candidate for demolition. That attitude has now infected all architecture and development. Low standards that wouldn't have been acceptable in our grandparents' day, when this was a less affluent country, are today perfectly normal. The new urbanism seeks to redress this substandard normality. It recognizes that a distinctive roofline is architecturally appropriate and spiritually desirable in the everyday environment. Pitched roofs and their accessories, including towers, are favored explicitly by codes. Roofing materials can also be specified if a community wants a high standard of construction.

Architectural codes should be viewed as a supplement to an urban code. Architectural codes are not intended to impose a particular style on a neighborhood—Victorian, neoclassical, Colonial, or whatever—though they certainly could if they were sufficiently detailed and rigorous. But style is emphatically not the point. The point is to achieve a standard of excellence in design for the benefit of the community as a whole. Is anything wrong with standards of excellence? Should we continue the experiment of trying to live without them?

GETTING THE RULES CHANGED

Replacing the crude idiocies of zoning with true civic art has proved to be a monumentally difficult task. It has been attempted in many places around the United States over the past fifteen years, mainly by developers, professional town planners, and architects who are members of the new-urbanist movement. They have succeeded in a few places. The status quo has remarkable staying power, no matter how miserable it makes people, including the local officials who support it and who have to live in the same jumk environment as everybody else. An enormous entrenched superstructure of bureaucratic agencies at state and federal levels also supports zoning and its accessories. Departments of transportation, the Federal Housing Administration, the various tax agencies, and so on all have a long-standing stake in policies that promote and heavily subsidize suburban sprawl. They're not going to renounce those policies without a struggle. Any change in a rule about land development makes or breaks people who seek to become million-

aires. Ban sprawl, and some guy who bought twenty acres to build a strip mall is out of business, while somebody else with three weed-filled lots downtown suddenly has more-valuable property.

I believe that we have entered a kind of slow-motion cultural meltdown, owing largely to our living habits, though many ordinary Americans wouldn't agree. They may or may not be doing all right in the changing economy, but they have personal and psychological investments in going about business as usual. Many Americans have chosen to live in suburbia out of a historic antipathy for life in the city and particularly a fear of the underclass that has come to dwell there. They would sooner move to the dark side of the moon than consider city life.

Americans still have considerable affection for small towns, but small towns present a slightly different problem: in the past fifty years many towns have received a suburban-sprawl zoning overlay that has made them indistinguishable from the sprawl matrix that surrounds them. In my town strip malls and fast-food joints have invaded what used to be a much denser core, and nearly ruined it.

Notwithstanding all these obstacles, zoning must go, and zoning will go. In its place we will re-establish a consensus for doing things better, along with formal town-planning codes to spell out the terms. I maintain that the change will occur whether we love suburbia or not.

Fortunately, a democratic process for making this change exists. It has the advantage of being a highly localized process, geared to individual communities. It is called the charette. In its expanded modern meaning, a "charette" is a week-long professional design workshop held for the purpose of planning land development or redevelopment. It includes public meetings that bring all the participants together in one room—developers, architects, citizens, government officials, traffic engineers, environmentalists, and so on. These meetings are meant to get all issues on the table and settle as many of them as possible. This avoids the otherwise usual, inevitably gruesome process of conflict resolution performed by lawyers—which is to say, a hugely expensive waste of society's resources benefiting only lawyers.

The object of the charette is not, however, to produce verbiage but to produce results on paper in the form of drawings and plans. This highlights an essential difference between zoning codes and traditional town planning based on civic art. Zoning codes are invariably twenty-seven-inch-high stacks of numbers and legalistic language that few people other than technical specialists understand. Because this is so, local zoning- and planning-board members frequently don't understand their own zoning laws. Zoning has great advantages for specialists, namely lawyers and traffic engineers, in that they profit financially by being the arbiters of the regulations, or benefit professionally by being able to impose their special technical needs (say, for cars) over the needs of citizens—without the public's being involved in their decisions.

Traditional town planning produces pictorial codes that any normal citizen can comprehend. This is democratic and ethical as well as practical. It elevates the quality of the public discussion about development. People can *see* what they're talking about. Such codes show a desired outcome at the same time that they depict formal specifications. They're much more useful than the reams of balderdash found in zoning codes.

An exemplary town-planning code devised by Andres Duany, Elizabeth Plater-Zyberk, and others can be found in the ninth edition of *Architectural Graphic Standards*. The code runs a brief fourteen pages. About 75 percent of the content is pictures—of street sections, blocks, building lots, building types, and street networks. Although it is generic, a code of similar brevity could easily be devised for localized conditions all over America.

The most common consequence of the zoning status quo is that it ends up imposing fantastic unnecessary costs on top of bad development. It also wastes enormous amounts of time—and time is money. Projects are frequently sunk by delays in the process of obtaining permits. The worst consequence of the status quo is that it actually makes good development much harder to achieve than bad development.

Because many citizens have been unhappy with the model of development that zoning gives them, they have turned it into an adversarial process. They have added many layers of procedural rigmarole, so that only the most determined and wealthiest developers can withstand the ordeal. In the end, after all the zoning-board meetings and flashy presentations and environmental objections and mitigation, and after both sides' lawyers have chewed each other up and spit each other out, what ends up getting built is a terrible piece of sprawl equipment—a strip mall, a housing subdivision. Everybody is left miserable and demoralized, and the next project that comes down the road gets beaten up even more, whether it's good or bad.

No doubt many projects deserve to get beaten up and delayed, even killed. But wouldn't society benefit if we could agree on a model of good development and simplify the means of going forward with it? This is the intent of the traditional town planning that is the foundation of the new urbanism.

Human settlements are like living organisms. They must grow, and they will change. But we can decide on the nature of that growth—on the quality and the character of it—and where it ought to go. We don't have to scatter the building blocks of our civic life all over the countryside, destroying our towns and ruining farmland. We can put the shopping and the offices and the movie theaters and the library all within walking distance of one another. And we can live within walking distance of all these things. We can build our schools close to where the children live, and the school buildings don't have to look like fertilizer plants. We can insist that commercial buildings be more than one story high, and allow people to live in decent apartments over the stores. We can build Main Street and Elm Street and still park our cars. It is within our power to create places that are worthy of our affection.

THE SPATIAL STRUCTURE
OF URBAN ETHNIC ECONOMIES

David H. Kaplan

The continued high immigration to the United States has transformed the composition and character of American society. In addition to its other effects, immigration has resulted in the establishment of numerous small businesses, often in previously blighted portions of metropolitan areas. The significance of ethnic economies to both the ethnic groups themselves and the cities within which they reside has sparked interest in the ingredients for business success and in the potential rewards of entrepreneurship. Certainly some ethnic groups have succeeded in creating small-scale urban economies that boast high levels of business ownership, predominate in a few key sectors, and employ substantial numbers of coethnics. Other groups have been far less successful owing to a lack of motivation, opportunities, or resources.

Ethnic economies usually arise under conditions of residential segregation. Most visibly, this distinguishes an ethnic economy from the mainstream economy—giving place identity to neighborhoods like "Chinatown" or "Little Havana." Several scholars go further in maintaining that spatial clustering, whether of residences or businesses or both, is vital to the success of ethnic economies (Portes and Manning, 1986; Logan et al., 1994). The question is, does space operate as an additional resource that facilitates the establishment and maintenance of ethnic businesses? Spatial concentration could indeed operate as a defined resource, or the connection could be more or less coincidental. And even should spatial concen-

tration have an independent effect, variations in the nature of the customer base, the nature of the labor force, the sectoral composition of the ethnic economy, and the maturity of the economy will generate multiple spatial patterns (Aldrich and Waldinger, 1990).

In this paper, I speculate on how spatial concentration may figure into the spectrum of individual and social resources that ethnic groups bring to bear in the formation of ethnic economies. I begin with some definitions of ethnic economies, followed by a more general discussion of demand conditions and the kinds of resources available to ethnic entrepreneurs. Following this, I present four ways in which the spatial structure of ethnic economies—either through the geographical concentration of residences or the clustering of businesses—may operate to enhance the prospects for individual firms. I then discuss how the types of spatial patterns generated by ethnic economic activity will vary depending on the type of resources utilized, the sectoral composition of the ethnic economy, and the maturity of the economy.

THE SIGNIFICANCE OF ETHNIC ECONOMIES

Portes and Jensen (1989) defined an ethnic economy as a group of businesses owned and operated by members of a single ethnic group, and other definitions have added the contribution of coethnic employees (Light et al., 1994; Logan et al., 1994). Within this deceptively simple construction lies a bewildering variety of forms, including the informal economy (Sassen-Koob, 1989), the enclave economy (Portes and Manning, 1986), and the middleman minority (Bonacich, 1973; Bonacich and Modell, 1980). Each carries implications as to the factors responsible for economic success, how the ethnic economy can be operationalized and measured, and the consequences of ethnic economic activity.

The form of the ethnic economy suggests the general mode of ethnic incorporation. A view of ethnic economies as vestigial owes much to the assimilationist perspective, with each group gradually blending into American culture and the American economy. A view of ethnic economies as disadvantaged, marked by a great deal of activity in informal (and sometimes illegal) activities, accords with a more general perspective of the exploitation of some ethnic groups by others.

Two additional views of ethnic economies place a more positive spin on ethnic economic activity. One view sees ethnic groups as utilizing cultural or situational advantages to insert themselves within the economy as intermediaries between dominant and subordinate groups (Bonacich and Modell, 1980). This view suggests a mode whereby certain ethnic groups broker between other groups and function effectively within other ethnic communities. Another view delineates an enclave economy operating within the ethnic community and offering rewards that equal or exceed those of the mainstream economy (Portes and Jensen, 1989). This type of ethnic economy focuses the entrepreneurial activities of an ethnic group within a defined geographic space and fosters linkages between ethnic businesses, customers, and employees.

It is important to note that these categories are not discrete but represent ideal types. Ethnic economies often share characteristics of two or more of these types, and the evolution of an ethnic economy could shift it from one category to another. Rogers (1992) distinguished between small-scale ethnic economies in neighborhoods that function as "ports of entry" and "transnational business enclaves." In the first case, ethnic businesses are severely undercapitalized and offer only the most minimal rewards to owners and employees. In the second case, one finds economies in which immigrant entrepreneurs invest in big-ticket items like hotels and shopping centers, and are wired into the global economy (Tseng, 1994).

Moreover, such categorical distinctions may get somewhat murky. Both undercapitalized and wealthy economies use immigrant labor and may to some extent rely on group resources and a protected market (Wilson and Portes, 1980; Lee, 1992; Gold, 1994), so that rather than describing wholly different types of ethnic economy, they may represent different stages of development (Auster and Aldrich, 1984; Waldinger et al., 1990).

RESOURCES IN ETHNIC ECONOMIES

Data on ethnic business activity demonstrate wide disparities in the entrepreneurship of ethnic groups (Goldscheider and Kobrin, 1980). Moreover, immigrants often exhibit higher rates of self-employment than native-born individuals within the same ethnic group (Borjas, 1986). And comparative research shows that the "same" immigrant group will have markedly different levels of self-employment and specialize in differing occupations in separate contexts (Razin, 1993; Ettlinger and Kwon, 1994). The questions of why some groups enjoy a higher propensity to start their own businesses in certain locales, why some economies have been more comprehensive than others, and why ethnic groups tend to concentrate in a few defined sectors are related to an array of factors. These factors can be conveniently lumped into "demand-side" aspects relating to the local opportunities available to the ethnic group and the "supply-side" factors relating to the characteristics of the group itself.

Conditions present within the local economy may favor or discourage economic activity among newcomers. First off, starting a business is risky, and a healthy local labor market renders this venture less attractive, since many individuals will choose the lower risk of working for others and receiving a wage (Dijst and Van Kempen, 1991). In some economies, the risk of entrepreneurship may be rewarded with greater income than a wage laborer would receive (Light and Karageorgis, 1994), although a study in Britain suggested that Asian entrepreneurs there experience few benefits (Aldrich et al., 1984). There may also be psychological satisfaction in starting a business, especially in light of conditions in the homeland (Light, 1984). Other arguments center on the potential for businesses resolving the status gap felt by many immigrants and others (Min, 1988). For those without appropriate professional credentials, business ownership can be a ticket into the middle class.

Since most ethnic entrepreneurs start small, they tend to concentrate in sectors where there is little advantage to great size—taxicabs being the case cited by Waldinger (1986). Relatively low levels of capital also mean that ethnic entrepreneurs initially confine themselves to businesses that require less capital, do not demand credentials, and can benefit from hard work and the use of family labor (Yoon, 1991). They may look for opportunities in areas that are underserved by chain stores (Light and Karageorgis, 1994). Ethnic entrepreneurs also may seek to supply a product or service that cannot be found anywhere else (Light, 1972; Aldrich and Waldinger, 1990).

For ethnic enterprise to attract labor, it needs to offer rewards unavailable within the host economy. The most controversial argument is whether an ethnic economy provides greater returns to human capital. In particular, Portes and Jensen (1989) and Jiobu (1988) have argued that it does. Other research has not shown this effect, especially for ethnic laborers (Sanders and Nee, 1987; Mar, 1991). Ethnic economies can confer other benefits, beyond the wages, to workers (Mar, 1991; Light et al., 1994). Ethnic enterprise can be more hospitable to women who need to watch their children while they work. It also may offer a springboard to later self-employment among laborers as they defer higher wages in favor of the greater opportunities for advancement, and it offers opportunities for employment where none may have existed.

If demand factors explain some of the differences between contexts, supply factors help explain why certain ethnic groups are disproportionately represented as business owners. Among supply factors, a distinction can be made between "class" and "ethnic" resources (Light, 1984). Some research finds that many of the differences between ethnic groups have to do with the fact that some enjoy better education, wealth, and experience (see Bates, 1994, and Lee, 1992, on the advantages of Korean immigrants).

Yet, as Light and Karageorgis (1994) pointed out, if simple access to capital endowments were the determining factor, immigrant groups would not equal or, in some cases, exceed the entrepreneurship of natives. Ethnic groups, especially recent arrivals, often have little money, little experience in the types of skills prized by the mainstream economy, and a tenuous grasp of the native language and culture. For ethnic businesses to flourish, additional resources must be available that accrue by virtue of group membership, and there must be incentives for individuals to participate in the ethnic economy.

Research points to the importance of ethnic or group resources in helping some ethnic groups. According to Portes and Zhou (1992), an ethnic group's sense of exclusion from the broader society aids potential entrepreneurs in acquiring investment capital, labor, and a customer base from within the community. What Portes and Zhou (1992) term "enforceable trust" assures coethnic investors of getting their money back, even without a written contract. One well-known means of bypassing the limited capital and access to credit is through revolving credit institutions whereby members of the group pool their money to help individual entrepreneurs begin their business (Light, 1972; Lee, 1995). Ethnic entrepreneurs demand considerable labor from themselves and their families (Light and Bonacich, 1988). In recruiting additional help, ethnic entrepreneurs often prefer individuals from within the community. Such a practice reduces employer risks, often reduces wage costs, and minimizes the chance of hiring an ineffective or corrupt employee (Bailey and Waldinger, 1991; Lee, 1992). It also promotes a greater comfort level within the firm as protocols are known and cultural norms prevail (Waldinger, 1986).

These ethnic resources vary by ethnic group. Boyd's (1990) comparison of Asian and Black self-employment suggests that Asians as a whole benefit from greater social and familial networks (see also Fratoe, 1988). What is more, while many Asian entrepreneurs can tap into a protected market of customers, African American entrepreneurs suffer from a reluctance among Blacks to patronize their establishments (Portes and Zhou, 1992).

While kept conceptually separate, demand and supply factors interact with one another in what Aldrich and Waldinger (1990) describe as "ethnic strategies." Ethnic groups enter into a particular situation and make their own luck given the parameters of the local economy. Successful entrepreneurs adapt to the needs of the market, the available labor supply, and the access to capital, and make up for a lack of previous training (Light and Karageorgis, 1994; Park and Kim, in press). Varying strate-

gies would explain why the same group fills different niches within similar urban economic contexts (Ettlinger and Kwon, 1994).

SPATIAL RESOURCES IN ETHNIC ECONOMIES

Discussions of ethnic economies often include a geographical aspect. This geographic issue makes sense considering that ethnic immigration and residential patterns do not occur uniformly over space, but tend to cluster in distinct regions and in particular neighborhoods. So-called "neighborhood effects" have been shown to be significant for the formation of political attitudes (O'Loughlin, 1981) and poverty (Wilson, 1987), and Borjas (1995) confirmed that spatial concentration independently influences general socioeconomic progress across generations. Definitions of ethnic economy have also used space as an important criterion, especially when trying to identify those ethnic economies that function as enclave economies. Logan et al. (1994, p. 694) stated that "clustering—in space and economic sectors—is essential to the concept of enclave economy." Portes and Manning (1986, p. 63) distinguished the enclave, which is "concentrated and spatially identifiable," from an economy based on middleman minorities, which are dispersed throughout the population.

Certainly, ethnic residential segregation often coincides with ethnic business activity. In Los Angeles, a strong correlation exists between the density of Koreans in Los Angeles and Korean-owned businesses (Lee, 1995), even though many Koreans live in suburban areas and many Korean businesses operate in Black or Latino neighborhoods (Waldinger et al., 1990). Similarly, Zhou (1992) noted that New York's Chinatown persists as a concentrated site for Chinese residence and the major focal point of the Chinese community, and Borjas (1986) has calculated the positive effect that living with other coethnics has on the self-employment rates of immigrants.

These correlations beg the questions (1) does space operate as a defined resource (like ready capital or education) at least at the early stages and (2) what is the nature of this resource? Concentration, either of individual households or of businesses, could influence ethnic business activity and its persistence. Factors related to spatial extent and concentration appear to have some effect. Evidence indicates that less-populous groups may be hindered in their business development (Evans, 1989). West Indians in Great Britain, for instance, are constrained by a small market, a small labor pool, and limited business contacts (Reeves and Ward, 1984). Internal dissension within a group also obstructs entrepreneurship. For instance, Villar (1994) reported that differences among Mexican entrepreneurs regarding the use of undocumented immigrants have limited the development of an ethnic economy in Chicago (Villar, 1994).

But does ethnic business development suffer in the absence of spatial concentration? In other words, is there a neighborhood effect "net" of other contributing factors? That is more difficult to gauge. While spatial concentration coincides with ethnic business activity, whether the two are intrinsically related has been speculated on but not empirically tested. Aldrich et al. (1985) showed that Asian stores benefit from a "protected market" and residential segregation reinforces that advantage. In a study of Los Angeles produce markets, Alvarez (1990, p. 107) maintained that "the unifying characteristic of all these markets is the ethnic concentration," which makes efficient exchange possible. But one example of where spatial concentration has not led to more business development is the African American population, often the most spatially segregated group in American cities. In this instance, is spatial isolation offset by other factors frustrating business development (Auster and Aldrich, 1984), or does spatial

isolation directly hinder business development much as it can damage labor-market prospects and increase poverty (Wilson, 1987; Massey, 1990)?

These diverging examples suggest that spatial location likely interacts with other factors that promote or prevent ethnic business development. At the most fundamental level, there needs to be some clarity about how spatial location is defined. Research on ethnic economies to date has indicated that it is important to distinguish between where ethnics live and where they work; the economic enclave is not always the same as the residential enclave (Portes and Jensen, 1989). While businesses within the ethnic enclave economy may be spatially fixed, more prosperous residents will often seek opportunities to buy property in more sedate locations (Rogers, 1992; Zhou, 1992; Tseng, 1994). It is also important to understand exactly how ethnic business or residential concentration may be utilized by existing and startup businesses to further their long-run prospects. Finally, since neither urban location nor economic activity is the same in each context or is static, there needs to be some understanding about how the nature of the spatial resource varies depending on different characteristics of the ethnic economy.

HOW SPATIAL CONCENTRATION MAY HELP ETHNIC BUSINESSES

Existing literature suggests four general ways in which spatial concentration may help ethnic businesses. Figure 1 (not shown here) notes four types of distributions:

A: Incubator with businesses concentrated along with labor but customers more distant

B: Linkages with only the businesses clustered

C: Agglomeration with businesses clustered and customers more distant

D: Focus with businesses in the middle with customers being distant, many quite distant

Distinctions are made between ethnic businesses (EB), ethnic customers (EC), and ethnic labor (EL). This typology is not meant to be exhaustive or exclusive; all four effects could operate at once. It is simply meant to elucidate some possible benefits of clustering.

A. There is a need for ethnic businesses to be close to their markets and close to an available labor supply of coethnics (Portes and Manning, 1986). Residential concentration provides a "cushion of customers" especially in the early stages (Auster and Aldrich, 1984). Likewise, potential coethnic employees will also live near the businesses and provide a desirable and reliable labor force (Zhou, 1992). Of course, this arrangement works best if both customers and employees lack access to automobiles. As such, the ethnic community operates as an *incubator* for small businesses, providing them with a protected market (Aldrich et al., 1985; Waldinger et al., 1990).

B. Ethnic businesses in close proximity have the opportunity to deal with each other to promote the exchange of information, credit, and other supports (Portes and Manning, 1986). This proximity may even facilitate *linkages* between coethnic suppliers and coethnic customers. This benefit, examined by Wilson and Martin (1982) in an input/output model of Cuban firms in Miami, has helped propel the Cuban ethnic economy into an alternative to the mainstream economy.

C. The de.velopment of several ethnic businesses within the same area may create conditions akin to *agglomeration economies* (Waldinger et al., 1990). In a study of Asian businesses in Great Britain, Aldrich et al. (1985) demonstrated that Asian shops in Asian neighborhoods increase the market for other Asian shops. The increased size of the ethnic market will facilitate more foot traffic, encour-

aging other businesses to open up and allowing highly specialized concerns to emerge as well.

D. The tendency for a concentrated ethnic economy to continue to service a more spatially dispersed ethnic residential community underlines its creation as a kind of ethnic central place, serving a much broader hinterland (Waldinger et al., 1990). It provides an *economic and cultural focus* for the ethnic population as a whole, buttressing ethnic cohesion by augmenting existing social and cultural ties with economic relations (Min, 1993), and it helps the community become "institutionally complete" (Breton, 1964). In this issue, Miyares notes how business signs and store names in Brooklyn's Russian enclave link the immigrant population to their native country.

It may be true that, in modern ethnic economies, the concentration of customers is less important. In many American cities, it is essential to have access to an automobile, and even poor families are often able to scrape together enough money to purchase one. In this case, the incubator effects (which rely on residential concentration and limited mobility) are less pronounced than the other effects, which are related more to the concentration of businesses. These incubator effects can still play a role in the crucial beginnings of ethnic economic activity, opening the door for businesses to establish a clear presence in a neighborhood.

HOW MIGHT THE SPATIAL EFFECT VARY?

Research on ethnic economies could benefit from a greater sensitivity to how spatial organization varies under different conditions. Influential factors include the nature of the resources utilized, the types of businesses, and the stage of business development. Some ethnic entrepreneurs thrive in an environment composed of members of other ethnic groups—the so-called "middleman minority" type of ethnic economy (Bonacich, 1973)—while other entrepreneurs rely more on coethnic customers as well as a coethnic labor force (Aldrich et al., 1985; Alvarez, 1990). Figure 2 depicts how the spatial effects may vary.

The nature of resources influences the constitution and geographical basis of the ethnic economy. The greater emphasis on individual resources suggests an economy made up of several successful entrepreneurs who, while possibly interacting for the moment, have fewer financial incentives to cohere spatially. They may be more likely to serve nonethnic markets, recruit outside the community, get credit from nonethnic banks, and conduct many business transactions outside the group. Reliance on group resources suggests an ethnic economy composed of business owners indebted to coethnics for startup capital, employees recruited through informal channels, and a customer base that is captive or loyal or both. These firms will have more reasons to secure ethnic territory and will benefit more from spatial clustering. This tendency is illustrated by the explicit spacing of Vietnamese businesses in Southern California to correspond with the market while also affording each entrepreneur a fair return (Gold, 1992).

Differences in the type of business sector relates to both of these previous attributes and influences spatial organization. Many businesses based around retail and services will locate within a market because they rely on the ethnic community for their customer base (an important exception would be in restaurants, which often appeal to customers outside the ethnic group). Ethnic economies based on manufacturing rely on a market beyond the ethnic community, but they realize cost and other labor advantages through their recruitment of a cheaper, more pliable coethnic labor force (Wong, 1987; Sassen-Koob, 1989). In this instance, the loca-

tion of firms may coincide with ethnic residences, but the residential clustering follows the locational demands of the factories (Waldinger et al., 1990; Zhou, 1992).

Because successful ethnic economies continue to attract more businesses, expand existing businesses, and develop more linkages, they will inevitably alter the nature of their market, employment, and spatial demands. At this point, ethnic businesses will begin to serve the nonethnic population and spatial dispersal will result (Waldinger et al., 1990; Park and Kim, in press).

Some ethnic economies, benefiting from a high capital base, leapfrog the traditional ethnic ghetto and establish themselves in suburban locations. In this issue, Zhou's paper contrasts Chinese business activity in New York and Los Angeles. For a variety of factors—ranging from the greater human capital endowments of Los Angeles's Chinese population, to the ethnic composition of the labor market in both venues, to the mass transportation accessibility of New York City—Chinese residents and Chinese firms are more spatially dispersed in Los Angeles than they are in New York. Li's paper in this issue looks closely at Chinese firms in Los Angeles's San Gabriel Valley. Here, an initially dispersed, suburban economy has altered its emphasis from consumer to producer services over the past 15 years. This change may result in even greater dispersal. Most Chinese firms in Los Angeles are multinuclear, as they look for locations that are cheaper and safer (Tseng, 1994). In this case, businesses and families locate within a broad swath of metropolitan Los Angeles, but are not confined to clustered neighborhoods. Even merchants that initially relied on ethnic resources will come to depend more and more on class resources over time (Yoon, 1991), a change that may diminish the need for ethnic business clustering.

CONCLUSION

The foregoing discussion argues that the success and nature of ethnic economies is predicated on an array of demand and supply conditions. Demand conditions depend on the opportunities present within the existing economy. Supply conditions are those resources the ethnic entrepreneur uses to establish her business, such as amount of capital, level of skills, and ethnic group affiliation. Moreover, demand conditions and supply conditions interact with one another to create an economy specific to each locale and each ethnic community.

Geographical location, especially clustering, seems to figure into the structure of most ethnic economies. Businesses frequently cluster together and this business concentration often correlates with ethnic residential patterns. The question is whether such clustering is coincidental or functional. Is spatial concentration a distinct resource for ethnic economies and does its function vary depending on the nature of the ethnic economy? While several studies point to the importance of the spatial element, the connection itself needs to be systematically examined. There exist a variety of ways in which spatial concentration could help the formation and maintenance of ethnic businesses, and which might help create the conditions necessary to transform a set of ethnic businesses into a truly integrated ethnic enclave economy.

Certainly, the number, complexity, and interplay of all such possible determinants make studying the geographical aspects of ethnic economies particularly challenging. But a more focused examination of these determinants could provide additional clues as to what breeds entrepreneurial success, while affording us greater insights into the possible value of urban segregation. It may be that segregation, long derided as a negative influence in the economic fortunes of some ethnic groups, turns out sometimes to play a positive role in fostering economic success among some ethnic groups.

LITERATURE CITED

Aldrich, H., Cater, J., Jones, T., McEvoy, D., and Velleman, P., 1985, Ethnic residential concentration and the protected market hypothesis. *Social Forces,* Vol. 63, 996–1009.

Aldrich, H., Jones, P.J., and McEvoy, D., 1984, Ethnic advantage and minority business development. In R. Ward and R. Jenkins, editors, *Ethnic Communities for Business: Strategies for Economic Survival.* Cambridge, UK: Cambridge University Press, 189–210.

Aldrich, H. and Waldinger, R., 1990, Ethnicity and entrepreneurship. *Annual Review of Sociology,* Vol. 16, 111–135.

Alvarez, R., 1990, Mexican entrepreneurs and markets in the city of Los Angeles: A case of an immigrant enclave. *Urban Anthropology,* Vol. 19, 99–124.

Auster, E. and Aldrich, H., 1984, Small business vulnerability, ethnic enclaves and ethnic enterprise. In R. Ward and R. Jenkins, editors, *Ethnic Communities for Business: Strategies for Economic Survival.* Cambridge, UK: Cambridge University Press, 39–54.

Bailey, T. and Waldinger, R., 1991, Primary, secondary, and enclave labor markets: A training systems approach. *American Sociological Review,* Vol. 56, 432–445.

Bates, T., 1994, Social resources generated by group support networks may not be beneficial to Asian immigrant-owned small businesses. *Social Forces,* Vol. 72, 671–689.

Bonacich, E., 1973, A theory of middleman minorities. *American Sociological Review,* Vol. 38, 583–594.

Bonacich, E. and Modell, J., 1980, *The Economic Basis of Ethnic Solidarity.* Berkeley, CA: University of California Press.

Borjas, G., 1986, The self-employment experiences of immigrants. *The Journal of Human Resources,* Vol. 21, 485–506.

Borjas, G., 1995, Ethnicity, neighborhoods, and human-capital externalities. *The American Economic Review,* Vol. 85, 365–390.

Boyd, R., 1990, Black and Asian self-employment in large metropolitan areas: A comparative analysis. *Social Problems,* Vol. 37, 258–274.

Breton, R., 1964, Institutional completeness of ethnic communities and the personal relations of immigrants. *American Journal of Sociology,* Vol. 70, 193–205.

Dijst, M. and Van Kempen, R., 1991, Minority business and the hidden dimension: The influence of urban contexts on the development of ethnic enterprise. *Tijdschrift voor Economische en Sociale Geografie,* Vol. 82, 128–138.

Ettlinger, N. and Kwon, S., 1994, Comparative analysis of U.S. urban labor markets: Asian immigrant groups in New York and Los Angeles. *Tijdschrift voor Economische en Sociale Geografie,* Vol. 85, 417–433.

Evans, M. D. R., 1989, Immigrant entrepreneurship: Effects of ethnic market size and isolated labor pool. *American Sociological Review,* Vol. 54, 950–962.

Fratoe, F., 1988, Social capital of black business owners. *The Review of Black Political Economy,* Vol. 16, 33–50.

Gold, S., 1992, *Refugee Communities: A Comparative Field Study.* Newbury Park, CA: Sage.

Gold, S., 1994, Chinese-Vietnamese entrepreneurs in California. In P. Ong, E. Bonacich, and L. Cheng, editors, *The New Asian Immigration in Los Angeles and Global Restructuring.* Philadelphia, PA: Temple University Press, 196–226.

Goldscheider, C. and Kobrin, F., 1980, Ethnic continuity and the process of self-employment. *Ethnicity,* Vol. 7, 256–278.

Jiobu, R., 1988, *Ethnicity and Assimilation.* Albany, NY: State University of New York Press.

Lee, D., 1992, Commodification of ethnicity: The sociospatial reproduction of immigrant entrepreneurs. *Urban Affairs Quarterly,* Vol. 28, 258–275.

Lee, D., 1995, Koreatown and Korean small firms in Los Angeles: Locating in the ethnic neighborhoods. *The Professional Geographer,* Vol. 47, 184–195.

Light, I., 1972, *Ethnic Enterprise in America: Business and Welfare Among Chinese, Japanese and Blacks.* Berkeley, CA: The University of California Press.

Light, I., 1984, Immigrant and ethnic enterprises in North America. *Ethnic and Racial Studies,* Vol. 7, 195–216.

Light, I. and Bonacich, E., 1988, *Immigrant Entrepreneurs: Koreans in Los Angeles, 1965–1982*. Berkeley, CA: University of California Press.

Light, I. and Karageorgis, S., 1994, The ethnic economy. In N. Smelser and R. Swedberg, editors, *The Handbook of Economic Sociology*. Princeton, NJ: Princeton University Press, 647–671.

Light, I., Sabagh, G., Bozorgmehr, M., and Der-Martirosian, C., 1994, Beyond the ethnic enclave economy. *Social Problems,* Vol. 41, 65–80.

Logan, J., Alba, R., and McNulty, T., 1994, Ethnic economies in metropolitan regions: Miami and beyond. *Social Forces,* Vol. 72, 691–724.

Mar, D., 1991, Another look at the enclave economy thesis: Chinese immigrants in the ethnic labor market. *Amerasia,* Vol. 17, 5–21.

Massey, D., 1990, American apartheid: Segregation and the making of the underclass. *American Journal of Sociology,* Vol. 96, 329–357.

Min, P., 1988, *Ethnic Business Enterprise: Korean Small Business in Atlanta*. New York, NY: Center for Migration Studies.

Min, P., 1993, Korean immigrants in Los Angeles. In I. Light and P. Bhachu, editors, *Immigration and Entrepreneurship: Culture, Capital, and Ethnic Networks*. New Brunswick, NJ: Transaction, 185–204.

O'Loughlin, J., 1981, The neighborhood effect in urban voting surfaces: A cross-national analysis. In A. D. Burnett and P. J. Taylor, editors, *Political Studies from Spatial Perspectives*. New York, NY: John Wiley & Sons, 357–388.

Park, S. and Kim, K. C., in press, Intrametropolitan location of Korean businesses: The case of Chicago. *Urban Geography.*

Portes, A. and Jensen, L., 1989, The enclave and the entrants: Patterns of ethnic enterprise in Miami before and after Mariel. *American Sociological Review,* Vol. 54, 929–949.

Portes, A. and Manning, R., 1986, The immigrant enclave: Theory and empirical examples. In S. Olzak and J. Nagel, editors, *Competitive Ethnic Relations*. Orlando, FL: Academic Press, 47–68.

Portes, A. and Zhou, M., 1992, Gaining the upper hand: Economic mobility among immigrant and domestic minorities. *Ethnic and Racial Studies,* Vol. 15, 491–522.

Razin, E., 1993, Immigrant entrepreneurs in Israel, Canada, and California. In I. Light and P. Bhachu, editors, *Immigration and Entrepreneurship: Culture, Capital, and Ethnic Networks*. New Brunswick, NJ: Transaction Publishers, 97–124.

Reeves, F. and Ward, R., 1984, West Indian business in Britain. In R. Ward and R. Jenkins, editors, *Ethnic Communities for Business: Strategies for Economic Survival*. Cambridge, UK: Cambridge University Press, 125–146.

Rogers, A., 1992, The new immigration and urban ethnicity in the United States. In M. Cross, editor, *Ethnic Minorities and Industrial Change in Europe and North America*. Cambridge, UK: Cambridge University Press, 226–249.

Sanders, J. and Nee, V., 1987, Limits of ethnic solidarity in the enclave economy. *American Sociological Review,* Vol. 52, 745–773.

Sassen-Koob, S., 1989, New York City's informal economy. In A. Portes, M. Castells, and L. Benton, editors, *The Informal Economy: Studies in Advanced and Less Developed Countries.* Baltimore, MD: The Johns Hopkins University Press, 60–77.

Tseng, Y.-F., 1994, Chinese ethnic economy: San Gabriel Valley, Los Angeles County. *Journal of Urban Affairs,* Vol. 16, 169–189.

Villar, M., 1994, Hindrances to the development of an ethnic economy among Mexican migrants. *Human Organization,* Vol. 53, 263–268.

Waldinger, R., 1986, *Through the Eye of the Needle: Immigrants and Enterprise in New York's Garment Trades.* New York, NY: New York University Press.

Waldinger, R., McEvoy, D., and Aldrich, H., 1990, Spatial dimensions of opportunity structures. In R. Waldinger, H. Aldrich, and R. Ward, editors, *Ethnic Entrepreneurs: Immigrant Business in Industrial Societies.* Newbury Park, CA: Sage, 106–130.

Wilson, K. and Martin, W. A., 1982, Ethnic enclaves: A comparison of the Cuban and the Black economies in Miami. *American Journal of Sociology,* Vol. 88, 135–160.

Wilson, K. and Portes, A., 1980, Immigrant enclaves: An analysis of the labor market experiences of Cubans in Miami. *American Journal of Sociology,* Vol. 86, 135–160.

Wilson, W. J., 1987, *The Truly Disadvantaged: The Inner City, the Underclass, and Public Policy.* Chicago, IL: University of Chicago Press.

Wong, B., 1987, The role of ethnicity in enclave enterprises: A study of the Chinese garment factories in New York City. *Human Organization,* Vol. 46, 120–130.

Yoon, I., 1991, The changing significance of ethnic and class resources in immigrant businesses: The case of Korean immigrant businesses in Chicago. *International Migration Review,* Vol. 25, 303–332.

Zhou, M., 1992, *Chinatown: The Socioeconomic Potential of an Urban Enclave.* Philadelphia, PA: Temple University Press.

B.
Socio-Demographic Views

MOVING INTO ADULTHOOD: FAMILY RESIDENTIAL MOBILITY AND FIRST-UNION TRANSITIONS

Scott M. Myers

Family sociologists have long believed that mobility interferes with normal family processes and introduces additional stressors into child and family development. Burgess, Locke, and Thomes (1963) argue that mobility introduces family members to new patterns of behavior and frees each of them from familial control through individualization and the breakdown of traditional norms and values that govern family life. Voydanoff (1980) contends that mobility is a potential stressor that disrupts the degree of family cohesion, social control, and integration. Indeed, research on mobility and divorce at the individual level, after controlling for compositional and individual-level variables, finds that divorce rates are higher among couples who live in large cities and in areas with high rates of mobility. The interpretations offered are Durkheimian—high levels of residential mobility disrupt social relations and are associated with low levels of social control, which decrease barriers to divorce.

The goal of this article is to examine the association between prior family mobility and

another specific domain of family life—movement of adult offspring into their first union. Mobility and first-union transitions may be linked directly, or indirectly through family processes that influence union-formation behaviors of adult offspring. In the following sections, I draw on social control theory and previous research on mobility, and argue that the most plausible family processes linking mobility and first-union transitions are parental supervision, parental support, and family structure.

MOBILITY, SOCIAL CONTROL, AND FIRST-UNION FORMATION

Social control has always been part of research on mobility. Social disorganization theorists argue that the connection between crime and poverty at the neighborhood and community levels is through the high mobility and population turnover rates in these areas (Bursick and

Grasmick, 1993). Mobility ruptures local attachments and weakens social control and the inhibiting influence of primary groups (Park, [1916] 1969). Research finds that mobility operates as a barrier to the development of social cohesion and control by decreasing levels of contact and increasing levels of anonymity among residents, net of urbanization, density, SES, and life cycle (Kasarda and Janowitz, 1974; Sampson, 1988). Mobility also affects union behaviors through similar social control mechanisms. At the macro level, divorce rates are greatest in the census regions with the highest mobility rates and in SMSAs that experienced rapid in-migration between 1975 and 1980 (Glenn and Shelton, 1985; South, 1987). South indicates that the most likely explanation for the divorce differentials is the lower levels of social integration and disruption of interpersonal relations in areas with high rates of mobility.

The relationship between mobility and social control mechanisms at the macro level guides research at the family level. Sampson and Laub (1993) find that frequent family mobility is associated with lower levels of maternal supervision, higher levels of parental indifference toward their children, and lower levels of parent-child attachment. In turn, these diminished family mechanisms are associated with elevated rates of delinquency among children. Parental indifference and parent-child attachment approximate another parenting variable— parental-child support. Together, parental supervision and parental support capture two important aspects of parenting and socialization and are associated with positive developmental outcomes in children and adolescents (Maccoby and Martin, 1983).

Mobility affects parenting in several ways. Relationships within the family are tied directly to the parents' relationships outside the family (e.g., school, community) because these institutions provide parents with a source of guidance and support. As frequent mobility re-

moves parents from these key societal institutions of control, mobility also affects intrafamily social control mechanisms (Hagan, MacMillan, and Wheaton, 1996; Sampson and Laub, 1993). This is essentially the basis of social capital, whereby parent-child relations and informal family control are contingent on the degree of parents' connection at extrafamilial levels (Hagan, MacMillan, and Wheaton, 1996). In recent research, Hagan, MacMillan, and Wheaton draw on Sampson and Laub's and Coleman's (1988) work on social capital, apply the concepts of parental supervision and support, and find that these two resources (i.e., family capital) account for the detrimental effects of childhood mobility on educational and occupational outcomes in adulthood.

What is the connection between parental supervision and support and union-formation behaviors? Two general paths are plausible. First, parental supervision and support are associated with other parental characteristics that influence offspring's first-union transitions. For example, parental support is greater when the parents have higher education and income levels and when the parents have a happy marriage (Amato and Booth, 1997). In turn, cohabitation, as well as marriage at early ages, is less likely among offspring from parents with high education, income, and marital-quality levels (Amato and Booth, 1997; Bumpass, Sweet, and Cherlin, 1991). There is some evidence that close parent-child relationships, which are more common at higher levels of parental support, deter entry into cohabiting unions (Clarkberg, Stolzenberg, and Waite, 1995). Explaining their finding, Clarkberg, Stolzenberg, and Waite argue that close ties to one's parents and family reinforce promarriage values, discourage cohabitation, and are part of marital roles.

Greater levels of parental supervision and support may also guide offspring into marriage and not into cohabitation. Most parents prefer their children to marry instead of to cohabit and think that couples should not live together before marrying. Most of their children, though, report that they think it is all right to live together before marrying (Thornton, 1989). Axinn and Thornton (1992) find later ages at first marriage among adult children from parents who prefer and are better able to impose their later-age marriage preferences on their children. Therefore, although adult children may prefer to cohabit or marry early, children's movement into a first union is guided to a greater extent, and resembles parents' preference for marriage, if parents are better able to supervise, coordinate, and support the activities of their children.

Second, parental supervision and parental support are associated with various offspring characteristics that influence first-union transitions. For example, Hogan and Kitagawa (1985) find significantly higher rates of premarital teenage pregnancy among girls whose parents exercise little supervision. Low levels of parental support and supervision are associated also with greater sexual risk taking and lower levels of religiosity and church attendance (Amato and Booth, 1997; Luster and Small, 1994; Myers, 1996). In turn, early sexual activity and low levels of religiosity increase the probability that the first union will be cohabitation (Clarkberg, Stolzenberg, and Waite, 1995; Cunningham and Antill, 1995). These few examples highlight the second potential relationship between parental supervision and support and first-union transitions.

In sum, I argue that family mobility influences first-union transitions, where most of the relationship is explained by individual differences in levels of parental supervision, parental support, and associated processes. The following hypotheses are derived.

1. *Hypothesis 1:* Offspring who moved frequently while living with their parents are more likely to enter into cohabitation than into marriage as a first-union experience than are offspring who moved less frequently.

2. *Hypothesis 2:* Offspring who moved most frequently while living with their parents are more likely to enter into cohabitation than into marriage as a first-union experience because more-mobile offspring were raised in households with lower levels of parental supervision and parental support.

The second hypothesis parallels research on social disorganization, social control, and parenting behaviors. Children who move more frequently experience lower levels of parental supervision and parental support. In turn, these low levels of parental supervision and support make it more likely that offspring will enter first into a cohabiting union than into a marital union. Therefore, the direct relationship between family mobility and first-union transitions proposed in the first hypothesis will disappear after adjusting statistically for parental supervision and parental support.

Parental supervision and support, mobility, and union formation may all be predicted by family structure. Thus, the relationships proposed in the hypotheses may be spurious because of a dependence on a third mechanism—family structure. For example, (a) single-parent and stepparent families generally have lower levels of parental monitoring, supervision, and support compared with those of intact households (Astone and McLanahan, 1991); (b) children who experience a parental divorce have significantly higher probabilities of delayed marriage (Li and Wojtkiewicz, 1994) and are more likely to enter into a cohabiting union (Thornton, 1991); and (c) children who experience divorce and remarriage are more likely to move and move more often than children in intact families (Astone and McLanahan, 1994; Long, 1992). In order to adequately evaluate the hypotheses, it is necessary to control for family structure and thereby control for the potential spurious relationships.

RESEARCH PROCEDURES

Sample. The data for this research come from the Study of Marital Instability over the Life Course (Booth et al., 1993). A national sample of 2,033 married persons in the United States were interviewed in 1980, and then again in 1983, 1988, and 1992. In 1980, sample households were chosen through a simple random-digit dialing procedure, and the husband or wife was selected for an interview using a second random process. Only married individuals under age 55 in 1980 were included in the sample. Completed interviews were obtained with 78% of the respondents in 1980. Reinterview rates were 78% in 1983, 84% in 1988, and 89% in 1992, yielding 1,193 completed interviews in 1992. These response rates are comparable to those obtained in studies using in-person interviews (Booth and Johnson, 1985).

In 1992, the fourth wave of data included a sample of offspring who had resided in the household in 1980 and who were 19 years of age or older in 1992. Among respondents reinterviewed in 1992, 575 had offspring 19 years of age or older who had been in the parental household in 1980, and 496 offered the names and telephone numbers of their offspring. Interviews were conducted with 471 offspring. In 1997, interviews were conducted with 426 of these offspring for a reinterview rate of 90%. In addition, interviews were conducted with all remaining offspring who reached age 19 or older in 1997 and who resided in the parental household in 1980 ($n = 220$). Therefore, the combined sample consists of 646 offspring who were age 19 or older in 1997 and who resided in the parental home in 1980. The combined sample is independent, as there are no sibling pairs. To ensure that all offspring are at risk of family mobility and to ensure the proper causal ordering of the family-of-origin variables, I exclude offspring who cohabited or married (7%) before 1983. There is no stan-dard method to fix full left censoring or to estimate any resulting selection bias (Yamaguchi, 1991). At best, ancillary analysis (not shown) suggests that the few omitted adult offspring do not differ significantly from those included, based on several variables: family structure history, family income, parental education, religious denomination in 1980, and the sex of the offspring.

Sample Selection. Two potential biases exist. First, the offspring interviewed in 1992 depended upon which parents were retained between 1980 and 1992. If there exists a theoretical connection between the variables predicting attrition (and thus the sample of offspring) and the dependent variable, then a control for sample selection may be necessary (Stolzenberg and Relles, 1990). I analyzed attrition patterns between 1980 and 1992 for all parents who would have a child eligible for interview in 1992. Attrition occurred in predictable categories: African Americans, renters, and persons in households in which husbands had no college education. In addition, mobility of the parents was a modest contributing factor to attrition.

Because these variables associated with attrition have theoretical connections to the dependent variable, I reestimated, according to procedures outlined in Berk (1983), all of the models presented in this paper with an instrumental variable for selection out of the sample between 1980 and 1992.

The second source of bias may occur because of the time intervals during which family mobility was measured. Family mobility was measured while the offspring lived at home between 1980 and 1992. This interval measures behaviors that are more continuous in nature. If this interval contained atypical mobility behaviors, then the ability to generalize my findings are compromised. I used data from the Current Population Reports to determine how closely the family mobility histories of the children represented the mobility behaviors of the nation. The result is reported below. Overall, I am confident that the results are not compromised by these two potential sources of data limitation.

Measurement of Variables

Mobility. The offspring mobility histories were created from parental reports of moving between 1980 and 1992. Using information on the age at which offspring left and returned to the parental home and the age at which offspring formed their first union, I was able to determine the specific interview intervals in which each offspring resided with his or her parents, was exposed to each family move, and had not yet entered into a first union. In cases of separation, divorce, or remarriage it was necessary to identify which parent the child lived with to ensure that any noncustodial parental moves did not count as an offspring move.

Three mobility intervals were possible: 1980–83, 1983–88, and 1988–92. Measures of residential mobility started with this question in the parent interview: "Have you moved to another residence since the fall of 1980 (fall of 1983, fall of 1988, fall of 1992)?" An affirmative response was followed by a query about the number of times movement took place and whether any move involved a change in community. For the purpose of this research, an offspring was considered to have moved *only if* that move required a change in community.

One measure of mobility was analyzed. Consistent with previous research on mobility (Coleman, 1988; Long, 1992; Sampson and Laub, 1993; Stack, 1994) and social capital (Coleman, 1988), I indicated the number of times a child had moved while residing in the parental home. Nearly 65% of the sample made at least one move, 20% made 3 or more moves, and 35% made no moves. The mean

number of moves made between 1980 and 1992 was about 1.5, with a range between 0 and 10. Given that the average offspring was in the household for eight years between 1980 and 1992, these rates approximate closely the national average. Among married-couple households with household heads under age 54 and with children present (similar to the population from which the sample of offspring were drawn), the average U.S. family moved once every 6.5 years or 1.23 times over an eight-year span (Hansen, 1995).

These mobility measures did not capture the full mobility histories of the offspring. Instead, they captured only the mobility experiences of the offspring while they resided in the parental home between 1980 and 1992. Because some offspring were older and resided in the parental home for shorter periods of time, they were at a substantially smaller risk of making a large number of moves. If anything, the effects of mobility may be underestimated since many moves occurred before 1980. Further biases may be reduced because all models included a variable for mother's age at marriage, which is associated with an offspring's age in 1980 and, subsequently, an offspring's risk of exposure to family mobility between 1980 and 1992.

Union Formation. The interviews with the adult children asked questions regarding their ages at and sequencing of union-formation behaviors. From these questions it was possible to determine whether the offspring exited singlehood through cohabitation or marriage. Overall, the distribution of first-union transitions was as follows: 39% exited the single state into cohabiting unions; 27% exited into marital unions; and 34% remained single.

Parental Supervision and Support. Three measures of parenting were used. Mother support and father support were based on a series of retrospective questions asked in the offspring interviews, in which young adults were asked to recall parental behaviors during their adolescence. Adult offspring were asked how often (never, sometimes, often) their mothers/fathers helped them with homework, helped them with personal problems, talked to them, and showed affection toward them. A fifth item rated the overall closeness of the mother/father-child relationship (very close, pretty close, not very close). Parental supervision was the third parenting measure, and again young adults were asked to recall parental behaviors during their adolescence. While these three variables were retrospective, they referenced periods when the offspring lived at home and made family moves. Similar to the prospective measures used in Hagan, MacMillan, and Wheaton (1996), these variables were not tied temporally to each specific act of mobility, but more to the general parent-child and family atmosphere of the household. In addition, these measures captured aspects of the parent-child relationship beyond those of supervision and support.

Family Structure.   Li and Wojtkiewicz (1994) contend that duration in a type of family structure is more important than whether one experienced a specific family structure or transition. This makes sense in the present framework. Arguably, time spent in a divorced, single-parent household is a better indicator of levels of parental supervision and support than simply whether one ever experienced a parental divorce. Two family structure measures were used: time spent in a divorced, single-parent family, and time spent in a stepparent family. The data did not contain a significant number of instances of widowhood, and these individuals were coded as time spent in single-parent households.

Control Variables.   I also controlled for family-of-origin variables that are associated consistently with union formation. These variables were measured in the baseline parental interview in 1980: average of mother's and father's education, mother's age at marriage, family income per capita, church attendance, religious denomination, and parents' attitudes toward marriage. The sample is composed mostly of whites (95%), so I was unable to test whether the effects of mobility differ across races. I did test whether the effects of mobility differ between men and women by reestimating all models separately by sex. No significant patterns emerged.

Strategy.   Cohabitation and marriage are defined by age-specific transition rates governing offspring's union-formation experiences, and hazard modeling is the appropriate analytical technique to estimate the effects of mobility history and family-of-origin variables. The analyses focused on person-years after age 16. During each of these person-years, individuals were coded according to whether their first-union experience was cohabitation or marriage, or if neither union-formation transition was experienced. Individuals were censored from subsequent person-years after experiencing either cohabitation or marriage. Because both cohabitation and marriage rates increase throughout the teenage and young-adult years, all models controlled for age. Thus, for each offspring, age was a time-varying covariate that changed by one year for each subsequent person-year, but other predictors were constant across all person-years. According to typical event history structure, all person-years were pooled together and analyzed simultaneously.

I followed previous research on first-union formation and examined four union-formation contrasts (Axinn and Thornton, 1993; Clarkberg,

Stolzenberg, and Waite, 1995; Thornton, 1991; Thornton, Axinn, and Teachman, 1995). First, I estimated the total union-formation rate ignoring whether the union was cohabitation or marriage. For the second and third analyses, cohabitation and marriage were two separate destinations (i.e., risks) that competed in terminating the single state. For the marriage rate, people who cohabited were included in the analysis up to the year of cohabitation, and then were censored at the time of their cohabitation. For the cohabitation rate, people who married were included in the analysis up to the year of marriage, and then were censored at the time of their marriage. The fourth analysis was based on only those individuals who formed a first union, and estimated the effects of mobility on the probability that the first union was cohabitation versus marriage.

RESULTS

(Table not shown.) Offspring who moved two times are 36% more likely to enter into a union, and those who moved three or more times are 63% more likely to enter into a union, compared with offspring who did not move. Remember, though, that this rate does not distinguish between marriage and cohabitation. The next three comparisons will decompose these effects.

Looking next at marriage, the results do not provide evidence that family mobility affects the rate at which adult offspring move into a marital union. On the other hand, the next comparison shows that mobility is associated with an increase in the odds of cohabiting as a first-union experience. Compared with the odds for offspring who made no moves between 1980 and 1992, the odds of cohabiting are 1.3 times greater for one move, 1.9 times greater for two moves, and 2.1 times greater for three or more moves. Put another way, the odds of cohabiting are 113% greater (100[2.133 − 1]) for offspring who made three or more moves than for offspring who made no moves.

The differential effects of mobility on cohabitation and marriage patterns are evident in the last contrast, which estimated the odds of cohabiting versus marrying among those who formed a first union. The results are particularly striking. Indeed, at all levels of mobility, offspring who move are more likely to cohabit in their first-union experience than nonmovers.

Overall, prior mobility experiences increase the rate at which one forms a first union in adulthood. However, as the results show, this is entirely due to the increased rate of entrance into cohabiting unions and the greater probability of forming a cohabiting union instead of a marital union. These results strongly support the first hypothesis.

I find that parental supervision and support and family structure differences are responsible for part or all of the effects of mobility.

The variables that account for the reduction in the effects of mobility are parental supervision, mother support, and both family structure measures. Higher levels of parental supervision and mother support are associated with lower rates of entry into a first union, whereas each additional year spent in a single-parent or stepparent family is associated with a higher rate of entry into a first union. The results indicate that offspring from single-parent and stepparent families enter into unions at earlier ages, and offspring from households with more supervision and support enter into unions at later ages. These patterns are supported in the next model, which estimated the marriage rate. Adult offspring have greater odds of marrying and at earlier ages for each unit increase in parental supervision and father support and for each year spent in a stepparent family.

Consistent with most research, higher levels of parental income, education, and marital quality are associated with lower rates of union formation and marriage. Few of the religion variables are significant, although Fundamentalists enter into unions and marriage at higher rates than do liberal and moderate Protestants.

In addition, neither the sex nor the race of the offspring explains the effects of mobility.

Parental supervision, parental support, and family structure influence movement into cohabiting unions. Looking first at the cohabitation rate, the annual probability of cohabiting is lower at greater levels of parental supervision and father support, but higher among adult offspring from single-parent and stepparent families. Yet, these variables are unable to explain all of the effects of mobility on the cohabitation rate. Although the effect of one prior move becomes nonsignificant, the coefficients for two and three or more moves remain significant. However, it is important to note that the decrease in the effect size for three or more moves is statistically significant. Still, adult offspring who moved at least two times between 1980 and 1992 have higher rates of cohabitation, compared with nonmovers and net of significant parenting and family structure effects. In the last comparison, similar patterns emerge. Each year spent in a single-parent family increases the odds of cohabitation by 24%, whereas each one-unit increase in parental supervision decreases the odds of cohabitation by 10% among adult offspring who have already formed a first union.

Unlike the results found in the first two comparisons, family background control variables do help to explain the effects of mobility on cohabitation rates and on the odds of cohabiting instead of marrying (results not shown). Parental education emerges as the primary explanatory variable and is associated with lower rates of cohabitation and the odds that cohabitation is the first-union transition.

DISCUSSION

This research uses a national and intergenerational data set to examine three questions: (a) How do prior mobility experiences with one's family influence movement into cohabitation and marriage in adulthood? (b) To what extent are the effects of mobility due to certain parenting practices—supervision and support? and (c) To what extent do family structure differences that are known to distinguish movers and nonmovers and that are associated with parenting practices and union formation confound the findings? The event history results indicate that offspring who moved frequently between 1980 and 1992 have higher annual probabilities of cohabiting and of cohabiting at earlier ages. In addition, offspring who moved frequently are more likely to cohabit than to marry among offspring who had already entered a first union.

Are these mobility effects explained by parenting practices and family structure? Not entirely. As suggested by previous research, higher levels of parental supervision and parental support are associated with later ages at marriage and decreased odds of entering into cohabiting unions. Time spent in single-parent and stepparent families increases the rate of entry into cohabitation and increases the odds that offspring choose cohabitation over marriage as their first-union transition. These family variables explain all of the significant effects of one move and significant parts of the effects of two and three or more moves. Therefore, higher levels of mobility have direct effects on union-formation transitions and indirect effects that operate through several family-of-origin variables. All models were estimated with additional controls for a wide range of family-of-origin variables that have been shown to affect union-formation behaviors among adult children.

Because this sample of offspring made moves at varying ages, I reestimated the series of full models to determine if the ages at mobility were associated with union transitions (results not shown). No consistent effects emerged, and it appears that the number of moves is more important than the age at which those moves occurred. I also reestimated marriage rates and included those with prior cohabitation experiences (results not shown). Unlike the results presented in this article, these results showed that offspring who made three or more moves have lower rates of marriage, or later ages at marriage, compared with offspring who made no moves. Additional analysis suggests that this result is explained entirely by the fact that offspring who moved more frequently as children are more likely to cohabit, which tends to delay marriage. This is consistent with Bumpass, Sweet, and Cherlin (1991), who find that recent delays in marriage are explained by increased rates of cohabitation. Therefore, mobility influences first-union transitions mainly through cohabitation, and not through marriage.

The relationship among mobility, cohabitation, and marriage is potentially complex. For example, I found that cohabitation rates are higher among those who moved as children, and cohabitation tends to delay marriage (Bumpass, Sweet, and Cherlin, 1991). Yet, premarital pregnancies among those who cohabit tend to accelerate movement into marriage (Manning, 1993), and childhood mobility is associated with a greater risk of premarital sex (Stack, 1994), and, perhaps, premarital pregnancy. Sorting out these complexities requires future research to examine one additional and important question: How do the contemporary and adult characteristics of the offspring alter the results? Childhood mobility may be predictive of adult outcomes that influence one's union-formation decisions. For example, extensive research finds that children who move have lower academic grades and achievement, are more likely to drop out of high school, and are less likely to earn a college degree than their nonmobile counterparts (Astone and McLanahan, 1994; Hagan, MacMillan, and Wheaton, 1996). In turn, lower levels of human and financial capital decrease the odds of entering into marriage and increase the odds of entering into cohabitation (Nakosteen and Zimmer, 1997; Thornton, Axinn, and Teachman, 1995). Therefore, offspring's adult characteristics may represent another indirect path linking prior mobility experiences and union-formation transitions. Research along these lines may provide additional insight into the results found in this article. It is clear, though, that offspring who moved frequently earlier in life proceed upon a different union-formation path than do offspring who did not move or moved infrequently.

REFERENCES

Amato, Paul R., and Alan Booth. 1997. *A Generation at Risk: Growing Up in an Era of Family Upheaval.* Cambridge, Mass.: Harvard University Press.

Astone, Nan M., and Sara S. McLanahan. 1991. "Family Structure, Parental Practices and High School Completion." *American Sociological Review* 56:309–20.

———. 1994. "Family Structure, Residential Mobility, and School Dropout: A Research Note." *Demography* 31:575–84.

Axinn, William G., and Arland Thornton. 1992. "The Influence of Parental Resources on the Timing of the Transition to Marriage." *Social Science Research* 21:261–85.

———. 1993. "Mothers, Children, and Cohabitation: The Intergenerational Effects of Attitudes and Behaviors." *American Sociological Review* 58:233–46.

Berk, Richard A. 1983. "An Introduction to Sample Selection Bias in Sociological Data." *American Sociological Review* 48:386–98.

Booth, Alan, Paul R. Amato, David R. Johnson, and John N. Edwards. 1993. *Marital Instability over the Life Course: Methodology Report for the Fourth Wave.* Lincoln: University of Nebraska Bureau of Sociological Research.

Booth, Alan, and David R. Johnson. 1985. "Tracking Respondents in a Telephone Interview Panel Selected by Random Digit Dialing." *Sociological Methods and Research* 14:53–64.

Bumpass, Larry L., James A. Sweet, and Andrew J. Cherlin. 1991. "The Role of Cohabitation in Declining Rates of Marriage." *Journal of Marriage and the Family* 53:913–27.

Burgess, Ernest W., Harvey J. Locke, and Margaret M. Thomes. 1963. *The Family: From Institution to Companionship.* New York: American Book Company.

Bursik, Robert J., and Harold G. Grasmick. 1993. "Economic Deprivation and Neighborhood Crime Rates, 1960–1980." *Law and Society Review* 27:263–83.

Clarkberg, Marin, Ross M. Stolzenberg, and Linda J. Waite. 1995. "Attitudes, Values, and Entrance into Cohabitational versus Marital Unions." *Social Forces* 74:609–34.

Coleman, James S. 1988. "Social Capital in the Creation of Human Capital." *American Journal of Sociology* 94:S94–S120.

Cunningham, J. D., and J. K. Antill. 1995. "Current Trends in Nonmarital Cohabitation: In Search of the POSSLQ." Pp. 148–72 in J. T. Wood and S. Duck, eds., *Under-Studied Relationships: Off the Beaten Track.* Thousand Oaks, Calif.: Sage.

Glenn, Norval D., and Beth A. Shelton. 1985. "Regional Differences in Divorce in the United States." *Journal of Marriage and the Family* 47:641–52.

Hagan, John, Ross MacMillan, and Blair Wheaton. 1996. "New Kid in Town: Social Capital and the Life Course Effects of Family Mobility on Children." *American Sociological Review* 61:368–85.

Hansen, Karen A. 1995. *Geographic Mobility: March 1993 to March 1994. U.S. Bureau of the Census, Current Population Reports, P20-485.* Washington, D.C.: GPO.

Hogan, Dennis P., and Evelyn M. Kitagawa. 1985. "The Impact of Social Status, Family Structure, and Neighborhood on the Fertility of Black Adolescents." *American Journal of Sociology* 90:825–55.

Kasarda, John, and Morris Janowitz. 1974. "Community Attachment in Mass Society." *American Sociological Review* 39:328–39.

Li, Jiang H., and Roger A. Wojtkiewicz. 1994. "Childhood Family Structure and Entry into First Marriage." *The Sociological Quarterly* 35:247–68.

Long, Larry L. 1992. "International Perspectives on the Residential Mobility of America's Children." *Journal of Marriage and the Family* 54:861–69.

Luster, Tom, and Stephen A. Small. 1994. "Factors Associated with Sexual Risk-Taking Behaviors among Adolescents." *Journal of Marriage and the Family* 56:622–32.

Maccoby, Eleanor, and J. M. Martin. 1983. "Socialization in the Context of the Family: Parent-Child Interaction." Pp. 1–101 in E. M. Hetherington, ed., *Handbook of Child Psychology: Socialization, Personality, and Social Development,* vol. 4. New York: Wiley.

Manning, Wendy D. 1993. "Marriage and Cohabitation following Premarital Conception." *Journal of Marriage and the Family* 55:839–50.

Myers, Scott M. 1996. "An Interactive Model of Religiosity Inheritance: The Importance of Family Context." *American Sociological Review* 61:858–66.

Nakosteen, Robert A., and Michael A. Zimmer. 1997. "Men, Money, and Marriage: Are High Earners More Prone Than Low Earners to Marry?" *Social Science Quarterly* 78:66–82.

Park, Robert E. [1916] 1969. "The City: Suggestions for Investigation of Human Behavior in the Urban Environment." Pp. 91–130 in R. Sennet, ed., *Classic Essays on the Culture of Cities.* New York: Appleton-Century-Croft.

Sampson, Robert J. 1988. "Local Friendship Ties and Community Attachment in Mass Society: A Multilevel Systemic Model." *American Sociological Review* 53:766–79.

Sampson, Robert J., and John H. Laub. 1993. *Crime in the Making: Pathways and Turning Points through Life.* Cambridge, Mass.: Harvard University Press.

South, Scott J. 1987. "Metropolitan Migration and Social Problems." *Social Science Quarterly* 68:3–18.

Stack, Steven S. 1994. "The Effect of Geographic Mobility on Premarital Sex." *Journal of Marriage and the Family* 56:204–208.

Stolzenberg, Ross M., and Daniel A. Relles. 1990. "Theory Testing in a World of Constrained Research Design." *Sociological Methods and Research* 18:395–415.

Thornton, Arland. 1989. "Changing Attitudes toward Family Issues in the United States." *Journal of Marriage and the Family* 51:873–93.

———. 1991. "Influence of the Marital History of Parents on the Marital and Cohabitational Experiences of Children." *American Journal of Sociology* 96:868–94.

Thornton, Arland, William G. Axinn, and Jay D. Teachman. 1995. "The Influence of School Enrollment and Accumulation on Cohabitation and Marriage in Early Adulthood." *American Sociological Review* 60:762–74.

Voydanoff, Patricia. 1980. "Work Roles as Stressors in Corporate Families." *Family Relations* 29:489–94.

Yamaguchi, Kazuo. 1991. *Event History Analysis.* Newbury Park, Calif.: Sage.

NEIGHBORHOOD RACIAL-COMPOSITION PREFERENCES: EVIDENCE FROM A MULTIETHNIC METROPOLIS

Camille Zubrinsky Charles

It is essential to understand the dynamics of racial residential segregation in multiethnic urban environments, as such settings will prevail in the future. Four of the five largest metropolitan areas—New York, Los Angeles, Chicago, and Houston—simultaneously have large numbers of Black, Latino, and Asian residents. According to Farley and Frey (1993), 37 metropolitan areas in the U.S. are now multiethnic, in the sense that the proportion of two or more racial minority groups exceeds their national representation. These cities span all regions of the country, highlighting the importance of moving beyond traditional two-group (usually Black-White) analyses. Of particular interest is Los Angeles, one of the largest, most racially and ethnically diverse cities in the world. According to figures from the U.S. Bureau of the Census (1990), L.A. County is 42% White, 11% Black, 37% Latino, and 10% Asian.

The racial and ethnic diversity that characterizes Los Angeles stands in sharp contrast to its high degree of racial residential segregation. Los Angeles is one of 29 cities in which Blacks are hyper-segregated from Whites—experiencing "extreme, multidimensional, and cumula-tive residential segregation" (Denton 1994:49). Table 1 summarizes residential segregation in Los Angeles using the Index of Dissimilarity, a measure of evenness, for the four major racial groups in Los Angeles. These figures illustrate the extreme nature of Black segregation from Whites, and from Latinos and Asians as well; they also reveal strikingly high Latino-White segregation and moderate Asian-White segregation.

Researchers have put forth several arguments to explain racial and ethnic residential segregation in the U.S. The *socioeconomic differences* argument—that groups live separately as a result of differences in economic resources—has for many years been discounted as a major determinant of Black-White segregation, as Blacks are severely segregated from Whites irrespective of socioeconomic resources (Taeuber and Taeuber 1965; Schnare 1977; Kain 1986; Massey and Denton 1993). By contrast, research on Latino and Asian segregation suggests that residential mobility and proximity to Whites increase with improved socioeconomic status (Massey and Mullan 1984; Massey and Fong 1990; Alba and Logan 1993). More recently, how-

TABLE 1 Racial Residential Segregation in Los Angeles County, 1990

	Black	Latino	Asian
White	.730	.611	.462
Black		.595	.693
Latino			.511

Source: U.S. Bureau of the Census.

ever, Logan and colleagues (1996:451) document a positive relationship between objective socioeconomic status (measured using income, education, and homeownership status) and the locational attainment of Blacks, as well as Latinos and Asians. Documenting a connection between socioeconomic status and residential segregation among Blacks for the first time, their findings, nonetheless, lead to the conclusion that "Assimilation processes—those linking socioeconomic with residential mobility—apply unequally to Blacks and to other minorities." Socioeconomic status indicators are least effective in predicting the percentage of non-Hispanic Whites in both poor and affluent Blacks' neighborhoods, and these differences are striking. Moreover, Blacks experience a smaller return on socioeconomic status when predicting tract median income, and are the only group for whom homeownership has negative consequences for proximity to Whites (Logan, et al. 1996). Finally, Jargowsky (1996) documents a trend toward increased economic segregation *within* both Black and Latino communities, but is unable to attribute this trend to changes in the metropolitan context, structural economic transformations, or shifts in social distance. All in all, research suggests that objective indicators of socioeconomic status are good predictors of Latino and Asian residential proximity to Whites and, at best, fair predictors of Black-White segregation.

The inability of the socioeconomic differences hypothesis to explain persisting racial residential segregation has shifted attention to group differences in neighborhood racial composition preferences (Clark 1986, 1992; Farley, et al. 1978, 1993). According to this line of reasoning, residential segregation persists because some group members prefer to live among their own. There is disagreement, however, about the extent to which these preferences indicate ethnocentric social preferences (Clark 1986:108–109, 1992), anti-out-group

affect (Farley, et al. 1993, 1994; Massey and Denton 1993), or an effort to preserve relative status advantages (Jankowski 1995; Bobo and Zubrinsky 1996; Gans 1999).

Some research suggests that active racial prejudice plays a role in reproducing racial residential segregation (Massey and Denton 1989, 1993). Some of the strongest evidence of this comes from two recent analyses: Farley and colleagues (1994) showed that anti-Black stereotypes strongly predict neighborhood racial composition preferences among Whites in Detroit. This analysis replicated the innovative Farley-Schuman showcard methodology developed for the 1976 Detroit Area Study (Farley, et al. 1978). Bobo and Zubrinsky (1996) analyzed multiethnic data from Los Angeles, concluding that negative out-group stereotypes reduced openness to integration among White, Black, Latino, and Asian respondents.

Nonetheless, our understanding of just how much and when prejudice matters is rudimentary at best. Recent research in this area faces three major shortcomings. First, prior studies have not directly assessed composition preferences in a multiethnic manner. Farley and colleagues rely on a Black-White dichotomy that, while possibly relevant to Detroit, is no longer representative of many U.S. metropolitan areas (Wood and Lee 1990; Farley and Frey 1993; Alba, et al. 1995). Moreover, the Farley-Schuman methodology is based on a series of questions that differ for Whites and non-Whites, making comparisons across racial groups difficult. Likewise, Bobo and Zubrinsky (1996) analyzed data on a multiracial sample, but measured attitudes toward just one out-group at a time, using a single forced-choice item, rather than measuring reactions to a variety of possible multiracial settings. Second, prior research tends to focus narrowly on stereotypes as predictors of neighborhood preferences, largely ignoring other possible factors. Finally, despite assertions that residential segregation is the result of mutually-expressed ethnocentric tendencies (Clark 1986, 1992; Patterson 1997; Thernstrom and Thernstrom 1997), prior studies have focused on preferences for out-group neighbors, never directly testing the effects of various factors on preferences for same-race neighbors.

This research addresses these lacunae in our understanding of the relationship between stereotyping and segregation, while also examining the utility of a major innovation on the Farley-Schuman showcard methodology. Respondents of a large (N = 4,025) multiracial sample were asked to create their own "ideal" multiethnic neighborhood instead of rating several predetermined alternatives. This measure: 1) allows respondents to consider integration with several out-groups simultaneously, solving the dilemma of a two-group measure in an increasingly multi-group society; 2) is based on a single question and is the same for all respondents; and 3) yields a measure of preferences that is less reactive, thus, reducing the likelihood of false, socially desirable responses. Analyses must also reflect, as accurately as possible, the diverse nature of respondents' communities, as well as society more generally. With these issues in mind, I examine the importance of several factors on neighborhood racial-composition preferences for both out-group and same-race neighbors, including some that have been neglected in the literature but that likely influence residential location decisions.

STAKE IN THE NEIGHBORHOOD

In an analysis of stable, integrated neighborhoods, Ellen (1997) found that Whites in racially-mixed neighborhoods tended to be young, single, and childless, and that White renters were more willing to move into and remain in racially mixed areas than White homeowners were. And research has consistently

shown that being a parent effects overall neighborhood satisfaction (Campbell, et al. 1976; Campbell 1981; St. John and Bates 1990). Yet, prior studies of preferences have failed to consider these important life-course issues (Harris 1999). Parents with minor children may be especially interested in maintaining cultural ties and passing their cultural heritage on to their children, which may result in preferences for more same-race neighbors. They may also place greater importance on certain criteria for determining neighborhood quality—the availability of recreational facilities, the quality of public schools, and levels of public safety—for which neighborhood racial composition often serve as a proxy. In the latter case, preferences for out-group neighbors may depend on the race of potential neighbors. Homeowners have a financial, as well as a psychic investment, to protect, making it more difficult to leave if the neighborhood changes in ways they find undesirable. If the presence of out-group members is perceived as undesirable for any reason (e.g., outright hostility, or fear of "neighborhood decline"), the "permanence" of homeownership might translate into active resistance to integration with those groups. For these reasons, parents of minor children and homeowners can be said to have a greater stake in their neighborhoods than non-parents (or parents of adult children) and renters.

Traditionally, close proximity to Whites is associated with high quality neighborhood amenities, and close proximity to Blacks (and increasingly Latinos) with poor quality amenities and neighborhood decay (Wilson 1987; Massey and Denton 1993). Given these associations, I expect that members of high-status groups (Whites and Asians) with a high stake in their neighborhoods will prefer fewer low-status-group neighbors (Blacks and Latinos) and more same-race or other high-status-group neighbors than those with a low stake in the neighborhood. Conversely, low-status-group homeowners and/or parents with a high neighborhood stake may prefer more out-group neighbors, especially high-status Whites, compared to low-status group members who rent and/or are childless. Nativity status may complicate this relationship for Latinos and Asians. Foreign-born members of each group may prefer more same-race neighbors irrespective of neighborhood stake. Such preferences could, again, reflect a desire to maintain cultural ties and pass them on to children, and a need for co-ethnic institutions and contacts. Another possibility, however, is that the desire for upward social mobility is more pronounced among the foreign-born, part of "making it" in America. If so, aversion to low-status neighbors (especially Blacks) and preferences for high-status neighbors (especially Whites) could be greater among the foreign-born compared to native-born co-ethnics and other groups.

NEIGHBORHOOD CONTEXT

It makes sense to think that the racial and socioeconomic composition of one's current neighborhood influences preferences in meaningful ways. According to the contact hypothesis, sustained contact with members of out-groups leads to more tolerant attitudes toward those groups (Allport 1954; Sigelman and Welch 1993; Ellison and Powers 1994). The evidence regarding the effect of actual neighborhood racial composition on racial attitudes, however, is mixed. Darden and Parsons (1981) and, more recently, Sigelman and Welch (1993) found that interracial contact in neighborhood settings positively impacts racial attitudes; the latter also concluded that such contact increases desires for integration. Alternatively, Farley and colleagues (1978) found no relationship between the two; Jackman and Crane (1986) suggest that the effects of interracial contact are selective and that intimacy is less important than a variety of contacts.

To the extent that issues of race and class are often entangled, the socioeconomic status of one's neighborhood might also influence neighborhood racial composition preferences. Economically disadvantaged neighborhoods are undesirable because they have higher rates of unemployment, criminal activity, and unkempt property (Leven, et al. 1976; Wilson 1987; Clark 1988). At the same time, these neighborhoods are likely to be largely populated by Blacks and Latinos, so that greater exposure to poverty (or an interest in avoiding increased exposure to poverty) may adversely impact preferences for integration with these groups.

Taken together, my expectation is that, across respondent- and target-group pairings, increased contact with out-groups increases preferences for integration. The degree of positive influence may vary, however, in conjunction with the relative status of groups (Bobo and Zubrinsky 1996). For example, among Whites, increased exposure to Asians may result in more positive attitudes than the same level of exposure to Blacks. Once again, nativity-status differences among Latinos and Asians might add an interesting twist. For example, Central American immigrants have settled in large numbers in south central Los Angeles, historically a predominantly Black community. This has led to some conflict between the two groups. In such a case, increased residential contact could negatively impact the preferences of each group (Blacks and foreign-born Latinos) for integration with the other.

RACE-RELATED ATTITUDES AND PERCEPTIONS

This class of factors includes two measures—perceived social class difference (as opposed to objective social class difference, discussed above) and racial stereotypes—that have received a good deal of empirical attention in the literature on racial attitudes and preferences, and a third that has not been tested empirically. First, it has been argued that groups *perceived* as economically disadvantaged (whether they, in fact, are or not) are less desirable neighbors. The reasons are similar to those discussed above regarding actual neighborhood socioeconomic status. The perception of social class disadvantage is not, it is argued, representative of an aversion to Black or Latino neighbors per se. Instead, it is said to represent a desire to avoid living among poor people (Clark 1988; Thernstrom and Thernstrom 1997:223). Concerns of this sort may be more salient among economically advantaged groups interested in maintaining their elevated social status (Leven, et al. 1976; Jankowski 1995; Bobo and Zubrinsky 1996; Gans 1999).

As such, it is expected that groups perceived as economically disadvantaged relative to one's own group will be less desirable neighbors than those perceived as economically advantaged. For minority group members—regardless of nativity status—this suggests that Whites will be the most desirable out-group and Blacks the least desirable. For Whites (majority group members), Asians are likely to be more desirable neighbors, followed by Latinos and finally Blacks. Economically advantaged groups (i.e., Whites and Asians) should also prefer more same-race neighbors than Blacks and Latinos, who are disproportionately poor.

The influence of negative racial stereotypes on preferences for out-group neighbors has received a great deal of empirical attention. Recent studies by Farley and colleagues (1994) and Bobo and Zubrinsky (1996), both conclude that racial stereotypes have a strong significant effect on preferences for out-group neighbors. The importance of stereotyping to our understanding of neighborhood racial composition preferences is twofold, each related to prejudice. At its most basic level, prejudice is imbued with negative affect and negative stereotypes that are unreceptive to reason and new information (Jackman 1994). This understanding of racial stereotypes is consistent with the traditional definition of prejudice, which emphasizes simple out-group antipathy (Allport 1954; Pettigrew 1982), and is the crux of Massey and Denton's (1993) argument in *American Apartheid*. The findings of both Farley and colleagues and Bobo and Zubrinsky (1996) support this argument.

As indicators of prejudice, racial stereotypes can also be examined in light of Blumer's (1958:3, 3–4) theory of race prejudice as a sense of group position. Blumer argues that prejudice "exists basically in a sense of group position, rather than in a set of feelings which members of one racial group have toward the members of another racial group." By viewing prejudice and stereotypes as more than simple out-group hostility, attention shifts away from individual feelings, focusing, instead, on a collective process in which "racial groups form images of themselves and of others . . . defining their positions vis-à-vis each other." From this perspective, prejudice has more to do with socially learned commitments to maintaining a particular group status or relative group position (Quillian 1996). With respect to racial stereotypes and neighborhood racial-composition preferences, then, what matters is the magnitude of difference that in-group members perceive between their own group and particular out-groups. Bobo and Zubrinsky's (1996) findings also support this definition of prejudice.

Accordingly, I anticipate that, as stereotypes of an out-group become increasingly unfavorable relative to one's own group (indicating the relative superiority of one's own group), preferences for integration with that group will decline. I expect that this is especially true for Whites as members of the dominant group, and least true for the lowest-status minority group—Blacks. Compared to native-born co-ethnics, the effect of stereotyping may be more extreme, particularly when potential neighbors are Black. Once again, this could be the result of heightened awareness among the foreign-born of who the "haves" and "have-nots" are and a concomitant interest in upward social mobility and acceptance.

Finally, Clark (1986, 1992) suggests that members of all racial/ethnic groups prefer to live in neighborhoods that are predominantly same-race, and that this preference is due to strong in-group attachment, rather than out-group hostility. If this is true, persisting racial residential segregation—particularly among Blacks—is to a substantial degree, a voluntary phenomenon unrelated to negative racial stereotypes or prejudice (Clark 1992; Patterson 1997; Thernstrom and Thernstrom 1997).

In this analysis, in-group attachment is measured as common fate identity—the belief that, "what happens to my group happens to me." Research suggests that feelings of common fate are important aspects of both African American and Asian American group identities (Gurin, Hatchett, and Jackson 1989; Espiritu 1992; Tate 1992; Dawson 1994, 1999; Tuan 1999), and that assumptions of common fate influence in-group favoritism (Tajfel 1982). Strong in-group attachment, then, should increase preferences for same-race neighbors, irrespective of respondent race or nativity-status; however, this relationship may be stronger among foreign-born Latinos and Asians. Conversely, preferences for out-group neighbors should be negatively impacted by strong in-group attachment. And, if, in fact, in-group attachment is not tied to hostility toward one or more out-groups—that is, if in-group attachment is race-neutral—I would also expect its influence on out-group preferences to be the same across target groups.

DATA AND METHODS

Data are from the *1993–94 Los Angeles Survey of Urban Inequality* (LASUI), a large, multi-faceted research project designed to explore in-

equality in Los Angeles County. The LASUI is a face-to-face household survey of adults 21 years of age or older living in Los Angeles County between September 9, 1993 and August 15, 1994. The primary sampling unit for the survey is the census tract stratified by 1) racial/ethnic composition, and 2) the percentage of the population with incomes below the poverty line.

Respondents identified as one of the following: Non-Hispanic/White (N = 863), African American/Black (N = 1,118), Latino (N = 988), or Asian (overwhelmingly of Korean, Japanese, or Chinese descent, N = 1,056), for a total of 4,025 respondents. In addition to generating over-samples of Blacks and Asians, efforts were made to fully capture the views, opinions, and experiences of Los Angeles' significant immigrant populations. To accomplish this, the English-language version of the survey instrument was also translated into Spanish, Korean, Mandarin, and Cantonese. Those respondents who either did not speak English or who preferred to conduct the interview in one of these other languages were interviewed using the appropriate foreign-language questionnaire. Race-matching occurred in 70% of the completed interviews. Within each major racial group, the distribution of sample characteristics on key social background factors closely resembles data from the 1990 Census (Bobo, et al. 1993).

RESULTS

Neighborhood Racial-Composition Preferences

To measure neighborhood racial-composition preferences in a multiethnic context, I introduce a major modification to the Farley-Schuman showcard methodology. All LASUI respondents were shown a blank neighborhood showcard similar to Figure 1 and asked to

Figure 1   Multi-Ethnic Neighborhood Experiment Showcard. Source: 1993–94 Los Angeles Survey of Urban Inequality.

specify the racial make-up of their ideal neighborhood. Respondents were instructed in the following manner:

> *Now I'd like you to imagine an ideal neighborhood that had the ethnic and racial mix you, personally, would feel most comfortable in. Here is a blank neighborhood card like those we have been using. Using the letters A for Asian, B for Black, H for Hispanic, and W for White, please put a letter in each of these houses to represent your ideal neighborhood where you would most like to live. Please be sure to fill in all of the houses.*

The variables—percent White, percent Black, percent Latino, and percent Asian—used in the analysis are simply the sum of each group represented on a respondent's card, divided by the total number of houses (including the respondent's house) and multiplied by 100.

Table 2 provides summary information for all respondent- and target-group pairings. The first row of each target-group block is the mean percentage of that group in each respondent category's ideal neighborhood. The percentage of respondents creating a neighborhood without any target-group members is presented in the second row of each target-group block. The percentage of respondents creating an entirely target-group neighborhood is located in the third row of each target-group block.

There is a tendency among all groups to specify substantially integrated neighborhoods, while at the same time preferring one where in-group representation always exceeds that of any particular out-group. Several other distinct patterns also emerge. First, while all groups prefer neighborhoods dominated by co-ethnics, this preference is strongest among Whites. The average ideal neighborhood among White respondents approaches 50% same-race, compared to mean same-race preferences of roughly 41% among Latinos and Asians and about 37% for Blacks. Moreover, Whites are the group most likely to prefer *entirely* same-race neighborhoods (11.16%)—a rate more than one and one-half times that of Latinos (6.60%) and Asians (7.06%), and four times that of Blacks (2.76%).

In addition, Blacks are *always* the least-preferred out-group neighbors. This is seen in two ways. First, Blacks are the most likely to be completely excluded from the ideal neighborhoods of Whites, Latinos, and Asians. Nearly one-fifth (18.91%) of Whites express integration preferences that exclude Blacks entirely, as do roughly one-third of Latinos and a striking 40% of Asians. Fewer than 1 in 10 Latinos or Asians insist on entirely same-race neighborhoods, but somewhere between 3 and 4 of 10 want no Black neighbors. Both the Latino and Asian samples are overwhelmingly foreign-born (73.5% of Latinos and 88.2% of Asians), and it is among this sub-sample of respondents that such high levels of Black exclusion occurs. Native-born Latinos and Asians prefer significantly more Black neighbors, on average, than their foreign-born co-ethnics, and have rates of Black exclusion similar to that of Whites (17%, and 15%, respectively). Among the foreign-born, however, 37% of Latinos and 43% of Asians exclude Blacks entirely. These striking differences between native- and foreign-born preferences for Black neighbors may reflect growing racial tensions between long-time Black residents and immi-

TABLE 2 Summary Statistics, Multi-Ethnic Neighborhood Showcard Experiment

Target Group	Respondent Race				
	Whites	**Blacks**	**Latinos**	**Asians**	**f/x²**
Whites					
Mean %	49.21%	23.67%	28.42%	32.98%	87.82***
No Whites	0.24%	10.10%	12.39%	7.24%	208.20***
All Whites	11.16	0	1.44	.52	192.03***
Blacks					
Mean %	16.15%	37.41%	13.76%	11.05%	182.83***
No Blacks	18.91%	0.72%	31.66%	39.94%	258.33***
All Blacks	0	2.76	0	0	93.36***
Latinos					
Mean %	17.07%	21.32%	41.23%	15.57%	146.63***
No Latinos	17.05%	8.55%	2.76%	26.42%	220.52***
All Latinos	0	0	6.60	0	166.20***
Asians					
Mean %	18.04%	17.77%	17.06%	40.98%	86.00***
No Asians	15.88%	15.57%	22.43%	0.54%	78.09***
All Asians	0	0	0.10	7.06	233.32***
All Out Groups					
Mean %	51.26%	62.72%	59.22%	59.60%	18.35***
No Out-Group	11.16%	2.76%	6.60%	7.06%	45.12***
All Out-Group	0.24	.72	2.76	.54	43.51***
N	818	1,082	982	1,027	

Notes: The percentage of each racial group in a respondent's "ideal" neighborhood is the sum of each group included in the experiment in Figure 1, divided by the sum of all houses, including the respondent's. ***$p < .001$.

Source: 1993–94 Los Angeles Survey of Urban Inequality.

grant newcomers (e.g., Central American immigrants settling in south central Los Angeles and Korean immigrants who own and operate small businesses in predominantly Black areas. See Johnson, Oliver, and Farell 1992). Despite their status at least-preferred neighbors, Black respondents appear least resistant to integration. Blacks have the lowest mean percentage of same-race neighbors (37.41%); are significantly more comfortable as the numerical minority in an integrated neighborhood (mean, all out-groups, 62.72%); and are significantly less likely than all other groups to create all-same-race neighborhoods (2.76%). These patterns

are consistent with previous research indicating that Blacks favor integration for reasons of racial harmony (Farley, et al. 1978). Finally, all minority groups prefer integration with Whites to other-race minorities.

Taken together, these preliminary results support the assertion that the race of potential out-group neighbors is important to our understanding of neighborhood racial composition preferences. While all groups express preferences for large numbers of co-ethnics, a rank-ordering of out-group neighbors is clearly evident: Whites are always the most desirable out-group neighbors, and Blacks are always the least desirable. In between these extremes are Asians and Latinos (with the exception of Black respondents, Asians are always more desirable neighbors than Latinos are). This hierarchical pattern is consistent with each group's social and economic position in contemporary American society (Jaynes and Williams 1989; Massey and Denton 1990; Bobo and Zubrinsky 1996).

The patterns are also consistent with findings from previous research based on the Farley-Schuman experiment (Zubrinsky and Bobo 1996), with some important differences. For example, Zubrinsky and Bobo found that 9% of Whites were unwilling to enter a neighborhood with a single Latino household, and 4% expressed discomfort with the entrance of a single Latino neighbor into a previously all-White neighborhood. By comparison, 17% of Whites completing the new experiment completely exclude Latinos. Similarly, less than 3% of Asians were unwilling to enter the least integrated neighborhoods presented to them (4 of 15 houses) irrespective of target-group race; but, when creating their own multiethnic neighborhoods, nearly 40% of Asians exclude Blacks completely, and 26% exclude Latinos completely. Such comparisons can be made across respondent-target-group combinations. More important, these new results suggest the persistence of much higher levels of aversion to integration than previously thought.

In an effort to improve our understanding of neighborhood racial-composition preferences, attention now turns to OLS regression analysis. In each set of models, the dependent measures are the neighborhood racial-composition preferences for each out-group; an additional set of models predicts preferences for same-race neighbors. The current analysis differs from the original Farley-Schuman experiment: The dependent measures for all models are based on a single, identical question, allowing easy, across-group comparisons; respondents have complete freedom in the racial make-up of their

neighborhoods; and are asked to consider several out-groups at once. Given these important differences and the inclusion of a broader range of predictors, it is hoped that this analysis offers a new and more powerful examination of the complex array of factors influencing preferences. Table 3 presents summary and coding information for all explanatory variables.

Four regression models are estimated for each outcome (not shown). For all dependent measures, interactions between race/nativity status and other factors and their impact on preferences for both out-group and same-race neighbors are considered.

PREFERENCES FOR VARIOUS OUT-GROUP NEIGHBORS

Multivariate analysis begins with a consideration of factors that influence preferences for particular out-groups as neighbors. In addition to the racial and nativity-status differences that are of central interest, there are important differences among respondents and across groups in the way that factors such as educational attainment, income, sex, age, and political ideology influence neighborhood racial composition preferences. Conservatives hold more traditional views on a range of issues, including matters of race such as stereotypes and social distance feelings; women are often found to express greater racial tolerance than men (Schuman, et al. 1997), and the better educated tend to express more positive racial attitudes than the less well educated (see Schuman, et al. 1997, though note Jackman and Muha 1984, for an important exception). There is no clear expectation regarding the effect of income on neighborhood racial composition preferences, since income effects vary depending upon the topic in question (Schuman, et al. 1997:236).

Of the social background characteristics, respondent race/nativity status is most consistently associated with neighborhood racial-

TABLE 3 **Summary Statistics, Explanatory Variables Examining "Ideal" Neighborhood Racial Composition Preferences**

	Whites	Blacks	Latinos	Asians	Total
Social background characteristics					
Born in the United States	84.2	91.0	26.5	11.8	59.8
Sex					
Male	49.3%	49.3%	50.4%	49.7%	49.7%
Age					
21–29	17.1%	26.5%	35.7%	19.2%	25.1%
30–39	24.9	28.7	28.1	22.9	26.4
40–49	22.5	18.8	17.9	23.3	20.4
50 and over	35.6	25.9	18.3	34.6	28.1
Education					
Less than high school	4.7%	11.5%	49.8%	15.5%	22.5%
High school graduate/GED	22.7	32.9	23.9	20.4	24.3
Some college	35.8	39.0	17.6	19.4	28.6
Bachelor's degree	26.1	9.2	6.8	32.0	17.4
Graduate/professional degree	10.8	7.4	1.9	12.7	7.3
Income					
Less than $20,000	14.6%	33.7%	44.1%	25.2%	28.1%
$20,000–39,999	27.5	30.7	34.2	33.1	30.6
$40,000–59,999	26.4	11.4	14.3	19.5	19.8
$60,000 and over	31.5	24.2	7.4	22.2	21.5
Political ideology					
Liberal	30.9%	43.7%	26.4%	32.1%	31.0%
Moderate	34.0	32.2	44.3	35.6	37.6
Conservative	35.1	24.1	29.3	32.3	31.4
Stake in the neighborhood					
Homeowner	52.6%	33.5%	27.3%	46.2%	40.6%
Parenting					
No/grown children at home	67.1%	62.7%	37.8%	53.7%	55.2%
Children 5 or younger at home	17.8	17.8	37.6	21.6	25.2
Children 6 to 12 at home	14.5	20.9	36.8	17.0	23.5
Children 13 to 18 at home	10.4	18.3	21.7	17.9	15.9
Neighborhood context					
Tract poverty level					
Less than 20%	96.1%	62.6%	54.6%	78.7%	75.8%
20–40%	3.7	32.2	42.0	20.9	22.2
Over 40%	0.2	5.2	3.4	0.3	2.0
Tract racial composition					
Mean % White in tract	63.5%	25.4%	24.4%	41.0%	43.2%
Mean % Black in tract	4.4	38.3	7.0	4.3	9.6
Mean % Latino in tract	21.1	27.7	58.1	28.3	35.7

(*continued*)

TABLE 3 **Summary Statistics, Explanatory Variables Examining "Ideal" Neighborhood Racial Composition Preferences (continued)**

	Whites	Blacks	Latinos	Asians	Total
Mean % Asian in tract	10.4	7.8	9.9	25.8	10.8
Race-related attitudes and perceptions					
Mean perceived SES difference score					
White target group	—	−2.1	−2.7	−0.5	−2.3
Black target group	1.6	—	−0.3	1.8	0.8
Latino target group	1.8	0.2	—	1.9	1.5
Asian target group	0.0	−1.8	−2.3	—	−1.1
Mean stereotype difference score					
White target group	—	0.0	−0.1	0.8	0.0
Black target group	1.2	—	1.1	1.8	1.2
Latino target group	1.0	0.2	—	1.4	0.9
Asian target group	0.1	−0.4	−0.7	—	−0.3
Mean common fate identity	1.5	1.9	1.6	1.6	1.6
TOTAL	863	1.119	988	1.055	4.025

Notes: Tract-level information obtained from the U.S. Bureau of the Census (1990). Due to space limitations, tract-level racial composition is reported here as a series of continuous variables. In the regression analyses, they are measured as a series of dummy variables (less than 10%, 10% to 30%, 31% to 50%, and over 50%) for each racial category. The SES and Stereotype Difference Scores are scaled from −6 to +6. High (positive) scores indicate unfavorable ratings of out-groups relative to one's in-group; low (negative) scores indicate favorable out-group ratings; 0 indicates no perceived difference. The Common Fate Identity measure ranges from 0 (no common fate identity) to 3 (strong common fate identity). $p < .001$, except Sex (n.s.).

Source: 1993–94 Los Angeles Survey of Urban Inequality.

composition preferences across target-groups. Blacks prefer fewer White neighbors than both Latinos and Asians do, irrespective of nativity status. As mentioned in the discussion of Table 2, foreign-born Latinos and Asians both prefer significantly fewer Black neighbors than Whites do; native-born Latinos and Asians do not differ significantly from Whites in their preferences for Black neighbors. It is possible that—either instead of, or in addition to—the racial tensions discussed previously—the extreme aversion to Black neighbors among the foreign-born is indicative of a heightened commitment to "making it" in America and embracing the view that socioeconomic success is equated with distance from Blacks (Portes and Rumbaut 1996). Both Blacks and native-born Asians prefer significantly more Latino neighbors than Whites do, and no significant

race/nativity status differences emerge in the Asian target-group model. Significant effects for the remaining social background variables are much less consistent and tend to be in the anticipated directions.

Research suggests that neighborhood racial composition preferences are influenced by peoples' stake in their neighborhoods (St. John and Bates 1990; Ellen 1997), and that objective characteristics of neighborhoods influence attitudes toward integration in important ways (Darden and Parsons 1981; Sigelman and Welch 1993; Ellison and Powers 1994).

Tract-level racial composition most consistently influences neighborhood racial composition preferences. Consistent with the contact hypothesis, increased contact with target-group members has a positive effect on preferences. This is especially true with respect to preferences for White and Asian neighbors, where varying degrees of exposure result in increased preferences for residential contact. When considering integration with either Blacks or Latinos, however, only respondents living in the most integrated tracts (over 50% target-group) show significantly greater preference for integration with these groups. Fewer than 1% of Whites and Asians and 5% of Latinos reside in tracts that are more than 50% Black and only between 4 and 12% of non-Latino respondents live in neighborhoods that are over 50% Latino. Thus, for the most part, target-group residential contact has no practical impact on preferences for integration with Blacks and Latinos, the two most segregated groups in Los Angeles County. Because these data are cross-sectional, however, it is not possible to say definitively whether actual neighborhood racial composition is a function of preferences or vice versa. The remaining measure of objective neighborhood characteristics has almost no effect on neighborhood racial composition preferences, reaching statistical significance only once: residents of high-poverty tracts (over 40%) prefer fewer Asian neighbors compared to residents of low-poverty tracts (less than 20%). These respondents are overwhelmingly Black and Latino (see Table 3). Here again, aversion to Asians may stem from tense relations between residents and Asian merchants.

Respondents' stake in their neighborhood also appears to have a very limited effect on neighborhood racial composition preferences. In keeping with the common belief that Blacks drive down property values, homeowners prefer significantly fewer Black neighbors than non-owners do. And, parents of teenaged children prefer significantly more Latinos in their ideal neighborhoods than parents with grown children or no children, net of other factors. In general, the addition of these four variables substantially reduces or eliminates significant social background effects of race/nativity status on preferences for both Black and Latino

neighbors. And, across target-group models there is a 22 to 40% increase in variance explained.

Charles builds on the previous analysis with three measures of race-related attitudes and perceptions: perceived social class difference, common fate identity, and racial stereo-typing. Whites (and others) may avoid neighborhoods with more than token numbers of Blacks and Latinos because these groups are more likely to be poor (Clark 1988; Quillian and Pager 1999). This behavior is said to reflect a rational desire to avoid downward social-class integration, not an aversion to Blacks or Latinos per se (Leven, et al. 1976; Clark 1988). Integration with Whites may be attractive; they are the group at the top of the economic and social hierarchy, and close proximity to Whites in "more desirable" communities represents upward social mobility. Perceived social class difference measures images of out-groups as "tending to be rich" or "tending to be poor" relative to one's own group. Respondents' out-group ratings are subtracted from their in-group ratings; possible scores range from -6 (favorable out-group perception) to $+6$ (unfavorable out-group perception), a score of 0 indicates a perception of no difference.

Common fate identity is included in this analysis based on evidence that feelings of common fate are important aspects of minority group identities (Gurin, et al. 1989; Espiritu 1992; Tate 1992; Dawson 1994, 1999; Tuan 1999), and of their influence on in-group favoritism (Tajfel 1982).

And, individuals may avoid residential contact with particular groups as the result of prejudice. Hostility can result from simple out-group antipathy (often expressed as negative stereotypes) or from socially learned expectations about group status and position (Blumer 1958; Jankowski 1995; Gans 1999), making both the presence of negative stereotypes and the magnitude of difference perceived between one's own group and particular out-groups relevant. The racial stereotyping measure is a "difference" score similar to the perceived social class difference measure that captures both aspects of prejudice. LASUI respondents rated all four racial groups on a series of stereotype traits: intelligence, preference for welfare dependence, difficulty to get along with socially, tendency to discriminate, and involvement in drugs and gangs. Scores range from −6 (favorable out-group perception) to +6 (unfavorable out-group perception), with a score of 0 indicating no perceived difference.

[R]esults provide strong support for the assertion that negative racial attitudes are potent predictors of neighborhood racial composition preferences, and that social class concerns and common fate identity are not. Of the three measures, only racial stereotyping emerges as a significant predictor of neighborhood racial composition preferences. Net of other factors, as stereotypes of out-groups become increasingly negative relative to one's own group, preferences for integration with those groups declines, irrespective of target-group race. The effect of racial stereotyping is strongest in the Black, Latino, and Asian target-group still, the effect of racial stereotyping on preferences for White neighbors satisfies rigorous statistical standards.

Perceived social class differences have no significant effect on preferences for particular out-group neighbors. Tract-level poverty is statistically significant only once, and its effect is the opposite of expectations: respondents living in high-poverty neighborhoods prefer *more* Black neighbors than their low-poverty counterparts. On the whole, then, social class concerns—whether real or perceived—do not influence preferences for out-group neighbors in any meaningful way. And, contrary to the suggestion that we avoid integration with others due to positive feelings toward our own group (Clark 1992; Patterson 1997), the sense of common fate identity has no significant effect on preferences for out-group neighbors. Results from a parametric table not shown reveal persisting respondent race/nativity status differences in preferences for particular out-groups as neighbors. Native-born Asians prefer significantly more Black and Latino neighbors than Whites do. Foreign-born Latinos and Asians appear to have more in common with each other than with their native-born co-ethnics: both prefer significantly more Whites and fewer Blacks in their ideal neighborhoods. These similarities may reflect knowledge of the American social and economic hierarchies and the desire to succeed: close proximity to Whites suggests socioeconomic success; close proximity to Blacks, socioeconomic failure. Positive education effects persist and often increase in both the White and Asian target-group models; income and political ideology continue to have only minimal effects on preferences. Sex and age have no significant effect on preferences.

The inclusion of the race-related measures reduces the negative effect of homeownership on preferences for Black neighbors by 16% and intensifies the effect of parenting teenagers on preferences for Latino neighbors (+8.7%); these remain the only significant neighborhood stake effects. In general, the effect of neighborhood characteristics on preferences for out-group neighbors is lessened, while the overall pattern of positive neighborhood racial composition associations persists. The now non-significant high-poverty tract effect in the Asian target-group model is additional evidence of the importance of racial attitudes. Finally, across target-group models, the amount of variance explained increases 14.3 to 38.9%; it should be noted, however, that the amount of variance explained is still fairly low.

PREFERENCES FOR SAME-RACE NEIGHBORS

Prior studies of neighborhood racial composition preferences (Farley, et al. 1978, 1993, 1994; Clark 1986, 1992; Bobo and Zubrinsky

1996; Zubrinsky and Bobo 1996) focus primarily on attitudes toward integration with various out-groups as neighbors. In these studies, dependent measures are based on considerations of integration with a single out-group; in the most recent of these (Clark 1992; Farley, et al. 1993; Zubrinsky and Bobo 1996), results consistently indicate that all groups prefer neighborhoods that are predominantly same-race. The interest has been in understanding the relative roles of ethnocentrism and prejudice (among other things). A new measure, where respondents consider integration with several out-groups simultaneously, however, reveals that, on average, all groups prefer neighborhoods that are predominantly out-group (e.g., a combination of the three out-group alternatives, see Table 2).

Furthermore, evidence both here and elsewhere (Bobo and Zubrinsky 1996) illustrates the elevated importance of prejudice over positive in-group attachment on out-group preferences. This suggests that prejudice is an important predictor of same-race preferences (since, in prior studies, the only alternative to avoiding one group is increasing the numbers of same-race neighbors). To date, however, there are no direct tests of factors influencing preferences for same-race neighbors; the second part of this analysis addresses this shortcoming in the literature.

(Parametric statistical table not shown.) All of the minority groups prefer fewer same-race neighbors than Whites do; and, contrary to the results presented in Table 2, Blacks do not prefer the smallest percentage of same-race neighbors, native-born Asians and Latinos do. Once again, foreign-born Latinos and Asians have more in common with each other than with their native-born co-ethnics, preferring more co-ethnic neighbors than all other non-White groups.

Age, education, and income all have less consistent effects on preferences for same-race neighbors. Respondents in their thirties and forties prefer significantly fewer same-race

neighbors than younger respondents do, and the most educated respondents prefer substantially fewer same-race neighbors than the least-educated. Respondents with $20,000 to $39,999 in annual income prefer fewer same-race neighbors than low-income respondents, and those not reporting any income in the previous year want more same-race neighbors. Sex and political ideology have no significant effect on same-race neighborhood preferences.

Respondents living in neighborhoods that are more than half same-race prefer roughly 8% more same-race neighbors in their ideal multi-ethnic neighborhoods. Sixty-one percent of all LASUI respondents—78.5% of Whites, 53.1% of Latinos, 47.7% of Blacks, and 7.3% of Asians—live in neighborhoods that are over half same-race; this is enough segregation to negatively impact preferences for out-group neighbors.

Racial stereotyping produces a significant effect on preferences for same-race neighbors. As stereotypes of out-groups become increasingly negative (positive scores reflect unfavorable ratings of out-groups), preferences for same-race neighbors increase, net of other factors. Contrary to assertions that a neutral ethnocentrism—shared by all groups—results in preferences for majority same-race neighborhoods (Clark 1992), an individual's sense of common fate identity does not significantly influence preferences for same-race neighbors.

Net of other factors, Whites still prefer the highest percentage of same-race neighbors, but are now followed by Blacks. Foreign-born similarities disappear as co-ethnics have more in common with each other: native- and foreign-born Asians prefer the fewest same-race neighbors and foreign-born and native-born Latinos fall in between Blacks and Asians.

Adding the race-related measures reduces the effect of living in a majority same-race neighborhood on preferences for such neighbors by about 15%. Middle-aged respondents continue to prefer fewer same-race neighbors than younger respondents do. A non-linear education effect emerges in which individuals with some college or with advanced degrees, prefer fewer same-race neighbors than those with less than a high school education; remaining measures of social background, neighborhood stake, and objective neighborhood characteristics are all non-significant.

RACE/NATIVITY-STATUS DIFFERENCES IN NEIGHBORHOOD RACIAL-COMPOSITION PREFERENCES

Finally, to what extent does the influence of these factors vary by respondent race/nativity status? The last part of this analysis attempts to answer this question, introducing interactions between race/nativity status and each of the measures of neighborhood stake, objective neighborhood characteristics, and race-related attitudes and perceptions to estimates of preferences for various out-group and same-race neighbors. Results demonstrate that the importance of respondent race/nativity status, neighborhood stake, neighborhood characteristics, and race-related attitudes and perceptions vary greatly by both respondent race/nativity status and target-group, and further strengthen race-based explanations of neighborhood racial-composition preferences.

DISCUSSION

In an effort to understand neighborhood racial-composition preferences in a multiethnic environment, this analysis introduces an innovation on the original Farley-Schuman showcard methodology that allows respondents to create neighborhoods with what they consider to be the ideal racial composition. Deceptively simple, this experiment elicits highly candid, easy-to-interpret responses that are comparable across respondent racial categories. Preferences are measured without constraining either in-group/out-group pairings or the degree of integration; it is entirely up to the respondent.

Analysis based on this technique 1) offers striking results that strengthen those of the original showcard research (Farley, et al. 1978, 1993, 1994; Zubrinsky and Bobo 1996); 2) demonstrates the complex nature of preferences across respondent- and target-group categories; and 3) illustrates the critical role of race in understanding neighborhood racial-composition preferences. Whites are clearly the most-favored out-group among all non-White groups. On average, Whites make up between 23 and 33% of minority's ideal neighborhoods. Equally clear, Blacks are always the least-preferred out-group neighbors. Fully 40% of Asians, nearly one-third of Latinos, and one-fifth of Whites create neighborhoods that completely exclude Blacks. Latinos are also excluded from a sizeable percentage of White (17%) and Asian (26%) neighborhoods.

These results exhibit a clearly defined racial-preference hierarchy and complicate explanations that rely primarily on social-class concerns or mutually expressed ethnocentric tendencies. Preferences for same-race neighbors are not the same across groups. Whites prefer a higher percentage of same-race neighbors on average, and are the most likely to specify all-same-race neighborhoods. Conversely, Blacks—the most segregated group in Los Angeles County and the U.S.—are the least likely to specify all-same-race neighborhoods.

In terms of overall residential patterns in Los Angeles, these results are both disturbing and cause for limited optimism. On one hand, these results reveal greater resistance to residential integration—particularly with Blacks—than previously thought. This seems to suggest that meaningful declines in residential segregation are unlikely. On the other hand, these responses also indicate that the average White and Asian respondents—who currently reside in neighborhoods that are roughly 4% Black could be comfortable with substantially more residential contact with Blacks than they currently experience. This latter pattern may help explain the slight decrease in Black-White segregation in Los Angeles between 1980 and 1990 (Farley and Frey 1994) and offers hope for more gains in the new millenium.

In addition to the development of a new measurement tool, my goal was the simultaneous analysis of a variety of factors thought to affect preferences for various out-group and same-race neighbors in important ways. Some have argued that these factors are not necessarily racially motivated (Clark 1988; Thernstrom and Thernstrom 1997); previous analyses of preferences have often ignored these factors or considered them separately. Results reveal the complexities of this issue—associations often vary by both respondent- and target-group race—while strengthening race-based arguments in several important ways.

First, it was hypothesized that individuals with a high degree of commitment to, or stake in, their neighborhoods would prefer less integration, net of other factors. As it turns out, however, the influence of homeownership and parenting on neighborhood racial-composition preferences is limited, having no significant effect on preferences for White or Latino neighbors. When significant effects emerge, their racial character is clear: all homeowners prefer fewer Black neighbors than non-owners do. This is consistent with the long-standing belief that when Blacks move into a neighborhood, crime and declining properties undoubtedly follow. Effects also vary to some degree by respondent race/nativity. Native-born Asian parents of teens prefer fewer Black neighbors compared to other parents of teens; native-born Latino parents of very young children prefer fewer Asian neighbors and more same-race neighbors (native-born Latinos with teens also prefer more same-race neighbors). These re-

sults do not suggest a simple desire to preserve one's cultural heritage; rather, they suggest that openness to integration varies by one's investment in their neighborhood, but more importantly by both respondent- and target-group race.

It was also hypothesized that the characteristics of individuals' actual neighborhoods might influence preferences in important ways. In the end, neighborhood socioeconomic status (measured as tract-level poverty) influences preferences only twice, again in the expected directions. Native-born Asians in medium-poverty neighborhoods prefer more Whites, and foreign-born Asians in high-poverty neighborhoods prefer fewer Blacks in their ideal neighborhoods. Both results are consistent with perceptions of the top and bottom of our society's social and economic hierarchy. And, in general, increased exposure to specific target-groups (measured as tract-level, target-group racial composition) is positively associated with preferences. For the two most segregated groups—Blacks and Latinos—a much higher rate of exposure is needed (over 50%); the average level of exposure is too low to reap this benefit of interracial contact. For native-born Latinos and Asians, however, the effect of increased exposure to Blacks is negative. It appears, then, that all groups do not experience the benefits of interracial contact in the same way. This, too, points to the importance of race. Again, because the data are cross-sectional, it is impossible to determine from these data whether preferences led to current residential locations, or if residential location comes to impact preferences. Most likely, there are reciprocal effects—preferences shape location decisions and the experience of particular neighborhoods then helps to shape preferences (Galster 1989; Sigelman and Welch 1993).

The potent effect of racial stereotyping and the non-significant role of common fate identity offer the most clear and convincing evidence of the role of race in understanding preferences for both out-group and same-race neighbors. Negative racial stereotyping—a constitutive element of racial prejudice—significantly decreases preferences for out-group neighbors, and increases preferences for same-race neighbors. Effects often vary by respondent race/nativity, but this overall pattern is clear. The measure of racial stereotyping used here captures not only simple out-group antipathy, but also the magnitude of difference that in-group members perceive between their own group and particular out-groups. As such, this measure may also capture the extent to which groups define themselves and their social positions vis-à-vis each other: prejudice as a sense of group position (Blumer 1958; Jankowski 1995; Bobo 1999; Gans 1999). The latter definition is consistent with 1) the rank-ordering of out-group neighbors found here; 2) the effect of stereotyping on preferences; and 3) the actual relative status positions of Whites, Blacks, Latinos, and Asians in U.S. society (Gans 1999; Jankowski 1995).

Contrary to the in-group preference hypothesis (Clark 1992; Patterson 1997), common fate identity—an indicator of positive in-group attachment—does not negatively influence preferences for out-group neighbors or positively influence preferences for same-race neighbors. Research by Tajfel (1982) suggests that common fate identity is the element of racial identification most likely to influence behavior. More recently, Bobo and Zubrinsky (1996) tested the effect of "mere in-group preference" on attitudes toward residential integration using a feeling thermometer—a widely used measure tapping affective reactions to social groups in sociology (Jackman 1977; Jackman and Muha 1984; Bobo 1988; Schuman, Steeh, Bobo, and Krysan 1997) and political psychology (Sears 1988:897)—concluding that "in-group favoritism is not a powerful determi-

nant" of attitudes toward integration. Racial identification, however, is a multi-faceted construct. Measures tapping other aspects of racial identification or in-group attachment—for example Black (or other group) nationalism—may well be significant predictors of neighborhood racial composition preferences. Future research should examine this possibility.

Finally, there is limited support for the role of perceived social class difference; however, the negative effect of perceiving Blacks as "tending to be poor" relative to one's own group (as native-born Latinos and foreign-born Asians do) is always smaller than the effect of racial stereotyping. More importantly, the lack of similar effects, at least with respect to Latinos (a group that also "tends to be poor") suggests that even this must be viewed through the prism of race.

There is growing, direct evidence that negative racial attitudes play an important role in aggravating racial residential segregation. This implies that the problem is unlikely to be ameliorated without sharply increasing the costs of discrimination or generally altering the social climate that sustains associated stereotypes. Active enforcement of anti-discrimination laws would do both. This analysis begins to tackle the complex nature of neighborhood racial-composition preferences and their likely relationship to racial residential segregation. While it is not my intention to reduce everything to race, the results of this analysis illustrate the enduring importance of race as an organizing principle in American society. As the nation becomes increasingly multiethnic, understanding the role of race becomes more challenging and, arguably, more important. Sadly, to the extent that Los Angeles represents the emerging "Prismatic Metropolis" (Zubrinsky and Bobo 1996) growing diversity may simply expand America's racial hierarchy while the top and bottom positions remain unchanged.

REFERENCES

Alba, Richard D., Nancy A. Denton, Shu-yin J. Leung, and John R. Logan 1995 "Neighborhood change under conditions of mass immigration: The New York City Region, 1970–1990." *International Migration Review* 29:625–656.

Alba, Richard D. and John R. Logan 1993 "Minority proximity to Whites in suburbs: An individual-level analysis of segregation." *American Journal of Sociology* 98(6):1388–1427.

Allport, Gordon W. 1954 *The Nature of Prejudice.* New York: Doubleday Anchor.

Blumer, Herbert 1958 "Race prejudice as a sense of group position." *Pacific Sociological Review* 1:3–7.

Bobo, Lawrence 1988 "Attitudes toward the Black Political Movement: Trends, meaning and effects of racial policy preferences." *Social Psychological Quarterly* 51:287–302.

———. 1999 "Prejudice as group position: Microfoundations of a sociological approach to racism and race relations." *Journal of Social Issues* 55(3):445–472.

Bobo, Lawrence, Eve Fielder, David Grant, Melvin L. Oliver, and James H. Johnson, Jr. 1993 *The Los Angeles Survey of Urban Inequality Sample Report on the Household Survey.* Los Angeles: UCLA Center for the Study of Urban Poverty.

Bobo, Lawrence and Vincent L. Hutchings 1996 "Perceptions of racial group competition: Extending Blumer's Theory of Group Position to a multiracial social context." *American Sociological Review* 61 (December):951–972.

Bobo, Lawrence D. and Devon Johnson. Forthcoming. "Racial attitudes in a prismatic metropolis: Mapping identity, stereotypes, competition and views on affirmative action." In *Prismatic Metropolis: Analyzing Inequality in Los Angeles,* ed. Lawrence D. Bobo, Melvin L. Oliver, James H. Johnson, and Abel Valenzuela, Jr., Chapter 3. New York: Russell Sage.

Bobo, Lawrence and Camille L. Zubrinsky 1996 "Attitudes toward residential integration: Perceived status differences, mere in-group preference, or racial prejudice?" *Social Forces* 74(3): 883–909.

Bok, Derek 1996 *The State of the Nation: Government and the Quest for a Better Society.* Cambridge, MA: Harvard University Press.

Campbell, Angus 1981 *The Sense of American Well-Being: Recent Patterns and Trends.* New York: McGraw Hill.

Campbell, Angus, Phillip E. Converse, and Willard L. Rodgers 1976 *The Quality of American Life: Perceptions, Evaluations, and Satisfactions.* New York: Russell Sage Foundation.

Clark, W.A.V. 1986 "Residential segregation in American cities: A review and interpretation." *Population Research and Policy Review* 5:95–127.

———. 1988 "Understanding residential segregation in American cities: Interpreting the evidence, a reply to Galster." *Population Research and Policy Review* 7:113–121.

————. 1992 "Residential preferences and residential choices in a multi-ethnic context." Demography 29(3):451–466.

Dawson, Michael C. 1994 *Behind the Mule: Race and Class in African American Politics.* Princeton, NJ: Princeton University Press.

————. 1999 "'Dis beat disrupts': Rap, ideology, and Black political attitudes." In *The Cultural Territories of Race: Black and White Boundaries,* ed. Michele Lamont, 318–342. Chicago and New York: University of Chicago Press and Russell Sage Foundation.

Darden, Joe T. and Margaret A. Parsons 1981 "The effect of neighborhood racial composition on Black and White attitudes." *The Urban Review* 13(2):103–109.

Denton, Nancy A. 1994 "Are African Americans still hyper-segregated?" In *Residential Apartheid: The American Legacy.* Los Angeles: UCLA Center for African American Studies.

Devine, P. G. and A. J. Elliot 1995 "Are racial stereotypes really fading: The Princeton Trilogy revisited." *Personality and Social Psychology* 21(11):1139–1150.

Ellen, Ingrid Gould 1997 "Welcome neighbors? New evidence on the possibility of stable racial integration." *The Brookings Review,* Winter: 18–21.

Ellison, Christopher G. and Daniel A. Powers 1994 "The contact hypothesis and racial attitudes among Black Americans." *Social Science Quarterly,* 75(2):385–400.

Espiritu, Yen Le 1992 *Asian American Pan-Ethnicity: Bridging Institutions and Identities.* Philadelphia, PA: Temple University Press.

Farley, John E. 1988 *Majority-Minority Relations, 2nd Edition.* Englewood Cliffs, NJ: Prentice Hall.

Farley, Reynolds and William H. Frey 1993 *Latino, Asian, and Black Segregation in Multi-Ethnic Metro Areas: Findings from the 1990 Census.* University of Michigan: Population Studies Center Research Report #93–278.

————. 1994 "Changes in the segregation of Whites from Blacks during the 1980s: Small steps toward a more integrated society." *American Sociological Review* 59(1):23–45.

Farley, Reynolds, Maria Krysan, Tara Jackson, Charlotte Steeh, and Keith Reeves 1993 "Causes of continued racial residential segregation in Detroit: 'Chocolate city, vanilla suburbs' revisited." *Journal of Housing Research* 4(1):1–38.

Farley, Reynolds, Howard Schuman, Suzanne Bianchi, Diane Colasanto, and Shirley Hatchett 1978 "'Chocolate city, vanilla suburbs': Will the trend toward racially separate communities continue?" *Social Science Research* 7:319–344.

Farley, Reynolds, Charlotte Steeh, Maria Krysan, Tara Jackson, and Keith Reeves 1994 "Stereotypes and segregation: Neighborhoods in the Detroit area." *American Journal of Sociology* 100(3):750–780.

Gans, Herbert J. 1999 "The possibility of a new racial hierarchy in the twenty-first century United States." In *The Cultural Territories of Race: Black and White Boundaries,* ed. Michele Lamont, 371–390. Chicago and New York: University of Chicago Press and Russell Sage Foundation.

Glazer, Nathan 1993 "A tale of two cities." *The New Republic* 209(5):39–41.

Gurin, Patricia, Shirley Hatchett, and James S. Jackson 1989 *Hope and Independence: Blacks' Response to Electoral and Party Politics.* New York: Russell Sage.

Harris, David R. 1999 "Property values drop when Blacks move in, because . . . ": Racial and socioeconomic determinants of neighborhood desirability." *American Sociological Review,* 64(June):461–479.

Hochschild, Jennifer 1995 *Facing Up to the American Dream: Race, Class and the Soul of the Nation.* Princeton, NJ: Princeton University Press.

Jackman, Mary R. 1977 "Prejudice, tolerance, and attitudes toward ethnic groups." *Social Science Research* 6:145–169.

———. 1994 *The Velvet Glove: Paternalism and Conflict in Gender, Class and Race Relations.* Berkeley and Los Angeles: University of California Press.

Jackman, Mary R. and Marie Crane 1986 "Some of my best friends are Black . . . ": Interracial friendship and Whites' racial attitudes. *Public Opinion Quarterly,* 50:459–486.

Jackman, Mary R. and Michael J. Muha 1984 "Education and inter-group attitudes: Moral enlightenment, superficial Democratic commitment, or ideological refinement?" *American Sociological Review* 49:751–769.

Jankowski, Martin Sanchez 1995 "The rising significance of status in U.S. race relations." In *The Bubbling Cauldron: Race, Ethnicity, and the Urban Crisis,* ed. Michael Peter Smith and Joe R. Feagin, 77–98. Minneapolis: University of Minnesota Press.

Jargowsky, Paul A. 1996 "Take the money and run: Economic segregation in U.S. metropolitan areas." *American Sociological Review,* 61 (December):984–998.

Jaynes, Gerald David and Robin M. Williams, Jr. 1989 *A Common Destiny: Blacks in American Society.* Washington, DC: National Academy Press.

Johnson, James H., Jr., Melvin L. Oliver, and Lawrence Bobo 1994 "Understanding the contours of deepening urban inequality: Theoretical underpinnings and research design of a multi-city study." *Urban Geography* 15(1):77–89.

Kain, John F. 1986 "The influence of race and income on racial segregation and housing policy." In *Housing Desegregation and Federal Policy,* ed. John M. Goering, 99–118. Chapel Hill: University of North Carolina Press.

Kinder, Donald R. and Tali Mendelberg 1995 "Cracks in American apartheid: The political impact of prejudice among desegregated Whites." *Journal of Politics* 57:402–424.

Krysan, Maria 1995 *White Racial Attitudes: Does it Matter How We Ask?* Ann Arbor, MI: Department of Sociology, University of Michigan.

Leven, Charles L., James T. Little, Hugh O. Nourse, and R. Read 1976 *Neighborhood Change: Lessons in the Dynamics of Urban Decay.* Ballinger.

Logan, John R., Richard D. Alba, Tom McNulty, and Brian Fisher 1996 "Making a place in the metropolis: Locational attainment in cities and suburbs." *Demography* 33(4):443–453.

Marger, Martin N. 1996 *Race and Ethnic Relations: American and Global Perspectives, 4th Edition.* San Francisco, CA: Wadsworth.

Massey, Douglas S. and Nancy A. Denton 1989 "Hyper-segregation in U.S. metropolitan areas: Black and Hispanic segregation along five dimensions." *Demography* 26(3):373–392.

———. 1993 *American Apartheid.* Cambridge, MA: Harvard University Press.

Massey, Douglas S. and Eric Fong 1990 "Segregation and neighborhood quality: Blacks, Hispanics, and Asians in the San Francisco metropolitan area." *Social Forces* 69(1):15–32.

Massey, Douglas S. and Brendan P. Mullan 1984 "Processes of Hispanic and Black spatial assimilation." *American Journal of Sociology* 89:836–873.

Patterson, Orlando 1997 *The Ordeal of Integration: Progress and Resentment in America's "Racial" Crisis.* Washington, DC: Civitas/Counterpoint.

Pettigrew, T. F. 1982 "Prejudice." In *Dimensions of Ethnicity: Prejudice,* ed. S. Thernstrom, A. Orlov, and O. Handlin, 1–29. Cambridge, MA: Belknap.

Portes, Alejandro and Ruben G. Rumbaut 1996 *Immigrant America: A Portrait, Second Edition.* Berkeley and Los Angeles: University of California Press.

Quillian, Lincoln 1996 "Group threat and regional change in attitudes toward African Americans." *American Journal of Sociology* 102:816–859.

Quillian, Lincoln and Devah Pager 1999 "Neighborhood racial makeup and neighborhood perceptions. Paper presented at the Annual Meetings of the Population Association of America, New York, New York, March 25.

Schuman, Howard, Chariotte Steeh, Lawrence Bobo, and Maria Krysan 1997 *Racial Attitudes in America: Trends and Interpretations, 2nd Edition.* Cambridge, MA: Harvard University Press.

Schnare, Ann B. 1977 *Residential Segregation by Race in US Metropolitan Areas: An Analysis across Cities and over Time.* Washington, DC: The Urban Institute.

Sears, David O. 1988 "Symbolic racism." In *Eliminating Racism: Profiles in Controversy,* ed. Phyllis A. Katz and Dalmas A. Taylor, 53–84. Plenum.

Sigelman, Lee and Susan Welch 1993 "The contact hypothesis revisited: Black-White interaction and positive racial attitudes." *Social Forces* 71(3):781–795.

Simpson, George Eaton and J. Milton Yinger 1985 *Racial and Cultural Minorities: An Analysis of Prejudice and Discrimination, 5th Edition.* New York: Plenum.

Smith, Tom W. 1991 "Ethnic images." *GSS Technical Report No. 19.* Chicago: National Opinion Research Center.

St. John, Craig and Nancy A. Bates 1990 "Racial composition and neighborhood evaluation." *Social Science Research* 19:47–61.

STATA 1999 *User's Guide.* College Station, TX: Stata Press.

Tajfel, Henri 1982 "Social psychology of inter-group relations." *Annual Review of Psychology* 33:1–39.

Tate, Katherine 1993 *From Protest to Politics: The New Black Voters in American Elections.* Cambridge, MA: Harvard University Press.

Taeuber, Karl E. and Alma F. Taeuber 1965 *Negroes in Cities: Residential Segregation and Neighborhood Change.* Chicago: Aldine.

Thernstrom, Stephan and Abigail Thernstrom 1997 *America in Black and White: One Nation, Indivisible, Race in Modern America.* New York: Simon and Schuster.

Tuan, Mia 1999 *Forever Foreigners or Honorary Whites?: The Asian Ethnic Experience Today.* New Brunswick, NJ: Rutgers University Press.

United States Bureau of the Census 1990 *Census of Population and Housing.*

Yinger, John 1995 *Closed Doors, Opportunities Lost: The Continuing Cost of Housing Discrimination.* New York: Russell Sage Foundation.

Wilson, William Julius 1987 *The Truly Disadvantaged.* University of Chicago Press.

Wood, Peter B. and Barrett A. Lee 1991 "Is neighborhood racial succession inevitable? Forty years of evidence." *Urban Affairs Quarterly* 26:610–620.

Zubrinsky, Camille L. and Lawrence Bobo 1996 "Prismatic metropolis: Race and residential segregation in the City of Angels." *Social Science Research* 24(4):335–374.

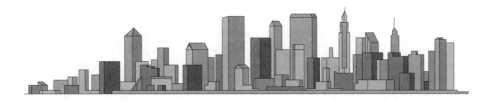

IV THE MODERN HOLISTIC STUDY

Molotch, Freudenburg, and Paulsen (2000) published a block-buster of an article, so good that I had to go to the two cities, Ventura and Santa Barbara, to see for myself. The only thing that could be better about the article is the photographic quality as printed in the journal; I hope mine come out better. One of the aspects of the article that I hope you will appreciate is the phenomenology and the idea that all elements are needed to understand how cities come to be what they are.

HISTORY REPEATS ITSELF, BUT HOW? CITY CHARACTER, URBAN TRADITION, AND THE ACCOMPLISHMENT OF PLACE

Harvey Molotch
William Freudenburg
Krista E. Paulsen

Geographic units—like cities and regions, but also like other types of social entities, such as corporations, academic departments, or whole societies—seem to exhibit overarching qualities that, however difficult to measure, make them durably distinct. Using "place difference" as our empirical focus, we strive here to make what might otherwise seem ineffable distinctions amenable to systematic empirical investigation.

In their personal lives, social scientists are as likely as anyone to be sensitive to holistic qualities that make Chicago the "city of the broad shoulders" rather than, like Paris, the "city of light." More prosaically, they presume that overarching attributes distinguish, say, Denver from Toledo as a place to live or work. Despite the fact that, in the words of geographer Entrikin (1991:13), "these differences are not imaginary, but rather are actual features of the world," social scientists, perhaps wary of facile descriptions of "national character" (Inkeles 1996) or the "invention" (Hobsbawn

1983) of hegemonic traditions, do not much take them up.[1] They more typically fall back on the apparent "solidity" of quantitative indictors—thus economic urban categories like "manufacturing center," "port town," "affluent suburb," or a position on the "center–periphery continuum" are common. Such material variables do matter in making up place differences, but they cannot, any more than would reliance on the symbolic or any other single element, explain the complex configurations that distinguish "place."

Based on a comparative study of two California localities, we rehabilitate the notions of *character* and *tradition* to offer a methodology for understanding the etiology of place distinctiveness: how places achieve coherence and how that coherence reproduces itself. Especially in contexts like the United States, where a lack of "ancient roots" make such qualities

---

[1]Williams ([1981] 1995:209) warns against such narratives as "surface froth and evanescence."

something other than self-evident, and at the present time, when late modernity supposedly has effaced place differences everywhere, an investigation of how place variations nevertheless take hold and persist offers a timely way to examine how social units take on durable distinctiveness.

First, we present two meta-problems that any explanation of identity and historical process (such as ours) must address. We then offer conceptual solutions for each problem from contemporary social theory. As a final preliminary step, we indicate how the ideas of character and tradition can lead to the empirical traces (i.e., data) that can bring these various abstract notions down to earth.

META-PROBLEMS

How Do Unlike Elements Conjoin?

Given that there is no single engine of history, places comprise an ensemble of forces that somehow must be examined together. In urban studies, aspects of this perspective go back at least to Firey's (1945) long unheeded insistence that "sentiment and symbolism" were "ecological variables" of equal standing to quantitative economic elements. Contemporary scholars studying cities and regions and their economies have returned to "culture" for a variety of explanatory programs (e.g., Amin and Thrift 1992; Lash and Urry 1994; Storper 1997; Zukin 1995). This "bringing of culture back in" corresponds to a still wider acceptance of other elements to be brought back as well: the state, organizations and (although somewhat less frequently) voluntary associations, the built environment, and nature (see Michelson 1977; Sack 1992:207; also see Agnew 1993; Maddox 1993; Putnam 1993; Somers 1993). But short of tediously and awkwardly listing a rash of "factors," how is all this bringing-back-in to be done? There have been a variety of helpful, albeit not completely

satisfactory, terms to imply this diverse intertwining. Braudel (1980:30) used the word "conjuncture"; Orum (1995:191) refers to "concatenation of circumstances"; McDaniel (1996:31) speaks of "interweaving"; Bourdieu (1990:66–68) uses "field"; Sack says "relational" (1992:180); Haydu (1998:366) works with "multiple registers." Regardless, we still need a conceptual frame-work to analyze just how all this combining occurs.

How Does Continuity Happen?

Somehow adjacent dependencies encourage past combinings to persist. Impressive scholarship documents long-term continuity in phenomena as diverse as rebelliousness in California's Owens Valley (Walton 1992), "virtuous circles" that "preserved . . . traditions of civic engagement through centuries" in parts of Italy (Putnam 1993:135), and "the agony of the Russian idea" as a "subterranean imprint" across the whole history of Russia (McDaniel 1996:93). But there is still relevance to Shils's (1981:7) complaint a generation ago that "the mechanism of recurrent self-reproduction is not sought,"[2] nor, in Suttles (1984:284) phrase, do social researchers investigate the way "cumulative texture" might operate. There is still the need, as Haydu (1998:351) more recently put it, to "pinpoint the mechanisms that transmute the influence of one sequence to the next." How exactly do textures "cumulate" such that virtuous circles are "preserved" or "imprints" carried?

Conceptual Solutions to The Meta-Problems

Thus we need conceptual guidance to explain (1) just how the unlike elements combine, and (2) how the continuity works. For the first

[2]Shils (1981) called explicitly for a study of "tradition" as the key for understanding social reproduction, but he pressed an ideational orientation, restricting tradition to ideas, religion, literature, and symbols (e.g., the British coronation).

problem (how unlike elements combine), our conceptual solution comes from actor-network theory. An array of physical and social elements cohere in a given locale through a "lash up" of co-occurrences (Law 1984,[3] also see Latour 1986, 1996). Rather than resulting from one kind of force over-powering another (e.g., the material versus the symbolic), things exist in the world through the "success" of connections among various forces and across material and ideational realms. To use a familiar and simplified example, thermometers as technical tools exist through scientists' (and others) reporting their findings according to their readings of them—a social activity. Each such act makes the thermometer "more" existing. Simultaneously, the category of "scientist" (and all its social paraphernalia) exists by virtue of material technologies like thermometers that scientists can use and "know all about." The physical thing and the social practice make each other up. Any identifiable *thing* in the world, be it a toaster, a norm, an ethnicity, a fact, or a city, gains its reality through an even more complex ecology of enrollments among diverse actors and the "stored-up" human activities represented by physical objects that also, in this sense, have a kind of agency (see Downey 1998). Any stroke of social practice, including one that directly shapes a material object, shores some things up and undermines others. As Pickering (1995) puts it, the existence of a "something" is evidence that "disciplined human agency and captured material agency are . . . *interactively stabilized*" (p. 17, emphasis in original). We can look for these kind of lash-ups that make up place identities.

Structuration Theory

We can approach the continuity problem by asking how a mode of "lash-up" at one time point moves to the next. *Structuration theory* provides

a conceptual solution: A social structure does not stand distinct from human action (i.e., as a separate "variable" in the determination of human behavior) but itself arises through human action, including mundane practices. In their structure-making actions, humans draw, per force, from existing conditions—that is, from structures resulting from their prior actions. Thus, as people take action they make structures, and every action is both enabled and constrained by the prior structures. All this occurs in an unending series of adjacent and recursive choice-point moves. Given the fact that every historic moment is unique, if for no other reason than that it includes the immediately prior events, and that every actor is unique given physical, biographical, and locational specificity, so it is that all actions and historic conditions are unique. Drawing upon what has come before entails continuity; the fact that at different times, what has come before is always different entails some change. The resulting configuration, at any moment or place, is thus not predetermined, but is formed in a path-dependent way as each actor, with more or fewer resources at his or her command,[4] shapes a new social structure by drawing upon the simultaneously enabling and constraining hand of the old.

Following this conceptualization from structuration theory, we look for the way particular urban structuration processes operate to make place distinctions durable.

Character and Tradition as Sources of Empirical Trace

We now can surmise that what is commonly sensed as overarching place attributes are the distinctive ways lash-up occurs in one place as opposed to others and the particular modes through which these lash-ups persist. The term "place character" represents, in our usage, the

---

[3]Law's essay was published later (1986) but with the "lash-up" phrase deleted.

[4]For a comprehensive treatment of how differential resources operate to perpetuate unequal access to the making of structure, see Tilly (1998).

mode of lash-up at a given time. "Tradition" stands in for how that character moves across time—how a mode of conjuncture at one point constrains or enables a particular mode of conjuncture at the next. People's sense of character and tradition make up the local "structure of feeling" (Williams 1973:131, passim) that itself enters, in ways we will show, as part of the lash-up and structuration process. We think character and tradition can be *observed*.

Putting our theoretical apparatus in summary form, in Table 1 we display, for each of our two meta-problems, their corresponding conceptual solutions and where to look for the relevant empirical trace. Row 1 of the table indicates the elements for understanding the statics of place, and Row 2 addresses the dynamic elements.

In our uses of the terms "character" and "tradition," we are rejecting not only the economic-engine view of history but also the dominance of the symbolic or sentimental themes often associated with the terms. In investigating how lash-up and structuration work differently across places, we substitute an action-based and more comprehensive view of what makes for collective distinction.[5] We do this to both exemplify how history works to create difference, and to propose a method, absent the

simplicities of old, for dealing with dynamic multiplicities of causation.

RESEARCH STRATEGY

To make these concepts tractable, we take a rather straightforward approach. We begin with two California urban areas—Santa Barbara and Ventura—that are quite similar by standard sociodemographic indicators and other evident characteristics. We then examine the very different ways these two places dealt with two outside forces: oil development and a freeway project. Comparing two places with many common attributes, including shared geographic region and broadly similar historical experiences, carries certain methodological advantages. External events are more or less equivalent in their *potential* impacts on both places.[6] In dealing with places that "could have" turned out more alike than they did (or even have had reversed outcomes) we meet the test of posing a "possible world" counter-factual (Elster 1978; Griffin 1993:1101, 1102), and we can trace

---

[5]In so doing, we depart from the usage not only of idealists like Shils, but also of others trying to show how it all counts. Both Maddox (1993:173, 191, 192) and Putnam (1993, passim), for example, treat "tradition" as idea-based, something that then intersects with other forces, like economy and class.

[6]We are not, in other words, comparing events that although nominally similar (e.g., "revolutions" in the Soviet Union, France, and China), have separations of centuries, vast geographies, and cultural gulfs that make comparison more troubling. Sewell (1996:259, citing Bloch 1967: 47) cautions on this score, and warns against turning history into mechanistic quasi-experiments that contradict the nature of historical events as mutually determinative and contingent.

Table 1   Theoretical Apparatus for Understanding Durable Distinction

Meta-Problem	Conceptual Solution	Empirical Trace
(1) How do unlike elements conjoin?	Lash-up (actor-network theory)	Character
(2) How does continuity happen?	Structuration	Tradition

how certain plausible paths were or were not taken.

In addition to the usual details of economic and social conditions, we researched other institutional realms. *Community voluntary associations* are linking devices, not only because their variety and social makeup "cover" so many substantive areas, but also because they harbor "memory traces" (Giddens 1984:17; also see Putnam 1993, passim; Sommers 1993:589) through which something like a social structure can transpose itself from one time or institutional realm to the next (March and Simon 1958; Walsh and Ungson 1991). These associations offer a space—sometimes a physical one with offices, chairs, photos, and paperwork—through which individuals make contact, convey know-how, and spread sensibilities. In this way, they bridge the somewhat ineffable "betweenness" of people's subjective experiences and the objective realities of locale (Entrikin 1991).

Physical trace material exists in still more obdurate form in the built environment and manipulations of nature (including development of large-scale public infrastructure) but also in the small details of shop signs, plantings, graffiti, and the kinds of goods displayed in store windows. Such environmental elements reveal to all, not just to the professional analyst, something of what Becker (1998:44) calls the "congealed social agreements" that lie behind them.[7]

Finally, we treat *nature* as something that also both influences and takes on different reality depending on how, as a continuous matter, it lashes up with the other aspects of the local milieu.

We now aim to diagnose how, across the realms of economy, politics, associational life, and the built and natural environments, our two urban areas differ in the way local actors "digest" phenomena over which they have only partial control. The pattern of the response reveals the very nature of the place; this pattern is our diagnostic tool for watching how the parts interact. Although we make extensive use of prominent events and trends reported in newspapers and other accounts, these events are primarily of methodological use. Our attention focuses primarily on the interplay; our challenge is to show how interactions across internal realms, linked to events outside each place, reinforce place differences in the very process of drawing upon those differences.

We do *not* do two things. First, we do not follow an agenda, suggested by some in historical sociology (e.g., Griffin 1993), that promotes searches for independent variables that, once "launched," cause place outcomes to be different. In structuration, as in other phenomenologically influenced approaches, variable independence and dependence are lost in each other because establishing causality involves tracing how path-dependent sequences of action structures emerge together.[8] Second, we do not try to name traditions or develop new typologies based upon traditions. We leave that task for others or for a later time. Instead, we strive toward a methodological contribution to the study of places by making more explicit the processes by which, to adapt Churchill's famous remark on architecture

---

[7]This is the basis for the famous "broken windows" theory of crime (Kelling and Coles 1996). Potential criminals, seeing an environment that is not cared for, putatively assume there is a general lack of surveillance and effective social control—factors making it more likely they will in fact then contribute to disorder.

[8]As Pred puts it (1984:281), we need to trace "how any given time-space specific practice can simultaneously be rooted in past time-space situations and serve as the potential roots of future time-space situations." For other discussions and applications of path dependence and related concepts, see Arthur (1988, 1994), Gramling and Freudenburg (1996), Inglehart and Baker (2000), North (1990), and Tilly (1989).

(James 1974), people shape their communities as their communities shape them—cumulating, as it turns out, in unmistakably different outcomes.

SANTA BARBARA AND VENTURA: SURFACE SIMILARITIES VERSUS DEEPER DIFFERENCES

Ventura and Santa Barbara are located 60 and 90 miles, respectively, northwest of Los Angeles, California. Both cities are the government seats and historic centers of their counties (of the same names). They have nearly identical (and ideal) climates, with little variation from the year-round average high temperature of 70 degrees in Ventura and 72 in Santa Barbara. Both cities have low humidity and many days of sunshine (an annual average of 252 in Ventura and 308 in Santa Barbara; by comparison, Seattle has 55), and they support an extraordinary diversity of natural and exotic fauna and flora (e.g., oak, palm, eucalyptus, citrus, hibiscus, cacti). The adjacent ocean waters of the Santa Barbara Channel, on which both cities front, are protected by a shield of scenic offshore islands—accessed by recreational boat service from Ventura (the closer of the two cities). Most of the coast is beach front, although Ventura's beaches stretch a greater distance than Santa Barbara's and are more consistently wide and sandy, like the idealized California beaches of travel brochures. The Los Padres National Forest provides a mountainous backdrop to both places, more visually dramatic from Santa Barbara.

Both cities derive from early Spanish mission settlements that later became Anglo or "Yankee" towns. Santa Barbara was the more important, as it had a larger and more significant mission and a strong military presidio. Santa Barbara incorporated as a U.S. city in 1850; Ventura 16 years later. The two cities' hinterlands share a history of cattle ranching and citrus agriculture, with other crops emerging later on. Although Santa Barbara had an earthquake in 1925 that was unmatched in its destructive severity by any Ventura experienced, the two places have otherwise been vulnerable to similar kinds of natural catastrophes, including periodic floods, droughts, and wildfires.

The two places also experience the political pressures waged by local business groups around issues of growth and development that characterize U.S. cities in general (Logan and Molotch 1987). And like other American cities, "growth machine" entrepreneurs are exceedingly active, striving to develop infrastructures and influence zoning decisions that will benefit their holdings and capacities for aggregate returns.

By standard indicators, such as population and income, Ventura and Santa Barbara are similar. Ventura has a somewhat larger population (97,000 vs. 87,000 for Santa Barbara in 1990) and a higher median family income ($46,361 vs. $40,912 for Santa Barbara)—an income level for Santa Barbara that may seem low to those who confuse the notoriety of the wealthy people there and in its suburbs with the city or country population as a whole.[9] Educational levels are high, although Santa Barbara's is somewhat higher than Ventura's (31.1 percent have a college degree in Santa Barbara—24.6 percent in Ventura). If socioeconomic status is measured by education and income combined, the cities balance out closely. These measures, moreover, have been generally stable over recent decades (see Table 2). Per capita retail sales are also about equal, with one or the other place taking the lead depending on year.[10] The cities do differ in minority

[9]Unless otherwise indicated, data correspond to central cities. We use the term "area" to denote the central city and immediate suburban ring, not the whole of the surrounding county.

[10]In 1989–1990, for example, per capita sales (in 1983 dollars) were $11,632 for Santa Barbara and $11,935 for Ventura. For 1993–1994, the order was reversed, with Santa

Table 2   Comparative Socioeconomic Characteristics, Ventura and Santa Barbara

Socioeconomic Variable	Year	Ventura	Santa Barbara
Percentage of residents with a four-year college degree	1970	15.1	18.1
	1990	24.6	33.1
Median family income (in dollars)	1970	11,552	9,514
	1990	46,361	40,912

population: Hispanics are the largest minority in both cities, but the percentage in Santa Barbara (31.5 percent) was almost double that of Ventura in 1990 (17.6 percent)—a ratio that has held roughly steady over the 1970–1990 period.

Thus, by standard indicators, one might consider these two cities to be virtually interchangeable. Judging by almost any other accounts of the two, however, dissimilarity would be the more likely conclusion. For example, Santa Barbara approximates development experts' contemporary ideal—a "learning economy" on the forefront of information, technology, and leisure services dubbed "Silicon Beach" to celebrate its emergence as a center of computer and internet innovations.[11] In the consumption patterns that result from and also enhance such economic activities, Santa Barbara is a place of "advanced tastes," with dense offerings in design-rich goods and services—proclaimed by a *Los Angeles Times* style editor as one of the "hip spots" (Romero

1995:D2). In civic life, Santa Barbara's downtown offers the kind of public space extolled by urban planners from Jane Jacobs in the early 1960s to contemporary advocates of the "New Urbanism" who prize vibrant central cores with diverse uses and users (e.g., Duany and Plater-Zyberk 1991; Langdon 1994). Outside commentators tout Santa Barbara for its planning accomplishments and levels of civic participation; planning consultants use video footage of the city's street life as a model for other cities to emulate.[12] While hardly free of the environmental problems (e.g., traffic and air pollution) or social problems found in most other parts of the United States, Santa Barbara's relative advantages have attracted wide notice.

Ventura's story has attracted little external adulation. However, it does have special qualities, including a county fair that outdraws any comparable event in Santa Barbara—a feature, as we will discuss, of some significance to local outcomes. But for economic development, civic participation, or land-use planning, Ventura has not offered much as a "model." To be sure, the area enjoys some of the charms of

---

Barbara having slightly higher per capita sales at $9,246 and Ventura having $8,904 (the early 1990's recession battered both places).

[11]A business-section front-page story in the *Los Angeles Times* declared: "Blading to work, surfing at lunch. No wonder Santa Barbara is the newest Mecca for high-tech companies" (Helft 1997:D1). By one measure (number of internet domain names per local employee), Santa Barbara County is the second-densest internet region in the United States (Zook 1998, table 4).

[12]For example, consultants who successfully advanced the Santa Monica's Third Street Mall used Santa Barbara as their exemplar. In their survey of California's natural and social landscapes, Brechin and Dawson (1999) single out Santa Barbara's "civitas" as virtually unique in California. For other acclamations, see Langdon (1994:161), Franklin (1926:42), and Plunket (1995).

small cities, including less downtown traffic and lower commercial rents than those found in major downtowns or in canonized places like Santa Barbara. But on most dimensions, Ventura more nearly typifies the qualities that preoccupy critics of U.S. urban places.

Thus, although Ventura and Santa Barbara overlap statistically on various measures, in natural endowments, and in regional location (being just 30 miles apart), they represent (at least within the boundaries of a more or less prosperous area of the country) very distinct versions of what a small city can be. Moreover, these perceptions are widely shared by those residing in the two areas. As revealed by the dozens of in-depth interviews we carried out in this research—including interviews with officials in the Ventura county planning department, the city tourist bureau, and the local California Coastal Commission office—the views of key observers in both cities have far more in common with the popular imagery of the two places than with the statistical profiles. Even the perception of what is ideal—and that Santa Barbara is closer to ideal than Ventura—is shared by numbers of Ventura officials, citizens group leaders, and business activists, many of whom explicitly hope to emulate what they refer to as Santa Barbara's "success." There are, of course, many residents, including some in Santa Barbara, who prefer Ventura as a place to live and work. For our purposes we are less interested in which is "better" or "preferred" than in the analytic utility the place differences can provide.

We have gone back over 100 years, examining memoirs, local media reports, and documents from election and assessor's offices, planning departments, citizens' groups, and many more private and public agencies. We interviewed more than 100 persons across the larger region. We also have developed a number of quantitative indicators as complementary sources of evidence. Finally, where appropriate, we draw from the results of our larger

investigation of 37 towns and cities in the two counties, plus one additional county to the north.[13]

We first take up the development of oil and show how, in each place, a distinctive early collective response set in motion particular trajectories. Then we take up the freeway project to illustrate how the prior handling of the oil issue influenced what the freeway would mean for each area and how these "freeway effects" reinforced, in turn, the patterns first observable in the local handling of oil. We add connecting details from other realms that indirectly tie oil and freeway dynamics to each other, and hence to place outcomes.

OIL DEVELOPMENT

Oil development rarely comes gently into regions; it can create vast wealth, launch new enterprises, and destroy existing ones. It typically brings in its own well-paid workers, who tend toward strong solidarity both with one another and, at least in recent times, the company that employs them (Beamish forthcoming a, forthcoming b; Freudenburg and Gramling 1994; Molotch and Woolley 1994; Quam-Wickham 1994; for detailed accounts of social and economic impacts of oil and related extractive industries, see Bunker 1984; Feagin 1990, Hallwood 1986; Lloyd and Newlands 1987). Oil also can be messy. Indeed, some of the world's

---

[13]We build toward a "consilience of induction" approximating the nonstatistical "confidence test" that, as in much of science (e.g., paleontology), substitutes for deductive reasoning. (see William Whewell as quoted in Gould 1986:86). Methodological details and extensive description of these places can be found in Beamish et al. (1998), Molotch, and Freudenburg (1996), Nevarez, Molotch, and Freudenburg (1996), Nevarez et al. (1998), Paulsen, Molotch, and Freudenburg (1996), Paulsen et al. (1998), as well as at http://www.mms.gov/omm/pacific/public/library .htm (reports are listed by title).

most publicized pollution events have involved oil spillage. With a rich iconography all its own, the industry provides petroleum producing regions with specific and potentially consequential imageries of tough work, rough settlements, and high-risk investing. Given its social distinctiveness, economic scale, political power, and physical impact, the industry presents a challenge to localities wishing to influence how it operates. In overall terms, the challenges have been comparable for Santa Barbara and Ventura; while their specific choices diverged, the two cities and their counties have been, in production volumes and timing, remarkably alike in their degree of involvement with oil production.

Oil Comes to Ventura

Commercial oil production first began in the hills of Ventura County in 1861, just 2 years after Titusville, Pennsylvania (site of the world's first commercial drilling) and 26 years before Santa Barbara. When oil prospectors arrived in Ventura County they found only a few scattered grazing and dry farming operations, with citrus orchards beginning to take root—the economies first of indigenous Chumash people and then of the Spanish-speaking Californios had both been vanquished (Almaguer 1994; Pitt 1966). Most of the early oil strikes were on hillside lands, sufficiently out of sight to avoid hindering an early tourist trade in the nearby valley hamlet of Ojai—a place the *Los Angeles Times* in 1878 called "the magnetic center of the earth" where "spirit-minded people come to reach the God centers in themselves" (quoted in Fry 1983:243). The oil pipelines through the citrus groves apparently did little damage to such sensibilities, and some citrus farmers benefited from oil royalties. Several farmers served on oil company boards, including that of the soon to be regionally dominant Union Oil Company (later the global giant Unocal).

Although the initial oil strikes were well outside the city of Ventura, they had important implications for the city. In particular, the city was the area's shipping port for oil (and also for agricultural produce), a role that encouraged oil-storage facilities and predisposed Ventura's waterfront to industrial use. Several decades later, oil would be discovered within a few hundred yards of the city center; this "Ventura Avenue" oil field hit its stride in the 1920s. Unlike other areas experiencing boom-bust cycles of oil development within the course of relatively few years, "the Avenue" experienced nearly continuous drilling through the 1950s and later because of technological advances in drilling and the discovery of ever-deeper oil deposits. This combination of factors, the marginally earlier oil discoveries and the geological happenstance of vertically stratified deposits, helped install oil service firms into areas adjacent to and even within the city of Ventura itself—an "industrial district," in Alfred Marshall's classic formulation, of mutually complementary functions (also see Scott 1988). This oil district ultimately sustained a support industry that also served sites elsewhere in California and, to a degree, other parts of the United States.

Ventura Avenue, also called "the oil patch" by locals, was the area's major artery running perpendicular to the ocean. As the oil industry developed, the Avenue became lined with oil service and supply firms, along with bars and restaurants frequented by oil workers. The Avenue area has also been home to low-income and, increasingly, Hispanic residents.

Ventura's beach is a natural feature of the city very different from the oil with which it has been in continuous interaction. Oil storage tanks and adjacent industrial facilities discouraged the settlement of affluent residents, tourist services, and upscale shopping that often accompany oceanfront development elsewhere along the California coast. One large ocean-oriented hotel (the Pierpont Inn) was constructed, but it was south of the downtown area and separated from much of the beachfront by the oil tanks.[14] In the 1950s, beachfront lots sold cheaply, even being-given away as promotional items with the purchase of a new car. In the 1960s, some ocean-oriented high-end homes and a recreational harbor were constructed, but these developments took place about three miles south of Ventura Avenue and the downtown.

Adjacent to the oil patch, the central business district was, as described in a Clark University geography dissertation, "hemmed in by blight on the west, hills on the north [and] the sea on the south" (Reith 1963:148). The only way for retail activity to expand was toward the east. Thus, department stores, national outlets, and other retailers expanded by leapfrogging adjacent built-up areas to land in areas miles away, effectively splitting Ventura's shopping district into two discrete units and moving retailing even farther away from the waterfront. More subtly, this movement to the periphery eliminated the high-end shops and services whose owners might have demanded a downtown and beach area clean-up, and would have had the clout to get it. Vacated downtown spaces became thrift shops, antique and used book stores—uses that persist to this day. Perhaps because of the devaluation of the city's core, county government had less reason to remain downtown—nor were there organizations demanding it remain. So when it needed new administrative and courthouse space, the county offices also migrated east, but to a still different part of the city, leaving the stately downtown courthouse (designed by Albert C. Martin in Beaux Arts classical style) to become the city hall in 1971.

The city configuration now was two distinct and separate retail districts, with the county government (the far largest of the public employers) outside of the downtown and separate from both retailing and the city government. Each element of dis-integration supported the other. In our research, we could find no evidence of organized groups surfacing to oppose oil operations in the city or the indirect consequences of the industry's presence. Even as the oil operations themselves began to wane, the industry's impact remained strong through the conjunctural elements that both affected it and that it helped induce (e.g., the devaluation of the oceanfront, dispersal of retailing, and public support for oil). The city, now acknowledged by locals as having "turned its back to the ocean," took its present shape.

Although these events in Ventura reduced the desirability of the coastal area, the effects were not predestined; there had been counter forces at work to make the downtown ocean-front an amenity. Through a gift from the region's most prominent banker, E. P. Foster, at the end of the nineteenth century the city gained a 62-acre "Seaside Park," "to fulfill Mr. Foster's dream of [it] becoming a miniature Golden Gate Park" (Percy 1957:6). In 1914, the park site became home to the Ventura County Fair and its annual judging of animals, produce, crafts, baking, and canning—first under tents and then in permanent structures. Over time, the fair's facilities, which now include an off-track betting structure (largely windowless to the sea) and parking for 2,500 cars, replaced the original trees, lawns, tennis courts, and stone barbecues. Writing in 1957, Foster's surviving friend ruefully remarked that Mr. Foster "would be very disappointed today if he could see what future management had done to his dream" (Percy 1957:6).

Even after the early 1900s, there were moments of possible reversal. During the 1970s the Ventura County Fair Board considered moving the attraction to a larger site to gain space for horse racing and gambling.[15] But the

---

[14]This hotel would later be separated from the beach by a freeway.

[15]As with other California fairs, Ventura's technically falls under the state's authority, but local board members manage it. In addition to general interviews (which included the fair-grounds' staff person with the longest tenure at the site), our information comes from 24 different news stories

controversy and "grave choice," as it was termed in the local newspaper editorial ("Whither the Fair?" 1978), turned on what would do more for downtown business—continuing with the fair or pursuing new options, such as high-rise apartments, hotels, and a new roadway at the fair's location (Paulsen 2000). Pressure from advocates of coastal access and from fair volunteers and enthusiasts, about 3,000 strong and by far the largest voluntary group we came across in the county, defended what they called the "homey feeling" of the fair as it stood, and forced the Board to retreat (Garnica 1980:1; Smith 1971:A6).[16]

Just south of the fairgrounds, along the coast, the city sponsored a high-rise Holiday Inn and parking garage, spanning the last remaining downtown ocean front. The hotel used a "generic" design—one common in high-rise Holiday Inns elsewhere. According to our communication from the son of the original developer, his father found it easy to gain building permission for this hotel, certainly compared with his tribulations in developing a similar project in Monterey at the time. Ventura's only high-rise structure, the Holiday Inn and parking garage closed off views from the beach to the mountains and from the city to the sea (see Photograph 2). These developments further nullified the Foster endowment. By now the downtown held few stakeholders for view preservation—no affluent residents or tourist businesses or organizations oriented toward the ocean as an amenity.

Throughout the fairground and hotel controversies, restoring the "Seaside Park" site to its original intended use never arose as an op-

tion. Even those fervently wanting to move the fair did not invoke park restoration as a possible advantage, despite the fact that the debate took place at a time when civic groups all over California vociferously agitated for coastal protection (resulting in the California Coastal Protection Act of 1972). The Ventura coast continued to serve industry rather than establishing alternative uses that might challenge historic orientations toward the oceanfront. Although the sentiment was voiced to retain public access to the fair site, we could find no record in organizational documents or informants' recollections of support for restoration of the park or for opposing the hotel proposal.

At each turn, the city and the county of Ventura welcomed oil development. Oil firm owners and employees took up prominent roles in civic life. Oil companies sponsored local activities, from concerts to little league teams. The local paper celebrated the industry with an annual "Oil Progress Week" supplement, including homage to the many oil company employees who volunteered in community groups.[17] Oil company officials and employees and their families also served in local government, including the Ventura City Council (in contrast, none ever served in Santa Barbara). During the great Santa Barbara Channel oil spill of 1969, which actually came ashore first in Ventura County before blackening 40 miles of beachfront in both counties, the Ventura City Council opposed a federal moratorium on ocean drilling—even as other California cities vociferously demanded (and gained) such a moratorium from the Nixon Administration.

Ventura's support for oil belied the ongoing decline in oil's local economic significance. As

published in the local newspaper and in the *Los Angeles Times*.

[16]One of the fair's board members was also board chair of a large oil company (Marlow 1988:A-4); the other members included two agriculturists, the owner of an equipment leasing firm, a welding company manager, a "housewife," a social service official, and one representative each from the fire department and law enforcement.

[17]See, for example, the Oil Progress Week Special Section of the *Ventura Star-Free Press* (October 18, 1950). The section contained long lists of oil industry workers and the groups in which they participated, including the Boy Scouts, Rotary, fraternal societies, and barbershop quartets.

noted earlier the two counties were virtually equal in the volume and pacing of oil exploitation, and the industry was in steep decline by the 1990s. Indeed, by 1970, shortly after the 1969 oil spill, Ventura County's ratio of oil jobs to tourism jobs was nearing the ratios in Santa Barbara County and California as a whole. Although the oil industry continued to be extolled as a bulwark of local economic and civic life, its political and social potency came not from economic *necessity*, but from an accumulated contextual fit that involved a broader range of issues than its share of economic base.

Here, then, are the cumulating path adjacencies that occurred in Ventura in response to oil development: Early oil production yields physical infrastructures (e.g., oil tanks on the oceanfront and an industrial thoroughfare); such infrastructures discourage recreational and affluent oceanfront development and help transform a donated oceanfront park into a fairgrounds (contrary to the donor's intent); the presence of the fairgrounds further diminishes orientation to the city's oceanfront as amenity, and a rare stretch of beachfront becomes a parking garage and franchise hotel; their design reinforces the apparent insignificance of the coast in official planning policy and local social life. Oil is present even in seemingly unrelated events, including the migration of retail and government offices to the perphery.

Oil Comes to Santa Barbara

When oil came to the Santa Barbara area, the city and the adjacent suburb of Montecito were already becoming tourist and retirement destinations, albeit on a rather small scale and well after tourism began in nearby Ojai. The local Arlington Hotel (at 150 rooms, far larger than any in Ventura County) was built in 1875—13 years after oil was first exploited in Ventura, but 12 years before oil came to Santa Barbara County. Both the Santa Barbara and Ventura areas, like Southern California in general, were

promoted widely for health restoration and the good life. Oil on the beaches and slicks occurring naturally at sea, evident from Chumash times to the present day, might seem to have put Santa Barbara at a tourism disadvantage, especially as Ventura lacked such contamination. Instead, Santa Barbara's boosters touted the fumes as good for respiratory ailments (Tompkins 1975: 56), portraying the oil they could not control as a health remedy.

As in the case of E. P. Foster's donation of a beachfront park to Ventura, a number of Santa Barbara's prominent citizens also acted to conserve the waterfront. Through gifts and public action, industrial facilities at the beach were gradually removed. Max Fleishmann (the "yeast king") funded a good part of the cost of building a harbor so he could berth his private yacht. Fearing "honky tonk" development at the ocean, a group of the area's wealthy residents bought up much of the city's beachfront and held it prior to city votes (in 1925, 1927, and 1931) supporting bonds to secure almost the entire oceanfront as public park. To catch views of the evolving amenity, developers gradually laid out housing and a main hillside boulevard to run parallel to the waterfront, roughly forming a vast amphitheater to the sea—thus mobilizing the natural aesthetics into an amenity-enhancing and commercially valuable infrastructure. In the end, Santa Barbara gained more benefactions—ocean-oriented as well as of other types—than did Ventura, plausibly because of the contrasting outcomes of the early donations. People tend to donate when they think their benefactions will have their intended effects, which means where they can sense that the social and environmental contexts (i.e., local character and tradition) will provide the appropriate support.

Santa Barbara's emerging orientation to amenities continuously generated tension between the locals and the oil industry (and other industries as, well). While residents tolerated oil development in those parts of the county distant from the city and its affluent suburb of Montecito, the closer-in projects soon met with a different response. The world's first "offshore" oil development (in shallow waters straddling the beach) was installed at adjacent Summerland in 1898 (Myric 1988), but in the summer of 1899, when oil development moved closer to Santa Barbara itself, residents took direct action. Here is an excerpt from the lead story in a local newspaper at the time:

> That the property owners on the sea front are determined that no unsightly oil derrick shall disfigure the beautiful views of land and sea was demonstrated last night, when a party of the best known society men of Santa Barbara armed to meet any resistance, and with workmen employed for the purpose, utterly demolished a new oil derrick. (Santa Barbara Morning Press, August 3, 1899, p. 1)

While the action indeed proved effective in blocking further expansion up the beach, approval of such tactics was not universal. A rival newspaper, the *Daily Independent* (August 3, 1899, p. 1) denounced this "vigilantism" as revealing an "animal instinct." The self-designated "business supporter" *Independent* also mocked the aesthetic concerns of oil's opponents, facetiously suggesting painting the derrick like a barber pole (August 7, 1899, p. 1). This sort of ridicule of fussy Santa Barbara residents, both from within the area and from outside, presages a theme that would continue for generations.

Although Santa Barbara had, and continues to have, prodevelopment political elements that support business of virtually any sort, the hardware of oil (so visible in Ventura) would simply never be established in those parts of Santa Barbara valued for other purposes. Oil was in the ground, but at least in certain locations, social and organizational features would keep it there or would alter the procedures used to bring it up. In 1953, the city banned all oil drilling within its borders. Lacking jurisdiction

over the ocean, all of which comes under state or federal authority, the city used litigation and political pressure to oppose the offshore drilling that nevertheless became prevalent later in the post-World War II era.

It was the 1969 oil spill, however, that unleashed the most intense opposition. World media attention amplified the outcry to a global level (Molotch and Lester 1975), forcing the Nixon Administration's temporary moratorium on offshore drilling. More permanent changes followed in oil and other forms of development, nationwide, under the newly passed National Environmental Policy Act (NEPA).[18] When the California electorate passed the 1972 state coastal protection act, Ventura county and city split almost equally on the vote; Santa Barbara city voters approved it by two-thirds, with county approval at 62 percent. The city of Santa Barbara banned any servicing of oil industry craft from the city pier, finishing the gradual deindustrialization of the water-front that had begun early in the century.

Besides providing bases for conflict, the Santa Barbara milieu had mechanisms for absorbing the riches of oil in ways different from Ventura's. Most notably, local politicians used oil property tax revenue to help finance the spectacular downtown Santa Barbara County Courthouse, completed just after the 1925 earthquake that leveled most of the downtown. Since 1922, the local "Plans and Planting"

---

[18]It was in response to his viewing of the oil spill damage that Senator Gaylord Nelson developed the idea of a national teach-in on the environment—the event that in 1970 became the first Earth Day. Various commentators see this oil spill—the "blowout heard 'round the world"—as a key spark in the modern environmental movement (e.g., Easton 1972; Freudenburg and Gramling 1994; Mowrey and Redmond 1993; Plunket 1995:39). Within the following year, Nixon's approval of the National Environmental Protection Act introduced the "environmental impact statement" as an element of the country's land development regime.

community group had been pressing for adopting a consistent "Spanish style" to supplant the city's then standard-American hodgepodge of architectural motifs (neoclassical, Tudor, "western," etc.). Under the group's urgings as well as pressure from other community associations, the city created, just after the quake, the country's first architectural board of review, requiring all new downtown buildings to conform to a Spanish motif. Although the controversial board was to go in and out of existence over the decades, the style decision triumphed over the years, sometimes to the chagrin of even enlightened local developers who found it and other planning requirements unduly burdensome.

The courthouse became the quintessential representation of the style and of Santa Barbara's commitment to beautification, with towers, tiled corridors, murals, and ornate ironwork—an ongoing ceremonial space for local civic and political events, as well as a tourist attraction and architectural feature used in television, movies, and on a variety of magazine covers (e.g., see Photograph 3). In effect, the county transformed oil money into physical forms that were to persist as an aesthetic and semiotic resource, emulated in still other structures and cumulating in an unusually dense stock of celebrated buildings.[19] In later years, when federal authorities forced offshore oil development, local agencies exacted special oil contributions toward improving shore-related recreation facilities, in effect, as before, offsetting rather than reinforcing the tendency for the oceanfront to bespeak industrial activities.

[19]In the *Guide to Architecture in Southern California* (Gebhard and Winter 1977), 178 Santa Barbara structures meet the authors' test of being "important," compared with only 29 in Ventura. A number of these structures, including the Santa Barbara Courthouse, are pictured at http://www.coolspots.com/spots/sba/page200002.html.

The preexisting range of place attributes in Santa Barbara also influenced how specific parts of the oil industry would distribute themselves. Numbers of oil company owners, and especially their heirs, made their home in the Santa Barbara area. For example, regional oil heiress Cynthia Wood (whose family's ranch sat atop the Ventura Avenue oil field) bred famous horses at her showplace Montecito stables; national oil heiress Alice Keck Park (of Keck Oil) lived in Santa Barbara, where she also endowed a public garden. Local retiree Samuel Mosher, founder of Signal Oil and early supporter (as a University of California Regent) of the creation of the University of California, Santa Barbara, also owned a local residence plus a large ranch outside the city. Environmental consulting firms, whose creation the city and county's high-regulatory regimes had helped bring about, were overwhelmingly centered in the Santa Barbara city area (Beamish and Paulsen 1999). Oil workers and suppliers, on the other hand, tended to settle in Ventura and other parts of the two counties (Molotch and Woolley 1994).

While Santa Barbara's civic leaders had serious reservations about the oil industry, they had a more positive consensus about higher education as a fitting kind of growth pole. The long-lived Thomas Storke published the local newspaper and was, at various times, also a University Regent, a friend of Franklin Delano Roosevelt and several California governors, and a U.S. Senator appointed to complete an incumbent's term (Storke 1958). With the help of his local allies, including oilman Mosher, he managed to have the federal government hand over its oceanfront Marine Base north of the city to the University of California Regents. The Regents, in turn, responding to the site's beauty and Santa Barbara's "long cultural background" (Storke 1958:435), and having strong support from local planning group leaders, designated Santa Barbara's prior existing public college as the core of a new general University of California campus to be built on the old military base (Kelley 1981:4, 6).

Constructed next to what had once been an oil field (Coal Oil Point), the university brought in students, staff, and faculty, who subsequently joined the anti-oil ranks, adding new levels of expertise and political energy to a place increasingly known as one of the country's environmentalist bastions.[20] The confrontation between oil and town-gown became direct when, in the mid-1990s, Mobil Oil proposed an onshore rig on university-owned land to slant-drill into an offshore field where special environmental rules precluded offshore platform construction. Under lobbying pressure from faculty, students, and local environmental groups, the university ultimately refused access to the former oil field, forgoing the revenue and, in effect, sealing in the deindustrialization of the site.

Symptomatic of the more subtle ways the character of places is constructed over time, the university's influence operates not just through big events but through micro-reinforcements of smaller ones. Here is an example involving a businessman's visits to his undergraduate daughter. Bega Lighting is a firm that designs and builds lighting projects around the world and also produces high-end fixtures for commercial applications (e.g., Washington, D.C.'s National Cathedral, the Mexico City subway system). The founder of the corporation's U.S. component (partnered with Bega of Germany) established the firm in Santa Barbara because he "was inspired to start a business after visiting his daughter, then a student at UCSB. He said he decided, 'This is a great place; I've got to find a way to live here'" (C. Ross 1994:B4). With a payroll of 75 employees and revenue above $26 million (in 1999),

Bega donated $100,000 of exterior decorative lighting for the Santa Barbara Courthouse.

This incident illustrates the path adjacencies making up the "character" of Santa Barbara: Citizen groups limit oil impacts, in part by using oil's tax contributions to build up the local ambiance (e.g., the courthouse); the local ambiance and social networks of its residents (e.g., Storke and his associates) induce the University's presence; the University attracts the CEO's daughter; the daughter (along with the ambiance) brings in the father, who locates the business; the business "gives back" with its donation of lighting, further enhancing the ambiance, which strengthens the anti-oil posture—which is where we started this tale of urban lash-up and structuration. Santa Barbara becomes even more like Santa Barbara, evidenced at any point along the way by the kinds of people who come to live there, the actions they take as individuals, as well as the local political and organizational decisions they enable. All along, and as in Ventura, the "look and feel" of the place are in continuous interaction with the other elements (see photo, page 317).

In natural endowments, both Ventura and Santa Barbara had oil, good weather, and attractive scenery. Indeed, in many ways Ventura's setting—with its closer proximity to Los Angeles tourist markets, wider and tar-free beaches, and boat access to the scenic offshore islands—provided better opportunities. That Ventura's oil wealth came a bit sooner contributed riches that its leaders could have used to set up Ventura for long-term economic and cultural innovation (something Norway did, but the Dutch failed to do in regard to North Sea oil; see Andersen 1993; Ellman 1977; Feagin 1990). In this long-term sense—at least in the hind-sight of the city's current leaders—Ventura's former elites, engaged in the oil-support mission, made the wrong move. How the natural environment operates as amenity or financial resource or both, turns on the cultural,

---

[20]For evidence that universities exert strong, but not inevitable, influences on local culture and economies, see Bassett et al. (1989) and Cowen et al. (1989).

political, and organizational context that interprets and shapes its meaning. "Geography matters," say Massey and Allen (1984), but contingently.[21]

FREEWAY PROJECT

As with oil development, freeways are high-impact operations. Funded and administered through federal and state sources, they are an element of urban life with which virtually every U.S. city has had to contend. At least until the early 1970s, when citizens began to rebel, localities welcomed freeways as a means of movement and as a mechanism for slum clearance (Gans 1968; Greer 1965; Whitt 1982). U.S. Highway 101 was the dominant thoroughfare in both our cities: By 1963, the state had upgraded the Ventura stretch to freeway standards, but the Santa Barbara portion took 30 years longer (owing to delays we will explain).

The Freeway Comes to Ventura

The old Highway 101 created traffic tie-ups as it cut through Ventura's downtown. For a new routing, the State acquired the commercial and residential land along the ocean and west of downtown (see photo, page 318)—by then an area of oil tanks, industrial uses, and low-amenity, primarily Hispanic residences ("Tortilla Flats"). Some low-lying oceanfront was filled in using earth excavated for the city's new recreational harbor. The resulting configuration was a freeway that squeezed between the downtown and the oceanfront, leaving room only for a narrow strip of grass along the beach, the future Holiday Inn, the fairgrounds complex, and parking. There would be no critical mass of

[21]In the words of Freudenburg, Frickel, and Gramling (1995:366), there is a "conjoint constitution" of the natural and social (also see Bunker 1984).

ocean-oriented residential, commercial, or recreational services near the central city. A prominent Southern California guidebook advises prospective visitors that the Ventura beach recreation area "is only tolerable if one is close enough to the beach so that the sound of the breakers can drown out the din of the freeway traffic" (Gebhard and Winter 1977:515).

In our interviews with local officials and planners, and in our inspection of media published when important decisions were made in the period 1955–1960, we found virtually no evidence of opposition to the highway's final route, much less to the fact of its creation (there was only one letter of complaint to the editor). Showing a seldom-expressed appreciation for ocean views, a newspaper editorial did congratulate the city for negotiating a partially depressed freeway that would preserve the vista from the then Ventura County Courthouse to the sea. But the main issue raised by "the public," as indicated by the news coverage of the time and by minutes of requisite hearings, was concern (expressed in 1956) that the lack of an exit into the old downtown would hurt merchants financially. As a result, the state constructed an extra freeway entrance, although its "make do" configuration was much inferior to the interchanges built where suburban malls were taking shape on the city's outskirts.

By the time of our interviews in the 1990s, and in contrast to the 1950s era, the freeway's impacts had become of major concern to planners and boosters, who now saw these as antithetical to a tourist or high-tech milieu (the city spends about $400,000 annually to attract visitors). The decision to depress a portion of the freeway created a canyon effect for cars coming through the heart of the city, meaning that neither the beach nor the historic Ventura mission can beckon to travelers. At the same time, the freeway cut off the city from the ocean. The highway's off-ramp configured a dangerous and uninviting pedestrian route from

Santa Barbara, relaxed and convivial.

downtown to the water, even though the physical distance is only a few blocks (see photo, page 319). To avoid blocking traffic in the freeway exit lane, cars spill into the city street, unimpeded by a traffic light or stop sign that might benefit pedestrians. The freeway, raised at various points, also obscures pedestrians' views of the ocean, as does an old railway bridge carrying train tracks that were moved during freeway construction and then, replaced *in situ* upon the freeway's completion. The attention to detail, either from city hall or community organizations, that might have mitigated these negative impacts, was not there.

Here, then, is an encapsulation of how response to the freeway project, itself induced by the way Ventura earlier responded to the coming of oil, continued to reinforce Ventura's character. Treating coastal land at the city's heart as utilitarian makes the land cheap and the residents vulnerable; a freeway is built right along the beach; the freeway further reinforces industrial uses and inhibits alternatives, even when possibilities arise, for ocean-oriented amenities. In these ways, Ventura sustains its path in the face of changing developments, whether in the form of a philanthropic gift, proposals to relocate its fair, or major declines in local oil production. Ventura's lash-up included acceptance of oil, an uncontested freeway, and a venerated county fair that reflected, in social and symbolic terms, the complementarity of agriculture with these other elements. Protesting activists did appear, but they focused on preserving access to downtown businesses and keeping the fair as it had been.

Ventura's Beachfront: condos but no people.

The Freeway Comes (Eventually) to Santa Barbara

For many years, Santa Barbara's "fussiness" was marked, for some, by its downtown congestion caused by the three adjacent traffic lights—the only signal lights stopping Highway 101 traffic between Los Angeles and Northern California. The city repeatedly rejected the state's "upgrading" proposals (e.g., a raised freeway of standard design) as damaging to beachfront and downtown, instead requesting a combined highway and rail corridor, sunk below ground where the main street crossed to the ocean—an option rejected by the State as unfeasible. Dozens of hearings were held through the 1970s and 1980s, and hundreds of citizens turned out. We found scores of letters to the editor of local newspapers (over 100 in 1971 alone) and many editorial comments, going back at least to 1965. The city's architectural review board provided detailed critiques and alternative proposals, as did the city's landmarks commission and planning-oriented citizens' associations. Business groups also were active, albeit often condemning the civic organizations for imposing costly delays in contesting what they considered the state's reasonable offers.

Finally, in 1986 city and state agencies compromised on a partially raised freeway, allowing the city's main street to pass under the freeway on its way to the beach area. The city contributed an extra $400,000 to upgrade landscaping and architectural detailing beyond state standards. The social and cultural capital of residents also kicked in—eminent experts

Ventura's troublesome access to the beach.

appeared, sometimes as paid consultants and sometimes providing *pro bono* service. Citizen groups scrutinized pedestrian experiences, views, and even the texture and tint of the concrete. The result, still offensive to some local critics, is a profusely landscaped freeway segment as it passes through downtown, and an auto and pedestrian underpass, done up as an ersatz medieval archway, that connects the downtown with the ocean. (The underpass, in particular, has been criticized as noisy and tunnellike.)

The downtown and seashore came to form a largely unbroken "T" of pedestrian access for recreation, shopping, government services (city and county), and tourism. Santa Barbara's downtown (see photo, page 320) remains the heart of retail activity in the area (the bulk of all sales occur there, not the in suburbs), and its shops include those selling the region's most expensive and stylish goods (a goodly number of thrift stores also exist). Near to the parks and beachfront recreation areas, the downtown is also the center for commercial entertainment (16 movie screens in five theater complexes are within a six-block strip) and cultural institutions (museums, live theaters, libraries). This concentration of complementary functions contrasts sharply with the dispersion of retail, government, and recreation in Ventura—a dispersion that inhibits a critical mass of civic activity either by day or by night.

Akin to the butterfly's incidental flutter in chaos theory, a string of successive and linked decisions each encouraged and constrained successive actions for Ventura. Had more sub-

Santa Barbara's downtown.

stantial tourism, even just a bit more, gotten "in the way," locals may have allowed Ventura's oil to have come out in the same volume but with different implications for local history. Similarly, if state or national coastal protection laws had been enacted sooner rather than later, Seaside Park might have been preserved, which might then have affected other local infrastructures, creating a basis for a different kind of economic and cultural "fix" in Ventura. Again, the evolving and strengthening complementarities in place at each historical moment insulated the oil-based trajectory in Ventura—and the recreation-environmental orientation in Santa Barbara. As oil development moved up the Santa Barbara coast, it met up with aesthetic vigilantes. The buy-up of the beachfront there was another timely intervention made meaningful not just by the wealthy people on hand, but also by local organizations and the public who were not especially rich but voted for the bonding debt. The end results, then, are not just a matter of "mere" chance but stem from the way initial events, some of them chance, interacted with deliberate and coherent choices, which the initial events influenced but did not determine (see Arthur 1988, 1994).[22]

However much it may be that "certain courses of development, once initiated, are hard to reverse" (Pierson 1994:181), they are not, as the term "lock-in" might imply, utterly

[22]Arthur (1994:109) argues that a "mixture of economic determinism and historical chance—and not either alone—has formed the spatial patterns" of the U.S. system of cities.

determinative. We prefer Haydu's (1998:353) image of "nudge" as opposed to his "steamroller." Even freeways, after all, have in a few cases been torn down, especially with help from earthquakes and aroused citizen groups (as in San Francisco, Oakland, Boston, and Munich). Santa Barbara's pre-1925-built environment (before the earthquake) itself represented a massive sunk cost in hardware, but because of individual action and organizational prowess, it was not rebuilt as it had been before—a typical post-disaster response of people anxiously needing to act quickly to restore lives and infrastructure (see Dynes and Tierney 1994; Quarantelli 1978). Rather than a long-term economic setback, the loss of so much capital stock became an opportunity for Santa Barbara. In Ventura, on the other hand, the pressure for a larger and more commercial fair could not be converted to an opportunity to restore the waterfront area, not because of the sunk costs in physical apparatus but because of the social enrollments to keep the fair intact and an absence of stakes in ocean-oriented amenity.

ORGANIZATIONAL AND CONSUMPTION MILIEUS: A COMPARISON OF DENSITIES

The presence (or absence) of mobilized community groups recurrently entered our accounts of links between events. Beyond whatever ennobling role participation in community organizations may have for individual participants or for the democratic process generally (Esman and Uphoff 1984; Gamm and Putnam 1999; Tocqueville 1990), voluntary associations also affect substantive outcomes. Preexisting networks can spread news and coordinate efforts across issue areas. These connections, which are classic examples of the strength of weak ties (Granovetter 1975), are

another form of social capital, highly consequential for the nature of place.[23]

We compared the strengths and types of the organizations that operate within Ventura and Santa Barbara.[24] Our data sources were the nonprofit directories maintained in each county by their respective voluntary sector associations, as well as the *Yearbook of California Charitable Organizations* (National Center for Charitable Statistics 1995). Between them, these three volumes list groups, by type, with each organization's annual budget and asset value; we standardized these figures for population size. We also interviewed leaders of the voluntary associations we thought would have a wide view (e.g., United Way officials and heads of local community foundations), to adjust the lists for any methodological inconsistencies across directories. The results for various cities in our larger study robustly reinforce our narrative: Whether in number of organizations, their aggregate revenues, or their assets, Santa Barbara has high densities, while Ventura, in comparison, is organizationally weak on all indicators.

Given the strength of Ventura's County Fair participation, we initially examined Wolpert's

---

[23]Coleman (1990) credits Loury (1977) for this idea, but the term "social capital" goes back, according to Putnam (2000), to an essay on rural schools by Hanifan (1916). Jacobs (1961) also used it: "If self-government in the place is to work, underlying any float of population must be a continuity of people who have forged neighborhood networks. These networks are a city's irreplaceable social capital" (p. 138).

[24]Ideally, we would have tracked organizations across time in both places, as we did in the oil and freeway histories described in the text, but appropriate data exist only for recent years. Even so, it is unlikely that strong contemporary differences developed "overnight," meaning that contemporary comparisons can offer telling evidence. Indeed, the patterns we report run parallel not only to the content of oral histories for the areas, but also to the historical accounts of outsider observers (see esp. Starr 1990:231–302).

(1988) hypothesis (also see Tiebout 1956) of "balanced generosity" across places—the idea that places "specialize" in different arenas of charity and service organizations (e.g., arts versus social services). Indeed, some of our informants said Santa Barbara's putative "elitism" led it to support the arts but not social service and health groups. To test these assertions, we broke down our place comparisons by the organizational functions used in the directories themselves: (1) health and human services, (2) arts and cultural organizations, (3) recreation and leisure, and (4) counseling and support organizations.

Contrary to our informants' impressions, our findings show no evidence of "trade-offs" in support of community organizations. The high density of Santa Barbara's health and human services organizations *parallels* its density in arts and cultural organizations. When we examined the other two categories (recreation/leisure and counseling/support), the pattern held as well. Perhaps this is yet another reason why place stratification so endures (Schneider and Logan 1981): Accrued advantage, evidenced here across even the nonprofit sector, grows through interaction with external forces.

As we suspected, and our interviews confirmed, "counts" such as these still miss one of the mechanisms that help organizations constitute the character and tradition of places—the way they create synergies through their connections with one another. For example, a Santa Barbara theater company, Access Theater, was initially funded by the Fund for Santa Barbara, a source of start-up dollars for "social change" projects. This theater company, headed by an actor-writer who had severe physical challenges, was committed to increasing handicapped people's life chances. Its considerable success depended on organizations in health, education, and social services to provide audiences and funding. These sources of support change the nature of what a theater

company can be, just as the theater alters what it means to be doing work in "health." These "horizontal networks of civic engagement" (Putnam 1993:175) build and sustain a kind of social capital that serves the common goals of these groups—goals that, as they are reached, help form the nature of the place.

Interorganizational links may also have physical impacts. Through the Santa Barbara Plans and Planting organization's early efforts to preserve historic adobe buildings, local groups captured what became office space for several different community nonprofit organizations (including the well-endowed Santa Barbara Foundation). Another small-scale physical change is the ongoing Community Flag Project, created by a former director of the city art museum, which commissions local artists to design flags for voluntary groups in the arts, welfare, health, environment, and social services (43 different flags have been designed to date). Each design can be repeated as a logo on stationery, in publicity efforts, on vehicles, and so forth. The flying flags, prominently displayed atop high poles at the city harbor, enhance the organizations visibility, and the city, in a locally characteristic way, gains a "beauty" asset. Thus the arts build other organizational realms, and vice versa. Beyond their external physical results, such projects create interpersonal links across organizational realms that strengthen the basis for future organizational action.

Part of local aura also consists of the goods and services available inside and flowing out of a city's buildings—the details of shop offerings, modes of window display, and mannerisms of service. Consumption is a "place creating activity" (Sack 1992:4; also see Zukin 1995). The type of "consumer's landscape" (Sack 1992:3) not only attracts and sustains workers in particular fields and of specific social types, but offers up more memory trace material. We compared our two cities, along with the other five primary towns and cities used in our more general studies, on the extent to which they offered goods and services we associate with consumers in advanced information, technology, and leisure service sectors. Using ratios of number of establishments to population size, we compared densities for each type of the following services: architectural services, bicycle shops, book stores, commercial art and graphic design, counseling services, and museums and art galleries. We used a computer phone directory data base, roughly equivalent to the "yellow pages."

While other indicators could perhaps be substituted for the ones we chose, the differences form a clear pattern that is consistent with our initial portrayal of the distinctions between the two places. In the patterning of consumption goods, Santa Barbara was first in architects, counseling services, and bicycle shops—the latter perhaps reflecting local commitment to environmentalism. In the two art categories (commercial art and graphic design, and museums and art galleries), it was surpassed, per capita, only by the art-colony town of Ojai. Number of book-stores was the only category in which Ventura out-scored Santa Barbara (albeit by a small margin), and in this case the count is affected by the many small used-book shops in low-rent Ventura compared with the large-scale bookstores in Santa Barbara.

The dynamics of local organizations, the built environment, and the consumption milieu add in recursively at every point, including just who is attracted and who is repelled. In addition to the economic deprivations that "push" people out of one location and the job opportunities that "pull" them to another, there is also a selective migration based on other, "softer" criteria that demographers typically ignore. Within the powerful macro forces of migration, people self-select on place character and tradition—a self-selection process that steers one type of person and functionary to Santa Barbara and a different type to Ventura. An indica-

tion of how typical socioeconomic measures can mislead, an environmental analyst makes no more money than an oil roustabout and has no more education than a petroleum field technician, but their effects on local character are dramatically different. Once attracted, migrants vote for the candidates, pass the tax measures, shop at the stores, and join the organizations that induced their own entry, thus carrying place character forward in time.

Our interviews revealed that our two places would differ even more if it were not for diffusion among them, as actors in one place mimic what is happening in the other. The "borrowing" was mostly in the direction of Ventura following Santa Barbara, evident, for example, in zoning, sign controls, or the type of trees used in downtown street plantings. In regard to an alternative newspaper, an AIDS-support organization, and a public interest law firm, the Ventura versions were established by the Santa Barbara "parents." Not only does this "following" put Ventura at least somewhat "behind the times" substantively, but the general order of events becomes another signal of place difference.

FINAL SPECULATIONS: PLACE AS ROLLING INERTIA

By reformulating character of place as the mode of connection among unlike elements, and tradition as the mode of perpetuating these links, we gain a way to explain how place differences develop and persist. Both Ventura and Santa Barbara experienced massive oil development and the freeway project—along with tract housing, fast food, the internet, and much of the other homogenizing paraphernalia of U.S. modernism. But surface similarities can mask underlying "more stable" differences in local unfoldings (Sewell 1992), because what is distinctive is not a list of attributes but the *way* these attributes lash-up and how the structuration process moves the resulting conjunctures forward through time.

Character and tradition serve as empirical proxies for lash-up and structuration. Methodologically, locating character and tradition requires keeping the agenda open, rather than focusing on, for example, the economic versus the political versus the ideational versus the natural. History occurs across *all* the realms, all the time, with no time out. Each element is, in ethnomethodological language, indexical vis-à-vis every other; they form a dynamic and coherent ensemble. Since all elements are part of what people put to use in taking action, they must all be available simultaneously to any analytic story of what those actions might "add up to" as they move through time.

The more "specialized" approaches to studying place differences have a liability in this regard, however elegant and useful they may be on other grounds. This criticism includes studies that encompass multiple realms but recommend treating each realm as alternating in their centrality (e.g., economic factors dominate at one time period, and political factors at another; see Mann 1986; Orum 1995). The analyst may fall victim to the historical sleight of hand as unanticipated forces enter in from unexpected directions. To perceive the "unbroken flow of local events" (Pred 1984:280) requires (and there are obvious limits to the accomplishment of this) eyes everywhere and all the time. One needs not a representative sample, but as with paleontological work, the capacity to spot the crucial links. Otherwise, one can easily miss the moves through which actions that are adjacent in time, but which come from different realms, shape history.

It further follows that if the local ways of doing things are "everywhere," there is no need to debate whether research should begin or center on the economy, civic organization, architecture, or nature. Given a focus on *connective tissues* among all of them, where to

start becomes a matter of research resources and accessibility. Oil development and a freeway project were useful to us because they were of similar magnitude in their potential effects on both places we studied, and they created a good deal of accessible data. Our search became not one of finding evidence to bolster one variable as opposed to another, but of following the tradition traces across the variables to see how each place worked.

Still another methodological implication of our effort derives from the suspicion that similar outside forces can have, as the development literature has long suggested (Hirschmann 1958), very different—even opposite—consequences, depending on local context. This view conflicts with Haydu's recommended agenda: to study what he takes to be the common problems of places and compare "sequences of problem solving" within them (Haydu 1998:349). Our study indicates, in a way inconsistent with Haydu's advice, that oil development and the freeway were seen as "problems" only in Santa Barbara; they provided "solutions" in Ventura. This core difference in what locals take to be problematic is itself a central research problem, the answer to which can clue researchers in to the nature of places. Such an analytic payoff reinforces our preference for investigating how different places deal with comparable external forces, and to leaving open the issue of whether or not the force is viewed as a problem (Haydu [1998] readily acknowledges that his strategy may not fit all instances).

Methodology aside, we think we have also illuminated some substantive issues of concern to urban analysts—notably, the issue of power. For local individuals and groups with only weak resources, the weight of accumulating conjunctures, and the routines they imply, set the terms for adjustments that must be made—however unhealthy, inegalitarian, or otherwise troubling these adjustments are. We thus reach, after a roundabout route, a possible contribution to ongoing Gramscian discussions of how hegemony works. It is not that a set of particular substantive and stable ideas "take hold" in a place and "drug the masses" (to caricature a Marxian view), but rather that so much can and does occur as people react to arrangements that appear normal (see Maddox 1993). Given persistent hierarchies of wealth and ideological control in places, reproduction requires all local actors to make adjustments, drawing on the configurations of place that have so durably come down. People live within the accustomed modes of things coming together, acting toward them as "going concerns" (Hughes 1971:52), naturalizing them as we now say. Such arrangements are further ratified through the assumption that others will presume and act similarly. Individuals, as Bourdieu (1990:65) remarks, "become the accomplices of the processes that tend to make the probable a reality." Even revolutionaries' actions, Calhoun (1983) thus observes, must draw on existing cultural arrangements even when otherwise scorned.

For the privileged as well, however, the not-so-dead hand of the past frames what is or is not in the cards locally. In Santa Barbara, some current projects of the rich and powerful must accommodate restrictions that carry the fingerprints of their predecessors who may never have meant for things to have "gone so far." More strikingly, Ventura's past elites, however unwittingly, were complicit in generating a future that their present-day counterparts would much like to alter. Even in narrow economic terms, Ventura's path is now judged to have been suboptimal.

Some traditions, perhaps those of the more open and diverse sorts, may be more likely than others to generate continuing innovation across cultural and economic content—at least this is what analysts like Porter (1990) and Jacobs (1984, 2000) would argue. Getting wind of the possibility that local ambiance has something to do with creating "miracles" like Silicon Valley (see Saxenian 1994), various

governmental and civic agencies have intensified their efforts to alter the texture and trajectory of places (see Massey, Quintas, and Wield 1992). Just as with previous efforts in urban renewal and convention center building, "change agents" continue seeking ways to manipulate locality to influence economic and social fates.

Our prism of character and tradition leads to doubts that very many could work. Plopping in a new museum, science park, or stadium, redesigning a streetscape, or injecting a new mission statement or community organization all carry the risk of artificiality. Without the needed complementary elements in place, they may not be viable interventions, something which has resulted in repeated project failures and mixed results (e.g., see Eisinger 1988; Squires 1989). It is not easy, in particular, to boost local standing vis-à-vis other places with a project here and another there. Especially when places try to imitate other locales (which is most often the nature of the case), it is *not the same thing* that is being done because the *context is different,* including the fact that the advantage of being the first to do it has been lost. By disregarding such realities, local subsidies only further enervate public budgets.

What about instances of radical urban shift that do occur, but that—both in geographic terms and conceptual framing—have been beyond our research purview? The mountains at Aspen, Colorado, once provided ore to the rough mining town that grew in their shadow. But the town collapsed when the ore ran out. Now the same topography provides ski runs for the rich and famous. South Beach in Miami is "back," very different from what it was when poor old people rocked on its porches or even what it was in its original art deco heyday. Bilbao, Spain, thanks to the new Gehry-designed Guggenheim Museum, seems to be shifting from an industrial hollow into a cultural capital of Europe. We suspect, but urge closer study of how it happens, that decay of social infrastructure and economic base can facilitate such transformations as underpinnings of prior lash-ups wither away. Ventura's steady upward swing in population and development (albeit modest compared to other parts of Southern California), we speculate, worked to maintain its continuity. But even Ventura may shift. We spell out here not an inevitable future, but what strong challenges its change-oriented actors are up against.

For reasons of building local economies and civic cultures, or just enhancing real estate profits from new developments, "character" and "tradition," albeit in different versions from our own, have conspicuously entered wide realms of city-building and place marketing. The New Urbanism movement is perhaps the most explicit and consequential as well as the most ambitious in its efforts to inject pervasive change in the way U.S. communities are built and lived in (Duany, Plater-Zyberk, and Speck 2000). In the prototypical case of the Disney Corporation's Celebration at Orlando, Florida, the company concentrated commercial and cultural activities in a downtown consciously designed to facilitate social interaction. "Old time" architecture, nostalgic street signs, and ersatz "mom and pop" storefronts, support the effort, as do ubiquitous front porches throughout the residential townscape. Compared with prior modes of development, these projects do coordinate across a wider range of elements to gain their effects—schools, business, iconography, and residence—but the New Urbanism may be an oxymoron. If nothing else, we have shown how an urban tradition arises through interactive layering and active enrollments over time, something that is difficult to produce all at once. Despite the skills of talented planners and architects, people can read the Disney landscape as "instant," and in that sense it is something entirely different from, say, a Santa Barbara that did its urbanizing over the longer interactive haul. Again, we are in no position to pronounce places like Celebration a success or a failure (but see A. Ross 1999); we can only indicate (again) what the creators are up against.

Similar challenges would confront those seeking to change any sort of institution or organization, all of which, in their way, have character and tradition. Beyond attributes having to do with the type of founder, time of founding, market share, type of environment, sunk costs, industrial sector or resource profile (common variables used by organizational analysts), organizations have specific textures and trajectories. Business gurus, as well as those who know organizations well from the inside or through repeated dealings with them, use a notion like "corporate culture" to represent the coherent and durable idiosyncrasies they think firms possess. Investigating character and tradition in our sense could augment such a gloss to help better understand continuities in organizations as well as why and how they differ. Such investigations would also help avoid the persistent tendency to anthropomorphize social units (a frequent problem in urban studies—e.g., Chicago "did" this, New York "did" that) by emphasizing concrete interactions as a basis for more holistic characterizations.

Both within the context of big events and mundane happenings, in regard to geographic units, but also, we suspect, a broader range of settings, interactional routines ratify differentiation and carry it forward. This is the blood of conjuncture and the life of what Becker (1995) calls the "inertia" of social organization. At least in regard to place, people know what to do, and in so doing, give identity to cities and regions; to use language that is neither active nor passive but both (what White and others call a "third voice"), *places make themselves up* (see White 1992:48). The resulting stabilities are neither preordained nor frozen in content. A kind of *rolling inertia* allows for continuous flux within a stable mode of operation.

Working with ideas borrowed from newer ways of understanding structure and agency, we have attempted to show how "place" happens and to offer ways of making the process of place structuration, otherwise vague and opaque, more accessible for study.

REFERENCES

Agnew, John. 1993. "Representing Space." Pp. 251–71 in *Place/Culture/Representation*, edited by J. Duncan and D. Ley. London, England: Routledge.

Almaguer, Tomas. 1994. *Racial Fault Lines: The Historical Origins of White Supremacy in California.* Berkeley, CA: University of California Press.

Amin, Ash and Nigel Thrift. 1992. "Neo-Marshallian Nodes in Global Networks." *International Journal of Urban and Regional Research* 16:571–87.

Andersen, Svein. 1993. *The Struggle over North Sea Oil and Gas: Government Strategies in Denmark, Britain, and Norway.* Oslo, Norway: Scandinavian University Press (Oxford, England: Oxford University Press, distributor).

Arthur, W. Brian. 1988. "Self-Reinforcing Mechanisms in Economics." Pp. 9–31 in *The Economy as an Evolving Complex System,* edited by P. W. Anderson, K. J. Arrow, and D. Pines. Redwood City, CA: Addison-Wesley.

———. 1994. *Increasing Returns and Path Dependence in the Economy.* Ann Arbor, MI: University of Michigan Press.

Bassett, Keith, Martin Boddy, Michael Harloe and John Lovering. 1989. Pp. 45–84 in *Localities,* edited by P. Cooke. London, England: Unwin Hyman.

Beamish, Thomas D. Forthcoming a. "Accumulating Trouble: Complex Organization, a Culture-of-Silence, and a Secret Spill." *Social Problems.*

———. Forthcoming b. *Silent Spill: The Organization of Industrial Crisis.* Cambridge, MA: MIT Press.

Beamish, Thomas D., Harvey Molotch, Randolph Bergstrom, and Perry Shapiro. 1998. "Petroleum Extraction in San Luis Obispo County: An Industrial History." Outer Continental Shelf Study MMS 98-004X (Contract No. 14-35-0001-30796). U.S. Department of Interior, Minerals Management Service, Pacific Outer Continental Shelf Region, Camarillo, CA.

Beamish, Thomas D. and Krista E. Paulsen. 1999. "The Santa Barbara Channel's Post-Petroleum Economy: Environmental Consulting Proliferates." Conference Proceedings, Channel Islands Symposium, March 29–April 1, Santa Barbara, CA.

Becker, Howard S. 1995. "The Power of Inertia." *Qualitative Sociology* 18:301–10.

———. 1998. *Tricks of the Trade.* Chicago, IL: University of Chicago Press.

Bloch, Marc. 1967. "A Contribution towards a Comparative History of European Societies." Pp. 44–81 in *Land and Work in Medieval Europe,* translated by J. E. Anderson. London, England: Routledge and Kegan Paul.

Bourdieu, Pierre. 1990. *The Logic of Practice.* Cambridge, England: Polity.

Braudel, Fernand. 1980. *On History.* Translated by S. Matthews. Chicago, IL: University of Chicago Press.

Brechin, Gray and Robert Dawson. 1999. *Farewell Promised Land.* Berkeley and Los Angeles, CA: University of California Press.

Bunker, Steve. 1984. "Modes of Extraction, Unequal Exchange, and the Progressive Underdevelopment of an Extreme Periphery." *American Journal of Sociology* 89:1017–64.

California Division of Oil and Gas. 1915–1992. *Annual Report of the State Oil and Gas Supervisor.* Vols. 1–78. Sacramento, CA: California Division of Oil and Gas.

Calhoun, Craig. 1983. "The Radicalism of Tradition." *American Journal of Sociology* 88:886–914.

Coleman, James Samuel. 1990. *Foundations of Social Theory.* Cambridge, MA: Harvard University Press.

Cowen, Harry, Ian L. Livingstone, Andy McNab, Steve H. Harrison, Laurie H. Howes, and Brian Jerrard. 1989. "Cheltenham: Affluence Amid Recession." Pp. 86–128 in *Localities,* edited by P. Cooke. London, England: Unwin Hyman.

Downey, Gary Lee. 1998. *The Machine in Me.* New York: Routledge.

Duany, Andres and Elizabeth Plater-Zyberk. 1991. *Towns and Town-Making Principles.* Edited by A. Krieger, with W. Lennertz. Cambridge, MA: Harvard University Graduate School of Design; New York: Rizzoli.

Duany, Andres, Elizabeth Plater-Zyberk, and Jeff Speck. 2000. *Suburban Nation: The Rise of Sprawl and the Decline of the American Dream.* New York: North Point.

Dynes, Russell R. and Kathleen J. Tierney. 1994. *Disasters, Collective Behavior, and Social Organization.* Newark, DE: University of Delaware Press.

Easton, Robert. 1972. *Black Tide: The Santa Barbara Oil Spill and Its Consequences.* New York: Delacorte.

Eisinger, Peter K. 1988. *The Rise of the Entrepreneurial State.* Madison, WI: University of Wisconsin Press.

Ellman, Michael. 1977. "Report from Holland: The Economics of North Sea Hydrocarbons." *Cambridge Journal of Economics* 1:281–90.

Elster, Jon. 1978. *Logic and Society: Contradictions and Possible Worlds.* New York: Wiley.

Entrikin, J. Nicholas. 1991. *The Betweenness of Place: Towards a Geography of Modernity.* Baltimore, MD: Johns Hopkins University Press.

Esman, Milton J. and Norman T. Uphoff. 1984. *Local Organizations: Intermediaries in Rural Development.* Ithaca, NY: Cornell University Press.

Family Service Agency of Santa Barbara. 1995. *The Community Resources Information Services Directory for 1995.* Santa Barbara, CA: Family Services Agency.

Feagin, Joe R. 1990. "Extractive Regions in Developed Countries: A Comparative Analysis of the Oil Capitals, Houston and Aberdeen." *Urban Affairs Quarterly* 25:591–619.

Firey, Walter. 1945. "Sentiment and Symbolism as Ecological Variables." *American Sociological Review* 10:140–48.

Franklin, Thomas J. 1926. "The Personality That Is Santa Barbara's." *Sunset Magazine,* July, pp. 42–43.

Freudenburg, William, Scott Frickel, and Robert Gramling. 1995. "Beyond the Nature/Society Divide: Learning to Think about a Mountain." *Sociological Forum* 10:361–91.

Freudenburg, William and Robert Gramling. 1994. *Oil in Troubled Waters.* Albany, NY: State University of New York Press.

Fry, Patricia L. 1983. *The Ojai Valley: An Illustrated History.* Ojai, CA: Matilija.

Gamm, Gerald and Robert D. Putnam. 1999. "The Growth of Voluntary Associations in America, 1840–1940." *Journal of Interdisciplinary History* 29:511–19.

Gans, Herbert J. 1968. *People and Plans.* New York: Basic Books.

Garnica, Cathy. 1980. "Fair-Move Opponents to Seek Ventura's Help." *Ventura County Star-Free Press,* October 27, p. 1.

Gebhard, David and Robert Winter. 1977. *A Guide to Architecture in Los Angeles and Southern California.* Santa Barbara, CA and Salt Lake City, UT: Peregrine Smith.

Giddens, Anthony. 1984. *The Constitution of Society: Outline of the Theory of Structuration.* Berkeley and Los Angeles, CA: University of California Press.

Gould, Stephen Jay. 1986. "Evolution and the Triumph of Homology, or Why History Matters." *American Scientist* 74:60–69.

Gramling, Robert and William Freudenburg. 1996. "Crude, Coppertone, and the Coast: Developmental Channelization and Constraint of Alternative Development Opportunities." *Society and Natural Resources* 9:483–506.

Granovetter, Mark. 1975. "The Strength of Weak Ties." *American Journal of Sociology* 78:1360–80.

Greer, Scott A. 1965. *Urban Renewal and American Cities.* Indianapolis, IN: Bobbs-Merrill.

Griffin, Larry J. 1993. "Narrative, Event-Structure Analysis, and Causal Interpretation in Historical Sociology." *American Journal of Sociology.* 98:1094–1133.

Hallwood, Paul. 1986. "The Offshore Oil Supply Industry in Aberdeen." North Sea Study Occasional Paper, No. 23, University of Aberdeen, Aberdeen, Scotland.

Hanifan, Lyda Judson. 1916. "The Rural School Community Center." *Annals of the American Academy of Political and Social Science* 67: 130–38.

Haydu, Jeffery. 1998. "Making Use of the Past: Time Periods as Cases to Compare and as Sequences of Problem Solving." *American Journal of Sociology* 104:339–71.

Helft, Miguel. 1997. "Sun, Sand, and Silicon." *Los Angeles Times,* January 20, pp. D1, D5.

Helpline. 1995. *Blue Book: The 1995 Directory of Health and Human Services throughout Ventura County.* Ventura, CA: Helpline, Interface Children, Family Services.

Hirschman, Albert 1958. *The Strategy of Economic Development.* New Haven, CT: Yale University Press.

Hobsbawm, Eric. 1983. "Introduction." Pp. 1–15 in *The Invention of Tradition,* edited by E. Hobsbawm and T. Ranger. Cambridge, England: Cambridge University Press.

Hughes, Everett C. 1971. *The Sociological Eye.* Chicago, IL: Aldine-Atherton.

Inglehart, Ronald and Wayne E. Baker. 2000. "Modernization, Cultural Change, and the Persistence of Traditional Values." *American Sociological Review* 65:19–51.

Inkeles, Alex. 1996. *National Character: A Psycho-Social Perspective.* New Brunswick, NJ: Transaction.

Jacobs, Jane. 1961. *The Death and Life of Great American Cities.* New York: Random House.

———. 1984. *Cities and the Wealth of Nations.* New York: Random House.

———. 2000. *The Nature of Economies.* New York: Modern Library

James, Robert Rhodes, ed. 1974. *Winston S. Churchill: His Complete Speeches, 1897–1963.* Vol. 7, *1943–1949.* New York, NY: Chelsea House.

Kelley, Robert. 1981. *Transformations: UC Santa Barbara, 1909–1979.* Santa Barbara, CA: Associated Students, University of California, Santa Barbara.

Kelling, George L. and Catherine M. Coles. 1996. *Fixing Broken Windows: Restoring Order and Reducing Crime in Our Communities.* New York: Martin Kessler.

Langdon, Philip. 1994. *A Better Place to Live: Reshaping the American Suburb.* Amherst, MA: University of Massachusetts Press.

Lash, Scott and John Urry. 1994. *Economies of Signs and Space.* London, England: Sage.

Latour, Bruno 1986. *Laboratory Life: The Construction of Scientific Facts.* Princeton, NJ: Princeton University Press.

———. 1996. *Aramis, or the Love of Technology.* Cambridge, MA: Harvard University Press.

Law, John. 1984. "Of Ships and Spices." Paris: Centre de Sociologie de l'Innovation, Ecole des Mines de Paris, Paris, France, March. Unpublished essay.

———. 1986. "On the Methods of Long-Distance Control: Vessels, Navigation, and the Portuguese Route to India." Pp. 234–63 in *Power, Action and Belief,* edited by J. Law. London, England: Routledge and Kegan Paul.

Lloyd, Martin G. and David Newlands. 1987. "Aberdeen." Department of Engineering, University of Aberdeen, Aberdeen, Scotland, Unpublished manuscript.

Logan, John and Harvey Molotch. 1987. *Urban Fortunes.* Berkeley, CA: University of California Press.

Louch, Hugh. 1995. "The Voluntary Sector and the Community: A Comparative Approach." Honors thesis, Department of Sociology, University of California, Santa Barbara, CA.

Loury, Glenn. 1977. "A Dynamic Theory of Racial Income Differences." Pp. 133–86 in *Women, Minorities, and Employment Discrimination,* edited by P. A. Wallace and A. Le Mund. Lexington, MA: Lexington Books.

Maddox, Richard Frederick. 1993. *El Castillo: The Politics of Tradition in an Andalusian Town.* Urbana, IL: University of Illinois Press.

Mann, Michael. 1986. *The Sources of Social Power.* New York: Cambridge University Press.

March, James G. and Herbert A. Simon. 1958. *Organizations.* New York: Wiley.

Marlow, Michael. 1988. "Ferris and the Squeaky Wheels." *Ventura County Star-Free Press.* January 17, pp. A1, A4.

Massey, Doreen and John Allen, eds. 1984. *Geography Matters.* New York: Cambridge University Press.

Massey, Doreen B., Paul Quintas, and David Wield. 1992. *High-Tech Fantasies: Science Parks in Society, Science, and Space.* New York: Routledge.

McDaniel, Tim. 1996. *The Agony of the Russian Idea.* Princeton, NJ: Princeton University Press.

Michelson, William M. 1977. *Environmental Choice, Human Behavior, and Residential Satisfaction.* New York: Oxford University Press.

Molotch, Harvey and William Freudenburg. 1996. "Santa Barbara County: Two Paths." Outer Continental Shelf study MMS 96-0036 (Contract No. 14-35-0001-30796). U.S. Department of the Interior, Minerals Management Service, Pacific Outer Continental Shelf Region, Camarillo, CA.

Molotch, Harvey and Marilyn Lester. 1975. "Accidental News: The Great Oil Spill as Local Occurrence and National Event." *American Journal of Sociology* 81:235–60.

Molotch, Harvey and John Woolley. 1994. *Evaluation of Current Programs to Identify and Mitigate Socioeconomic Impacts in the Santa Barbara Channel: An Analysis of SEMP.* Camarillo, CA: U.S. Department of Interior, Minerals Management Service, Pacific Outer Continental Shelf Region.

Mowrey, Marc and Tim Redmond. 1993. *Not in Our Backyard: The People and Events that Shaped America's Modern Environmental Movement.* New York: William Morrow.

Myrick, David F. 1988. "Summerland: The First Decade." *Noticias* 34:65–111.

National Center for Charitable Statistics. 1995. *Yearbook of California Charitable Organizations.* Washington, DC: National Center for Charitable Statistics.

Nevarez, Leonard, Harvey Molotch, and William Freudenburg. 1996. "San Luis Obispo County: A Major Switching." Outer Continental Shelf Study MMS 96-96-0037 (Contract No. 14-35-001-30663). U.S. Department of Interior, Minerals Management Service, Pacific Outer Continental Shelf Region, Camarillo, CA.

Nevarez, Leonard, Harvey Molotch, Randolph Bergstrom, and Perry Shapiro. 1998. "Petroleum Extraction in Santa Barbara County: An Industrial

History." Outer Continental Shelf Study MMS 98-0048 (Contract No. 14-35-0001-30796). U.S. Department of Interior, Minerals Management Service, Pacific Outer Continental Shelf Region, Camarillo, CA.

North, Douglas. 1990. *Institutions, Institutional Change, and Economic Performance.* New York: Cambridge University Press.

Orum, Anthony M. 1995. *City-Building in America.* Boulder, CO: Westview.

Paulsen, Krista. 2000. *Fairgrounds as Battle-grounds: Rationality, Community, and the Reproduction of an American Cultural Institution.* Ph.D. dissertation, Department of Sociology, University of California, Santa Barbara, CA.

Paulsen, Krista, Harvey Molotch, Randolph Bergstrom, and Perry Shapiro. 1998. "Petroleum Extraction in Ventura County: An Industrial History." Outer Continental Shelf Study MMS 98-0047 (Contract No. 14-35-0001-30796). U.S. Department of Interior, Minerals Management Service, Pacific Outer Continental Shelf Region, Camarillo, CA.

Paulsen, Krista, Harvey Molotch and William Freudenburg. 1996. "Ventura County: Oil, Fruit, Commune and Commute." OCS Study MMS 96-0035 (Contract No. 14-35-001-30663). U.S. Department of Interior, Minerals Management Service. Pacific Outer Continental Shelf Region, Camarillo, CA.

Percy Richard G. 1957. "The Fosters." *Ventura County Historical Society Quarterly* 2(3):2–9.

Pickering, Andrew. 1995. *The Mangle of Practice: Time, Agency, and Science.* Chicago, IL: University of Chicago Press.

Pierson, Paul. 1994. *Dismantling the Welfare State?* New York: Cambridge University Press.

Pitt, Leonard. 1966. *The Decline of the Californios: A Social History of the Spanish-Speaking Californians, 1846–1890.* Berkeley, CA: University of California Press.

Plunket, Robert. 1995. "A Nice Place to Visit." *Atlantic Monthly,* August, pp. 36–39.

Porter, Michael. 1990. *The Competitive Advantage of Nations.* New York: Free Press.

Pred, Alan. 1984. "Place as Historically Contingent Process: Structuration and the Time-Geography of Becoming Places." *Annals of the Association of American Geographers* 74:279–97.

Putnam, Robert D. 1993. *Making Democracy Work: Civic Traditions in Modern Italy.* Princeton, NJ: Princeton University Press.

———. 2000. *Bowling Alone: The Collapse and Revival of American Community.* New York: Simon and Schuster.

Quam-Wickham, Nancy Lynn. 1994. *Petroleocrats and Proletarians: Work, Class, and Politics in the California Oil Industry, 1917–1925.* Ph.D. dissertation, Department of History, University of California, Berkeley, CA.

Quarantelli, Enrico, ed. 1978. *Disasters: Theory and Research.* Thousand Oaks, CA: Sage.

Reith, Gertrude M. 1963. *Ventura: Life Story of a City.* Ph.D. dissertation, Department of Geography, Clark University, Worcester, MA.

Romero, Dennis. 1995. "Location, Location, Location." *Los Angeles Times,* March 2, p. D2.

Ross, Andrew. 1999. *The Celebration Chronicles.* New York: Ballantine Books.

Ross, Cissy. 1994. "Courthouse Lighting Reflects Favorably on Carpinteria Firm." *Santa Barbara News-Press,* February 5, p. Ft.

Sack, Robert. 1992. *Place, Modernity, and the Consumer's World.* Baltimore, MD: Johns Hopkins University Press.

Saxenian, AnnaLee. 1994. *Regional Advantage: Culture and Competition in Silicon Valley and Route 128.* Cambridge, MA: Harvard University Press.

Schneider, Mark and John R. Logan. 1981. "The Fiscal Implications of Class Segregation." *Urban Affairs Quarterly* 17:23–36.

Scott, Allen J. 1988. *Metropolis.* Berkeley: University of California Press.

Sewell, William. 1992. "A Theory Of Structure-Duality, Agency, and Transformation." *American Journal of Sociology* 98:1–29.

———. 1996. "Three Temporalities: Toward an Eventful Sociology." Pp. 245–80 in *The Historic Turn in the Human Sciences,* edited by T. J. McDonald. Ann Arbor, MI: University of Michigan Press.

Shils, Edward Albert. 1981. *Tradition,* Chicago, IL: University of Chicago Press.

Smith, Wally. 1971. "Relocate County Fair? Race Track Complex Aired." *Ventura County Star-Free Press,* October 3, pp. A1, A5–8.

Somers, Margaret. 1993. "Citizenship and the Place of the Public Sphere: Law, Community, and Political Culture in the Transition to Democracy." *American Sociological Review* 58:587–620.

Squires, George D., ed. 1989. *Unequal Partnerships: The Political Economy of Urban Redevelopment in Postwar America.* New Brunswick, NJ: Rutgers University Press.

Starr, Kevin. 1990. *Material Dreams: Southern California through the 1920s.* New York: Oxford University Press.

Storke, Thomas More (with Walker A. Tompkins). 1958. *California Editor.* Los Angeles: Westernlore.

Storper, Michael. 1997. *The Regional World.* New York: Guilford.

Suttles, Gerald. 1984. "The Cumulative Texture of Local Urban Culture." *American Journal of Sociology* 90:283–304.

Tiebout, Charles M. 1956. "A Pure Theory of Local Expenditures." *Journal of Political Economy* 64:416–24.

Tilly, Charles. 1998. *Durable Inequality.* Berkeley, CA: University of California Press.

———. 1989. "State and Counterrevolution in France." *Social Research* 56:71–97.

Tocqueville, Alexis de. [1835] 1990. *Democracy in America.* Reprint, New York: Vintage.

Tompkins, Walker A. 1975. *Santa Barbara Past and Present.* Santa Barbara, CA: Tecolote Books.

Walsh, James P. and Gerardo Ungson. 1991. "Organizational Memory." *Academy of Management Review* 16:57–91.

Walton, John. 1992. *Western Times and Water Wars.* Berkeley, CA: University of California Press.

White, Hayden. 1992. "Historical Emplotment and the Problem of Truth." Pp. 37–53 in *Probing the Limits of Representation,* edited by S. Friedlander. Cambridge, MA: Harvard University Press.

"Whither the Fair?" 1978. *Ventura County Star Free Press,* July 23, p. C-10.

Whitt, Allen J. 1982. *Means of Movement: Urban Elites and Mass Transportation.* Princeton, NJ: Princeton University Press.

Williams, Raymond. 1973. *The Country and the City.* New York: Oxford University Press.

———. [1981] 1995. *The Sociology of Culture.* Chicago, IL: University of Chicago Press.

Wolpert, Julian. 1988. "The Geography of Generosity: Metropolitan Disparities in Donations and Support for Amenities." *Annals of the Association of American Geographers* 78:665–79.

Zook, Mathew. 1998. "The Web of Consumption: The Spatial Organization of the Internet Industry in the United States." Paper presented at the Association of Collegiate Schools of Planning Conference, November 5–8, Pasadena, CA.

Zukin, Sharon. 1995. *The Cultures of Cities.* Boston, MA: Blackwell.

Bibliography

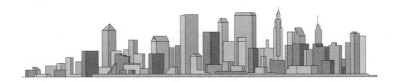

Selections in
The Urban Community

Burgess, Ernest W. 1925. "The Growth of the City: An Introduction to a Research Project." Pp. 47–62 in Robert E. Park *The City*, Chicago: University of Chicago Press.

Park, Robert Ezra 1936. "Human Ecology." *The American Journal of Sociology* 62 (July): 1–15.

Tönnies, Ferdinand. 1887. Translated by Charles P. Loomis 1957. *Community and Society* East Lansing: Michigan State University Press.

Simmel, Georg. 1903. Translated by Karoline Jacobs 2002. "The Bulk Cities and Mental Life."

Wirth, Louis. 1938. "Urbanism as a Way of Life." *American Journal of Sociology* 64 (July): 3–24.

Warren, Roland L. 1963. (3rd Ed. 1978). Chapter 2: "Older and Newer Approaches to the Community." *The Community in America*. Chicago: Rand McNally, Pp. 21–51.

Hunter, Albert. 1978. "Chapter 5: "Persistence of Local Sentiments in Mass Society." Pp. 134–156 in David Street and Associates, *Handbook of Contemporary Life.*

Merton, Robert K. 1949. IV-VI "Types of Influentials: The Local and the Cosmopolitan." In *Communications Research, 1948–1949*, edited by Paul F. Lazarsfeld and Frank Stanton.

Drayton, William. 1998. "Secret Gardens." *Atlantic Monthly*. June: 108–110.

Marcus, Clare Cooper. 2001. "The Neighborhood Approach to Building Community." *Western City Magazine* March.

Steuteville, Robert. 2000. "The New Urbanism: an alternative to modern, automobile-oriented planning and development." *New Urban News*. June 28.

Bridger, Jeffrey C. and A. E. Luloff. 2001. "Building the Sustainable Community: Is Social Capital the Answer?" *Sociological Inquiry* 71:4 (Fall):458–472.

Raijman, Rebeca and Marta Tienda. 2000. "Training Functions of Ethnic Economies: Mexican Entrepreneurs in Chicago." *Sociological Perspectives* 43:3:439–456.

Silverman, Robert Mark. 2001. "Neighborhood Characteristics, Community Development Corporations and the Community Development Industry System: A Case Study of the American Deep South." *Community Development Journal* 36:3 (July):234–245.

Wuthnow, Robert. 1998. "The Larger Picture." *Loose Connections: Joining Together in America's Fragmented Communities*. Cambridge, Mass.: Harvard University Press, pp. 213–224.

Lemann, Nicholas. 1996. "Kicking in Groups." *Atlantic Monthly*. April: 22–26.

Sucoff, Clea A. and Dawn M. Upchurch. 1998. "Neighborhood Context and the Risk of Childbearing Among Metropolitan-Area Black Adolescents." *American Sociological Review* 63 (August):571–585.

Rankin, Bruce H. and James M. Quane. 2000. "Neighborhood Poverty and the Social Isolation of Inner-City African American Families." *Social Forces* 79:1:139–164.

Small, Mario Luis and Katherine Newman. 2001. "Urban Poverty After *The Truly Disadvantaged*: The Rediscovery of the Family, the Neighborhood, and Culture." *Annual Review of Sociology* 27:29–34.

Mesch, Gustavo S. and Kent P. Schwirian. 1998. "The Effectiveness of Neighborhood Collective Action." *Social Problems* 43 (November):467–483.

Etzioni, Amitai. 1996. "The Responsive Community: A Communitarian Perspective." (1995 Presidential Address) *American Sociological Review* 61 (February):1–11.

Mitchell, Jerry T., Deborah S. K. Thomas, and Susan L. Cutter. 1999. "Dumping in Dixie Revisited: The Evolution of Environmental Injustices in South Carolina." *Social Science Quarterly* 80:2 (June):229–243.

Kunstler, James H. 1996. "Home from Nowhere." *Atlantic Monthly*. September: 43–66.

Kaplan, David H. 1998. "The Spatial Structure of Urban Ethnic Economies." *Urban Geography* 19:6:489–501.

Myers, Scott M. 2000. "Moving into Adulthood: Family Residential Mobility and First-Union Transitions." *Social Science Quarterly* 81:3 (September):782–797.

Charles, Camille Zubrisky. 2000. "Neighborhood Racial-Composition Preferences: Evidence from a Multiethnic Metropolis." *Social Problems* 47:3:379–407.

Molotch, Harvey, William Freudenburg, and Krista E. Paulsen. 2000. "History Repeats Itself, But How? City Character, Urban Tradition, and the Accomplishment of Place." *American Sociological Review* 65 (December):791–823.

Selected Bibliography

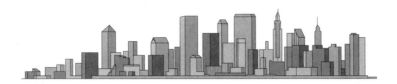

Banfield, Edward C. 1968. The Unheavenly City. Boston: Little, Brown.

Childe, V. Gordon. 1950. "The Urban Revolution." *Town Planning Review* 21 (April):3–17.

Davis, Kingsley. 1965. "Human Population." *Scientific American* (September):41–53

Kaplan, David H. 1997. "The Creation of an Ethnic Economy: Indochinese Business Expansion in Saint Paul." *Economic Geography* 73:2:214–233.

Lynd, Robert S. and Helen M. Lynd. 1937. *Middletown in Transition: A Study in Cultural Conflict*. New York: Harcourt, Brace, Javanovich.

Lyon, Larry. 1987. *The Community in Urban Society*. Chicago, IL: The Dorsey Press.

Martin, W. Allen. 1988. "Entrepreneurship Among the Vietnamese of Port Arthur, Texas." Presented at the American Sociological Association meeting, August, Atlanta.

Martin, W. Allen and Darrel L. McDonald. 1995. "Introducing Geographic Information Systems for Neighborhood Analysis." Presented at the American Sociological Association meeting, August, Washington, D. C.

Marx, Karl and Friedrich Engels. 1848/1993. The Manifesto of the Communist Party. New York: International Publishers.

Nisbet, Robert A. 1966. *The Sociological Tradition*. New York: Basic Books.

Warren, Roland L. 1983. New Perspectives on the American Community. Homewood, IL: The Dorsey Press.

Wilson, Kenneth L. and W. Allen Martin. 1982. "Ethnic Enclaves: A Comparison of Cuban and Black Economies in Miami." *American Journal of Sociology* 88:135–160.

Wilson, Kenneth L. and Alejandro Portes. 1980. "Immigrant Enclaves: An Analysis of the Labor Market Experiences of Cubans in Miami." *American Journal of Sociology* 86 (September): 295-319.

Wilson, William J. 1987. *The Truly Disadvantaged: The Inner City, the Underclass, and Public Policy*. Chicago: University of Chicago Press

DATE DUE

PRINTED IN U.S.A.